Abstracts
of the
Balance Books
of the
PREROGATIVE COURT
of **MARYLAND**

Libers 4 *and* 5

1763–1770

Vernon L. Skinner, Jr.

HERITAGE BOOKS
2011

HERITAGE BOOKS
AN IMPRINT OF HERITAGE BOOKS, INC.

Books, CDs, and more—Worldwide

For our listing of thousands of titles see our website
at
www.HeritageBooks.com

Published 2011 by
HERITAGE BOOKS, INC.
Publishing Division
100 Railroad Ave. #104
Westminster, Maryland 21157

Originally published 1995

All rights reserved. No part of this book may be reproduced or transmitted in any form or by any means, electronic or mechanical, including photocopying, recording or by any information storage and retrieval system without written permission from the author, except for the inclusion of brief quotations in a review.

International Standard Book Numbers
Paperbound: 978-1-58549-382-1
Clothbound: 978-0-7884-8682-1

PREFACE

The probate records of the Prerogative Court of Maryland contain several types of records: testamentary proceedings, wills, administration accounts, inventories, inventories and accounts, and distributions. Each kind of record has value for the genealogist. Prior to 1777, all probate records were required to be filed with the Prerogative Court of Maryland.

The Balance Books are a separate series of probate records established in 1751 and continued until 1777. They are closely aligned with the Accounts. Whereas, the Accounts are a citation of payments from the estate (and, in some cases, distributions), the Balance Books show how the remainder of the estate had been distributed to the heirs or representatives, after all other payments had been made.

The abstracts of the balances cite the following:

> Name of the decedent.
> Liber and folio reference.
> "D" - distribution of the estate.
> County. (See the table below for abbreviations.)
> Amount cited in the balances. The amount is in currency specified in pounds, shillings, and pence (a number preceded by "£"). In some cases, the amount cited included part of a pence; this part has been dropped. Additional amounts may be cited in pounds of tobacco (a number preceded by "#") or sterling (a number in pounds, shillings, and pence, preceded by a "£"), or gold (a number in pounds, shillings, and pence, preceded by a "£").
> Date of the balances.
>
> Name(s) of the sureties.
> Name(s) of the heirs/representatives. If all of the heirs/representatives are children (and so stated), and the surname is the same as that of the deceased, then the surname(s) here are not printed. However, note that often the accounts do not state a surname; in which case, the surname of the deceased is assumed as a default (When in doubt, the reader should check the original document for the actual wording.) The reference "1/3" indicates one-third; "1/2", one-half; etc.
> Name(s) of the executor(s)/administrator(s).
> Name(s) of other persons mentioned.

The following table cites the abbreviations used for the counties. The date of establishment for the county is shown in parentheses.

Anne Arundel	AA	(1650)
Baltimore	BA	(1659)
Calvert	CA	(1654)
Caroline	CR	(1773)
Cecil	CE	(1674)
Charles	CH	(1658)
Dorchester	DO	(1668)
Frederick	FR	(1748)
Harford	HA	(1773)
Kent	KE	(1642)
Kent Island	KI	
Montgomery	MO	(1776)
Prince George's	PG	(1695)
Queen Anne	QA	(1706)
St. Mary's	SM	(1637)
Somerset	SO	(1666)
Talbot	TA	(1661)
Washington	WA	(1776)
Worcester	WO	(1742)

All names are cited in the index; however, a name may appear more than once on a particular page. All efforts have been made to correctly interpret the names. However, sometimes the handwriting was difficult or impossible to read. The reader should refer to the original liber or photo-copy thereof when possible. No attempt has been made to resolve differences in the spelling of names. Entries such as "his Lordship" or "the Secretary", where no specific name was cited, have been omitted.

The following method was used when the folios of the original libers were numbered. This methodology has been carried forth as the page numbers:

- Liber 2 - Each page number has a left-side and a right-side.
- Liber 3 - Each page number has a left-side and a right-side.
- Liber 4 - Each page number has a left-side and a right-side.
- Liber 5 - Folios 1-157, each has a left-side and a right-side.
  Folios 158-403, conventional page numbering, except where noted.
- Liber 6 - Conventional page numbering, except where noted.
- Liber 7 - Each page number has a left-side and a right-side.

Copies of any particular distribution(s) can be obtained on microfilm by loan through a local Family History Center (FHC) from the library of the Church of Jesus Christ of the Latter Day Saints, or by means of photoduplication from the Maryland State Archives (350 Rowe Boulevard, Annapolis, Maryland 21401).

All dates prior to 14 September 1752 have been recorded in Old Style format. However, the denotation "(OS)" has not been specified. (Thus, the date January 1, 1751/2 will be written as Jan 1 1751.)

Liber 1 of the Balance Books was previously abstracted by Debbie Moxey, and is not included in this abstraction. Copies of Liber 1 can be obtained from her, by writing to:

Ms. Debra S. Moxey
1058 Taylor's Island Road
Madison, Maryland 21648

John Atkinson   4.1   D   QA   £269.13.11   Jul 22 1763
    Legatees: John (accountant), Timothy Lane.
    Distribution to: Widow (unnamed, 1/3). Residue to 4 children (equally): Mary
       Young, Ann Meredith, Juliana Meredith, John.
    Administrators/Executors: John Atkinson, Mary Atkinson.

William Goe   4.1   D   PG   £270.9.6   Jan 24 1763
    Legatees: Elisabeth Goe (granddaughter), Mary Hatton (granddaughter), Mary Goe
       (granddaughter), John Goe.
    Residue to (equally): William Goe, Margaret Hatton.
    Executors: William Goe, Richard Hatton.

Sarah Hammond   4.1   D   BA   £447.0.8   Apr 27 1763
    Distribution to: Representatives unknown to this Office.
    Administrators: Bryan Philpot, Thomas Harrison.

James Clare   4.2   D   CA   £231.19.5   Apr 14 1763
    Legatees: Isaac Clare, John Clare, Mary Sedgwick, Ann Sedgwick, Edmond Clare.
    Residue to (equally): Edmond and his 4 sisters: Sarah, Elisabeth, Hannah,
       Christian.
    Administrator: Benjamin Sedwick.

Peter Gibson   4.2   D   CA   £177.14.0   Apr 15 1763
    Distribution to: accountant.
    Executor: John Gibson.

Eleanor Linch   4.2   D   BA   £1589.14.8   Mar 9 1763
    Legatees: Joshua Linch, Sarah Linch, Deborah Lince, Eleanor Linch, Ann Linch,
       Eleanor Cromwell.
    Residue to 2 last sons & 4 daughters (equally): William, Joshua, Sarah, Deborah,
       Nelly, Ann.
    Executor: John Ensor, Jr.

Joshua Grason   4.3   D   TA   £64.15.10   Apr 5 1763
    Sureties: Francis Neale, John Jenkinson.
    Legatees: Elisabeth Elston, Rachel Elston.
    Residue to: Elisabeth Elston, Mary Carslake.
    Administrators (de bonis non): Peter Denny, Emanuel Jenkinson.

Edward Collison   4.3   D   TA   £241.0.3   Apr 13 1763
    Sureties: Benjamin Cooper, James Hews.
    Legatees: George Collison, James Collison, Edward Collison, Benjamin Collison,
       Mary, Sarah, Frances Collison, Rachel Crawford & Elisabeth Chap.
    Residue to children (equally): George, James, Edward, Benjamin, Mary, Sarah,
       Frances.
    Executor: George Collison.

John Hellen   4.3   D   CA   £422.10.0   Apr 30 1763
    Distribution to (equally): Charles, John, Richard, Penelope, Jesse, Nicholas,
       Mary, Rebecca.
    Administrator: Walter Hellen.

Andrew White   4.3   D   CA   £447.18.5   Apr 6 1763
The amount of the accounts also included £160.16.5 sterling.
    Distribution to (equally): accountant, James White, Ann White.
    Administratrix: Hannah White.

Dilah Catterton   4.4   D   CA   £111.5.9   Apr 30 1763
    Distribution to: Widow (unnamed, 1/3). Residue to (equally): Jeremiah Catterton,
       Ann Taylor, Michael Devawn (?), Daniel Price.
    Administratrix: Susannah Catterton.

Robert Etherington   4.4   D   CA   £119.19.0   May 4 1763
    Distribution to: Robert Etherington (son of Thomas Etherington).
    Administrator: Capt. John Barnes.

John Roberts   4.4   D   CE   £131.10.0   May 11 1763
    Sureties: James Wroth, Robert Walmsley.
    Distribution to: Representatives unknown to this Office.
    Administratrix: Dorothy Roberts.

John Duke   4.4   D   CA   £551.7.0   May 21 1763
    Distribution to: Widow (unnamed, 1/3). Residue to (equally): James Duke, Mary
       Duke.
    Administratrix: Esther Bourn, wife of Jacob Bourn.

George Thompson   4.4   D CA   £205.17.11   May 14 1763
    Distribution to: Widow (unnamed, 1/3). Residue to: Dorcas Thompson, Araminta
        Thompson, Martha Thompson.
    Administratrix: Mary Thompson.

Mathew Barnes   4.5   D CH   £1193.16.10 Jan 29 1763
    Sureties: Richard Barnes, Thomas Reid Cooksey.
    Legatees: Katherine Barnes, Mary Ann Barnes, Ann Barnes, Catherine (wife),
        Violetta Barnes, Richard Barnes, Thomas Cooksey, Burr Barnes, James Barnes.
    Distribution to: Catherine Barnes (1/3). Residue to children (equally):
        Violetta, Mary Ann, Ann, Jane, Burr.
    Executrix: Katherine Barnes.

John Beall   4.6   D CH   £36.14.1   Feb 14 1763
    Distribution to: Widow (unnamed, 1/3). Residue to children (unnamed, equally).
    Administratrix: Elisabeth Beall.

Thomas Mudd   4.6   D CH   £431.1.9   Mar 16 1763
    Sureties: Ignatius Gardiner, Richard Gardiner.
    Legatees: Richard Mudd, Luke Mudd, Mary Johnson.
    Residue to children (equally): Thomas, Ignatius, Joseph, Francis.
    Executor: Henry Mudd.

Aquilla Scot   4.6   D BA   £602.2.5   Mar 7 1763
This entry is crossed out.
    Sureties: Thomas Wheeler, Benjamin Wheeler.
    Distribution to: Elisabeth (widow), 3 sons & 4 daughters (unnamed).
    Administrator (de bonis non): Ignatius Wheeler.

Elisabeth Scott   4.6   D BA   £223.9.9   May 8 1763
This entry is crossed out.
    Sureties: Thomas Wheeler, Benjamin Wheeler.
    Distribution to children (equally): James, Elisabeth, Rebecca, Sarah.
    Administrator: Ignatius Wheeler.

Peter Lettick   4.7   D BA   £90.12.4   May 16 1763
    Sureties: Andrew Stiger.
    Distribution to: Widow (unnamed, 1/3). Residue to 4 children (unnamed, equally).
    Administratrix: Elisabeth Seigler, wife of John Seigler.

James Course   4.7   D KE   £232.9.0   Apr 9 1763
    Distribution to: Representatives unknown to this Office.
    Administratrix: Susannah Piner, wife of Bartus Piner.

Benjamin Knock   4.7   D KE   £281.17.2   Jun 11 1763
    Legatees: William Knock, widow (unnamed).
    Distribution to: Widow (unnamed, 1/3). Residue to children (unnamed).
    Executors: John Blackiston, John Spearman and his wife Elisabeth Spearman.

Thomas Johns   4.7   D CE   £81.0.0   May 25 1763
    Sureties: Peter Bower, John Lewis.
    Distribution to: Representatives unknown to this Office.
    Administratrix: Elisabeth Johns.

Alexander Fulton   4.8   D CE   £50.8.9   May 25 1763
    Sureties: Andrew Porter, William Ewing.
    Legatees: John Fulton, Francis Fulton, John (son, under age), Francis (son, under
        age).
    Distribution to: Widow (unnamed, 1/3). Residue to: accountant.
    Executor: Samuel Fulton.

George Hall   4.8   D KE   £760.4.1   Jun 8 1763
    Distribution to: Representatives unknown to this Office.
    Executors: John Hall, Christopher Hall.

John Hooper   4.8   D DO   £570.7.10   Feb 22 1763
    Sureties: Henry Traver, Mathew Traver.
    Legatees: John Hooper, Roger Ashcomb Hooper, Samuel Ashcomb Hooper, Thomas
        Hooper, May Hooper, "child his wife was pregnant with".
    Distribution to: Widow (unnamed, 1/3).
    Executor: John Ashcomb Hooper.

William Hadaway   4.9   D TA   £430.16.1   May 17 1763
    Sureties: Robert Lambden, Joseph Harrison.
    Distribution to: Widow (unnamed, 1/3). Residue to children (equally): Elisabeth,
        William, Thomas Lambden Hadaway.
    Administratrix: Mary Hadaway.

John Catrop   4.9   D   TA   £154.16.0   Jun 28 1763
    Sureties: Philip McManus, Richard Turbut.
    Legatees: Mary Ann Catrop, Elisabeth Catrop, John Catrop, William Marsh Catrop.
    Executor: John Catrop.

Thomas Osment   4.9   D   TA   £170.10.9   Jun 9 1763
    Sureties: Richard Osment, John Dobson.
    Distribution to: Widow (unnamed, 1/3). Residue to 3 children (equally): Thomas,
        Jonathon, Priscilla.
    Administratrix: Priscilla Turner, wife of Joseph Turner.

Samuel Queen   4.10   D   PG   £470.19.2   --- -- 1763
The amount of the accounts also included #7411.
    Legatees: Edward Queen.
    Distribution to: Widow (unnamed, 1/3). Residue to children (equally): Walter,
        Henry, Catharine, Henrietta, Mary Ann.
    Executors: Henrietta Jameson wife of Henry Jameson, Henry Queen.

John Pollard   4.10   D   BA   £26.15.7   --- -- 1763
    Distribution to: Representatives unknown to this Office.
    Administrator: William Pollard.

Daniel McComas   4.10   D   BA   £114.15.6   --- 27 1763
    Distribution to: Representatives unknown to this Office.
    Administratrix: Ann Poteet, wife of John Poteet.

David Stewart   4.10   D   AA   £504.5.11   --- 13 1763
The amount of the accounts also included £98.16.3 sterling.
    Legatees: David Steuart.
    Distribution to: David Steuart, Thomas Mayo who married one of the daughters
        (unnamed), Joseph Duvall, Elisabeth Steuart.
    Executrix: Mary Stewart.

Stephen Horsey   4.11   D   SO   £1045.8.9   May 17 1763
    Legatees: John Horsey.
    Executor: Revell Horsey.

Joy Walston   4.11   D   SO   £34.9.0   May 25 1763
    Executor: Boz Walston.

Isaac Adams   4.11   D   SO   £228.8.10   Jun 1 1763
    Distribution to: Representatives unknown to this Office.
    Administrator: Ephraim Adams.

Joshua Cooke   4.11   D   QA   £21.16.7   Jun 30 1763
    Sureties: Nathan Samuel Turbut Wright.
    Distribution to: William Cooke, Samuel Cooke.
    Administrator (de bonis non): Thomas Miller.

James Andrews   4.11   D   QA   £94.2.0   Jun 30 1763
    Distribution to: Widow (unnamed, 1/3). Residue to 3 children (equally): Mary,
        James, Joseph.
    Administratrix: Jemima Boone.

Esther Comegys   4.12   D   KE   £233.8.0   May 19 1763
    Sureties: William Whaley (Kent County), Alexander Lee (Queen Anne's County).
    Legatees: Joseph Whaley, William Heath, Sarah Heath (daughter of William),
        Abraham Waley (son of Joseph Waley), Sarah Waley (daughter of Joseph).
    Residue to children of Joseph Waley (equally): Joseph, Daniel, Abraham, Mary,
        Esther, Hannah, Sarah, Rachel.
    Executor: Joseph Whaley.

John Carman   4.12   D   QA   £135.17.6   Apr 14 1763
    Legatees: William Burton Carman.
    Distribution to: Widow (unnamed, 1/3). Residue to: Henry Cully Carman.
    Executrix: Rachel Bolton, wife of William Bolton.

John Sparks   4.12   D   QA   £55.3.7   Apr 14 1763
    Sureties: Benjamin Sparks, James Ruth.
    Distribution to: Widow (unnamed, 1/3). Residue to 7(!) children (equally): John,
        Rebecca, William, James, Mary, Samuel.
    Administrator: Edward Sparks.

James Pearman   4.13   D   AA   £21.8.6   Jun 19 1760
    Distribution to: child (unnamed) in possession of Mrs. Ann Pearman.
    Administratrix: Ann Pearman.

Nathaniel Phipps   4.13   D AA   £79.14.0   Jun 15 1763
    Sureties: John Brown, Peter Faris.
    Distribution to: Widow (unnamed, 1/3). Residue to 9 children (unnamed, equally).
    Executrix: Sarah Phipps.

Richard Taylor   4.13   D AA   £818.12.1   Mar 9 1763
    Sureties: Benjamin Williams, William Ijams, Hezekiah Linthicum, Henry Oneal
        Welsh.
    Distribution to 8 children: Samuel, Richard, Mary wife of John Green, Sophia,
        Caleb, Isaac, Joseph, Jemima.
    Executor: Richard Taylor.

Joseph Fenwick   4.14   D SM   £85.10.8   Nov 29 1760
    Distribution to: Representatives unknown to this Office.
    Administrator: Robert Fenwick.

James Broadaway   4.14   D DO   £118.13.6   Jun 11 1763
    Legatees: widow (unnamed), James Broadaway, Mary Broadaway, Sarah Broadaway.
    Distribution to: Widow (unnamed, 1/3).
    Executrix: Mary Sands, wife of Thomas Sands.

John Lotan   4.14   D AA   £27.5.9   Aug 5 1763
    Distribution to: Representatives unknown to this Office.
    Administrator: Valentine Douglas.

William Wright   4.15   D AA   £51.4.11   Jul 6 1763
    Administratrix: Elisabeth Wright.

Abell Crandell   4.15   D AA   £86.10.7   Jun 15 1763
    Distribution to: Widow (unnamed, 1/3). Residue to 5 children (equally):
        Margaret, Esther, Joseph, John, Francis.
    Administrator (de bonis non): Walter Gott.

Bartholomew Shean   4.15   D CA   £340.5.4   Mar 29 1763
    Distribution to (equally): Sarah Shean, Arthur Shean, Ann Shean.
    Administrator: Jonathon Slater.

James Dossey   4.16   D CA   £283.19.2   Jul 22 1763
    Executors: James Dossey, John Dossey.

Edward Newton   4.16   D DO   £820.16.1   Jun 15 1763
    Distribution to: Widow (unnamed, 1/3). Residue to (equally): Willis Newton,
        Richard Newton, Betty Newton.
    Executors: Mary Newton, Willis Newton.

Harrison Ayres   4.17   D WO   £169.17.5   Aug 7 1760
    Distribution to (equally): widow (unnamed), 2 children (unnamed).
    Executrix: Rachel Hudson, wife of John Hudson.

George Willson   4.17   D KE   £1019.11.0   Oct 17 1763
    Distribution to: Widow (unnamed, 1/3). Residue to 6 children (equally): George,
        Mary, James, John, William, Sarah.
    Administrator: William St. Clair.

Jacob Alwell   4.17   D AA   £212.13.6   Nov 8 1763
    Sureties: John Todd, Thomas Alwell.
    Distribution to: Widow (unnamed, 1/3). Residue to (equally): Thomas, John,
        William, Jacob, Elisabeth, Mary, Nathan, Stephen, Sarah.
    Administratrix: Sarah Allwell.

John Galwith   4.18   D   £122.5.3
    Distribution to: Widow (unnamed, 1/3). Residue to (5 parts, equally): John
        Galwith, Ignatius Galwith, Jonas Galwith, Sophiah Swallow, Absalom Beddah &
        Elisabeth Lawson.
    Administratrix: Elisabeth Galwith.

John Dickenson   4.18   D TA   £1074.16.3   May 18 1755
    Legatees: Rebecca Dickenson, Rachel Dickenson, William Dickenson, John Dickenson.
    Residue to 5 children (equally): Daniel, William, Rebecca, John, Rachel.
    Executor: Daniel Dickenson.

William Thomas   4.19   D KE   £1380.14.11   Sep 18 1750
    Sureties: William Trew, Edward Beck.
    Legatees: Mary (daughter).
    Distribution to: Widow (unnamed, 1/6). Residue to: Henry, William, Mary, James
        Thomas.
    Administrators: James Ringgold & Henry Hosier who married with the executrices
        (unnamed) of William Thomas & Henry Thomas (executors of the deceased).

Jervis Spencer   4.19   D KE   £2092.9.6
    Legatees: Isaac Spencer, Hannah Spencer, Ann Blackiston, Sarah Comegys,
        Christopher Williams.
    Residue to (equally): Isaac Spencer, Elisabeth Maxwell, Ann Blackiston, Sarah
        Comegys, Hannah Spencer.
    Executor: Isaac Spencer.

Aquilla Scott   4.20   D BA   £873.17.7
    Legatees: James.
    Representatives: Widow (unnamed), 7 children (unnamed).
    Distribution to: Lemuel Howard in right of his wife (unnamed), Joshua Bond
        guardian for Daniel Scott, Mordecai Ames guardian for 6 children (unnamed),
        widow's (unnamed) part added to her estate.
    Administrator (de bonis non): Ignatius Wheeler.

Elisabeth Scott   4.20   D BA   £248.7.8   Mar 8 1763
    Sureties: Thomas Wheeler, Benjamin Wheeler.
    Mentions: her part of estate of Aquilla Scott.
    Distribution to children (equally): James, Elisabeth, Rebecca, Sarah.
    Administrator: Ignatius Wheeler.

Richard Porter   4.21   D TA   £136.18.0   Mar 23 1763
    Distribution to: Ann Elbert, Mary Aarden, Alice Porter.
    Administrator (de bonis non): Mr. Peter Comeford.

Thomas Richardson   4.21   D PG   £383.2.5   Aug 24 1759
    Legatees: Mary, Thomas.
    Distribution to: Widow (unnamed, 1/3). Residue to: Thomas.
    Executrix (acting): Susanna Richardson.

Amey Tolson   4.22   D QA   £203.16.10   Nov 12 1763
    Sureties: John Tolson, Isaac Winchester.
    Legatees: John Tolson, Rachel Elliott, accountant, Ann Stephens, Andrew Tolson.
    Residue to (equally): John Tolson, Rachel Elliott.
    Executor: Benjamin Tolson.

Elisabeth Taylor   4.23   D KE   £81.18.8   Mar 10 1764
    Distribution to: Representatives unknown to this Office.
    Administrator: John Burk, Jr.

Philip Brookes   4.23   D KE   £471.12.2   Mar 10 1764
    Distribution to: Representatives unknown to this Office.
    Administrator: Rizden Bishop.

Eliza Thom   4.23   D KE   £45.5.3   Mar 1 1764
    Distribution to: (sister). Residue to: John (son).
    Administrator: John Burk, Jr.

James Lynch   4.24   D KE   £81.9.5   Mar 12 1764
    Distribution to: Representatives unknown to this Office.
    Administrator: Thomas Ringgold.

Jervis Gilbert   4.24   D BA   £132.11.6   Mar 5 1764
    Distribution to: Representatives unknown to this Office.
    Administrators: Ruth Gilbert, John Love.

Jos. England   4.24   D BA   £370.9.5   Feb 27 1764
    Distribution to: Widow (unnamed, 1/3). Residue to 7 children (equally): Robert,
        Hannah, Joseph, George, John, Samuel, Elisabeth.
    Administrators: Elisabeth England, William Ames.

Christ. Sutton   4.25   D BA   £296.9.11   Feb 27 1764
    Sureties: Luke Raven, John Buck.
    Distribution to: Representatives unknown to this Office.
    Administrator: Benjamin Buck.

Luke Raven   4.25   D BA   £694.9.10   Mar 10 1764
    Sureties: Capt. William Bond, Goldsmith Presbury.
    Executor: Luke Raven.

George Clark   4.25   D BA   £235.9.9   Mar 10 1764
    Sureties: Henry Thomas, Samuel Forwood.
    Distribution to: Representatives unknown to this Office.
    Administratrix: Mary Clark.

Shadrack Claywell   4.25   D WO   £158.19.0   Dec 6 1763
    Administratrix: Sarah Mitchell.

Elisabeth White   4.26   D WO   £7.0.2   Dec 2 1763
    Executors: Josiah Mitchell, Levin Hill.

William Collins   4.26   D WO   £45.6.3   Dec 20 1763
    Distribution to: Representatives unknown to this Office.
    Administrator: John Collings.

Mathew Purnell   4.26   D WO   £1070.7.2   Dec 8 1763
    Executors: Thomas Purnell, Martha Purnell.

James Owins   4.26   D WO   £139.1.1   Jan 6 1764
    Executrix: Keziah Fowler, wife of Arthur Fowler.

Smith Mills   4.27   D WO   £334.16.11   Dec 31 1763
    Administrator (de bonis non): Robert Mills.

Archibald Smith   4.27   D WO   £105.10.7   Mar 6 1764
    Executors: Turner Smith, George Smith.

Solomon Jarman   4.27   D WO   £177.15.4   Mar 23 1764
Reads "Should be Rachel Jarman administratrix of William Jarman".
    Distribution to: Widow (unnamed, 1/3). Residue to 6 children (unnamed, equally).
    Administratrix: Rachel Jarman.

John Edwards   4.28   D SM   £517.12.6   Feb 6 1764
    Distribution to: Representatives unknown to this Office.
    Administratrix: Elisabeth Edwards.

Thomas Broom   4.28   D SM   £1341.2.9   Feb 3 1764
    Legatees: Mathew Traverse, John Hooper Broome.
    Distribution to: Widow (unnamed, 1/3). Residue to 6 children (equally): Sarah,
        Mary, Elisabeth, Thomas, Hooper, Nancy.
    Executrix: Dorcas Broome.

Samuel Abel   4.28   D SM   £217.3.5   Feb 2 1764
    Distribution to: Representatives unknown to this Office.
    Administrator: Samuel Abell.

Cuthbert Fenwick   4.29   D SM   £417.4.4   Feb 10 1764
    Executor: Bennett Fenwick.

Cyranius Cheseldine   4.29   D SM   £338.1.10   Feb 10 1764
    Distribution to: Representatives unknown to this Office.
    Administrator: Knelem Cheseldine.

John James   4.29   D SM   £393.13.3   Feb 4 1764
    Distribution to: Widow (unnamed, 1/3). Residue to 4 children (equally): Hannah,
        Margaret, John, Jane.
    Administratrix: Margaret James.

Jane Powell   4.30   D KE   £51.0.9   Mar 2 1764
    Executor: Ch. Minskee.

William Copper   4.30   D KE   £194.14.6   Mar 13 1764
    Distribution to: Representatives unknown to this Office.
    Administrator: George Copper.

Henry Brooks   4.30   D KE   £826.1.3   Mar 2 1764
    Distribution to: Representatives unknown to this Office.
    Administrator (de bonis non): Henry Bodein.

Daniel Few   4.30   D KE   £8.11.4   Mar 3 1764
    Distribution to: Representatives unknown to this Office.
    Administratrix (de bonis non): Issabella Parsons.

Nicholas Parsons   4.31   D KE   £48.14.10   Mar 31 1764
    Distribution to: Representatives unknown to this Office.
    Administratrix: Issabella Parsons.

John Grant   4.31   D KE   £189.11.7   Apr 6 1764
    Distribution to: Representatives unknown to this Office.
    Administratrix: Elisabeth Grant.

Nicholas Crouch   4.31   D KE   £17.10.0   Apr 7 1764
    Administrator: William Murray.

John Tucker   4.31   D CA   £34.19.5   1764
    Administrator: John Kent.

John Hungerford   4.32   D CA   £263.6.11   Apr 8 1764
    Administrator: Thomas Cleverly Dare.

Walter Reed   4.32   D   QA   £112.10.10   Mar 29 1764
    Sureties: Ezekiel Hunter, Henry Thompson.
    Distribution to: Widow (unnamed, 1/3). Residue to 3 children (equally): Thomas,
        William, James.
    Administrator: Nathaniel Knotts.

William Goldsborough   4.32   D   QA   £246.5.7   Feb 23 1764
    Sureties: William Kent, John Kent.
    Executor: Daniel Griffith.

James Bowden   4.32   D   QA   £8.17.4   Mar 27 1764
    Executor: Thomas Davis of Kent County in Delaware.

Margaret Keene   4.33   D   PG   £1540.13.0   Aug 2 1763
    Executor: Capt. Francis Keene.

William Hutchings   4.33   D   TA   £31.15.9   Mar 27 1764
    Sureties: Thomas Benny of Kent County, Christopher St. Tee.
    Distribution to: Widow (unnamed, 1/3). Residue to 2 children (equally): William,
        James.
    Administratrix: Rachel St. Tee, wife of Christopher St. Tee.

John Robinson   4.33   D   AA   £197.17.1   May 3 1764
    Distribution to: Representatives unknown to this Office.
    Administratrix: Sophiah Robinson.

Susanna Hardy   4.33   D   SO   £53.19.1   Mar 19 1764
    Distribution to: Representatives unknown to this Office.
    Administrators: William Tully, Joshua Moore.

Ruth Williams   4.34   D   AA   £167.0.10   May 17 1764
    Distribution to: Representatives unknown to this Office.
    Administrator: Benjamin Williams.

Joseph Fenwick   4.34   D   SM   £27.12.4   Jun 26 1764
    Distribution to: Representatives unknown to this Office.
    Administrator: Robert Fenwick.

Edward Pritchet   4.34   D   DO   £104.13.11   Jan 16 1764
    Distribution to: Representatives unknown to this Office.
    Administrator (de bonis non): William Pritchet.

John Eccleston   4.34   D   DO   £1264.6.4   May 28 1764
    Sureties: Hall Caile, Henry Ennalls, Jr.
    Residue to 4 children (unnamed, equally).
    Executor (surviving): Hugh Eccleston.

James Tippett   4.35   D   KE   £14.16.6   May 26 1764
    Executrix (acting): Grace Tippet.

Henry Semans   4.35   D   KE   £550.12.6   May 25 1764
    Legatees: Henry Semans (grandson), Solomon Semans (son), William Semans (son),
        Jeremiah Semans (son), Elisabeth Boyer (daughter), Hannah Jarvis (daughter),
        Mary Burris (daughter).
    Distribution to: Widow (unnamed, 1/3). Residue to 2 sons (equally): Daniel,
        Fowler.
    Executor: Solomon Semans.

Nathaniel Strong   4.36   D   KE   £87.7.5   Jun 5 1764
    Distribution to: Representatives unknown to this Office.
    Administratrix: Rachel Wilson (late Rachel Strong), now wife of William Wilson.

James Frazier   4.36   D   KE   £72.13.1   Jun 13 1764
    Distribution to: Representatives unknown to this Office.
    Administratrix: Mary Rewell (late Mary Frazier), now wife of John Rewell.

Thomas Hebbron   4.36   D   KE   £33.0.   Jun 17 1764
    Distribution to: Representatives unknown to this Office.
    Administrator: Thomas Hebbron.

William Briscoe   4.36   D   KE   £198.19.8   Jun 22 1764
    Distribution to: Representatives unknown to this Office.
    Administratrix: Mary Ann Briscoe.

John Booth   4.37   D   KE   £187.2.0   Jun 30 1764
    Executrix: Elisabeth Thomas, wife of William Thomas.

Henry Miles   4.37   D   SO   £69.12.9   Jul 11 1764
    Executors: William Miles, Henry Miles.

George Raisin   4.37   D KE   £551.14.8   Jul 6 1764
    Mentions: widow (unnamed) was pregnant.
    Executrix: Sarah Raisin.

Thomas Acre   4.38   D KE   £173.8.10   Jul 7 1764
    Distribution to: Representatives unknown to this Office.
    Administrator (de bonis non): Abraham Acre.

Conrad Resior   4.38   D CE   £32.5.8   Apr 21 1764
    Administrator: Edward Mitchel.

Rosanna Thomas   4.38   D KE   £36.10.8   May 19 1764
    Legatees: John Arnold, Elisabeth Gosh and her daughter Mary.
    Residue to children (unnamed).
    Executor: John March.

John Watson   4.39   D KE   £335.18.5   May 4 1764
    Distribution to: Widow (unnamed, 1/3). Residue to 4 daughters (equally): Eliza,
        Catherine, Margaret, Jane.
    Executors: Hester Watson, Edward Watson.

William Price   4.39   D TA   £256.10.10   Jun 5 1764
    Sureties: Francis Baker, George Prouse.
    Distribution to: Widow (unnamed, 1/3). Residue to 6 children (equally): James,
        Evan, William, Andrew, Nathan, Jacob.
    Administratrix: Rebecca Price.

Abner Parratt   4.40   D TA   £409.8.4   Jun 26 1764
    Sureties: James Berry, Thomas Jenkins.
    Legatees (children): Mary, Elisabeth, Abner, William, ------ (daughter, unnamed).
    Distribution to: Widow (unnamed, 1/3). Residue to 5 children (aforesaid,
        equally).
    Executors: Margaret Parratt, Mathew Jenkins.

Philip Melton   4.41   D KE   £265.2.3   May 8 1764
    Distribution to: Representatives unknown to this Office.
    Administratrix: Mary Read, wife of Benjamin Read.

Bartus Garnett   4.41   D KE   £219.10.0   May 4 1764
    Executrix: Henrietta Blackiston, wife of Ebenezar Blackiston.

Martin Trush   4.41   D BA   £58.19.9   My 19 1764
    Executrix: Eliza Enimice, wife of Philip Enimice (?).

George Clark   4.41   D BA   £145.9.4   May 21 1764
    Distribution to: Representatives unknown to this Office.
    Administratrix: Mary Clarke.

William Greenfield   4.42   D BA   £192.7.3   May 14 1764
    Mentions: Distribution for estate of Nicholas Van Horn, which belongs on Folio
        65: Barnet Van Horn (son), Jacob Harper (son-in-law), Nicholas Van Horne
        (son), Jacob Van Horne (son), children (unnamed) of Robert Walmsley by
        Elisabeth (daughter), Jane Nowland (daughter), Mary Hutchinson (daughter),
        Letitia McCombs (daughter), Rachel Rice (daughter), William Rice (son-in-law),
        Jacob Everte (son-in-law) and his wife Esther.
    Legatees: Micajah (son).
    Distribution to: heirs (unnamed) of wife (unnamed) of John Coatney, heirs
        (unnamed) of wife (unnamed) of John Deavers, heirs (unnamed) of wife (unnamed)
        of William Debruler, James Greenfield, William Greenfield, John Walters,
        Micajah Greenfield.
    Executor: Micajah Greenfield.

Michael Taney   4.43   D CA   £1243.0.7   May 14 1764
    Distribution to: Widow (unnamed, 1/3). Residue to children (unnamed).
    Executrix: Jane Wheeler, wife of George Wheeler.

William Dawkins   4.43   D CA   £602.0.1   May 19 1764
    Executrix: Mary Dawkins.

Abraham Bowen   4.43   D CA   £355.1.0   Jun 12 1764
    Executor: Abraham Bowen.

Thomas Ireland   4.44   D CA   £2056.0.2   May 11 1764
The amount of the accounts also included £284.14.6 sterling.
    Legatees: widow (unnamed), Thomas (son), John John (son), Richard (son), Gideon
        (son), George (son), "child wife is pregnant with", Sarah Johnson (wife's
        daughter).
    Distribution to: Widow (unnamed, 1/3). Residue to children (equally): Richard,
        Gideon, George, "child wife is pregnant with".
    Executrix: Mary Ireland.

Mathew Hawkins   4.45   D QA   £837.2.10   Jan 7 1764
    Sureties: James Gould, Benjamin Gould.
    Distribution to: Widow (unnamed, 1/3). Residue to 6 children (equally): John,
        Mathew, Frances, James, Elisabeth, Ernault.
    Administratrix: Frances Gould.

Solomon Seeney   4.45   D QA   £258.6.11   Apr 5 1764
    Sureties: James Hackett, Joel Brown.
    Legatees (children): John, Nevil, Solomon.
    Distribution to: Widow (unnamed, 1/3).
    Executor (acting): John Seeney.

John Wallace   4.46   D QA   £160.0.0   May 12 1764
    Executrix: Hannah Warner, wife of Philip Warner.

John Sunderland   4.46   D CA   £138.10.8   Jul 26 1763
    Legatees: John Sunderland.
    Distribution to: Widow (unnamed, 1/3). Residue to 2 children (unnamed, equally).
    Executrix: Sarah Marquis (late Sarah Sunderland), now wife of William Marquis.

John Elder   4.47   D AA   £521.2.3   Oct 18 1764
    Legatees (children): Elisabeth, Honor, Jemima.
    Distribution to: Widow (unnamed, 1/3). Residue to 7 children (equally): John,
        Owen, Charles, Eli, Honor, Jemima, Elijah.
    Administratrix: Jemima Hobbs, wife of Joseph Hobbs.

Samuel Parker   4.47   D WO   £354.19.1   May 6 1763
    Legatees: widow (unnamed), Tabitha (daughter), Abigail (daughter), Samuel (son).
    Distribution to: Widow (unnamed, 1/3). Residue to children (unnamed, equally).
    Administratrix: Elisabeth Parker.

Sarah Parran   4.48   D CA   £242.15.6   Nov 29 1764
    Sureties: Josep Vansweringen, Aaron Williams.
    Administrator: Samuel Parran.

John Dorrumple   4.48   D CA   £208.11.5   Nov 5 1764
    Sureties: Alexander Somervill, Rousby Miller.
    Administratrix: Ann Dorrumple.

John Burk   4.48   D QA   £8.5.7   Nov 29 1764
    Sureties: Andrew Hynson, James Hynson.
    Distribution to: Representatives unknown to this Office.
    Administrators: Mathew Griffith, Thomas Hall.

William Luckett   4.48   D CH   £137.18.10   Jun 30 1764
    Sureties: Francis Ware, Thomas Husey.
    Administratrix: Susannah Maddox, wife of Cornelius Maddox.

Thomas Keybert   4.48   D CH   £306.13.11   Jul 7 1764
    Sureties: John Kinsman, Wharton Philbert, William Cooper.
    Administrator: John Keybert.

John McKee   4.49   D DO   £28.2.0   Aug 10 1764
    Sureties: William Byus, Benjamin Woodward.
    Administrator: John Stewart.

Joseph Bullock   4.49   D DO   £71.6.7   Aug 18 1764
    Sureties: Thomas Perry, Francis Bullock.
    Administratrix: Sarah Warrington, wife of Nathaniel Warrington.

Roger Adams   4.49   D DO   £883.2.3   Oct 29 1764
    Sureties: William Cannon, James Adams.
    Administrator: Richard Clarkson, Roger Adams, William Fountain.

Ambrose Mitchell   4.49   D DO   £60.0.0   Jun 14 1764
    Sureties: Felix Summers, John Mitchell.
    Administratrix: Elisabeth Mitchell by her surety John Mitchell.

James Broadaway   4.50   D DO   £7.12.4   Dec 6 1764
    Sureties: Thomas Baynard, James Lecompte.
    Legatees: wife (unnamed), children: James, Mary, Sarah.
    Executrix: Mary Sands, wife of Thomas Sands.

Kensey Sparrow   4.50   D AA   £23.0.0   Oct 24 1764
    Sureties: Jonathon Selman, Martin Norris.
    Administratrix: Dianah Sparrow.

James Davis   4.50   D AA   £20.18.0   Nov 13 1764
    Administrator: William Davis.

Mary Wright   4.50   D AA   £79.15.6   Oct 18 1764
    Sureties: Caleb Dorsey, Samuel Dorsey.
    Administrator (de bonis non): Thomas Wright.

Robert Gordon   4.51   D CH   £68.16.4   Oct 13 1764
    Executrix: Rebecca Wall, wife of Robert Wall.

Jane Langley   4.51   D SM   £238.1.9   Oct 28 1764
    Administrator: John Langley.

Francis Scale   4.51   D TA   £126.10.1   Nov 27 1764
    Administrator: Peter Shanahan.

Philip Hall   4.51   D AA   £90.0.5   Nov 15 1764
    Sureties: Joseph Cowman, Joseph Watkins.
    Administratrix: Mary Hall.

John Cornish   4.51   D CH   £307.5.11   Feb 13 1764
    Sureties: William Douglass, William Franklin.
    Administratrix: Ann Cornish.

Edward Trippe   4.52   D DO   £301.13.5   Sep 3 1764
    Sureties: John Griffith, William Trippe.
    Distribution to: Mary (daughter).
    Executor: John Trippe.

William Carter   4.52   D DO   £43.16.11   Aug 12 1764
    Sureties: Alexander Frazier, Thomas Taylor.
    Administrator: Edward Carter.

John Andrew   4.52   D DO   £9.2.8   Mar 26 1764
    Sureties: Thomas Gray, William Gray.
    Legatees: Jane Cannon, William Andrew, James Andrew, Tamsey Nuton.
    Residue to (equally): John Andrew, Jr., Thomas Andrew, Joseph Andrew, Mary
        Griffith.
    Executor: John Andrew, Jr.

Stephen Fleaharty   4.53   D DO   £130.14.1   --- 26 1764
    Sureties: Alexander Frazier, Joseph Chezum.
    Legatees: Mary (sister).
    Residue to (equally): Rebecca (child), children (John & Ann) of John (son),
        children (Sarah, William, & Deborah) of Ann Perry (daughter).
    Executrix: Rebecca Chipley.

Thomas Bourk   4.53   D KE   £435.18.4   Aug 8 1764
    Sureties: Andrew Hynson, James Hynson.
    Distribution to: Representatives unknown to this Office.
    Administrator (de bonis non): Isaac Freeman.

John Rasin   4.53   D KE   £538.18.1   Aug 2 1764
    Sureties: Razin Gale, Macal Medford.
    Distribution to: Representatives unknown to this Office.
    Administratrix: Rosa Rasin, wife of Abraham Rasin.

John Waters   4.54   D KE   £37.12.0   Aug 7 1764
    Distribution to: Representatives unknown to this Office.
    Administrator: Charles Reed.

Peter Green   4.54   D KE   £44.17.3   Jul 24 1764
    Sureties: Samuel Rogers, Henry Thomas.
    Distribution to: Representatives unknown to this Office.
    Administrator (acting): Alexander Green.

Thomas Wyatt   4.54   D QA   £123.2.8   Jun 21 1764
    Sureties: James Ewen, John Ewen.
    Distribution to: Widow (unnamed, 1/3). Residue to: Thomas (son).
    Administratrix: Elisabeth Wyatt.

Mary Benston   4.54   D AA   £5.18.10   1764
    Distribution to: Representatives unknown to this Office.
    Administrator (de bonis non): Joseph Frazier.

Francis Green   4.55   D CH   £54.17.0   Apr 7 1764
    Sureties: William Clements, James Mudd.
    Distribution to: Representatives unknown to this Office.
    Administrator: Leonard Green.

Thomas Dubberly   4.55   D WO   £74.15.10   May 25 1764
    Sureties: Isaac Payne, Jacob Payne.
    Distribution to: Widow (unnamed, 1/3). Residue to 9 children (unnamed, equally).
    Administratrix: Esther Dubberly.

George Hurry   4.55   D CH   £102.9.2   1764
    Sureties: William Lindsey, James Thompson.
    Administratrix: Ann Skinner, wife of Jeremiah Skinner.

Elisabeth Brandt   4.55   D CH   £108.15.7   1764
    Sureties: Joseph Thompson, Richard Thompson.
    Distribution to: Representatives unknown to this Office.
    Administrator: Henry Thompson.

James Sutherland   4.56   D CH   £175.19.2   May 12 1764
    Sureties: Jos. Brawner, John Fagg.
    Administrator: Joseph Tims.

John Gibson   4.56   D CE   £256.15.4   Aug 20 1764
    Sureties: Johannas Arrants, James Veazey.
    Distribution to: Widow (unnamed, 1/3). Residue to 4 children (equally):
        Elisabeth, Rachel, Robert, Mary.
    Administratrix: Ann Hutchison (late Ann Gibson).

Caleb Guthry   4.56   D KE   £36.13.7   Sep 8 1764
    Administrator: Thomas Ringgold.

Thomas Price   4.56   D QA   £322.14.9   Jul 26 1764
    Sureties: Solomon Kenton, Barthol. Fiddeman.
    Representatives: Elisabeth (mother, accountant), Jane (sister) wife of Samuel
       Pennington, Ann (sister) wife of Thomas Pennington, Margaret (sister) wife of
       Robert Noble.
    Administratrix: Elisabeth Price.

John Dolvin   4.57   D TA   £156.19.3   Sep 20 1764
    Sureties: George Noble, Thomas Cassaway.
    Distribution to 4 children: Richard (accountant), Daniel, Mary wife of Patrick
       Hart, Frances wife of John Powell.
    Administrator: Richard Dolvin.

Robert Anderson   4.57   D CH   £249.12.5   Apr 4 1764
    Sureties: James Anderson, Robert Glanding.
    Distribution to: Representatives unknown to this Office.
    Administratrix: Mary Anderson.

William Jeffers   4.57   D QA   £213.16.1   Aug 30 1764
    Sureties: Benjamin Tanner, Absalom Davis.
    Distribution to: Widow (unnamed, 1/3). Residue to 7 children (equally): John,
       William, Mary, Peter, Reuben, Jacob, Bazil.
    Administratrix: Elisabeth Joiner, wife of William Joiner.

Job Newton   4.58   D WO   £68.4.5   Apr 6 1764
    Sureties: Joshua Evans, Levin Newton.
    Distribution to: Widow (unnamed, 1/3). Residue to 9 of children (unnamed,
       equally).
    Administratrix: Comfort Newton.

Isaac Flemming   4.58   D WO   £215.18.3   Aug 11 1764
    Sureties: David Long, William Moore.
    Distribution to: Representatives unknown to this Office.
    Administratrix: Elisabeth Flemming.

John Butler   4.58   D CH   £129.6.6   Aug 9 1764
    Sureties: John Brookes, John Fagg.
    Distribution to: Widow (unnamed, 1/3). Residue to 6 children (unnamed, equally).
    Administratrix: Elisabeth Higgins, wife of William Higgins.

David Crawford   4.58   D CH   £74.17.6   Jun 13 1764
    Sureties: John Sanders, John Perry, Jr.
    Distribution to: Representatives unknown to this Office.
    Administratrix: Ann Crawford.

William Whittington   4.59   D AA   £125.4.2   Sep 20 1764
    Distribution to: Representatives unknown to this Office.
    Administrator: Thomas Whittington.

John Guybert   4.59   D SM   £236.13.0   Aug 1 1764
    Sureties: William Hammersley, Samuel Lee.
    Distribution to: Representatives unknown to this Office.
    Administratrix: Dorothy Martin, wife of Thomas Green Martin.

Mathew Henikin   4.59   D CH   £103.13.11   Aug 2 1764
    Sureties: Blaw Posey, Mark Brafield.
    Distribution to: Representatives unknown to this Office.
    Administratrix: Elisabeth Henkin.

James Townsend   4.59   D QA   £34.19.7   Oct 4 1764
    Distribution to 7 children: Mary wife of Thomas Swann, Thomas, Solomon, James,
        Aaron, Sarah, Jane wife of William Roe.
    Administratrix: Jane Barwick.

John Barwick   4.60   D QA   £43.19.3   Oct 4 1764
    Sureties: Edward Barwick, Thomas Swann.
    Distribution to 4 children: Edward (of age), William (of age), Eleanor wife of
        Richard Bond, John.
    Administratrix: Jane Barwick.

George Foxon   4.60   D KE   £74.9.1   Jul 25 1764
    Distribution to: Martha Green (sister), Martha (daughter) wife of Joseph Copper.
    Executor: Joseph Copper.

John Day   4.60   D KE   £288.0.4   Sep 8 1764
    Sureties: John Monsh, John Beuly.
    Distribution to: Widow (unnamed, 1/3). Residue to children (equally): John,
        Araminta.
    Executrix: Susannah Piner, wife of Benjamin Piner.

Robert Breakenbridge   4.61   D CE   £48.8.7   Sep 8 1764
    Distribution to: widow (unnamed), "child (if any) wife is pregnant with", Barbara
        (niece).
    Executor: Samuel Whan.

John Stavely   4.61   D KE   £444.12.9   Aug 11 1764
    Sureties: Joseph Briscoe, Joseph Stavely.
    Distribution to: Widow (unnamed, 1/3). Residue to 3 children (equally): James,
        John, Mary.
    Executors: James Stavely, Margaret Stavely.

Margaret Gaither   4.61   D AA   £638.7.2   Oct 1 1764
    Sureties: Henry Howard, Edward Gaither.
    Distribution to (equally): Margaret (daughter) wife of Joseph Howard, their 4
        children: Margaret Howard, Joseph Howard, Margery Howard, Benjamin Howard.
    Executor: Joseph Howard, Sr.

Thomas Conn   4.62   D FR   £228.10.10   Nov 8 1764
    Sureties: Thomas Miles, Joseph Miles.
    Legatees: Thomas (son).
    Residue to: Martha (wife).
    Executor: Thomas Conn.

Richard Adams   4.62   D CH   £623.13.4   May 19 1764
    Sureties: James Greenfield Wood, John Stone Hawkins.
    Legatees: John (son), Margaret Burch, Samuel (son).
    Residue to 6 children ("then living with him").
    Executor: John Adams.

Thomas Buswell   4.62   D KE   £145.4.0   Oct 28 1764
    Sureties: Stephen Bordley, Abraham Milton.
    Executor: Arthur Miller.

John Cooper   4.63   D QA   £526.4.0   Aug 20 1764
    Sureties: Daniel Wheatley, Solomon Kenton.
    Legatees: George (son), Deborah Emory (daughter), Thomas (son), Ann Everit
        (daughter), Richard Roe (grandchild), Elisabeth Roe (grandchild), Abner Roe
        (grandchild), Thomas Roe (grandchild), Richard Cooper (son of Richard,
        grandchild), James Cooper (son of Richard, grandchild), Richard (son).
    Executor: Richard Cooper.

Edward Piner   4.63   D KE   £99.0.6   Oct 23 1764
    Distribution to: Bartus (brother).
    Administrator: Bartus Piner.

Mary Graham   4.64   D CE   £466.4.11   Aug 15 1764
    Sureties: John McCoy, James Arbunkill.
    Legatees: Catrin Graham, William (son), Robert (son).
    Residue to 3 children (equally): William, Robert, Catrin.
    Executor: George Corry.

Elisabeth Birkhead   4.64   D AA   £42.0.0   Sep 13 1764
    Sureties: Samuel Chew, Samuel Birkhead.
    Distribution to: Samuel Birkhead (brother).
    Administrator: Elisabeth Birkhead, Nehemiah Birkhead.

Hudson Wathen   4.64   D CH   £284.8.0   Dec 12 1763
    Sureties: Philip Edelin, Ignatius Simpson.
    Executrix: Sarah Wathen.

John Basil Greenwell   4.65   D SM   £171.5.11   Aug 1 1764
    Legatees: Eleanor (widow), daughter-in-law (unnamed), Richard Clark (son-in-law).
    Distribution to: Widow (unnamed, 1/3). Residue to 2 sons (equally): Joshua,
        James.
    Executrix: Eleanor Wheatly, wife of James Wheatly.

John Elder   4.65   D AA   £521.2.3   1764
    Sureties: Vachel Dorsey, James Elder.
    Legatees: Honor (daughter), Jemima (daughter).
    Distribution to: Jemima (widow, 1/3). Residue to 7 children (equally): John,
        Owen, Charles, Ely, Elijah, Honor, Jemima.
    Administrators: Joseph Hollis and his wife Jemima Hollis.

Nicholas Vanhorne   4.65   D CE   £114.17.8   Sep 1 1764
    Sureties: Barnett Vanhorne, Charles Heath.
    Distribution to: see Folio 42.
    Executors: Jacob Evertson, Jacob Vanhorne.

Joseph Nicholson   4.66   D SO   £192.6.3   Sep 14 1763
    Sureties: George Dashiell, Doubty Collier.
    Distribution to (equally): Mary Nicholson, Peggy Nicholson.
    Administratrix: Sarah Nicholson.

Winder Jacobs   4.66   D SO   £93.3.4   1763
    Sureties: Panther Laws, Hugh Porter.
    Distribution to: Representatives unknown to this Office.
    Administratrix: Ann Jacobs.

Elisabeth Callaway   4.66   D SO   £52.1.0   Mar 30 1763
    Sureties: William Robinson, Southy King.
    Distribution to: Representatives unknown to this Office.
    Administrator: Peter Callaway.

Isaac Noble   4.66   D SO   £95.11.9   1764
    Sureties: Marthillas Hobbs, John Noble.
    Distribution to: Representatives unknown to this Office.
    Administratrix: Alice Noble.

Abraham Barklet   4.67   D SO   £103.4.0   Jun 30 1764
    Distribution to: Representatives unknown to this Office.
    Administratrix: Rachel Barklet.

James Laramore   4.67   D SO   £206.11.11   May 14 1764
    Distribution to: Representatives unknown to this Office.
    Administratrix: Sarah Laramore.

Bloys Harris   4.67   D SO   £98.16.3   1764
    Distribution to: Representatives unknown to this Office.
    Administratrix: Ann Harris.

Philip Adams   4.67   D SO   £53.2.2   Dec 10 1763
    Sureties: Bell Maddox, Jacob Adams.
    Distribution to: Representatives unknown to this Office.
    Administratrix: Sarah Adams.

Solomon Collins   4.67   D SO   £19.10.3   Mar 25 1763
    Sureties: Richard Knowles, Thomas Walker.
    Distribution to (equally): Nathan Collins, Patrick Collins.
    Administratrix: Elisabeth Collins.

Nehemiah Hearn   4.68   D SO   £221.16.6   May 20 1764
    Sureties: Isaac Moore, Thomas Hearn, Jr.
    Legatees (sons): Joshua, Elisha, William.
    Distribution to: Widow (unnamed, 1/3). Residue to children (equally): Elisha,
        William, Joshua, Thomas, Mary.
    Executrix: Betty Day Hearn.

Solomon Hitch   4.68   D SO   £187.12.2   1764
    Sureties: Thomas Humphris, John Hitch.
    Legatees: Elisabeth (widow), Risdon (son, under 18), Susannah (daughter),
    Residue to (equally): Elisabeth (widow), son (unnamed), daughter (unnamed).
    Executrix: Elisabeth Hitch.

Alexander Munroe   4.69   D SO   £32.10.8   Aug 16 1764
    Sureties: James Polk, John Tull.
    Distribution to 2 of children (equally): Isaac, Matthias.
    Executor: William Pullett.

Mathew Wallace   4.69   D SO   £384.4.10   Jul 13 1764
    Sureties: Gowen White, Francis White.
    Legatees: William (son), Bridget Reveall (daughter), Richard (son), George
        Traverse (grandson), Mathew (son), Mary Roe (daughter), Elisabeth Traverse
        (daughter), Leah (daughter), Ann Winder (daughter).
    Residue to: Mary (wife). She is to provide schooling for: Joseph, David, Jane,
        Mary.
    Executrix: Mary Roberts, wife of Rencher Roberts.

Thomas Hearn   4.70   D SO   £631.8.3   Jul 2 1764
    Sureties: Isaac Meek, John Martin.
    Legatees: George (son), Ebenezar (son), Thomas (son), Elisabeth Moore (daughter),
        to grandsons Elisha & William & Joshua (sons of son Nehemiah), Jemima
        (daughter), John Hearn (grandson), Mary Morgan (daughter), Sarah (daughter),
        Ann (daughter), Esther Vinnent (daughter).
    Residue to all children (unnamed, equally).
    Executor: Thomas Hearn.

Whittington King   4.71   D SO   £452.6.9   Nov 4 1763
    Sureties: Jesse King, William Furnis.
    Executor: John King.

Ahab Costen   4.71   D SO   £281.9.3   Nov 2 1763
    Sureties: Jacob Costen, Matthias Costen.
    Executors: Matthias Costen and his wife Abigail Costen.

John White   4.71   D FR   £237.1.0   Dec 12 1760
    Legatees: Martha (wife), children: Peter, Leonard, James, Catherine (cites "her
        mother"), Ruth (cites "her mother"), John (eldest son).
    Distribution to: Widow (unnamed, 1/3). Residue to (equally): John, Peter,
        Leonard, James, Abigail, Sarah, Catherine, Ruth White.
    Executrix: Martha Terrence (formerly Martha White), wife of Hugh Terrence.

Zebulon Hollingsworth   4.72   D CE   £952.12.0   Dec 11 1764
    Sureties: Joseph Gilpin, Jesse Hollingsworth.
    Legatees: Henry (son), Lydia (daughter), Mary (wife).
    Distribution to (equally): Zebulon, Henry, Levy, Jacob, Lydia, Thomas, Stephen,
        John, Samuel Hollingsworth.
    Executors: Mary Hollingsworth, Henry Hollingsworth, Jacob Hollingsworth.

Mary Pennington   4.72   D CE   £205.10.6   Feb 13 1765
    Sureties: William Pearce, William Beedle, Jr.
    Distribution to 7 children: John, Mary Conn, Isaac, Rebecca Pearce, Elisabeth
        Hyland, Sarah, Robert. To daughters of Rachel Tule (daughter of deceased):
        Alice Tule, Ann Tule, Rachel Tule, Rebecca Tule. To: William Button (son of
        Susanna daughter of Rachel Tule (daughter of deceased)).
    Administrator: John Pennington.

John Thompson   4.73   D CE   £763.12.1   Nov 12 1764
    Sureties: Adam Van Bebber, Sidney George.
    Legatees (children): John Dockwra Thompson (eldest son), Mary (under 20), Joshua
        (under 21), Edward (under 21), George.
    Distribution to: Widow (unnamed, 1/3). Residue to children (equally): Mary, John
        Dockwra, Joshua, Edward.
    Executrix: Jane Brown (late Jane Thompson).

James Bryson   4.74   D CE   £139.8.5   Nov 21 1764
    Sureties: Joseph Taylor, John Getty.
    Distribution to: Representatives unknown to this Office.
    Administratrix (de bonis non): Hester Hukill.

Daniel McLane   4.74   D CE   £85.18.2   Oct 26 1764
    Sureties: Mathew Taylor, Mathew Thompson.
    Distribution to: Representatives unknown to this Office.
    Administrator: Daniel McLane.

Guilder Hukill   4.74   D   CE   £29.1.11   1764
    Sureties: Joseph Taylor, John Getty.
    Distribution to: Representatives unknown to this Office.
    Administratrix: Hester Hukill.

Alexander Broom   4.74   D   CA   £212.2.9   Sep 10 1764
    Sureties: Henry Brome, Thomas Brome.
    Legatees: Mary Brome (daughter of John Brome), Ann Brome (daughter of John
        Brome), Ann Wilson, Thomas Brome (brother), William Brome (nephew).
    Executor: Capt. John Brome.

William Harrison   4.75   D   CA   £574.11.9   Oct 2 1764
    Sureties: Henry Hewes, James Sawell.
    Distribution to: Widow (unnamed, 1/3). Residue to 4 children (equally): Henry,
        Mary Hunt, William, James.
    Executor: Henry Harrison.

John Robinson   4.75   D   CA   £174.5.6   Sep 26 1764
    Sureties: John Robinson, Samuel Worthy.
    Distribution to: Widow (unnamed, 1/3). Residue to 7 children (equally): John,
        Nathaniel, Abraham, Isaac, Jacob, Elisabeth, Richard.
    Administratrix: Sarah Robinson.

John Ward   4.76   D   CA   £104.0.0   Nov 9 1764
    Sureties: Rousby Miller, William Dorrumple.
    Legatees: Thomas (son), one of the daughters (unnamed).
    Distribution to: Widow (unnamed, 1/3). Residue to children (unnamed, equally,
        not including the above).
    Executor (surviving): James Ward.

Robert Freeland   4.76   D   CA   £1611.7.3   Sep 13 1764
    Sureties: Francis Freeland, James Sawell.
    Legatees: Rebecca Wilson (daughter), Elisabeth & Robert Freeland (children of
        Benjamin Freeland (son)).
    Distribution to: Rebecca Wilson (late Rebecca Freeland). Residue to 6 of the
        children (equally): Robert, Francis, Jacob, Sarah, Frisby, Peregrine.
    Executor: Robert Freeland.

Francis Middlemore   4.77   D   BA   £2377.17.7   Oct 14 1764
The amount of the accounts also included #12627 and £1016.12.1 sterling.
    Sureties: Col. John Hall, Robert Adair.
    Legatees: children (Garret, Goldsmith, George, Pheneta, Mary) of George & Mary
        Garretson, George Goldsmith Garretson, children (William Robinson, George,
        Martha) of George Presbury, daughters (Mary, Elisabeth, Martha, Frances,
        Hannah) of John & Elisabeth Paca, George Presbury, Sr., Martha Garretson wife
        of George Garretson, Richard Dallam, Josias Dallam, Catherine Bradford wife of
        William Bradford, Elisabeth Webster wife of Michael Webster.
    Residue to (equally): Richard Dallam, Josias Dallam.
    Executor: John Paca.

James Garretson   4.78   D   BA   £505.2.0   Nov 7 1764
    Sureties: Samuel Griffith, Edward Garretson.
    Legatees: Garret (son).
    Distribution to: Widow (unnamed, 1/3). Residue to 7 children (equally): Garret,
        Elisabeth, Frances, Martha, Mary, James, Bennett.
    Executors: Catharine Garretson, James Garretson.

James Brown   4.78   D   BA   £377.4.2   1764
    Sureties: Edward Morgan, Robert Dunn.
    Distribution to: Representatives unknown to this Office.
    Administratrix: Elisabeth Lynn, wife of Josias Lynn.

Thomas Lytle   4.78   D   BA   £286.9.11   Aug 10 1764
    Sureties: William Anderson, William Wyley.
    Distribution to: Widow (unnamed, 1/3). Residue to 7 children (equally): James,
        George, Elisabeth, Henrietta, Margaret, Thomas, Mary.
    Administratrix: Eleanor Lytle.

William Beedle   4.79   D   CE   £996.17.4   Oct 17 1764
    Sureties: Edward Price Wilmer, John Ward.
    Distribution to: Representatives unknown to this Office.
    Administratrix: Jane Glenn, wife of Samuel Glenn.

Mathew Heniken   4.79   D   CH   £103.13.11   Aug 2 1764
    Sureties: Blain Posey, Mark Brafield.
    Distribution to: Representatives unknown to this Office.
    Administratrix: Elisabeth Heniken.

Andrew Thompson   4.79   D BA   £69.18.4   Oct 29 1764
    Sureties: Andrew Martin, William Rigdon.
    Legatees (daughters): Sarah Durham wife of Jacob Durham, Elisabeth Bush wife of
        Isaac Bush, Hannah.
    Residue to: Elisabeth (widow).
    Administratrix: Elisabeth Thompson.

John Hart   4.79½   D KE   £91.9.6   Nov 23 1764
    Sureties: Griffith Jones, John Angier.
    Distribution to: Representatives unknown to this Office.
    Administrator: John Mitchell.

Francis Mauldin   4.79½   D CE   £720.4.5   Oct 10 1764
    Sureties: Henry Baker, Peter Sluyter.
    Legatees: Francis (son), Benjamin (son), William (son), Henry (son), Rebecca
        (daughter), Elisabeth (daughter), Mary Kitridge Mauldin, "child wife pregnant
        with".
    Distribution to: Widow (unnamed, 1/3). Residue to children (unnamed, "those then
        living", equally).
    Executrix: Mary Mauldin.

James Davis   4.80   D AA   £11.17.8   Feb 20 1765
    Sureties: Nicholas Boone, Thomas Moss.
    Distribution to: Representatives unknown to this Office.
    Administrator: William Davis.

John Young   4.80   D BA   £657.19.5   Nov 3 1764
    Sureties: Edward Bussey, Michael Jenkins.
    Distribution to 6 children (equally): William, George, Rebecca, Mary, Sarah,
        Elisabeth.
    Executrix: Rebecca Young.

William Whaley   4.80   D KE   £127.0.0   Dec 21 1764
    Sureties: Joseph Whaley, Nicholas Mason.
    Distribution to: Representatives unknown to this Office.
    Administratrix: Martha Whaley.

Charles Grindage   4.80   D KE   £13.3.0   Dec 13 1764
    Sureties: Sanders Bostick, Ebenezar Massey.
    Distribution to: Representatives unknown to this Office.
    Administrator: Thomas McDermot.

Elisabeth Stinson   4.81   D CA   £39.13.10   Feb 16 1765
    Sureties: William Harris, Jr., Ellis Slater.
    Distribution to (equally): Thomas Polson, William Polson.
    Administrator (surviving): Benjamin Sedwick.

Nehemiah Covington   4.81   D KE   £259.19.0   Dec 11 1764
    Sureties: Daniel Jones, Philip Covington.
    Distribution to: Representatives unknown to this Office.
    Administratrix: Rachel Covington.

Benjamin Blackston   4.81   D KE   £1043.12.3   Sep 7 1763
    Sureties: John Blackston, Benjamin Knock.
    Legatees (children): William, Priscilla, George.
    Distribution to: Widow (unnamed, 1/3). Residue to children (unnamed, equally).
    Executors: Sarah Blackston, William Blackston.

Christopher Hall   4.82   D KE   £910.4.6   1764
    Sureties: John Maxwell, Isaac Freeman.
    Distribution to: Representatives unknown to this Office.
    Administrator: William St. Clair.

Isaac Taylor   4.82   D CA   £203.16.4   Aug 7 1764
    Sureties: Richard Gibson, Peter Dowell.
    Legatees: James (son).
    Distribution to: Widow (unnamed, 1/3). Residue to 4 of children (equally):
        Isaac, Elisabeth Sunderland, Sarah Sunderland, Mary.
    Administrator: Benjamin Sunderland (administrator of Elisabeth Taylor (executrix
        of deceased)).

Benjamin Mead   4.82   D BA   £219.19.7   Jul 23 1764
    Sureties: Jonathon Starkey, John Jones, Jr.
    Legatees (daughters): Ann Dulany, Susannah Buck, Hannah Crock.
    Distribution to: Widow (unnamed, 1/3). Residue to: Benjamin (son).
    Executor: Benjamin Mead.

Benjamin Knock   4.83   D KE   £211.15.8   Jan 21 1764
    Sureties: John Falconer, Benjamin Scully.
    Legatees: widow (unnamed), William (son).
    Distribution to: Widow (unnamed, 1/3). Residue to "child or children" (unnamed).
    Executor (acting): John Blackiston.

James Andrews   4.83   D BA   £135.12.7   Jun 18 1764
    Sureties: Samuel Bowen, Edward Bowen.
    Distribution to: Representatives unknown to this Office.
    Administratrix: Agnes Andrews.

Peter Cornelius   4.83   D QA   £336.3.7   1764
    Sureties: Francis Bright, John Thurlow.
    Distribution to: Widow (unnamed, 1/3). Residue to 4 children (equally): Mary
        Ann, Eve, Rebecca, Mary.
    Administratrix: Mary Cornelius.

Charles Clark   4.84   D KE   £136.17.11   Feb 18 1764
    Sureties: John Woodall, John Clark.
    Distribution to: Representatives unknown to this Office.
    Administratrix: Rachel Clark.

Ann Smith   4.84   D KE   £67.15.10   Jan 21 1764
    Sureties: John Hatchison, John Henslough.
    Distribution to: Representatives unknown to this Office.
    Administrators (de bonis non): Charles Ringgold, Samuel Wickes.

John Johnson   4.84   D FR   £88.15.9   Jul 12 1764
    Sureties: Michael Jessarang.
    Distribution to: Representatives unknown to this Office.
    Administrator: Thomas Johnson.

Joseph Bouston   4.84   D CE   £13.9.8   Jun 27 1764
    Sureties: Nathaniel Buchanan, George Vansant.
    Distribution to: Representatives unknown to this Office.
    Administratrix: Sarah Street.

Michael Whiteford   4.84   D BA   £116.6.6   Jun 11 1764
    Sureties: Hugh Whiteford, John Walch.
    Legatees: Mary (daughter) in Pennsylvania currency.
    Distribution to: Widow (unnamed, 1/3). Residue to children (unnamed, except
        Mary, equally).
    Executors: Mary Whiteford, Hugh Whiteford.

Robert Crute   4.85   D BA   £176.5.5   Aug 29 1764
    Sureties: Richard Johns, John Barnes.
    Distribution to: Widow (unnamed, 1/3). Residue to 3 children (equally): Rebecca,
        Richard, Francis.
    Administratrix: Rachel Stevenson, wife of William Stevenson.

Cornelius Hurt   4.85   D KE   £431.7.2   Dec 29 1763
    Sureties: George Browning, Cornelius Harkins.
    Distribution to: Representatives unknown to this Office.
    Administratrix: Hannah Hurt.

James Thomas   4.85   D KE   £133.12.9   1764
    Sureties: Thomas Thomas, Edward Ferrill.
    Legatees (children): Sarah, Rebecca, Philip.
    Executor: Daniel Ferril.

Jacob Baker   4.86   D CA   £27.11.3   1764
    Sureties: Ellis Dixon, John Mannyngsimmons.
    Distribution to: Widow (unnamed, 1/3). Residue to 4 (!) children (equally):
        Isaac, Christopher, Jacob, Jesse, Dorcas.
    Administrator: William Allen.

Joshua Sewall   4.86   D BA   £40.11.11   Sep 3 1764
    Sureties: Sewall Young, William Towson.
    Distribution to: Representatives unknown to this Office.
    Administrator: Christopher Sewall.

James Scott   4.86   D BA   £898.12.0   Jul 4 1764
    Distribution to: Widow (unnamed, 1/3). Residue to children (unnamed, equally).
    Administratrix: Ann Scott.

Thomas Sheard   4.87   D CE   £29.4.10   Dec 3 1763
    Distribution to: Free School of Cecil County.
    Administrator: John Roberts.

James Bozley   4.87   D BA   £1491.7.2   Jun 7 1762
See also Liber MM#2, Folio 134 (Liber 3).
    Legatees (5 representatives): B. Price, Daniel Bond, Prud Bozley, William Bozley.
        (One name is missing.)
    Distribution to: Widow (unnamed, 1/3). Residue to remaining 7 representatives
        (unnamed, equally).
    Administratrix: Elisabeth Bozley.

Gunby Taylor   4.87   D SO   £48.17.6   Jun 6 1765
    Sureties: William Kersley, Elijah Wood.
    Distribution to 3 of the children: Sarah, Esther, Mary Gunby Taylor.
    Administratrix: Naomi Taylor.

Edward Hale   4.88   D DO   £152.11.4   Nov 2 1764
    Sureties: Thomas Steuart, Henry Saunders.
    Distribution to: Representatives unknown to this Office.
    Administrator: John Hale.

Ann Devorix   4.88   D WO   £25.13.0   Dec 10 1764
    Distribution to: Representatives unknown to this Office.
    Administrator: Cornelius Devorix.

William Melson   4.88   D WO   £50.3.10   Nov 29 1765
    Sureties: John Evans, Jr., John Evans, Sr.
    Distribution to: Widow (unnamed, 1/3). Residue to 4 children (equally): Wharton,
        Hannah, Betty, Luke.
    Administratrix: Nanny Melson.

William Byrd   4.88   D SO   £262.14.0   Nov 6 1764
    Sureties: Joshua Hitch, James Hitch.
    Distribution to: Representatives unknown to this Office.
    Administratrix: Philis Humphrys, wife of Thomas Humphrys.

Edward Burch   4.89   D PG   £504.1.9   1765
    Sureties: Thomas Blacklock, Thomas Bean.
    Legatees (children): Ann, Mary, Stacy, Winifred, Edward, Justinian.
    Residue to: Stacy (widow).
    Executrix: Annastatia McDonald, wife of Alexander McDonald.

Thomas Noble   4.89   D PG   £847.18.8   1764
    Sureties: Enoch Magruder, Robert Wade.
    Distribution to: Representatives unknown to this Office.
    Administratrix: Mary Ann Gilbert, wife of Francis Gilbert.

James Winson   4.90   D DO   £53.19.4   1764
    Sureties: Waitman Goslin, Daniel Vinson.
    Legatees (children): Bruffit, Barsheba, Celia, Mary Morris.
    Residue to (equally): Eliab Vinson, James Vinson, Barsheba Vinson, Celia Vinson.
    Executor: Eliab Vinson.

Edmund Knowles   4.90   D SO   £75.5.10   Apr 7 1765
    Sureties: John Collins, Moses Spear.
    Distribution to: Edmund Knowles.
    Administrator: Richard Knowles.

Thomas Gray   4.90   D CA   £380.4.1   1765
    Sureties: Joseph Vansweringen, John Mills.
    Legatees (children): Thomas, Ann Freeman, William, Henry, John.
    Distribution to: Widow (unnamed, 1/3). Residue to 2 youngest sons (equally):
        Henry, John.
    Executor (acting): Henry Gray.

Thomas Jones   4.91   D QA   £119.16.5   1764
    Sureties: Thomas Jackson, Jr., James Jones.
    Legatees (children): Elisabeth Herring, Sarah Herring, Jane Coper, Rebecca
        Barcos.
    Residue to: widow (unnamed) during her widowhood.
    Executrix: Sarah Jones.

David Melvill   4.91   D DO   £261.5.5   Nov 16 1764
    Sureties: Thomas Smith, Thomas Smith, Jr.
    Executrix: Rachel Smith, wife of Thomas Smith.

Abraham Bull   4.91   D BA   £128.7.0   Feb 14 1765
    Sureties: The name is either Luke Jacob or Luke Jacob Bond.
    Distribution to: Widow (unnamed, 1/3). Residue to 2 daughters (equally): Hannah,
        Rachel.
    Administratrix: Martha Bull.

William Hollis   4.92   D   BA   £199.6.6   Feb 10 1765
    Sureties: John Paca.
    Legatees: Ann Hollis, Catherine Hollis.
    Residue to children (unnamed, equally).
    Executor: William Hollis.

Eleanor Slaughter   4.92   D   DO   £21.15.6   Apr 30 1765
    Sureties: Levin Wale, Stapleford Wallace.
    Distribution to: Representatives unknown to this Office.
    Administrator: Thomas Slaughter.

Nathaniel Moore   4.92   D   QA   £111.13.11   Mar 4 1765
    Sureties: John Ruth, Hezekiah Betts.
    Distribution to: Joseph Moore (son of Samuel Moore of Kent County), Mary Ware,
        John Ware (son of James Ware), James Ware (son of James Ware), Ann Moore
        (widow).
    Executrix: Ann Ruth, wife of John Ruth.

Thomas Wilson   4.93   D   DO   £61.11.11   Nov 17 1764
    Sureties: Joseph Hicks, Peter Hubbert.
    Distribution to: Representatives unknown to this Office.
    Administratrix: Elisabeth Wilson.

Thomas Trego   4.93   D   DO   £59.13.4   1765
    Sureties: Levin Woolford, John Warren.
    Legatees (children): William, Thomas, Priscilla Wheeler, Esther Willis, James,
        Henry.
    Distribution to: Widow (unnamed, 1/3); then to 3 sons: Newton, James, Henry.
    Administrators: Elisabeth Trego, Newton Trego.

Thomas Baden   4.94   D   PG   £521.11.10   Nov 29 1764
    Sureties: John Brightwell, Mason Crim, Jr.
    Legatees: widow (unnamed), John Baden, Thomas Baden, Martha Baden, Letitia Baden.
    Distribution in 3 parts: widow (unnamed), Martha Baden, Letice Baden.
    Executrix: Eleanor Baden.

Nathan Smith   4.94   D   PG   £78.15.7   Feb 15 1765
    Sureties: Zachariah Elias, Robert Whitmore.
    Distribution to: Representatives unknown to this Office.
    Administrator: James Smith.

Aaron Tilghman   4.94   D   SO   £566.7.2   Dec 20 1764
    Sureties: John Tull, John Gwinn.
    Distribution to: Representatives unknown to this Office.
    Administratrix: Catherine Tilghman.

Thomas Thompson   4.95   D   PG   £63.7.7   1762
    Sureties: James Edelin, Jos. Clarke.
    Distribution to: widow (unnamed).
    Executrix: Chloe Thomas.

Thomas Potter   4.95   D   SO   £105.14.2   1762
    Sureties: Henry Caldkins, William Willson.
    Distribution to: Representatives unknown to this Office.
    Administratrix: Sarah Potter.

William Kimble   4.95   D   BA   £159.15.0   Apr 9 1765
    Sureties: Samuel Kimble, James Osborn.
    Distribution to (equally): widow (unnamed), 3 children: Richard, Martha, Frances.
        Mentions the "child wife is pregnant with"
    Executrix: Sarah Pike, wife of William Pike.

William Kitely   4.96   D   BA   £815.16.2   Apr 25 1765
    Sureties: Alexander McComas, Robert Adair.
    Legatees (children): William, Rebecca Norris, Rachel.
    Distribution to: Widow (unnamed, 1/3). Residue to 3 children (unnamed, equally).
    Executrix: Elisabeth Kitely.

Mary Henderson   4.97   D   PG   £255.11.3   May 28 1765
The amount of the accounts also included £1028.17.11 sterling.
    Sureties: Mark Mareen Duvall, John McGill.
    Legatees: Mary Whitehead (daughter-in-law), Susannah Lamar (daughter-in-law),
        Priscilla Wickham (daughter-in-law), Mary Magruder wife of Jeremiah Magruder,
        Ruth Hall wife of Isaac Hall, Susannah Gray wife of John Gray, John Duvall,
        Jeremiah Magruder, Margaret Hutton wife of Richard Hutton, Robert Tyler son of
        her son-in-law Robert Tyler (dead), John Piddle son of Pindle.
    Residue to: Daniel Stanton (son of her brother Daniel Stanton in Philadelphia).
    Executor: John Duvall.

James Weatherly 4.98 D SO £369.18.8 Jun 24 1765
 Sureties: John Weatherly, David Polke.
 Legatees: Eleanor (daughter), Mary (daughter), Sarah (daughter), James (son),
  Charles (son), Jesse (child), Charles Hopkins.
 Residue to 6 children (unnamed, equally).
 Executor: Joseph Weatherly.

Webb Prior 4.98 D WO £43.8.9 Jun 28 1765
 Sureties: William Bishop, Jos. Bishop, Jr.
 Distribution to 6 children: Comfort, Mary Littleton, Sturgis, Betty, Esther,
  Andesia.
 Administratrix: Rebecca Prior.

George Robinson 4.99 D WO £51.16.8 Jun 26 1765
 Sureties: William Waples, John Waples.
 Distribution to 3 children (unnamed).
 Administratrix: Mary Robinson.

Leonard Wheeler 4.99 D PG £477.13.8 May 28 1765
 Sureties: Alexander Norton, William Gibbs.
 Distribution to: Representatives unknown to this Office.
 Administratrix: Elisabeth Wheeler.

Thomas Waters 4.99 D PG £324.19.4 Jun 29 1765
 Sureties: Jos. Isaac, John Fowler.
 Distribution to: Widow (unnamed, 1/3). Residue to children (equally): Richard,
  Rachel, John, Ann, Thomas, Mathew, Casandra.
 Administratrix: Sarah Watters.

Margaret Brannock 4.100 D DO £106.5.4 May 11 1765
 Sureties: Solomon Bryan, Charles Beckwith.
 Legatees: Robert Spedden (grandson), Hugh Spedden (grandson), John Spedden
  (grandson), Robert Spedden (grandson), Margaret Mathews (daughter), Nehemiah
  Lecompte (son), Ann Payne (granddaughter), Joseph Pain (grandson), Mary
  Lecompte (granddaughter).
 Residue to: Ann Pain (daughter).
 Executors: Joseph Payne and his wife (unnamed).

William Evans 4.101 D WO £79.11.11 Jun 25 1765
 Sureties: Walter Evans, Benjamin Schoolfield.
 Legatees: widow (unnamed), Mary (daughter), Elisabeth (daughter), Esther
  (daughter), Caleb (son), Sally (daughter), Bathsheba (youngest daughter).
 Distribution to: widow (unnamed), children (unnamed).
 Executrix: Esther Evans.

Richard Manklin 4.102 D WO £75.5.6 May 6 1765
 Sureties: James Mumford, John Kennett.
 Legatees: Comfort Mathews (daughter), Martha Mason (daughter).
 Distribution to: Widow (unnamed, 1/3). Residue to: Leah Burton (granddaughter).
 Administrator: William Burton.

Charles Dean 4.102 D SO £146.5.3 Jun 20 1765
 Sureties: Thomas Walker, John Moore.
 Distribution to: Representatives unknown to this Office.
 Administratrix: Sarah Dean.

Thomas Nixon 4.102 D BA £126.12.3 Jun 10 1765
 Sureties: Christopher Divers, John Colret.
 Distribution to: Representatives unknown to this Office.
 Administratrix: Sarah Davies, wife of Christopher Davies.

James Gibbs 4.102 D PG £276.5.11 May 28 1765
See Folio 103. This entry is crossed out.
 Sureties: William Bayne, Charles Fenby.
 Distribution to: Representatives unknown to this Office.
 Administratrix: Ann Gibbs.

James Gibbs 4.103 D PG £276.5.11 May 28 1765
 Sureties: William Bayne, Charles Fenby.
 Distribution to: Representatives unknown to this Office.
 Administratrix: Ann Gibbs.

John Davis   4.103   D SO   £318.1.6   1764
    Sureties: John Sherwood, 3rd, William Sharpe.
    Legatees: Mary Cox (sister), Samuel Cox (nephew), Sarah Flemming (niece) wife of
        John Flemming, Elisabeth Colbourn (niece) wife of William Colbourn, Mary Gould
        formerly widow of one John Randall to be paid by Thomas Handy & Samuel Cox,
        Enclin Salsbury.
    Residue to (equally): Mary Cox (sister), Thomas Handy (nephew), Samuel Cox
        (nephew), Sarah Flemming (niece), Elisabeth Colbourn (niece).
    Executor (acting): Thomas Handy.

Stephen Whinright   4.104   D SO   £109.8.3   May 12 1765
    Sureties: Samuel Flewelling, William Whinright.
    Legatees (children): Stephen, ------ (name not given), Sarah Thomas.
    Distribution to: Widow (unnamed, 1/3). Residue to 6 children (equally): Evans,
        Elander, John, Cannon, Stephen, Rebecca.
    Executrix: Mary Winright.

John Page   4.104   D KE   £1484.16.6   Aug 13 1757
    Sureties: Sutter Burgain, John Reid, Jr.
    Representatives: Ruth (widow), children: Mary, Aquila, Araminta, Hannah,
        Temperance.
    Executors: Robert Maxwell, Jr., Ruth Page.

Jacob Lowe   4.104   D DO   £47.18.4   Nov 30 1764
    Sureties: Richard Glover, John Elliott.
    Distribution to: Widow (unnamed, 1/3). Residue to (equally): Jane, Rebecca,
        Margaret, Sarah, Isaac.
    Administratrix: Rebecca Croneen, wife of Daniel Croneen.

Samuel Taylor   4.105   D WO   £112.3.6   Jun 28 1765
    Sureties: Solomon Taylor, Thomas Selby.
    Legatees: widow (unnamed), Samuel (son).
    Residue to children (unnamed, equally). Cites married and unmarried children.
    Administratrix: Ann Beavins.

John Vickers (Bridge)   4.105   D DO   £75.18.7
    Sureties: William Jones, Isaac Lee.
    Distribution to: Widow (unnamed, 1/3). Residue to children (equally): Mary,
        Sarah, Solomon, Thomas, John, Benjamin, William.
    Administratrix: Ann Vickers.

Patrick Hew   4.105   D CE   £158.4.2   Jan 4 1764
    Sureties: Charles Rumsey, William Withers.
    Distribution to: Representatives unknown to this Office.
    Administrator: James Boyle.

Henry McCoy   4.106   D CE   £23.4.9   May 22 1765
    Sureties: James McCoy, William Chick.
    Distribution to: Widow (unnamed, 1/3). Residue to (equally): John McCoy, Henry
        McCoy.
    Administratrix: Rebecca McCoy.

John Silson   4.106   D DO   £21.6.0   Aug 9 1764
    Sureties: William Killman, William Hamilton.
    Distribution to: Representatives unknown to this Office.
    Administrator: Charles Eccleston.

Shadrack Keene   4.106   D DO   £17.9.0
    Sureties: Thomas Wheatly, Philip Keene.
    Administrator: Zebulon Keene.

William Worsley   4.106   D DO   £47.1.4   Sep 30 1764
    Sureties: James Woolford, James Branklin.
    Representatives: none.
    Administratrix: Ann Worsley.

Elisabeth Manship   4.107   D DO   £37.12.2   1765
    Sureties: Thomas Manning, William Dingle.
    Distribution to: Representatives unknown to this Office.
    Administrator: Charles Manship.

David Rathell   4.107   D DO   £20.11.4   Nov 6 1764
    Sureties: John Turner, William Jones.
    Distribution to: Representatives unknown to this Office.
    Administrator: George West.

Thomas Bullen   4.107   D TA   £29.17.0   Aug 2 1765
    Sureties: Powell Cox, William Cox.
    Distribution to: Widow (unnamed, 1/3). Residue to 4 children (equally): Mary,
        Henry, Thomas, Elisabeth.
    Administratrix: Sarah Bullen.

George McKinley   4.107   D CE   £11.12.10   May 7 1765
    Sureties: John Harper (farmer), Henry Pennington.
    Distribution to: Representatives unknown to this Office.
    Administrator: Jacob Harper.

John Watts   4.108   D TA   £119.16.8   Apr 30 1765
    Sureties: Moses Hopkins, Richard Hopkins, James Hopkins.
    Distribution to: Widow (unnamed, 1/3). Residue to children (equally): Thomas,
        James, Rachel, John.
    Administratrix: Penelope Hopkins, wife of Moses Hopkins.

James Paden   4.108   D DO   £52.0.0   Nov 12 1764
    Sureties: William Jones, Joseph Robson.
    Distribution to: Widow (unnamed, 1/3). Residue to 2 children (equally): Nancy,
        John.
    Administratrix: Sarah Paden.

Jonas Bowen   4.108   D BA   £46.5.0   Apr 29 1765
    Sureties: Samuel Bowen, Edmond Bowen.
    Administratrix (de bonis non): Mary Green.

Hannah Rutledge   4.108   D BA   £13.3.7   Jun 3 1765
    Distribution to: Representatives unknown to this Office.
    Administrator: John Rutledge.

Joshua Jackson   4.109   D SO   £271.15.1   May 29 1765
    Sureties: George Collier, James Jackson.
    Legatees: Rachel Donohoe, Samuel (brother), ------ (son, name not given).
    Distribution to: Widow (unnamed, 1/3). Residue to (equally): John Jackson,
        Sophia Jackson, George Jackson, Elihu Jackson, William Jackson.
    Executrix: Sarah Jackson.

Peter Corkran   4.109   D DO   £42.11.10   Nov 15 1764
    Sureties: George Hutton, James Irving.
    Distribution to: Widow (unnamed, 1/3). Residue to 3 children (equally): James,
        Peter, Timothy.
    Administratrix: Elisabeth Corkran.

Thomas Nutter   4.110   D DO   £79.14.9   Nov 11 1764
    Sureties: Henry Camplin, William Addams.
    Distribution to: Widow (unnamed, 1/3). Residue to 4 children (equally): Charles,
        Nelly, James, William.
    Administratrix: Ann Nash.

John Tull   4.110   D DO   £86.9.10   Nov 15 1764
    Sureties: Edward Smith, Noble Covey.
    Distribution to: Widow (unnamed, 1/3). Residue to 4 children (equally): Richard,
        Priscilla, William, Levin.
    Administratrix: Mary Tull.

Randolph Brandt   4.110   D CH   £565.17.10   Dec 11 1745
    Distribution to: Widow (unnamed, 1/3). Residue to (equally): Randolph Brandt,
        Richard Brandt.
    Administratrix: Ann Harriss, wife of Nathan Harriss.

Edward Beatty   4.111   D FR   £1019.12.1   Apr 10 1756
    Sureties: Thomas Beatty, John Kimbol.
    Distribution to (equally): Ezekiel, Ezra, Elijah, Edward.
    Executor (surviving): Thomas Beatty.

Charles Beavin   4.111   D PG   £685.8.3   Dec 27 1762
    Sureties: John Clagett, John Miles.
    Legatees (children): Charles, Richard, Edward.
    Distribution to: Widow (unnamed, 1/3). Residue to children (unnamed, equally).
    Executrix: Rebecca Beavin.

Samuel Taylor   4.112   D WO   £112.3.6   Jun 28 1765
    Sureties: Solomon Taylor, Thomas Selby.
    Legatees: Samuel (son), widow (unnamed).
    Residue to children (equally). Cites some married, some unmarried.
    Administratrix: Ann Beavins (late Ann Taylor).

Richard Scrivener   4.112   D QA   £68.17.7   Jun 14 1765
    Sureties: John Scrivener, Henry Council.
    Distribution to: Widow (unnamed, 1/3). Residue to children (unnamed, equally).
    Executrix: Hesther Scrivener.

Susannah Elliott   4.113   D QA   £373.3.4   Jun 6 1765
    Sureties: John Tolson, John Elliott.
    Legatees (children): Samuel, Benjamin, Elisabeth.
    Executor: Henry Elliott.

Jeremiah Semans   4.113   D KE   £387.11.11   Jun 17 1765
    Sureties: Solomon Semans, William Semans.
    Distribution to: Representatives unknown to this Office.
    Administratrix: Sarah Semans.

Samuel Middleton   4.113   D CH   £1005.10.1   Jul 6 1765
    Sureties: Thomas McPherson, Benjamin Ward.
    Distribution to: Representatives unknown to this Office.
    Administratrix: Elisabeth Middleton.

John Leverton   4.113   D QA   £168.3.0   Jun 20 1765
    Sureties: Thomas Meads, Bartholomew Fiddeman.
    Distribution to: Widow (unnamed, 1/3). Residue to children (equally): John
        Foster, Thomas, Ann.
    Administratrix: Ann Dwiggens, wife of James Dwiggens.

Jane Nowland   4.114   D CE   £34.7.1   Aug 21 1765
    Sureties: Isaac Gibbs, Nicholas Vanhorne.
    Distribution to: Rachel (only child).
    Administratrix: Rachel Nowland.

Mark McLane   4.114   D CH   £34.15.7   Jun 12 1765
    Sureties: Archibald Johnson, John Melson.
    Distribution to: Widow (unnamed, 1/3). Residue to 2 of children (unnamed,
        equally).
    Administratrix: Elisabeth McLane.

George Robinson   4.114   D WO   £51.16.8   Jun 25 1765
    Sureties: William Waples, John Waples.
    Distribution to 3 of children (equally): Betty, John, Joshua Waples.
    Administratrix: Mary Robinson.

John Pippen   4.115   D CE   £31.0.0   Jun 24 1765
    Sureties: Mathias Henderson, John Cox.
    Distribution to: Representatives unknown to this Office.
    Administrator/Executor: Charles James.

William Falkner   4.115   D DO   £24.5.6   Jun 13 1765
    Sureties: James Willson, David Clark.
    Distribution to: Widow (unnamed, 1/3). Residue to children (equally): James,
        William.
    Administratrix: wife (unnamed) of Andrew Sullivane.

Matthias Pippen   4.115   D CE   £330.16.9   Jun 26 1765
    Sureties: Matthias Hendrickson, John Cox.
    Distribution to: Representatives unknown to this Office.
    Administrator (de bonis non): Charles James.

William Falkner   4.115   D DO   £24.5.6   Jun 13 1765
This entry is crossed out.
    Sureties: James Willson, David Clark.
    Distribution to: see above.
    Administratrix: wife (unnamed) of Andrew Sullivane.

Andrew Crocker   4.116   D CE   £41.7.2   Sep 7 1765
    Sureties: Robert Porter, Jr., Philip Stoop.
    Distribution to: Rachel Tully (mother), Thomas Crocker (brother), William Crocker
        (brother), Mary Crocker (sister).
    Administrator (surviving, de bonis non): Jacob Jones, Jr.

William Evans   4.116   D WO   £79.11.11   Jun 25 1765
    Sureties: Walter Evans, Benjamin Schoolfield.
    Legatees: widow (unnamed), Elisabeth (daughter), Esther Evans, Caleb (son), John
        (son), Sally (daughter).
    Distribution to: Widow (unnamed), children (unnamed).
    Executrix: Esther Evans.

Samuel Gillet   4.117   D WO   £219.15.3   Jun 28 1765
    Sureties: William Gillet, Robert Mills.
    Distribution to: widow (unnamed) during her lifetime or widowhood.
    Executrix: Sarah Gillet.

James Blades   4.117   D WO   £42.14.11   Apr 12 1765
    Sureties: Elisha Jones, George Green.
    Distribution to: Widow (unnamed, 1/3). Residue to 4 children (equally): Samuel,
        Ann, Mary, Isabella.
    Administratrix: Elisabeth Blades.

William Campbell   4.117   D QA   £2069.7.3   Jul 1 1765
    Sureties: Gideon Emory, John Willson.
    Legatees: Ann Walter (daughter), Frances Walter (granddaughter), Sarah Walter
        (granddaughter), Ann Cedar (granddaughter) wife of John Cedar, Elisabeth Green
        (granddaughter), James Walters (grandson), Robert Walters (grandson), Sarah
        Sullivane (daughter), William Hammond (grandson), Mary Roberts
        (granddaughter), James Mooth (grandson), Elisabeth Mooth (granddaughter),
        Margaret Mooth (granddaughter), Sarah Meredith (granddaughter), John (son),
        William Campbell (grandson), William Hackett (grandson), Thomas Hackett
        (grandson).
    Residue to 3 daughters (equally): Ann Walters, Sarah Sullivane, Mary Mooth.
    Executors: Philemon Green, Thomas Emory.

James Heighe   4.118   D CA   £1489.8.8   Jul 29 1760
    Sureties: Joseph Wilkinson, Thomas Johns.
    Legatees: James (son), Thomas Holdsworth Heighe, Ann Gantt wife of George Gantt,
        Barbara Heighe, Mary (daughter).
    Executrix: Betty Heighe.

Webb Price   4.118   D WO   £43.8.9   Jun 28 1765
    Sureties: William Bishop, Joseph Bishop.
    Distribution to: Widow (unnamed, 1/3). Residue to 6 children (equally): Comfort,
        Mary, Littleton, Sturgis, Betty, Esther.
    Administratrix: Rebecca Price.

John Mannery   4.118   D CH   £79.19.1   May 27 1765
    Sureties: Francis Ware, Edward Ware.
    Distribution to: Widow (unnamed, 1/3). Residue to 2 of children (unnamed,
        equally).
    Administratrix: Mary Mannery.

Mathew Smallwood   4.119   D CH   £340.7.6   1765
    Sureties: James Griffin, Richard Roby.
    Legatees (children): Beans, Priscilla, Francis Green, Martha, Benjamin, Philip,
        James.
    Executors: John Harriss, Jr., Priscilla Smallwood.

Alexander McDaniel   4.119   D CH   £194.13.5   Jun 8 1765
    Sureties: John Smallwood, William Lindsay.
    Distribution to: Widow (unnamed, 1/3). Residue to 7 children (unnamed, equally).
    Administratrix: Mary Ann McDaniel.

Samuel Jones   4.120   D CH   £378.5.5   1765
    Sureties: John Chapman, Alexander McPherson.
    Distribution to: Widow (unnamed, 1/3). Residue to 3 children (equally):
        Precious, William, Samuel.
    Administratrix: Sarah Beck, wife of William Beck.

Nathaniel Parran   4.120   D CA   £479.11.3   Sep 9 1765
    Sureties: Young Parran, Benjamin Parran.
    Legatees: none.
    Executrix: Ann Taylor, wife of Ignatius Taylor.

John Bull (blacksmith)   4.120   D BA   £253.13.10   Jun 26 1765
    Sureties: Robert Adair, Thomas Treadway.
    Administratrix: Elisabeth Bull.

Josiah Wynn   4.120   D PG   £98.7.10   Apr 18 1765
    Sureties: William Martiny, William Fourd.
    Legatees: widow (unnamed), John Sharpe (son), Chloe (one of the daughters).
    Residue to: widow during her lifetime.
    Executrix: Ann Higdon, wife of Benjamin Higdon.

John Smith   4.121   D AA   £48.12.6   Jul 5 1765
    Sureties: John Campbell, Charles Bryan.
    Distribution to: Widow (unnamed, 1/3). Residue to: Eleanor (daughter).
    Administratrix: Esther Smith.

Peter Parsons   4.121   D   WO   £69.4.4   Apr 5 1765
    Sureties: Thomas Purnell, William Porter.
    Legatees: Joshua (son).
    Residue to: widow (unnamed) during lifetime.
    Administratrix: Martha Parsons.

James Lucas   4.121   D   SO   £972.13.10   Jul 17 1765
    Administratrix: Jane Lucas.

Stephen Walton   4.122   D   WO   £489.17.2   Apr 25 1765
    Legatees: Wise (daughter), William Walton.
    Distribution to: Widow (unnamed, 1/3). Residue to children (unnamed, equally).
    Executrix: Mary Walton.

George Brown   4.122   D   BA   £429.19.6   Jun 11 1765
    Distribution to: widow (unnamed) during her lifetime.
    Executrix: Mary Brown.

James Cassey   4.123   D   QA   £201.3.10   Apr 13 1765
    Legatees: Elisabeth (daughter).
    Distribution to: Widow (unnamed, 1/3). Residue to children (unnamed, equally).
    Executor (surviving): Othaniel Cassey.

Margaret Brannock   4.123   D   DO   £186.5.4   May 11 1765
    Sureties: Solomon Bryan, Charles Beckwith.
    Legatees: Robert Spedden (grandson), Hugh Spedden (grandson), John Spedden
        (grandson), Mary Mathews (daughter), Nathaniel Lecompte (son), Ann Pain
        (granddaughter), Mary Lecompte (granddaughter), Ann Payne (daughter).
    Executors: Joseph Payne and his wife (unnamed).

Robert Patterson   4.124   D   CE   £945.10.0   Dec 7 1763
Several legacies cited in Pennsylvania currency.
    Sureties: John McCoy, Joseph Rutherford.
    Legatees: Samuel (son), Martha Humphries (daughter), Elisabeth (daughter), John
        (son), Esther (daughter), Elisabeth Patterson.
    Residue to children (equally): 3 daughters (unnamed), John.
    Executor: Samuel Patterson.

Nicholas Gassaway   4.125   D   AA   £215.1.8   Feb 25 1761
    Sureties: George Shipley, William Hall.
    Legatees: Elisabeth Selman (daughter), heirs (unnamed) of Ann Peirpoint, Susannah
        Mansill (daughter), Nicholas (son).
    Distribution to: Widow (unnamed, 1/3). Residue to children (equally): Thomas,
        James, Hannah Foster, Mary Gassaway, Lucy Nicholson, Benjamin, Sarah, Richard,
        Robert, Rachel.
    Executrix: Rachel Sewall (widow), now wife of James Sewall.

Charlotte Harrison   4.125   D   QA   £637.18.1   Mar 11 1765
The amount of the accounts also included £237.7.10 sterling and #1865.
    Sureties: John Jackson, James Hollyday.
    Distribution to: Representatives unknown to this Office.
    Administrator: James Hacket.

Richard Harrison   4.126   D   QA   £1033.18.5   Mar 11 1765
The amount of the accounts also included £448.7.4 sterling and #45376.
    Sureties: John Jackson, James Hollyday.
    Distribution to 5 children: Ann, John, William, Mary, Richard Everingham.
    Administrator (surviving): James Hackett (administrator of Charlotte Harrison
        (executrix of deceased)).

James Dawkins   4.126   D   BA   £222.10.6   Jun 16 1766
    Sureties: Richard Taylor, Thomas Floyd.
    Legatees: Ann & Mary & Allin (grandchildren), John Sergeant in right of his wife
        Mary Sergeant, Sabret & Joseph & John Sollers.
    Executor: Joseph Taylor.

Elisabeth Boone   4.127   D   AA   £429.5.3   1766
    Sureties: Benjamin Beall, William Reynolds.
    Legatees: Humphrey (son), John Boone (grandson, son of Thomas), Thomas (son),
        Charles Boone (grandson, son of Humphrey).
    Executor: Humphrey Boone.

Joseph Lusby   4.127   D   BA   £1551.3.0   Apr 22 1766
    Sureties: John Paca, John Mathews.
    Legatees: Milcah Mathews (sister), Anthony Drew (nephew).
    Residue to: Josiah (son).
    Executor: William Ringgold.

Joseph Smith Nailor　　　　　4.128　　D　BA　£16.15.7　　May 1 1766
    Sureties: George Botts, Edward Wiggens.
    Distribution to: Representatives unknown to this Office.
    Administrator: Thomas Pribble.

Jacob Hoopman　　　　　　　　　4.128　　D　BA　£74.15.6　　Jun 7 1766
    Sureties: John Kittinger.
    Distribution to 7 children (unnamed, equally).
    Administratrix: Barbara Hoopman.

John Hyland　　　　　　　　　　4.128　　D　CE　£461.2.8　　Sep 8 1765
    Sureties: Col. Nicholas Hyland, Capt. William Rumsey.
    Distribution to: Representatives unknown to this Office.
    Administratrix: Mary Hyland.

John Hurt　　　　　　　　　　　4.128　　D　KE　£940.2.3　　Oct 30 1765
The amount of the accounts also included £48.13.5 sterling.
    Sureties: Thomas Smith, Darius Dunn.
    Distribution to: Representatives unknown to this Office.
    Administrator (de bonis non): Nathan Hatcheson.

Samuel Adams　　　　　　　　　　4.129　　D　SO　£1096.2.10　Aug 20 1765
    Sureties: Elias White, William Warrick.
    Legatees (children): Philip Collins, Sarah, Mary, Betty, Samuel.
    Distribution to: Widow (unnamed, 1/3). Residue to children (unnamed, equally).
    Executor: Samuel Adams.

Joseph Chunn　　　　　　　　　　4.130　　D　SM　£310.18.10　Jul 2 1765
    Sureties: Thomas Barber, Henry Morris.
    Distribution to: Representatives unknown to this Office.
    Administrators: Edward Barber, Catherine Chunn.

Eleanor Gardiner　　　　　　　4.130　　D　SM　£960.14.5　　Aug 6 1765
    Sureties: John Smith, Jean Gardiner.
    Legatees: Monica Queen (daughter), Ann Boarman (daughter), first child after date
       of will of Ann Boarman (daughter), Mary Boarman, Sarah.
    Residue to 3 daughters (unnamed, equally).
    Executor: Richard Boarman.

Cornelius Wildman　　　　　　　4.131　　D　SM　£931.13.7　　Jul 28 1765
    Sureties: John Reeder, Jr., Athanatius Ford.
    Legatees (children): John (items belonging to his mother (unnamed)), Cornelius,
       Mary Ann Snowden, Susanna, Monica.
    Distribution to: Widow (unnamed, 1/3). Residue to children (equally): Mary Anne,
       Cornelius, Susanna, Monica.
    Executors: Cornelius Wildman, Henry Hudson Wathin and his wife Ann Wathin.

John Derochbrune　　　　　　　4.131　　D　QA　£122.18.7　　Sep 5 1765
    Sureties: Samuel Osburne, Lewis Derochbrune.
    Distribution to: Widow (unnamed, 1/3). Residue to children (equally): John, Ann.
    Administratrix: Mary All, wife of Robert All.

Charles Ralston　　　　　　　　4.132　　D　QA　£100.0.0　　Aug 30 1765
    Sureties: Matthias Wickes, Isaac Comegys.
    Distribution to: Widow (unnamed, 1/3). Residue to: Mary (daughter).
    Administratrix: Mary Seyrims, wife of Thomas Seyrims.

Richard Bruff　　　　　　　　　4.132　　D　QA　£109.11.0　　Sep 25 1765
    Sureties: James Benson, John Thomas.
    Legatees: widow (unnamed), William (son), Mary (daughter), Lucy (daughter),
       Richard (son), Rachel (daughter), Rebecca (daughter), Jonathon (no surname,
       wife's son).
    Executor: William Bruff.

Edward Barber　　　　　　　　　4.133　　D　SM　£735.17.8　　Jun 25 1765
    Sureties: John Watson, Samuel Swan.
    Legatees: widow (unnamed), Elisabeth Barber, Mary (daughter), Sarah (daughter),
       Rebecca (no surname given, granddaughter), Edward & John Miphert & Elisabeth &
       Sarah (children of Sarah (widow)).
    Residue to children (unnamed, equally).
    Executors: John Mevert Barber, Elisabeth Barber.

Edward Cole　　　　　　　　　　4.134　　D　SM　£1734.5.0　　Sep 14 1765
    Sureties: Enoch Fenwick, Raphael Taney.
    Legatees: John Smith (grandson), Jane Smith (granddaughter, her mother's
       (unnamed) part), Francis Brooke (grandson), Joseph (son), Robert (son), Mary
       Fenwick (daughter), Elisabeth Brooke (daughter).
    Residue to (equally): children (unnamed, except Ignatius Fenwick & Edward Fenwick
       (sons)) of Mary Fenwick (daughter).
    Executrix: Ann Cole.

Jacob Lusby   4.134   D BA   £1008.0.3   Sep 11 1765
    Sureties: Joseph Lusby.
    Distribution to: Representatives unknown to this Office.
    Administratrix: Betty Lusby.

Levi Brittingham   4.135   D SO   £231.16.1   Dec 18 1765
    Sureties: Jefery Long, Coulbourn Long.
    Distribution to: Sarah Brittingham.
    Administratrix: Orpha Turpin, wife of Nehemiah Turpin.

Frederick Garrison   4.135   D FR   £37.13.4   Oct 1 1765
    Sureties: Jacob Young, Casper Sharf.
    Distribution to: Representatives unknown to this Office.
    Administrator: Frederick Garrison.

Thomas Allynn   4.135   D AA   £132.14.4   Sep 13 1765
The amount of the accounts also included £13.8.6 sterling.
    Sureties: James Brown, Stephen Steuart.
    Distribution to: Representatives unknown to this Office.
    Administrator: Benjamin Allyn.

Charles Chambers   4.135   D QA   £121.2.3   Oct 4 1765
    Sureties: Francis Woolahand, Andrew Belgrave.
    Distribution to: Representatives unknown to this Office.
    Administratrix: Rebecca Blunt, wife of Laban Blunt.

Thomas Parsons   4.136   D QA   £128.11.9   Oct 29 1765
    Legatees: Elisabeth Dodd (daughter).
    Distribution to: Tabitha Parsons (1/2). Residue to grandchildren: Thomas Taylor,
        John Taylor, Joseph Taylor, Elisabeth Taylor.
    Executrix (acting): Tabitha Parsons (since deceased), was wife of Thomas Davis.

William Rowles   4.136   D BA   £262.17.7   Sep 24 1765
    Sureties: David Rowles, Stephen Wilkinson.
    Legatees (children): John, William.
    Residue to: widow (unnamed) during her natural life.
    Executor: Jacob Rowles.

David Graham   4.137   D QA   £93.3.8   Oct 17 1765
    Sureties: Thomas Jackson, Dennis Carey.
    Distribution to: Representatives unknown to this Office.
    Administrator: Philemon Murphy (Wye).

John Sturrum   4.137   D FR   £54.6.0   Sep 16 1765
See folio 156.
    Sureties: Henry Shever.
    Distribution to: Representatives unknown to this Office.
    Administrator: Peter Daffer.

Henry Hickman   4.137   D FR   £145.8.0   Oct 25 1765
The amount of the accounts also included #4127. Cites items in Pennsylvania currency.
    Sureties: William Luckett, Ezekiel Gosling.
    Legatees: widow (unnamed), David (son), Solomon (son), Joshua (son), Bety
        (daughter), Director (no surname given).
    Distribution to: Widow (unnamed, 1/3). Residue to 4 children (equally): Solomon,
        Joshua, Betty, Director.
    Executor: Solomon Hickman.

John Thompson   4.138   D BA   £95.2.0   Jun 20 1766
    Sureties: Richard Johns.
    Distribution to: Representatives unknown to this Office.
    Administratrix: Mary Thompson.

Thomas Parsons   4.138   D QA   £128.11.9   Oct 29 1765
See folio 136.
    Legatees: Elisabeth Dodd (daughter).
    Distribution to: Tabitha Parsons (1/2). Residue to grandchildren: Thomas Taylor,
        John Taylor, Joseph Taylor, Elisabeth Taylor.
    Executrix (acting): Tabitha Parsons (since deceased), was wife of Thomas Davis.

John Williams   4.138   D KE   £299.14.5   Oct 30 1765
    Sureties: Samuel White, Sanders Bostick.
    Distribution to: Representatives unknown to this Office.
    Administratrix: Mrs. Elisabeth Williams.

Ann Scott   4.139   D CH   £441.9.11   Aug 10 1765
    Sureties: Charles Love, William McPherson.
    Distribution to: Representatives unknown to this Office.
    Executrix: Mrs. Elisabeth Love.

Nicholas Browning   4.139   D KE   £172.14.3   Oct 30 1765
    Sureties: Wilson Browning, George Browning.
    Distribution to: Representatives unknown to this Office.
    Administratrix: Mrs. Cornelia Browning.

Mathew Martin   4.139   D CH   £65.3.4   Sep 21 1765
    Sureties: Thomas Beale, Richard Slater.
    Distribution to: Representatives unknown to this Office.
    Administratrix: Mrs. Elisabeth Martin.

Charles Trail   4.139   D FR   £71.19.7   Oct 16 1765
    Legatees: Jane (daughter).
    Distribution to: Widow (unnamed, 1/3). Residue to 8 children (unnamed, equally).
    Administratrix: Mrs. Susannah Trail.

Thomas Beech   4.140   D CH   £85.0.4   Sep 14 1765
    Sureties: Joseph Hanson Harrison, Avery Dye.
    Distribution to: widow (unnamed), 4 children (unnamed).
    Administratrix: Lydia Beech, now wife of Mr. Henry Davis.

George Keplinger   4.140   D FR   £149.1.4   Sep 6 1765
    Sureties: Stephen Ransberg, Mathias Ringer.
    Distribution to: Widow (unnamed, 1/3). Residue to 3 children (unnamed, equally).
    Administratrix: Mrs. Eve Keplinger.

John Coe   4.140   D PG   £102.12.7   Sep 12 1765
    Sureties: James Alder, William Stevens.
    Distribution to: Representatives unknown to this Office.
    Administratrix: Mrs. Mary Coe.

William Jones   4.140   D BA   £34.11.4   Oct 14 1765
    Sureties: Richard Jones, John Hendrickson.
    Distribution to: Representatives unknown to this Office.
    Administratrix: Mrs. Ann Jones.

Elisabeth Price   4.141   D BA   £253.10.6   Oct 15 1765
    Sureties: Samuel Price.
    Distribution to: administrator.
    Administrator: Mr. Mordecai Price.

Richard Fenwick   4.141   D SM   £556.13.0   Oct 31 1765
    Sureties: Henry Sewall, Bennett Hopewell.
    Distribution to: Representatives unknown to this Office.
    Administrator: Mr. George Fenwick.

Joseph Burroughs   4.141   D SM   £332.19.4   Oct 3 1763
    Sureties: Jonathon Edwards, Stourton Edwards.
    Distribution to: Representatives unknown to this Office.
    Administratrix: Mrs. Elisabeth Burroughs.

William Sanders   4.141   D KE   £327.3.4   Oct 30 1765
    Sureties: Thomas Sanders, Sanders Bostick.
    Distribution to: Representatives unknown to this Office.
    Administrators: Mrs. Ann Sanders, John Sanders.

William Comegys   4.142   D KE   £370.16.0   Sep 23 1765
    Sureties: Cornelius Vansant, John Comegys.
    Distribution to: Representatives unknown to this Office.
    Administrator (de bonis non): Mr. Jesse Cosden.

Thomas Denwood   4.142   D SO   £812.15.0   Sep 23 1765
    Sureties: Arnold Elsey, Jr., Thomas Sloss.
    Distribution to: Representatives unknown to this Office.
    Administratrix: Mrs. Mary Denwood.

Christopher Bellican   4.142   D KE   £836.10.1   Oct 31 1765
    Sureties: Samuel Griffith, Paul Witchcote.
    Distribution to: Representatives unknown to this Office.
    Administratrix: Hannah Wallis, wife of Mr. Hugh Wallis.

John Windsor   4.142   D SO   £33.17.1   Oct 24 1765
    Representatives: Rebecca Windsor, John Windsor, Reatherford Windsor, William
        Windsor, Catherford Windsor,
    Administratrix: Mrs. Margaret Windsor.

Thomas Williams, Jr.   4.143   D DO   £32.0.11   Aug 14 1765
    Sureties: Thomas Connerly, Allan Williams.
    Representatives: widow (unnamed), 8 children: Major, Job, William, Polly,
        Rebecca, Nelly, Jesse, Celia.
    Administratrix: Mrs. Mary Williams.

John Aaron   4.143   D   DO   £197.2.4   Oct 12 1765
    Sureties: Ambrous Aaron, Joseph Robinson.
    Representatives: widow (unnamed), 4 children (minors): Mary, Nancy, John, Sally.
    Administratrix: Sarah Keene, wife of Mr. Capewell Keene, Jr.

Timothy Barnhouse   4.143   D   SM   £143.11.2   Oct 31 1765
    Sureties: George Biscoe, Richard Barnhouse.
    Distribution to: Representatives unknown to this Office.
    Administratrix: Mrs. Elisabeth Barnhouse.

Christopher Cox   4.143   D   CH   £13.16.1   Oct 8 1765
    Sureties: Joseph Hanson Harrison, Ignatius Sims.
    Representatives: none.
    Administrator: Mr. Ignatius Ryan.

Thomas Wilson   4.144   D   DO   £52.19.8   Aug 6 1765
    Sureties: Joseph Hicks, Nehemiah Hubbert.
    Representatives: widow (now wife of the accountant), 2 children (minors): John,
       Aramintha.
    Administratrix: wife (unnamed) of Mr. Lewis Spike.

Samuel Turner   4.144   D   CH   £1037.14.0   Oct 2 1765
    Sureties: Robert Hooe, Alexander McPherson.
    Distribution to: Widow (unnamed, 1/3). Residue to children (equally): Zephaniah,
       Hezekiah, Dorcas, Deborah, Martha, Anna, Mary, John Beal.
    Executor: Mr. Zephaniah Turner.

Amey Gibbens   4.145   D   SO   £103.8.1   Oct 24 1765
    Sureties: Michael Cluff, Sampson Wheatly.
    Legatees: John Perkins (son of John Perkins (dead)), Sarah Perkins (daughter of
       John Perkins (dead)), Mary Perkins (daughter of John Perkins (dead)), William
       Perkins (son of John Perkins).
    Residue to (equally): John Perkins, William Perkins, Sarah Perkins, Mary Perkins.
    Administrator: John Broughton.

Philip Ricketts   4.146   D   KE   £372.9.6   Oct 30 1765
    Sureties: Nathaniel Ricketts, William Cowarden.
    Distribution to: Representatives unknown to this Office.
    Executrix: Mrs. Charlotte Ricketts.

John Laurance   4.146   D   CA   £167.7.5   Oct 22 1765
    Sureties: Thomas Holland, Henry Harrison.
    Representatives: accountant, Joseph Smith.
    Executor: Mr. John Laurance.

Abraham Fowler   4.146   D   KE   £30.4.10   Oct 31 1765
    Sureties: Samuel Davis, Thomas Browning.
    Distribution to: 4 brothers: Jacob, John, Jonathon, Josiah. Residue to: widow
       (unnamed).
    Executrix: Mary Fowler.

Elisabeth Wiseman   4.147   D   SM   £299.8.6   Oct 30 1765
    Sureties: Jeremiah Rhodes, Mark Heard.
    Legatees: John (son), Ann Vanrishwick (daughter) then to Monica Vanrishwick &
       Milford Vanrishwick (grandchildren), Richard (son), Robert Wiseman (grandson,
       son of Richard), Elisabeth Downie (daughter), Peggy Leigh (granddaughter).
    Residue to children (equally): John, Richard, Mary Leigh, Ann Vanrishwick,
       Elisabeth Downie.
    Executor: Mr. Richard Wiseman.

Nathaniel Truman Greenfield   4.148   D   SM   £1488.11.10   Oct 30 1765
    Sureties: Thomas Greenfield, Henry Jernagan.
    Legatees: widow (unnamed), Thomas Truman Greenfield (son).
    Distribution to: widow (unnamed), children (unnamed). Except a Negro given by
       deceased's mother (unnamed) to Nanny (daughter).
    Executrix: Mrs. Rebecca Greenfield.

Jacob Duckett   4.148   D   FR   £333.14.5   Oct 31 1765
    Sureties: Thomas Prather, Stephen Newton Chiswell.
    Legatees: Ann Botelar (daughter), 5 sons (unnamed).
    Distribution to: Widow (unnamed, 1/3). Residue to 4 daughters (unnamed,
       equally).
    Executors: Mr. Thomas Duckett, Mrs. Sarah Duckett.

John Walker   4.149   D   TA   £57.17.2   Oct 17 1765
    Sureties: Powel Cox, John Harding.
    Distribution to: Widow (unnamed, 1/3). Residue to 4 children (equally): Ann,
       Jane, Sarah, Nathan.
    Administratrix: Catherine Walker.

Walter Jenkins   4.149   D TA   £279.11.8   Oct 29 1765
    Sureties: Nicholas Goldsborough, Jr., Thomas Skinner.
    Distribution to: Widow (unnamed, 1/3). Residue to 6 children (equally): Rachel
        Pritchard, Henry, Sarah, Thomas, Lewis, Margaret.
    Administrators (de bonis non): Thomas Jenkins, Matthew Jenkins.

Thomas Taney   4.149   D SM   £30.0.0   Oct 30 1765
    Sureties: William Combs, Jeremiah Edwards.
    Distribution to: Representatives unknown to this Office.
    Administrator: Raphael Taney.

John Dolbee   4.150   D WO   £500.18.2   Oct 11 1765
    Sureties: William Boyce, John Houston.
    Distribution to: Widow (unnamed, 1/3). Residue to 3 children (equally):
        Susannah, Mary, Isaac.
    Administratrix: Mary Dolbee.

Edward Dingle   4.150   D WO   £484.14.8   Aug 20 1765
    Sureties: Joseph Gray, James Mumford.
    Distribution to: Widow (unnamed, 1/3). Residue to 6 children (unnamed, equally).
    Administratrix: Elisabeth Gibbins, wife of John Gibbins.

Edward Nowell   4.151   D SM   £35.0.3   Oct 31 1765
    Sureties: James King, Henry Nowell.
    Distribution to: Representatives unknown to this Office.
    Administratrix: Lydia Nowell.

John Bay   4.151   D BA   £111.15.2   Oct 15 1765
    Sureties: Thomas Canaday, Alexander Young.
    Distribution to: Representatives unknown to this Office.
    Administrator: Thomas Bay.

John Denton   4.151   D BA   £76.5.4   Oct 14 1765
    Sureties: James League, John Hendrickson.
    Distribution to: Representatives unknown to this Office.
    Administratrix: Rachel Denton.

John Stephens   4.151   D PG   £41.17.1   Sep 10 1765
    Sureties: Abram Devinport, Richard Stevins.
    Distribution to: Representatives unknown to this Office.
    Administratrix: Eleanor Stephens.

William Tyler   4.152   D CH   £317.18.0   Apr 26 1765
    Sureties: William Eilbeck, John T. stoddert.
    Legatees (children): John, Elisabeth, Sarah.
    Distribution to 3 children: John, Elisabeth, Sarah.
    Executor: John Tyler.

Elisabeth Williams   4.152   D SM   £253.16.8   Oct 31 1765
    Sureties: Hopewell Adams, James King.
    Legatees (daughters): Mary, Susanna. Susanna is to received the remainder of the
        deceased's 1/3 of her husband's (unnamed) estate.
    Administratrix: Susanna Williams.

John Beard   4.153   D FR   £102.8.5   Sep 18 1765
    Sureties: George Winter, Nicholas Beard.
    Distribution to: widow (unnamed) during her widowhood, or until Nicholas (eldest
        son) comes of age.
    Executrix: Chloe Beard.

Jacob Gore   4.153   D TA   £98.1.2   Oct 29 1765
    Sureties: James Hendricks, Robert Hunter.
    Distribution to: Representatives unknown to this Office.
    Executrix: Elisabeth Gore.

William Coulbourn   4.153   D SO   £375.16.1   Oct 30 1765
    Sureties: Elisabeth Coulbourn, William Miles, William Roach.
    Distribution to: widow (unnamed) during lifetime or widowhood.
    Executrix: Elisabeth Coulbourn.

William Bowland   4.154   D SO   £14.8.5   Oct 29 1765
    Sureties: William Snulling, John Phillips.
    Distribution to: Representatives unknown to this Office.
    Administrator: William Furnice, Jr.

Samuel Broadaway   4.154   D TA   £278.1.1   Oct 15 1765
    Sureties: Henry Clark, James (no surname given).
    Legatees: Mary (widow), Isaac (son), John Miles (son), Samuel (son).
    Residue to: widow (unnamed) during her natural life.
    Executrix: Mary Broadaway.

Edward Perkins   4.155   D TA   £81.7.1   Sep 17 1765
    Sureties: William Ratcliffe, Robert Howard.
    Legatees: Rebecca (daughter).
    Distribution to: Widow (unnamed, 1/3). Residue to children (unnamed, equally).
    Executor: Solomon Perkins.

William Warring   4.155   D TA   £210.2.10   Oct 29 1765
    Sureties: Henry Clark, Edward Turner.
    Legatees (children): Basil, Henry, Hannah Turner wife of Edward Turner, Mary
        Kerby, Betty, William, Marson.
    Distribution to: Widow (unnamed, 1/3). Residue to 4 youngest children (equally):
        Sarah, Clark, James, Thomas.
    Executrix: Betty Warring.

David Crawford   4.156   D CH   £50.3.4   Aug 14 1765
    Sureties: John Sanders, John Perry, Jr.
    Distribution to: Representatives unknown to this Office.
    Administratrix: Ann Crawford.

John Sturrum   4.156   D FR   £54.6.0   Sep 16 1765
    Sureties: Henry Shover.
    Legatees: Barbara Sterm (wife), John Sterm (son).
    Distribution to: widow (unnamed) for maintenance of children (under age): John,
        Jacob, Catherine.
    Executor: Peter Duffler.

Christopher Cox   4.157   D QA   £746.15.3   Jul 30 1760
    Sureties: Arthur Emory, Philemon Emory.
    Legatees: Thomas (son), Ann (daughter), Lucy (daughter), Margaret (daughter),
        John (son), James (accountant), widow (unnamed).
    Residue to 8 children (equally, except Martha).
    Executors: Margaret Cox, James Cox.

Levin Hicks   4.158   D DO   £705.3.6   May 8 1758
    Distribution to: Widow (unnamed, 1/3). Residue to children (equally): Mary,
        Levin.
    Administratrix: Mary Hicks.

Brickhus Townsend   4.158   D WO   £1044.5.9   Dec 10 1764
    Sureties: William Fassit, William Richards.
    Representatives: Luke, John, William, Mary Townsend.
    Executors: Jeremiah Townsend, Mary Townsend.

Mary Hart   4.158   D KE   £701.8.9   Sep 22 1766
    Distribution to: Representatives unknown to this Office.
    Administrator: Nathan Hatchenson during the minority of Morgan Hart.

James Stuart   4.159   D WO   £131.2.5   Oct 25 1766
    Sureties: William Whittington, William Hayward.
    Distribution to: Hannah Morris Steuart (daughter, infant).
    Administrator: Mr. Isaac Morris.

John Creswall   4.159   D CE   £121.13.8   Jun 7 1766
    Sureties: Patrick McGarrity, James Carson.
    Distribution to: James Creswall, David Creswall, Robert Creswall, Isaac Creswall,
        Margaret Creswall, Mary Carson.
    Administrator: Robert Creswall.

Thomas King   4.159   D DO   £25.10.10   Feb 7 1766
    Sureties: John Trice, Ezekiel Cavender.
    Distribution to: Widow (unnamed, 1/3). Residue to 3 children (equally): Jenny,
        Rachel, Betty.
    Administratrix: Mrs. Catherine King.

Samuel Taylor   4.160   D CE   £72.0.10   Jun 4 1766
    Sureties: George Beaston, Andrew Craw.
    Distribution to: Widow (unnamed, 1/3). Residue to children (equally): Mary,
        Elisabeth, James, William, John, Ann, Benjamin.
    Administratrix: Mrs. Sarah Taylor.

Samuel Simmons   4.160   D CE   £178.1.10   Jun 4 1766
    Sureties: Menaper Logar, Andrew Laurenson.
    Distribution to: Widow (unnamed, 1/3). Residue to children (equally): Sarah,
        Mary, Laurenson, Benjamin.
    Administratrix: Mrs. Mary Simmons.

William Hammilton   4.160   D BA   £21.4.3   Aug 6 1766
    Sureties: John Parks, Aquilla Methugh.
    Distribution to: Representatives unknown to this Office.
    Administrator: Mr. William Murphy.

```
John Robinson                    4.161    D   CA    £111.8.6      Jun 14 1766
     Sureties: John Robinson, Samuel Northerly.
     Distribution to: Widow (accountant, 1/3).  Residue to (equally): John Spikernall
         (son of John Spikernall), Joseph (son), John (son).
     Administratrix: Ann Robinson.

Sarah Massey                     4.161    D   QA    £1738.10.2    1766
She is the residuary legatee of Samuel Massey.
     Sureties: Mathew Dockery, Sollomon Seeney, Timothy Mountseir.
     Distribution to: accountants.
     Executors: John Birstall, Jane Farmer.

Anthony Greggory                 4.162    D   TA    £257.2.6      Aug 26 1766
     Sureties: James Benny, Edward Turner.
     Distribution to: Widow (accountant, 1/3).  Residue to 6 children (equally): Mary
         wife of William Grace, Elisabeth wife of Aquila Hutchins, Lidia, Ann, Grace,
         Esther.
     Executrix: Lidia Kinnimont (executrix of John Gregory (executor of deceased)),
         wife of Ambrose Kinnimont.

William Alexander                4.162    D   TA    £187.5.6      Aug 20 1766
     Sureties: Howell Powell, George Parrot, Sr.
     Distribution to: William Alexander (age 15).
     Executor: Mr. Howell Powell (executor of Hannah Alexander (executrix of
         deceased)).

Solomon Massey                   4.162    D   KE    £188.9.5      Sep 2 1766
     Sureties: Ebenezer Massey, William Spearman.
     Distribution to: Representatives unknown to this Office.
     Executor: Mr. Joseph Massey.

Henry Addams                     4.163    D   BA    £335.0.3      Aug 4 1766
     Sureties: Abraham Reesin, Thomas Gittings.
     Distribution to: Widow (unnamed, 1/3).  Residue to child (unnamed, equally).
     Administrator: Mr. Joseph Sutton.

Joseph Riley                     4.163    D   KE    £385.14.8     Aug 5 1766
     Sureties: John Riley, James Shawhan.
     Distribution to: Representatives unknown to this Office.
     Administratrix: Mrs. Sarah Riley.

John Knock                       4.163    D   KE    £482.0.3      Aug 4 1766
     Sureties: James Denning, John Kennard.
     Distribution to: Representatives unknown to this Office.
     Executrix: Mary Glenn, wife of Mr. Johannus Glenn.

Joseph Pearce                    4.163    D   KE    £111.14.7     Aug 11 1766
     Sureties: Henry Thomas, Richard Simmons.
     Distribution to: Representatives unknown to this Office.
     Administrator: John Pearce.

Nicholas Massey                  4.164    D   KE    £673.17.7     Sep 2 1766
     Sureties: Nicholas Massey, Zorababel French.
     Legatees: 2 persons (unnamed).
     Distribution to: William Massey (minor), James Massey (minor), these accountants.
     Executors: Joseph Massey, Ebenezar Massey.

Michael Robson                   4.164    D   KE    £365.1.10     Aug 11 1766
     Sureties: Samuel Mansfield, Dennis Shawn.
     Distribution to: Representatives unknown to this Office.
     Administrator (acting): John Robson.

James Greenwood                  4.164    D   KE    £364.3.6      Aug 16 1766
     Sureties: James Staples, Joshua Staples.
     Distribution to: Representatives unknown to this Office.
     Administratrix: Mrs. Rebecca Greenwood.

Robert Berry                     4.164    D   KE    £169.1.7      Aug 14 1766
     Sureties: John Wheland, John Toward.
     Distribution to: Representatives unknown to this Office.
     Administratrix: Mrs. Susannah Berry.

Walmsly Baynes                   4.165    D   FR    £36.3.11      Jun 13 1766
     Mentions: no children.
     Administratrix: Mrs. Elisabeth Beans.

John Goddart                     4.165    D   PG    £367.9.10     Jun 14 1766
     Sureties: William Bayne, Charles Tenley, Jr.
     Distribution to: Representatives unknown to this Office.
     Administratrix: Mrs. Jane Goddart.
```

Samuel Conn   4.165   D PG   £321.19.9   Jul 1 1766
    Sureties: Zachariah Scott, Josiah Shaw.
    Executor: Mr. Jesse Conn.

George Woolhater   4.165   D PG   £137.19.1   Aug 12 1767
    Sureties: Bartholomew Tiperary, Michael Tiperary.
    Distribution to: Widow (unnamed, 1/3). Residue to: George Evan Woolhater (son).
    Administratrix: Mrs. Barbara Woolhater.

George Boaz   4.166   D DO   £30.6.8   Jun 11 1766
    Sureties: George Boaz, Jacob Gouttee.
    Distribution to: Widow (unnamed, 1/3). Residue to 8 children (equally): Henry,
        George, James, William, Nancy, Joseph, John, Mary.
    Administratrix: Mrs. Bridget Boaz.

Richard Richardson   4.166   D FR   £905.3.7   Jun 17 1766
    Sureties: William Richardson, Samuel Swearingen.
    Distribution to 6 children: Richard, Thomas, Milcah, John, William, Lucretia.
    Administrator (de bonis non): Richard Richardson (administrator of Edward Mathews
        & Samuel Richardson (administrators of deceased)).

Thomas Trego   4.167   D DO   £71.18.5   Aug 15 1766
    Sureties: Theodore Matkins, Theodore Matkins, Jr.
    Distribution to: Widow (unnamed, 1/3). Residue to 7 children (unnamed, equally).
    Administratrix: Mrs. Elisabeth Trego.

George Boaz   4.167   D DO   £30.6.8   Jun 11 1766
    Sureties: George Boaz, Jacob Gouttee.
    Distribution to: Widow (unnamed, 1/3). Residue to 8 children (unnamed, equally).
    Administratrix: Bridget Boaz.

Babbington Cook   4.167   D DO   £93.12.1   Sep 6 1766
    Sureties: Thomas Cook, Peter Ratcliff.
    Distribution to: Widow (unnamed, 1/3). Residue to 4 children (equally): Sarah,
        Ann, Andrew, Thomas.
    Administratrix: Mary Hubbert, wife of William Hubbert.

Sarah Massey   4.168   D QA   £1102.16.10   Sep 1 1766
    Sureties: Swetnam Burn, John Primrose.
    Representatives: accountants.
    Executors: John Birster, Jane Farmer.

John Oakly   4.168   D CH   £266.16.5   Jun 11 1766
    Sureties: John Maddox, John Serogen.
    Distribution to: Widow (unnamed, 1/3). Residue to 7 of the children (unnamed,
        equally).
    Administratrix: Mrs. Sarah Oakly.

Benjamin Gwynn   4.168   D CH   £668.5.11   Jun 28 1766
    Sureties: John Gwynn, Edward Ford.
    Distribution to: Representatives unknown to this Office.
    Administratrix: Mrs. Ann Gwyn.

William Lovely   4.168   D CH   £57.1.3   May 10 1766
    Sureties: Thomas Hyde Skelton, Joseph Puckrell.
    Representatives: only child (unnamed).
    Administratrix: Mrs. Mary Smallwood.

Thomas Tongue   4.169   D AA   £672.1.11   --- 12 1766
    Distribution to: Representatives unknown to this Office.
    Administratrix: Mrs. Ann Dare.

Lewis Stinchcomb   4.169   D AA   £102.14.4   Aug 21 1766
    Sureties: Rezin Hammond.
    Distribution to: Representatives unknown to this Office.
    Administrator: Mr. Nathan Hammond.

John Robinson   4.169   D AA   £197.5.10   Sep 13 1766
    Sureties: Charles Robinson, Thomas Rockall.
    Distribution to: Representatives unknown to this Office.
    Administratrix: Mrs. Sophia Robinson.

James Anderson   4.169   D CE   £21.14.6   Feb 5 1766
    Sureties: Patrick McGarritty, Isaac Decon Watson.
    Distribution to: Widow (unnamed, 1/2). Residue to children (equally): Samuel,
        Elisabeth, Robert, Agness.
    Administratrix: Mrs. Elisabeth Anderson.

William Boulding   4.170   D   CE   £282.12.6   Sep 3 1766
    Sureties: Edward Armstrong, Noble Beedle.
    Distribution to: Widow (unnamed, 1/3). Residue to 5 children (unnamed).
    Administratrix: Rebecca Armstrong, wife of John Armstrong.

Thomas Besswick   4.170   D   TA   £46.5.0   Nov 11 1766
    Sureties: John Pitts, John Cullen, Jr.
    Distribution to: Widow (unnamed, 1/3). Residue to 4 children (unnamed, equally).
    Administratrix: Mrs. Mary Besswick.

Henry Baily   4.170   D   TA   £83.15.4   Sep 24 1766
    Sureties: James Berry, James Barnwell.
    Distribution to: Widow (accountant, 1/3). Residue to 3 children (unnamed,
        equally).
    Administratrix: Margaret Snelling, wife of William Snelling.

Thomas Banning   4.171   D   DO   £15.8.2   Sep 29 1766
    Sureties: John Cullens, James Cullens.
    Distribution to: Representatives unknown to this Office.
    Administratrix: Mrs. Mary Ingram.

Basil Barry   4.171   D   AA   £87.17.3   Aug 29 1766
    Sureties: William Ijams, John Ijams.
    Distribution to: Widow (unnamed, 1/3). Residue to 4 children (equally): Sarah,
        Mordecai, Jacob, Basil.
    Administratrix: Rachel Sullyvane.

Paul Ingram   4.171   D   DO   £76.14.3   Sep 29 1766
    Sureties: Philemon Lecompte, Stephen Gary Warner.
    Distribution to: Widow (unnamed, 1/3). Residue to 7 children (unnamed, equally).
    Administratrix: Mrs. Mary Ingram.

James Burn   4.172   D   DO   £43.12.6   Oct 21 1766
    Sureties: Henry Ennalls, Thomas Ennalls.
    Representatives: 2 children (unnamed).
    Administrator: William Burn.

Richard Chance   4.172   D   DO   £62.0.3   Oct 16 1766
    Sureties: Ebenzer Vaul, Daniel Chance.
    Distribution to: Widow (unnamed, 1/3). Residue to 9 children (unnamed, equally).
    Administratrix: Martha Chance.

Ann Boyce   4.172   D   WO   £80.6.4   Nov 7 1766
    Sureties: William Boyce, John Boyce.
    Distribution to: Ann Boyce (infant).
    Executor: Joseph Boyce.

Samuel Dorman   4.173   D   WO   £33.13.10   Sep 4 1766
    Sureties: John Donohoe, Major Townsend.
    Distribution to: Widow (unnamed, 1/3). Residue to 3 children (unnamed, equally).
    Administratrix: Mrs. Rachel Dorman.

William Woodcraft   4.173   D   WO   £278.16.0   Sep 19 1766
    Sureties: William Holland, William Loughinhouse.
    Distribution to: Widow (unnamed, 1/3). Residue to 8 children (unnamed, equally).
    Administratrix: Mrs. Mary Woodcraft.

Thomas Collier   4.173   D   WO   £52.17.11   --- -- 1766
    Distribution to: Representatives unknown to this Office.
    Administratrix: Ann Addams, wife of George Addams.

Archibald Smith   4.174   D   PG   £255.3.0   Aug 18 1766
    Distribution to: Representatives unknown to this Office.
    Administrator: Zachariah Lyles.

Louther Dashiel   4.174   D   SO   £1335.17.8   Oct 8 1766
    Sureties: Thomas Dashiel.
    Distribution to (equally): Arthur Dashiel, William Dashiel, Mathias Dashiel,
        Louther Dashiel.
    Executrix: Mrs. Ann Dashiel.

Christopher Everhart   4.174   D   FR   £206.0.9   Nov 4 1766
    Sureties: Henry Shover, Abraham Linganfeller.
    Distribution to: Widow (unnamed, 1/3). Residue to 4 children (unnamed, equally).
    Administrators: Valentine Addams, Barbara Everhart.

Thomas Tinnally   4.175   D   FR   £46.5.0   Nov 19 1766
    Distribution to: Representatives unknown to this Office.
    Administratrix: Eleanor Loflin, wife of Richard Loflin.

Peter Stilley   4.175   D FR   £415.19.0   Dec 5 1766
    Sureties: Martin Keplinger, Charles Hedge.
    Distribution to: Representatives unknown to this Office.
    Executors: Mrs. Mary Stilly, Jacob Stilly.

John Kandell Boone   4.175   D FR   £72.7.0   Aug 24 1766
    Sureties: Martin Smith, Addam Smith.
    Distribution to: Widow (unnamed, 1/3). Residue to children (unnamed).
    Administrator: Nicholas Boone.

William Partridge   4.175   D BA   £13.6.10   Nov 21 1766
The amount of the accounts also included £55.6.2 sterling.
    Representatives: accountant, Jacob Bond, Joshua Bond, Hugh Sollers.
    Administrator: Daubrey Buckley Partridge.

Lancelot Watson   4.176   D BA   £16.16.5   Sep 8 1766
    Distribution to: accountant.
    Executor: Mr. David Gorsuch.

Charles Blackmore   4.176   D FR   £169.7.5   Nov 18 1766
    Distribution to: Widow (accountant), 6 children (unnamed).
    Administratrix: Mrs. Mary Blackmore.

Christopher Layman   4.176   D FR   £179.14.0   Nov 4 1766
    Distribution to: Widow (accountant), 2 children (unnamed).
    Administratrix: Mrs. Rachel Laymon.

John Warfield   4.177   D FR   £72.9.6   Nov 20 1766
    Sureties: John Holland, Solomon Turner Bergman.
    Distribution to: Widow (unnamed, 1/3). Residue to 4 children (unnamed).
    Administratrix: Elisabeth Saffle, wife of Peter Saffle.

Richard Goodman   4.177   D QA   £462.0.5   Oct 2 1766
    Sureties: William Horn, Alexander Walters.
    Representatives: Richard Goodman, this accountant, 7 children (unnamed).
    Administratrix: Mrs. Sarah Goodman.

Valentin Hufnagle   4.177   D FR   £36.4.6   Aug 26 1766
    Distribution to: Widow (unnamed, 1/3). Residue to 3 children (unnamed).
    Administratrix: Eve Hufnagle.

Richard Richardson   4.178   D FR   £1321.17.9   Feb 23 1767
    Sureties (1st set): William Richardson, Samuel Swearingen.
    Sureties (2nd set): John Darnall, Francis Pierpoint.
    Legatees: Sophia Mathews, Samuel (son, since dead)--distributed to Richard &
        Thomas & John & William Richardson.
    Distribution to 6 of the children: Richard, Thomas, Milcah, John, William,
        Lucretia.
    Administrator (de bonis non): Mr. Richard Richardson (administrator of Edward
        Mathews & Samuel Richardson (administrators of deceased)).

Nehemiah Birkhead   4.179   D AA   £703.11.1   Oct 1 1766
Note: the right hand folio appears as Folio 180.
    Sureties: Samuel Chew, Samuel Birkhead.
    Legatees: Elisabeth (widow), Joseph Birkhead, Francis Birkhead, Samuel Birkhead,
        John Birkhead, Mary Birkhead, Susannah Batson.
    Executors: Mrs. Elisabeth Birkhead, Nehemiah Birkhead.

         List of Desperate Debts - sent to County Courts October 4, 1765

This is located on folio 179, right side.

Dr. Benjamin Crockett, Baltimore, Gilbert Crocket (administrator).
Joseph Cockran, Cecil, Joseph Cockran (administrator).
John Bull, Baltimore, Elisabeth Bull (administrator).
James Anderson, Baltimore, John Anderson (administrator).
Andrew Price, Cecil, Richard Thompson, Jr. (administrator).
Charles Ford, Cecil, Cornelia Ford & John Veazey (executors).
Patrick Reed, Dorchester, Rosannah Reed (administratrix).
John Hyland, Cecil, Mary Hyland (administratrix).
James Reid, Kent, Sarah Creag (administratrix).
James Mills, St. Mary's, John Eden (executor).
Jeremiah Semans, Kent, Sarah Semans (administratrix).
Caleb Litton, Frederick, Margaret Litton (administratrix).
Joseph Porter, Worcester, Ezekiel Fookes (administrator).
Christopher Billican, Kent, Hugh Wallace and his wife Hannah (administratrix).
John Morrison, Baltimore, William Dunlop (administrator).
Robert Nairne, Worcester, John Nairn (administrator).
Daniel Campbell, Dorchester, Levin Traverse (administrator).
Alexander Frazier, Dorchester, Sarah Frazier (executrix).

Nathaniel Dare   5.1   D   AA   £1098.3.0   Mar 4 1767
    Sureties: Thomas Beall, Abraham Fisher.
    Distribution to: Nathaniel Dare, Gideon Dare, Ann Dare, Richard Dare.
    Executrix: Mrs. Ann Dare.

Peter Cole   5.1   D   KE   £96.19.8   Aug 14 1766
    Sureties: George Vansant, Benjamin Cole.
    Legatees: George Cole, John Cole, Benjamin Cole, Rebecca Cole, Ann Cole, Mary
       Cole, Sarah Murphy.
    Residue to: Elisabeth (wife), Francis (daughter).
    Executrix: Mrs. Elisabeth Cole.

Henrietta Shaw   5.1   D   PG   £84.7.11   Sep 10 1766
    Distribution to 4 children: Josiah, Rebecah, Henrietta, Zachariah.
    Executor: Joseph Shaw.

William Cannon   5.2   D   DO   £537.15.3   Aug 10 1766
    Sureties: Clement Bailey, Thomas Cannon.
    Legatees: Cartis Cannon, Levin Cannon, Nicy Hooper.
    Distribution to: Widow (unnamed, 1/3). Residue to (equally): William Cannon,
       Constant Cannon, Jesse Cannon.
    Executrix: Mrs. Mary Cannon.

Joseph Dawson   5.2   D   CE   £43.7.5   Jun 18 1766
    Sureties: Feryus Smith, William Wallace.
    Distribution to: Mary Dawson, Rebecca Dawson.
    Executor: Thomas Kilgore.

William Cord   5.2   D   WO   £635.17.10   Jun 17 1766
    Sureties: John Selby, Parker Selby.
    Distribution to: Widow (unnamed, 1/3). Residue to: representatives (unnamed).
    Executrix: Mrs. Rachel Cord.

William Morgan   5.3   D   CE   £606.8.1   Aug 12 1766
    Sureties: John Roberts, John Beedle, Jr.
    Distribution to: Widow (unnamed, 1/3). Residue to 4 children (equally): James,
       Elisabeth, Sarah, Ann.
    Executrix: Elisabeth Welch, wife of Richard Welch.

Richard Price   5.3   D   CE   £315.11.3   Aug 20 1766
    Sureties: Thomas Wallace, John Veazey, Jr.
    Legatees (children): John, Rebecca, Sarah, Mary, Lydia.
    Residue to: widow (accountant) for lifetime or widowhood; then to Hyland (son).
       Hyland is to care for James Price.
    Executrix: Mrs. Sarah Price.

Andrew Patton   5.3   D   CH   £31.19.9   1766
    Distribution to: accountant.
    Executor: Mr. Walter Hanson.

Esther Ann Hudson   5.4   D   DO   £450.12.5   Oct 5 1766
    Sureties: Bariah Clarkson, Julius Augustin.
    Legatees: Ann Cannon (niece), Alethea Cannon, Lucretia Cannon, Ann Lookerman,
       Elisabeth Lookerman, Mary Lookerman, Lilly Lookerman, William Smith.
    Residue to (equally): John Hudson, Whittington Cannon.
    Executor: John Cannon.

John Cannon   5.4   D   DO   £203.11.2   Sep 2 1766
    Sureties: George Smith, Jacob Cannon.
    Legatees: John (son), Charity (daughter), William Turpin (grandson).
    Distribution to: Widow (unnamed, 1/3). Residue to (equally): widow (unnamed),
       John, Charity.
    Executor: John Cannon.

Roger Addams   5.4   D   DO   £883.2.3   1766
    Sureties: William Cannon, James Adams.
    Distribution to: Representatives unknown to this Office.
    Executors: Richard Clarkson and his wife Betty Clarkson, Roger Addams, William
       Fountain.

Solomon Chaplain   5.5   D   DO   £868.13.4   Sep 29 1766
    Sureties: Benjamin Todd, Jr., Levin Todd.
    Legatees: Susanna Conway.
    Distribution to: Widow (unnamed, 1/3). Residue to (equally): Susanna Conway, Ann
       Chaplain.
    Executrix: Mrs. Bridget Chaplain.

John Reed   5.5   D   KE   £295.2.11   Aug 11 1766
    Sureties: executors.
    Distribution to: Widow (unnamed, 1/3). Residue to 4 of children (equally):
        Benjamin, Amos, Shadrack, Ruth.
    Executors: Mrs. Ann Reed, Shadrack Reed.

John Meekins   5.5   D   DO   £78.0.11   Jun 12 1766
    Sureties: John Burn, Raymond Shenton.
    Legatees: John (son).
    Distribution to: wife (accountant).
    Executrix: Mrs. Catharine Meekins.

Sarah Blackiston   5.6   D   KE   £185.1.10   Sep 11 1766
    Sureties: William Blackiston, Nathaniel Knock.
    Legatees: George (son), Sarah Blackiston (granddaughter), Sarah Comegys
        (granddaughter), John Shermond (grandson), Ann Worell (granddaughter), John
        Porter (orphan boy).
    Administrator: John Blackiston.

John Willis   5.6   D   DO   £19.0.6   Jun 11 1766
    Sureties: John Willis, John Nichols.
    Legatees: John (son), Mary Clift, Elisabeth Kellim.
    Distribution to: widow (unnamed) during life; then to John 3rd (son).
    Executrix: Mrs. Elisabeth Willis.

William Haddon   5.6   D   BA   £376.17.1   Jun 9 1766
    Distribution to (equally): Jannet Haddon (mother), John (brother), Jannet
        (sister), Elisabeth (sister).
    Executor: Mr. William Dunlop.

Ann Richardson   5.6   D   KE   £601.7.0   Aug 22 1766
    Executrix: Mrs. Sarah Rasin (executrix of William Rasin (executor of deceased)).

Thomas Whitely   5.7   D   DO   £101.13.1   Aug 13 1766
    Sureties: Solomon Whiteley, James Jarish (?).
    Legatees: Solomon Whiteley, Abraham Whiteley, Daniel Whiteley.
    Residue to: Thomas Whitely (accountant), paying Jemima Lewis (at age 18), William
        Reed (at age 20), Mary Bramble (at age 18).
    Executor: Thomas Whitely.

Edmond McCattee   5.7   D   CH   £580.17.0   Aug 9 1766
    Sureties: John Smallwood, Thomas Maccatee, Jr.
    Legatees: James McCatee (grandson), John (son), Edmond McCattee (grandson),
        William (son), Thomas (son), Elisabeth (daughter).
    Distribution to: Widow (unnamed, 1/3). Residue to (equally): John McCattee,
        William McCatee, Thomas McCattee, Mary Dyer, Eleanor Sanders, Ann Osbourn,
        Rosamond McCattee, Agness McCattee.
    Executor: Thomas McCatee.

Jacob Boon   5.7   D   QA   £615.17.8   Sep 23 1766
    Sureties: James Ginn, William Boon.
    Legatees (daughters): Rachel, Jemimah.
    Residue to: widow (unnamed) during widowhood.
    Executrix: Jemmima Boon.

Joseph Mahew   5.8   D   FR   £381.2.3   Nov 14 1766
    Sureties: George Clim, George Clem.
    Distribution to: Widow (unnamed, 1/3). Residue to: heirs (unnamed) of Ann
        (daughter).
    Executrix: wife (unnamed) of Martin Keplinger.

Josiah Jenkins   5.8   D   FR   £66.16.0   Sep 28 1766
    Sureties: James Good, Charles Hoskinson.
    Legatees (sons): Edward, Phillip.
    Residue to: widow (unnamed).
    Executrix: Anna Wood, wife of John Wood.

Peter Bond   5.8   D   BA   £369.0.9   Sep 1 1766
    Sureties: Samuel Bond (son of Peter Bond), Joseph Osbourn.
    Distribution to: Widow (unnamed, 1/3). Residue to children (equally): Sophia
        Karenhappuch, Edward, Benjamin, Henry, Elisabeth, Christopher, Joshua,
        Susanna.
    Executrix: wife (unnamed) of John Pott.

George Loy   5.8   D   FR   £224.10.11   Oct 17 1766
    Sureties: Peter Hofman, Jacob Staley.
    Distribution to: Jacob Loy, Peter Shaver, Rosinah Loy, Sebastian Dare, Frederick
        Trexell, Benedict Stone, Adam Loy, Frederick Loy, Charles Loy.
    Executor (surviving): Peter Shaver.

John Mace   5.9   D DO   £14.15.2   Jul 14 1766
    Sureties: Robert Willson, Joseph Fooks (?).
    Distribution to: Widow (unnamed, 1/3). Residue to: only child (unnamed).
    Administrator: Robert Ewing.

George Saltner   5.9   D FR   £114.18.6   Sep 3 1776
    Sureties: Robert Willson, Joseph Fooks (?).
    Distribution to: Catharine Saltner (cousin).
    Executor: Caspar Shaaf.

William Nicholson   5.9   D FR   £351.19.8   May 7 1767
    Legatees: Elisabeth Connell, Dorothy Elton.
    Distribution to: Mary Nicholson (widow).
    Executrix: Mary Hall, wife of Elisha Hall.

John Welch   5.9   D QA   £327.15.2   Oct 2 1766
    Sureties: Charles Clayton, Arthur Emory, 3rd.
    Distribution to: Widow (unnamed, 1/3). Residue to children (equally): John
       McClean, William, "child widow was big with".
    Executrix: Mrs. Mary Welch.

Edward Brown   5.10   D QA   £303.8.10   Sep 1 1766
    Sureties: Samuel McCosh, Bartholomew Jacobs.
    Legatees: John (son), Elisabeth (daughter), Mary Brown Hawkins.
    Residue to: widow (unnamed) during widowhood; then to children (unnamed).
    Executor: Mr. Morgan Brown.

George Tate   5.10   D QA   £307.9.0   Oct 2 1766
    Sureties: Jonathon Culbreath, John Rasin.
    Distribution to: widow (unnamed) during her widowhood.
    Executrix: Mrs. Catharine Tate.

Henry Rochester   5.10   D QA   £391.5.9   March 7 1759
    Legatees (sons): John, James, Henry.
    Distribution to: Elisabeth (widow, now Elisabeth Hall, 1/3). Residue to children
       (equally): Hannah, John, James, Henry.
    Executor: Francis Rochester.

Peter Ford, Jr.   5.11   D SM   £232.14.10   Mar 3 1767
    Distribution to: Representatives unknown to this Office.
    Administratrix: Mary Ford.

Robert Whiteman   5.11   D SM   £33.4.8   May 8 1767
    Sureties: Thomas Jenison.
    Distribution to: Representatives unknown to this Office.
    Administrator: Joseph Briscoe.

Cornelius Manning   5.11   D SM   £1088.4.5   Dec 15 1766
    Sureties: Peter Ford, Jr., Robert Fenwick.
    Legatees: John Manning, Robert Manning, Cornelius Fenwick, Ann Elisabeth Fenwick,
       Monica Manning, Francis Manning, Mary Manning, John Greenwell, Jane Manning
       (widow).
    Note: Robert Manning received 1/5th part of stock and 1/6th part of household
       furniture.
    Residue to: Jane Manning (widow).
    Executrix: Jeane Manning.

Peter Maxwell   5.12   D QA   £364.2.3   Sep 1 1766
    Sureties: Alexander Walter, John Bostick.
    Distribution to: Widow (unnamed, 1/2). Residue to (equally): "To the same Mary
       Maxwell deceased her part", Rachel Maxwell, John Maxwell, Sarah Maxwell,
       Alexander Maxwell.
    Executrix: Mrs. Sarah Flower.

Conrad Brust   5.12   D BA   £54.7.6   Dec 8 1766
    Sureties: John Shavers, James Hardwick.
    Distribution to: Representatives unknown to this Office.
    Administrator: Adam Baine.

John McCubbin   5.13   D AA   £149.17.4   Mar 16 1767
    Sureties: John Ridgley, Cornelius Barry.
    Distribution to: William McCubbin, John McCubbin, Joseph McCubbin, Hamutal
       Homwood, Jasper Halmsley, Jane Milbury.
    Administrator: William McCubbin.

Lewis Lewin				5.13	D AA	£1476.5.10	Mar 4 1764
    Legatees: widow (unnamed) then to 3 young children (unnamed), Richard (son),
        Henrietta (daughter), Margaret (daughter), Lewis (son), Frances (daughter),
        Christian (daughter), Sarah (daughter), Samuel (son).
    Distribution to: Widow (unnamed, 1/3). Residue to children (equally): Richard,
        Henrietta, Margaret, Lewis, Frances, Christian, Sarah, Samuel.
    Executors: Elisabeth Lewin, William Simmons.

Elisabeth Gott				5.13	D AA	£359.13.6	Feb 29 1767
    Distribution to (equally): Walter Gott, Virlinda Willson, Ezekiel Gott, John
        Gott, Samuel Gott.
    Administrators: Walter Gott, Ezekiel Gott.

Robert Gott				5.14	D AA	£460.13.8	Feb 12 1767
    Distribution to: Elisabeth Gott (widow, 1/3) during natural life; then equally to
        5 children (unnamed).
    Executors: Elisabeth Gott, Walter Gott.

John Chake				5.14	D BA	£531.17.0	Nov 11 1766
    Sureties: Thomas James, Thomas Mill.
    Legatees (6 daughters): Margaret, Mary, Elisabeth, Sarah, Martha, Priscilla.
    Distribution to: Widow (unnamed, 1/3). Residue to children (unnamed, except Mary
        (daughter)).
    Executrix: Mary Cheeke.

Thomas Floyd				5.14	D DO	£26.13.4	Dec 22 1764
    Sureties: Jonathon Hays, William Trippe.
    Distribution to: Widow (unnamed, 1/3). Residue to: 1 child (unnamed, minor).
    Administratrix: Susannah Floyd.

John Leverton				5.15	D QA	£128.7.2	Feb 5 1767
    Sureties: Bartholomew Fidleman, Thomas Meeds.
    Distribution to: Widow (unnamed, 1/3). Residue to (equally): John Foster
        Leverton, Thomas Leverton, Ann Leverton.
    Administratrix: Ann Dwiggens, wife of James Dwiggens.

James Hammond				5.15	D QA	£1736.11.3	Dec 25 1766
    Sureties: Charles Clayton, John Brown.
    Legatees (children): Mary, James, John.
    Distribution to: Widow (unnamed, 1/3). Residue to above-named (equally).
    Executors: Rachel Hammond, John Hammond.

William Peele				5.15	D AA	£208.17.2	Feb 16 1766
    Distribution to: Representatives unknown to this Office.
    Executor (surviving): James Dick.

Joseph Freeman				5.16	D CA	£118.18.3	May 9 1767
    Sureties: Francis Kershaw, James Marriott.
    Distribution to: Mary Freeman (widow).
    Executrix: Mary Freeman.

John Cumming				5.16	D AA	£17.14.0	Mar 2 1767
    Sureties: John Golder, Wright Mills.
    Distribution to: Representatives unknown to this Office.
    Administrator: John Campbell.

Edward Meade				5.16	D BA	£532.4.8	Apr 13 1767
    Sureties: Spencer Legar, Walter James.
    Distribution to: Representatives unknown to this Office.
    Administrator (de bonis non): Samuel Rickets.

Moses Chapline				5.16	D FR	£730.11.11	Apr 30 1767
    Sureties: Joseph Helms, Henry Boteler.
    Legatees: widow (unnamed), Ruth Lindsay, Elisabeth Chapline.
    Distribution to: Widow (unnamed, 1/3). Residue to children (equally): Josias,
        Moses, William, Elisabeth, Mary, Agness, Ester, Lydia, Levica.
    Executors: Joseph Chapline, Jennet Chapline.

James Armstrong				5.17	D SM	£157.2.7	Mar 25 1767
    Sureties: John Bennett, William Hammett.
    Legatees: Catherine Crane (daughter), Christian Crabb (daughter), Robert (son),
        John (son), George (son), Dinah Armstrong (wife).
    Residue to 5 children (equally): James, Robert, John, George, Hellen.
    Executrix: Dinah Armstrong.

Edward Lanham				5.17	D	PG	£495.18.1	1767
    Legatees: Josiah Lanham, Mary Lanham, Arsenah Lanham, Mildred Lanham, Henry
      Lanham, Bersheba Lanhan, Edward Lanham, Susannah Lanham, Rachel Lanham, Sarah
      (daughter), Sarah Bias Wilder Lanham.
    Residue to: widow (unnamed).
    Executrix: Catharine McKinnon, wife of Daniel McKinnon.

Annanias Grear				5.18	D	PG	£74.5.10	Mar 26 1767
    Sureties: John Stone Hawkins.
    Distribution to: Widow (unnamed, 1/3). Residue to (equally): Hezekiah, James,
      Elisabeth, Benjamin, Annanias, William Johnson.
    Executrix: Margret Grear.

Thomas Soaper				5.18	D	PG	£242.5.0	Mar 26 1767
    Sureties: David Ross.
    Distribution to: Representatives unknown to this Office.
    Administrator: John Cooke, Esq.

Richard Coleman				5.18	D	BA	£24.14.6	Jun 18 1767
    Distribution to: Representatives unknown to this Office.
    Administratrix: Mary Croney, wife of Jeremiah Croney.

Robert Fisher				5.18	D	BA	£58.9.6	Jun 12 1767
    Distribution to: Widow (unnamed, 1/3). Residue to 2 children (unnamed, equally).
    Administratrix: Hannah Fisher.

Benjamin Brook				5.19	D	PG	£688.13.1	Feb 10 1767
    Sureties: Mathew Everfield, William Everfield.
    Distribution to: Representatives unknown to this Office.
    Administratrix: Mary Brook.

William Cox				5.19	D	BA	£176.6.0	May 19 1767
    Sureties: Nathan Johnson, Jacob Cox.
    Distribution to: Widow (unnamed, 1/3). Residue to 8 children (equally).
    Administratrix: Ruth Cox.

William Button				5.19	D	DO	£10.8.9	Jul 16 1767
    Sureties: Philemon Phelps, James Brite.
    Distribution to: Representatives unknown to this Office.
    Administrator: Roger Button.

Elisabeth Selman				5.19	D	AA	£22.5.1	Apr 30 1767
    Sureties: Edmund Wayman, John Ijams.
    Distribution to: Benjamin Selman, Williams Selman, John Selman, Elisabeth
      Edwards.
    Administrator: John Selman (son of Son Selman).

Richard Dorsey				5.20	D	AA	£1309.16.9	Apr 8 1767
    Sureties: Basil Dorsey, John Dorsey.
    Distribution to: Representatives unknown to this Office.
    Administratrix: Elisabeth Dorsey.

Jacob Goutee				5.20	D	DO	£41.13.1	Mar 18 1767
    Sureties: John Goutee, George Cole.
    Distribution to: Widow (unnamed, 1/3). Residue to 3 children (unnamed).
    Administratrix: Rosannah Trego, wife of Solomon Trego.

Mary Evans				5.20	D	DO	£3.0.4	Mar 16 1767
    Sureties: George Middleton, Thomas Killman.
    Distribution to: Representatives unknown to this Office.
    Administratrix: Francis Evans.

Patrick Meed				5.20	D	DO	£100.18.7	Mar 27 1767
    Sureties: Levin Woolford, John Reed.
    Distribution to: Widow (unnamed, 1/3). Residue to 5 children (equally): John,
      William, Patrick, Thomas, Elisabeth.
    Administratrix: Rosannah Reed.

Nicholas Baker				5.21	D	FR	£1134.3.10	Aug 25 1767
The amount of the accounts also included #804.
    Sureties: David Lynn, Charles Jones.
    Legatees (children): John, Ignatius, Walter, William, Eleanor, Cassandra, Rachel,
      Margret.
    Administrator: John Baker.

William Spalding				5.21	D	SM	£226.8.1	Apr 14 1767
    Sureties: George Fenwick, Bennett Fenwick.
    Distribution to: Representatives unknown to this Office.
    Administratrix: Elisabeth Spalding.

George Hardon John James   5.21   D AA   £6.11.3   Jun 10 1767
    Sureties: Stocket Williams, Philip Richardson.
    Distribution to: Representatives unknown to this Office.
    Administrator: Richard Linthicumb.

Charles Robinson   5.21   D PG   £53.7.10   Mar 22 1767
    Sureties: Jeremiah Piles, Thomas Frazer.
    Distribution to: Representatives unknown to this Office.
    Administratrix: Ann Robinson.

Bennett Posey   5.21½   D CH   £65.15.11   May 20 1767
    Sureties: Edward Hubbert, Barton Philpot.
    Distribution to: Widow (unnamed, 1/3). Residue to 4 children (equally): Ann,
        John, Benjamin, Bennett.
    Administratrix: Elisabeth Posey

Henry Bryon   5.21½   D SM   £390.2.8   Apr 4 1767
    Sureties: Peter Todd, Jr., Robert Mattingly.
    Distribution to: Representatives unknown to this Office.
    Administratrix: Eleanor Bryon.

Francis Kersey   5.21½   D TA   £683.10.3   Mar 4 1767
    Sureties: Edward Trippe, James Wrightson, Jr.
    Legatees (children): John, Mary.
    Distribution to: Widow (unnamed, 1/3). Residue to children (equally): Mary,
        John, Eleanor, Elisabeth, Anna, Sarah.
    Executrix: Margaret Kersey.

John Brooke   5.22   D CH   £268.6.4   Sep 14 1767
    Legatees (4 daughters): Elisabeth Stewart, Mary Harrison, Sarah Roby, Jane Roby.
    Distribution to: Widow (unnamed, 1/3). Residue to 5 youngest children (equally):
        William, Charity, Walter, Chloe. (Only 4 names given.)
    Executors: Sarah Brooke, Peter Robie.

Sarah Crandal   5.22   D AA   £27.15.6   Feb 19 1767
    Sureties: John Norriss.
    Distribution to: Representatives unknown to this Office.
    Administrator: Walter Gott.

Thomas Hackett   5.22   D DO   £47.19.9   Mar 11 1767
    Sureties: David Harper, Oliver Hackett.
    Distribution to: Rebeccah Hackett (widow).
    Administratrix: Rebeccah Hackett.

Caleb Litton   5.22   D FR   £190.19.6   Apr 24 1767
    Sureties: Daniel Clay, Benjamin Johnson.
    Legatees: Grace (wife), Grace Sammons (daughter), John (son), Michael (son),
        Johannah Hall (daughter).
    Residue to: Grace (wife).
    Executrix: Grace Litton.

Bethulia Wallace   5.23   D DO   £16.0.9   Feb 6 1767
    Sureties: Isaac Partridge, John Griffith.
    Legatees: Stapleford Wallace, Richard Wallace, Joseph Wallace, Thomas Wallace,
        Mathew Wallace, Charles Wallace, Amelia Wallace.
    Executor: Mathew Wallace.

William Robins   5.23   D TA   £1565.4.3   May 24 1767
    Legatees: Margaret Robins (niece).
    Residue to: Standley Robinson (nephew).
    Executor: John Goldsborough.

James Oldrick   5.23   D TA   £31.4.1   Mar 5 1767
    Sureties: Thomas Skinner, Henry Delahay.
    Distribution to: widow (unnamed).
    Executor: Joseph Harding.

William Tucker   5.24   D AA   £35.9.8   May 27 1767
    Sureties: Benjamin Carr, Samuel Wood.
    Distribution to: Widow (unnamed, 1/3). Residue to: 1 child (unnamed).
    Administrator: Joseph Ward.

Daniel Campbell   5.24   D DO   £117.0.2   Mar 12 1767
    Sureties: Robert How, Bartholomew Ennalls.
    Distribution to: Representatives unknown to this Office.
    Administrator: Levin Traverse.

Thomas Fisher   5.24   D   QA   £122.11.6   Apr 20 1767
    Sureties: John Mayne, Anthony Harrington.
    Distribution to: Widow (unnamed, 1/3). Residue to only child: William.
    Administrator: John Fisher.

John Bryan   5.24   D   QA   £123.7.3   Apr 22 1767
    Sureties: John Winchester, John Diamont.
    Distribution to: Widow (unnamed, 1/3). Residue to 4 children (unnamed).
    Administratrix: Rebeccah Jackson, wife of George Jackson.

Edward Bourk   5.25   D   QA   £210.3.8   Apr 23 1767
    Sureties: Robert Ross, Robert Noble.
    Distribution to: Representatives unknown to this Office.
    Administrator: James Bourk.

Alexander Wallace   5.25   D   FR   £150.3.10   Mar 2 1767
    Distribution to: Representatives unknown to this Office.
    Administrator: Edward Talbot of Calvert County.

John Crain   5.25   D   CH   £55.18.3   Dec 11 1766
The amount of the inventory also included #1486.
    Distribution to: Widow (unnamed, 1/3). Residue to 3 children (equally): Mark,
        Brafield, Bateman.
    Administratrix: Elisabeth Bateman, wife of John Bateman.

William Wheeler   5.25   D   BA   £308.15.5   Jun 29 1767
    Legatees: widow (unnamed) 1/3 of payment to William Benjamin Wheeler, Charles
        Vaughan, William Wheeler, Elisabeth Perigoy, Nathaniel Wheeler.
    Distribution to: Widow (unnamed, 1/3).
    Administrator: Nathan Wheeler.

Ann Norriss   5.26   D   SM   £130.17.8   May 4 1767
    Legatees: Thomas Norriss, John Norriss, William Norriss, Mathew Norriss, Clement
        Norriss, Stephen Norriss, John Baptist Norriss, Susannah Gough, Monica Stone.
    Residue to (equally): Mathew Norriss, Clement Norriss, Stephen Norriss, John
        Baptist Norriss.
    Executors: Mathew Norriss, Clement Norriss.

Jacob Hanson   5.26   D   BA   £645.6.7   May 10 1767
    Sureties: James Greenfield, Edward Ward.
    Distribution to: Representatives unknown to this Office.
    Executor: Micajah Greenfield.

John Foord   5.26   D   SM   £25.12.2   Apr 6 1767
    Sureties: John Booth, George Booth.
    Distribution to: Jesse Ford to maintain the widow (unnamed).
    Executor: Jesse Ford.

John Newton   5.27   D   SM   £479.2.1   Apr 19 1767
    Sureties: James Bredon, John Simmonds.
    Legatees: Catharine Newton (daughter of Robert Newton and his wife Elisabeth),
        John Newton (son of the same), Leonard (brother).
    Residue to: Frances (widow).
    Executors: Frances Newton, Mathew Wise.

Richard Millard   5.27   D   SM   £361.11.0   Apr 22 1767
    Sureties: Benjamin Hudson Watkins, Bennett Wheeler.
    Legatees: Elisabeth Howe (daughter).
    Residue to: widow (unnamed) during life.
    Executrix: Mary Millard.

James Brice   5.27   D   BA   £448.1.8   Mar 6 1767
    Sureties: Thomas Johnson, Jr., Barnet Johnson.
    Distribution to: Widow (unnamed, 1/3). Residue to children (unnamed, except
        Samuel & James Brice, equally).
    Executrix: Mary Brice.

Joseph Hall   5.28   D   AA   £657.12.4   Mar 11 1767
    Sureties: William Coale, Joshua Griffith.
    Legatees: Joseph Hall, Edward Hall, Sophia Hall, Sarah Hall, Ann Hall.
    Residue to: widow (unnamed) during lifetime; then to 3 daughters (unnamed).
    Executor: Joseph Hall.

William Comegys   5.28   D   KE   £879.4.5   May 14 1767
    Legatees: John (son), Alphon (son).
    Distribution to: Widow (unnamed, 1/3). Residue to (equally): Nathaniel, Jesse,
        Edward, Jonathon, Cornelius, Alethea, Ann.
    Executor: John Comegys.

Philip Ricketts   5.28   D KE   £330.10.4   Feb 26 1767
    Distribution to: Widow (unnamed, 1/3). Residue to children (unnamed, equally).
    Executrix: Charlotte Griffith, wife of Samuel Griffith.

John Stone   5.29   D CA   £33.4.8   Mar 4 1767
    Sureties: James Hardesty, Henry Hardesty.
    Legatees: Susannah Stone (granddaughter), Martha Griffith (granddaughter), Mary &
        Margaret & Rebecca & Littleton (grandson).
    Residue to 9 children (equally): Margret, Elisabeth, Mary, Rachel, Ann,
        Priscilla, Samuel, Thomas, William.
    Executor: Thomas Stone.

Nicholas Boone   5.29   D AA   £441.18.11   Jun 4 1767
    Sureties: Joseph Jacobs, Richard Jacobs, Sr.
    Legatees: John Boone, Richard Boon.
    Distribution to: Widow (unnamed, 1/3). Residue to (equally): John Boone, Richard
        Boon.
    Executrix: Susannah Fowler, wife of Benjamin Fowler.

William Nicholson   5.29   D BA   £351.19.8   May 9 1767
    Sureties: John Ridgley, William Lux.
    Legatees: Elisabeth Connell, Dorothy Elton.
    Residue to: widow (unnamed).
    Executrix: Mary Hall, wife of Elisha Hall.

William Nelson   5.30   D SO   £320.14.9   Apr 9 1767
    Sureties: Thomas Holbrooke, William Pollitte.
    Legatees: William Atkison (grandson), Joshua Atkison, Betty Atkison.
    Residue to: widow (unnamed) during life.
    Administrator: Isaac Atkison.

Francis Parrot   5.30   D TA   £148.0.3   Mar 8 1767
    Sureties: Mathew Jenkins, William Carey.
    Legatees (children): Abner, Mary.
    Residue to remaining children (unnamed).
    Executor (acting): George Jenkins.

Barber Oldfield   5.30   D TA   £25.0.11   Feb 21 1767
    Sureties: Francis Daley, William Waring.
    Distribution to: Widow (unnamed, 1/3). Residue to children (equally): Henry,
        Lucretia.
    Administratrix: Margaret Oldfield.

Thomas Harriss   5.31   D QA   £2793.7.9   Aug 31 1767
    Sureties: William Clayton, Nathan Wright, Edward Clayton.
    Legatees: Thomas, Margaret, "unborn child", son (unnamed), Elisabeth and her
        husband (accountant).
    Distribution to: Elisabeth (widow, now Elisabeth Kane, 1/3). Residue to
        (equally): William Harriss, Edward Harriss, Sarah Harriss, Mary Harriss.
    Executor: Dr. George Garnett, Jr.

John Kinnemont   5.31   D TA   £518.0.10   Dec 15 1763
    Sureties: Rev. John Gordon, James Benson.
    Mentions: Richard Parrott.
    Distribution to: Widow (unnamed, 1/3). Residue to 2 children (equally):
        Susannah, John.
    Administratrix: Mrs. Elisabeth Kinnemont.

William Peele   5.32   D AA   £71.8.0   Nov 12 1767
    Legatees: Hannah Brown (daughter) wife of Capt. Brown in London, John Peele (son
        of Richard Peele in London), Roger (nephew), Robert (nephew), Samuel (nephew),
        William Alridge (son of Nicholas Alridge), Henry Caton of Annapolis.
    Executor (surviving): Mr. James Dick.

Joseph Hall   5.32   D AA   £657.12.4   Mar 11 1767
    Sureties: William Coale, Joshua Griffith.
    Legatees: Joshua Hall.
    Residue to: widow (unnamed) during lifetime; then to 3 daughters (unnamed,
        equally).
    Executor: Joseph Hall.

John Sappington   5.33   D AA   £163.4.6   Sep 8 1767
    Sureties: Richard Sappington, Thomas Sappington.
    Legatees: Rebeccah (daughter).
    Distribution to: Widow (unnamed, 1/3). Residue to 4 children (equally):
        Rebeccah, John, Caleb, Richard.
    Executrix: Ann Ridgley, wife of Nicholas Ridgley.

Thomas Morgan   5.33   D CA   £425.18.6   Jan 28 1768
   One-third of balance of estate of Richard Roberts devised by deceased to accountant.
   Legatees: accountant in consideration for her paying off her children (unnamed)
      by her former husband (unnamed), Elisabeth (daughter), Mary (daughter),
      Elisabeth Roberts, Thomas Morgan, Jonathon Morgan.
   Executrix: Mrs. Elisabeth Morgan.

Sarah Miller   5.34   D KE   £137.19.7   Jul 21 1763
   Sureties: Charles Groome, William Cowarden.
   Distribution to: children (unnamed).
   Administrator: Samuel Groome, Jr.

Samuel Miller   5.34   D KE   £545.11.3   Jul 21 1763
   Sureties: Gustavus Hanson, John Shield.
   Distribution to: Widow (unnamed, 1/3). Residue to children (unnamed, equally).
   Administrator (de bonis non): Samuel Groome, Jr.

John Pope   5.34   D WO   £447.19.11   Jul 15 1759
   Legatees: Mary Pope (granddaughter), Naomy Pope (granddaughter), Joyce Pope
      (granddaughter), Ann (widow), Joshua Mitchell (son-in-law), Robert Mitchell
      (grandson).
   Administrator (de bonis non): John Martin.

Jean Hill   5.35   D SM   £149.10.7   Jun 15 1767
   Distribution to: Representatives unknown to this Office.
   Administrator: Joseph Edwards assignee of Elisabeth Hill (administratrix of
      deceased).

Philip Edelin   5.35   D CH   £1113.14.8   Jul 6 1767
   Sureties: James Middleton, John Gardner.
   Distribution to: Representatives unknown to this Office.
   Administratrix: Mrs. Jane Edelin.

Cornelius Dickenson   5.35   D WO   £921.10.2   Oct 26 1767
   Sureties: William Barkley Townsend, Solomon Townsend.
   Legatees (children): Cornelius, Joshua, Josiah, Grace, Sophia.
   Residue to: above 5 representatives.
   Administrator: Josiah Dickenson.

William Briley   5.36   D QA   £59.13.10   Sep 7 1767
   Sureties: Aaron Yoe, James Carter.
   Distribution to: Representatives unknown to this Office.
   Administratrix: Lucretia Briley.

John Campbell   5.36   D QA   £266.2.11   Oct 18 1767
   Sureties: William Durding, Robert Walters.
   Distribution to: Representatives unknown to this Office.
   Administratrix: Elisabeth Benton, wife of John Benton.

Mary Ching   5.36   D CH   £45.15.7   Feb 11 1768
   Sureties: Philip Briscoe, John Andrews.
   Distribution to: Representatives unknown to this Office.
   Administrator: Luke Nicholas.

Isaac Chittum   5.36   D CH   £73.16.2   Feb 13 1768
   Sureties: John Brooks, Thomas Hopewell.
   Distribution to: Representatives unknown to this Office.
   Administratrix: Ann Quade, wife of John Quade.

Samuel Middleton   5.36   D CH   £1063.8.9   Feb 3 1768
   Sureties: Thomas McPherson, Benjamin Ward.
   Distribution to: Representatives unknown to this Office.
   Administratrix: Elisabeth Middleton.

John Hays   5.37   D QA   £53.12.7   Jan 11 1768
   Distribution to: Representatives unknown to this Office.
   Administratrix: Elisabeth Hinds.

John Sutton   5.37   D QA   £171.3.7   Jan 13 1768
   Sureties: John Deford, James Byrn.
   Distribution to: Representatives unknown to this Office.
   Administratrix: Elisabeth Hinds.

John Raitt   5.37   D AA   £526.15.5   Oct 1 1767
   The amount of the accounts also included #6633 and £4239.9.9 sterling.
   Sureties: John Carnan, Christopher Carnan.
   Distribution to: widow (accountant, 1/3). Residue to (equally): Ann Raitt wife
      of John Ducket, Barbara Raitt, Hariott Wivell, John Raitt, George Raitt.
   Administratrix: Ann Hammond, wife of Mr. Nathan Hammond.

John Woolen   5.37   D   DO   £144.19.3   Jun 23 1767
    Sureties: Ezekiel Johnson, Patrick Brawhawn.
    Distribution to: Widow (unnamed, 1/3). Residue to 9 children (equally): Lettice,
        Anne, John, Elisabeth, Levin, William, Amelia, Edward, Benjamin.
    Administratrix: Elisabeth Woolen.

Joseph Whitely   5.38   D   DO   £87.17.11   Jun 13 1767
    Sureties: Thomas Wall, Edward Whitely.
    Distribution to: Representatives unknown to this Office.
    Administrator: William Whitely.

Jacob Hooper   5.38   D   CA   £387.8.0   Jan 30 1768
The amount of the accounts also included £2.1.5 sterling and £12.3.3 gold.
    Distribution to: Representatives unknown to this Office.
    Administrators: John Willin, Rachel Willin.

Mary Haycraft   5.38   D   AA   £47.8.4   Feb 4 1768
    Sureties: Zachariah Gray, John Phillips.
    Distribution to: Representatives unknown to this Office.
    Administrator: Humphrey Phillips.

James Preston   5.38   D   BA   £318.11.3   Dec 29 1767
    Sureties: Joseph Lusby, Robert Lusby.
    Distribution to: Representatives unknown to this Office.
    Administratrix: Ann Preston.

Joseph Frost   5.38   D   BA   £220.0.6   Dec 19 1767
    Sureties: Charles Baker.
    Distribution to: Representatives unknown to this Office.
    Administratrix: Mary Frost.

Lewis Pottee, Jr.   5.39   D   BA   £27.1.5   Feb 12 1768
    Sureties: John Taylor, Jos. Norris.
    Distribution to: Representatives unknown to this Office.
    Administrator: Thomas Norriss (son of Benjamin Norriss).

Thomas Burch   5.39   D   CH   £724.8.6   Jan 27 1768
    Sureties: Joseph Dyson, Bennett Dyson.
    Distribution to: Representatives unknown to this Office.
    Administrator: Thomas Burch.

John Meredith   5.39   D   QA   £238.12.7   Jan 6 1768
Amended on 27 March 1770.
    Sureties: John Scrivner, William Hammond.
    Legatees: Thomas (son), Sarah Costin (daughter), James Meredith (grandson, son of
        William (son)), John (son).
    Distribution to 4 children (equally): William, John, Thomas, Sarah.
    Executor: John Meredith.

John Rochester   5.39   D   QA   £44.18.6   Mar 2 1768
    Sureties: John Seeney, William Ruth.
    Distribution to: Representatives unknown to this Office.
    Administrator: Francis Rochester.

Joseph Joy   5.40   D   CH   £567.15.8   Oct 7 1767
    Sureties: Charles Allison Ford, John Scrogan.
    Distribution to: Representatives unknown to this Office.
    Administratrix: Elisabeth Joy.

William Smallwood Faglor   5.40   D   CH   £312.17.3   Oct 30 1767
    Sureties: Richard Speake, Joseph Hanson.
    Distribution to: Representatives unknown to this Office.
    Administrator: John Maddox.

James Skinner   5.40   D   CH   £155.15.4   Nov 6 1767
    Sureties: Edward Maddox, Jr., John Maddox.
    Distribution to: Representatives unknown to this Office.
    Administrator: James Skinner.

Daniel Wright   5.40   D   CH   £62.3.9   Nov 5 1767
    Sureties: William Lindsay, John Blackwood.
    Distribution to: Representatives unknown to this Office.
    Administratrix: Prudence Wright.

Alexander McDaniel   5.40   D   CH   £30.16.11   Oct 9 1767
    Sureties: John Stromatt, Alexander Williams.
    Distribution to: Representatives unknown to this Office.
    Administratrix: Mary Ann McDaniel.

Benjamin Adams, Jr.　　　　　　　5.41　　　D　CH　£84.15.3　　　Sep 2 1767
　　　Sureties: Thomas Adams, Archibald Johnson.
　　　Distribution to: Representatives unknown to this Office.
　　　Administratrix: Elisabeth Hudson, wife of William Hudson.

Elisabeth Hungerford　　　　　　5.41　　　D　CH　£48.8.6　　　Sep 2 1767
　　　Sureties: Samuel Lowe, William Penn.
　　　Distribution to: Representatives unknown to this Office.
　　　Administrator: William Brown.

James Deale　　　　　　　　　　5.41　　　D　BA　£8.1.8　　　Nov 6 1767
　　　Sureties: Thomas Renshaw, Joseph Renshaw.
　　　Distribution to: Representatives unknown to this Office.
　　　Administrator: William Fisher, Jr.

Thomas Gilpin　　　　　　　　　5.41　　　D　CH　£152.19.8　　Sep 2 1767
　　　Sureties: Thomas Contee, Thomas Hopewell.
　　　Distribution to: Representatives unknown to this Office.
　　　Administrator: James Gilpin.

William Hamilton Smith　　　　　5.41　　　D　CA　£933.17.2　　Dec 17 1767
　　　Sureties: John Hamilton, Richard Bond.
　　　Distribution to: Representatives unknown to this Office.
　　　Administrators: Thomas Blake and his wife Barbara Blake.

Richard Johns　　　　　　　　　5.42　　　D　BA　£369.14.9　　Feb 3 1767
　　　Sureties: Jacob Giles, Nathan Rigbie.
　　　Distribution to: Representatives unknown to this Office.
　　　Administrator (de bonis non): Richard Johns.

John Barton Miles　　　　　　　5.42　　　D　SM　£71.0.6　　　Nov 24 1767
　　　Sureties: Enoch Fenwick, Cornelius Wildman.
　　　Distribution to: Representatives unknown to this Office.
　　　Administratrix: Elisabeth Miles.

Rubin Cheseldine　　　　　　　　5.42　　　D　QA　£5.12.9　　　Nov 15 1767
　　　Sureties: Owen Allen, Kenelum Cheseldine.
　　　Distribution to: Representatives unknown to this Office.
　　　Administrator: Kenelum Cheseldine, Sr.

Paul Rawlings　　　　　　　　　5.42　　　D　PG　£50.10.6　　Aug 24 1767
　　　Sureties: Richard Hutton, Paul Rawlings.
　　　Distribution to: Representatives unknown to this Office.
　　　Administratrix: Ann Rawlings.

Sarah Kent　　　　　　　　　　5.42　　　D　AA　£22.17.6　　Dec 4 1767
　　　Sureties: Edmund Jenings.
　　　Distribution to: Representatives unknown to this Office.
　　　Administrator: Thomas Mayo.

Benjamin Whittington　　　　　　5.43　　　D　QA　£929.0.11　　Sep 9 1763
The amount of the estate also included £7.13.1 sterling.
　　　Sureties: John Brown (son of James Brown), Edward Wright.
　　　Legatees: Benjamin Whittington, Joseph Whittington, William Whittington, Mary
　　　　Whittington, Elisabeth Whittington.
　　　Distribution to: Widow (unnamed, 1/3). Residue to 5 children (unnamed, equally).
　　　Executrix: Jane Whittington.

Thomas Airey　　　　　　　　　5.43　　　D　DO　£1432.2.3　　Oct 26 1768
　　　Legatees: John Pitt Airey, Thomas Hill Airey, Richard Hill Airey, Mary Airey,
　　　　Elisabeth Gale, Sarah Haskins, Leah Hicks Airey, Louisa Airey, Milcah Airey,
　　　　Thomas Ennalls, Mary Herbert.
　　　Distribution to children: Mary Airey, John Pitt Airey, Elisabeth Gale, Sarah
　　　　Haskins, Leah Hicks Airey, Louisa Airey, Thomas Hill Airey, Richard Hill
　　　　Airey, Milcah Airey.
　　　Executors: MM John Pitt Airey, William Haskins.

Caleb Dorsey　　　　　　　　　5.44　　　D　AA　£560.13.4　　Aug 13 1767
　　　Sureties: Henry Ridgely, John Burgess.
　　　Distribution to: Representatives unknown to this Office.
　　　Administrator: Mr. Thomas Dorsey.

John Jones　　　　　　　　　　5.44　　　D　DO　£26.2.6　　　Jun 1 1767
　　　Sureties: Philemon Phillips, Jr., Philemon Phillips.
　　　Distribution to: Widow (unnamed, 1/3). Residue to 3 children (equally): Mary,
　　　　Solomon, David.
　　　Administratrix: Rosannah Jones.

James Maddox   5.44   D CH   £78.16.2   Nov 15 1767
    Sureties: Richard Speake, John Manning.
    Distribution to: Representatives unknown to this Office.
    Administratrix: Theodocia Maddox.

James Provin   5.44   D CH   £71.19.4   Dec 21 1767
    Sureties: William Warden, James French.
    Distribution to: Representatives unknown to this Office.
    Administrator: Francis Robinson.

John Carpenter   5.44   D CH   £169.1.8   Aug 20 1767
    Sureties: William Woodward, Henry Woodyard.
    Distribution to: Representatives unknown to this Office.
    Administratrix: Priscila Addams, wife of Richard Addams.

John Kent   5.45   D AA   £103.2.3   Apr 9 1767
    Sureties: John Kent, Joseph Joyce.
    Distribution to: Representatives unknown to this Office.
    Administrator (de bonis non): Mr. Thomas Mayo.

John Clarkson   5.45   D DO   £31.6.8   May 18 1767
    Sureties: Absolem Thompson, Ezekiel Johnson.
    Distribution to 2 children: accountant, John Clarkson.
    Administrator: Mr. Joseph Clarkson.

Jacob Lockerman   5.45   D DO   £99.7.7   May 1 1767
See Folio 159.
    Sureties: Thomas Howell, James Woolford Stewart.
    Distribution to: Representatives unknown to this Office.
    Administratrix: Rosannah Gray.

Thomas Barnett   5.45   D QA   £51.6.0   Jun 4 1767
    Sureties: Robert Smith.
    Distribution to: Representatives unknown to this Office.
    Administratrix: Barbara Copeland, wife of Lawrence Copeland.

John Staples   5.45   D DO   £42.12.8   Nov 11 1767
    Sureties: John Gouttee, William Edger.
    Distribution to: Representatives unknown to this Office.
    Administratrix: Margaret Staples.

Charles Lowd   5.46   D DO   £124.17.0   Aug 19 1767
    Sureties: Obed Dixon, Nehamiah Andrew.
    Distribution to: Representatives unknown to this Office.
    Administratrix: Mary Aaron.

Joseph Cox Gray   5.46   D DO   £605.9.7   Oct 24 1767
This entry crossed out. See new balance in Liber EV#2 (Liber 6).
    Sureties: John Stewart, Levin Woolford.
    Distribution to: Representatives unknown to this Office.
    Administratrix: Rosannah Gray.

John Rochester, Jr.   5.46   D QA   £114.17.3   Nov 26 1767
son of Henry Rochester.
    Sureties: John Seeney, William Ruth.
    Distribution to: Representatives unknown to this Office.
    Administrator: Francis Rochester.

John Coniken   5.46   D QA   £123.5.10   Aug 20 1767
    Sureties: Philemon Tanner, John Legg.
    Distribution to: Representatives unknown to this Office.
    Administratrix: Mary Horsley, wife of Thomas Horsley.

Thomas Walker   5.46   D QA   £66.3.7   Aug 6 1767
    Sureties: William Walker, James Phillips.
    Distribution to: Representatives unknown to this Office.
    Administratrix: Tamesin Walker.

James Bowling   5.47   D CH   £66.18.7   Aug 22 1767
    Sureties: William Hamilton, John Manning.
    Distribution to: Representatives unknown to this Office.
    Administratrix: Mary Ann Bowling.

George Boaz, Jr.   5.47   D DO   £22.16.3   Aug 12 1767
    Sureties: George Boaz, Jacob Goutte.
    Distribution to: Representatives unknown to this Office.
    Administratrix: Bridget Boaz.

John Tollin   5.47   D   DO   £155.16.6   Aug 13 1767
    Sureties: Jonathon Patridge, John Bramble.
    Distribution to: Representatives unknown to this Office.
    Administratrix: Rachel Jefferson, wife of John Jefferson.

Jeremiah Leech   5.47   D   CH   £171.1.11   Sep 2 1767
    Sureties: Lancelot Chun, Thomas Bond. Both of St. Mary's County.
    Distribution to: Representatives unknown to this Office.
    Administratrix: Mrs. Elisabeth Leech.

Joseph Barnett   5.47   D   QA   £77.15.5   Aug 26 1767
    Sureties: William Ratcliffe, William Thompson.
    Distribution to: Representatives unknown to this Office.
    Administratrix: Rebecca Barnett.

Samuel Norriss   5.48   D   FR   £22.8.0   Nov 5 1767
    Sureties: James Brand.
    Distribution to: Representatives unknown to this Office.
    Administrator: John Carey.

Jacob Loy   5.48   D   FR   £138.10.2   Nov 30 1767
    Sureties: Thomas Shley, Valentine Stackle.
    Distribution to: Representatives unknown to this Office.
    Administrators: John Jeremiah Myers, Mary Loy.

Jonathon Stevens   5.48   D   DO   £9.3.8   Aug 12 1767
    Sureties: Naher Goodwine, George Stockly.
    Distribution to: Representatives unknown to this Office.
    Administrator: John Stevens.

Ayres Nunam   5.48   D   DO   £138.5.11   Aug 13 1767
    Sureties: William Low, Stephen Andrews.
    Distribution to: Representatives unknown to this Office.
    Administratrix: Frances Nunam.

John Clark   5.48   D   BA   £54.3.5   Jul 13 1767
    Distribution to: Representatives unknown to this Office.
    Administrator: John Hammond Dorsey.

Joseph Paulson   5.48   D   BA   £64.16.3   Jul 20 1767
    Distribution to: Representatives unknown to this Office.
    Administrator (de bonis non): Charles Lynn.

Roger Hodson   5.49   D   DO   £80.15.3   May 24 1768
    Sureties: John Hicks.
    Distribution to: accountant in right of his deceased wife Mary (1/3). Residue to
        children (equally): Thomas, Ann.
    Administrator: Mr. Isaac Lloyd who intermarried with Mary Hodson (widow,
        administratrix of deceased).

John Smith Prather   5.49   D   PG   £888.2.5   Dec 4 1767
    Sureties: Thomas Chittam, Henry Hillary.
    Distribution to (equally): Jeremiah Prather and his 2 daughters Martha Odell &
        Rachel Prather.
    Executrix: Elisabeth Deakins, wife of William Deakins.

Thomas Carradine   5.49   D   QA   £1021.13.2   Aug 20 1767
See Folio 85.
    Sureties: Henry Costin, John Costin.
    Legatees (children): Richard, John, Eleanor, Hannah, Susannah, Thomas, William.
    Mentions: estate of William Scandrett (uncle to sons Thomas & William).
    Distribution to: Widow (unnamed, 1/3). Residue to children (equally): Richard,
        John, Eleanor, Hannah, Susannah.
    Executrix: Henrietta Caradine.

Edward Killium   5.50   D   SO   £655.0.6   Sep 9 1767
Amended on 19 May 1769 by George Hayward.
    Sureties: Joseph Copeland, George Brown.
    Legatees: Edward Killum.
    Distribution to: Widow (unnamed, 1/3). Residue to (equally): Elisabeth
        Huffington, John Killum (accountant).
    Executor: John Killium.

Bartholomew Jesserang   5.50   D   FR   £252.16.6   Aug 22 1767
    Sureties: Caspar Shaff, John Carey.
    Legatees: Daniel (son).
    Distribution to 5 parts (equally): Barbara Woolhaton (daughter), Catherine Cooper
        (daughter), George Michael Jesserang (son), Eve Catharine Lambert (daughter),
        Peter & Lewis & Catharine (children of son Daniel).
    Executor: Michael Jesserang.

Abraham Porter   5.50   D KE   £129.1.10   Feb 19 1767
    Distribution to: Representatives unknown to this Office.
    Administratrix: Ruth Porter.

Joseph Basill   5.50   D KE   £32.11.8   May 7 1767
    Distribution to: Representatives unknown to this Office.
    Administrator (de bonis non): William Hollingsworth.

Amos Hollingsworth   5.51   D KE   £268.3.5   May 9 1767
    Sureties: Nathaniel Stennard, John Kinnard.
    Distribution to: Representatives unknown to this Office.
    Administrator: William Hollingsworth.

Peter Cole   5.51   D KE   £331.17.0   May 8 1767
    Sureties: Michael Corse, John Lamb.
    Distribution to: Representatives unknown to this Office.
    Administratrix: Martha Cole.

Ebenezar Perkins   5.51   D KE   £546.3.7   Dec 30 1767
    Sureties: Thomas Perkins, Abraham Woodland.
    Distribution to: Representatives unknown to this Office.
    Administratrix: Margaret Eccleston, wife of John Eccleston.

Richard Warfield   5.51   D AA   £687.2.7   Mar 6 1768
    Sureties: Alexander Warfield, John Marriott.
    Legatees: Rachel (daughter), 3 children (unnamed) of John (son) when eldest
       daughter (unnamed) comes of age, Richard (son), Luke (son), Joseph (son).
    Executors: Seth Warfield, Joseph Warfield.

Theophilus Swift   5.52   D CH   £1507.19.1   Nov 5 1767
    Sureties: Daniel of St. Thomas Jenifer, John Semple.
    Distribution to: Mary (widow, 1/2). Residue to siblings (equally): John Swift,
       Meade Swift, Thomas Swift, Susannah Jubbs, Elisabeth Boor.
    Administrator: Goodwin Swift.

John Wallis   5.52   D KE   £748.1.4   Jan 20 1767
    Distribution to: Representatives unknown to this Office.
    Administratrix: Hannah Warner, wife of Philip Warner.

George Cole   5.52   D KE   £394.3.1   Jun 22 1767
    Sureties: Ephraim Vansant, Joseph Redgrave.
    Distribution to: Representatives unknown to this Office.
    Administratrix: Jane Cole.

Amos Johnson   5.52   D BA   £151.12.7   Nov 8 1762
    Sureties: William Ball, Richard Williams.
    Distribution to: Representatives unknown to this Office.
    Administrators: William Bayne and his wife Lydia Bayne, Peter Miles.

Ann Johns   5.52   D BA   £84.12.4   Mar 11 1768
    Distribution to: Representatives unknown to this Office.
    Administrator: Richard Johns.

William Richey   5.53   D FR   £145.3.1   Mar 28 1768
    Distribution to: Representatives unknown to this Office.
    Administratrix: Mary Ann Richey.

Edward Northcraft   5.53   D FR   £454.9.1   Apr 25 1768
The amount of the accounts also included #2826.
    Distribution to: Representatives unknown to this Office.
    Administratrix: Elisabeth Hook (formerly Elisabeth Northcraft).

Jane Medford   5.53   D KE   £1350.9.8   Jun 5 1767
    Sureties: Thomas Chandler, Andrew Tolson.
    Distribution to: Representatives unknown to this Office.
    Administrator: Thomas Medford.

William Bruffitt   5.53   D KE   £56.10.10   Mar 19 1767
    Sureties: John Kinnard, Robert Meeks.
    Distribution to: Representatives unknown to this Office.
    Administrator: John Abell.

Alexander Gordon   5.53   D SO   £98.13.11   Feb 10 1768
    Sureties: John Malone, William Kibble, Jr.
    Distribution to: Representatives unknown to this Office.
    Administrator: William Kibble.

Arraminta Box   5.53   D KE   £13.11.6   Jan 10 1767
    Distribution to: Representatives unknown to this Office.
    Administrator: Richard Frisby.

Stephen Kendall   5.54   D   KE   £97.13.7   Oct 5 1767
    Sureties: Daniel Shehawn, John Ambrose, Sr.
    Distribution to: Representatives unknown to this Office.
    Administratrix: Sarah Morgan, wife of Charles Morgan.

John Sewell   5.54   D   KE   £79.3.5   May 31 1767
    Distribution to: Representatives unknown to this Office.
    Administrator: John Spargo.

James Whittington   5.54   D   KE   £287.13.4   Jul 13 1767
    Sureties: Luke Miers, John Bateman.
    Distribution to: Representatives unknown to this Office.
    Administratrix: Christian Whittington.

Robert Layfield   5.54   D   SO   £37.4.10   Mar 14 1768
    Distribution to: Representatives unknown to this Office.
    Administratrix: Rebeccah Layfield.

Thomas Caldwell   5.54   D   SO   £100.16.5   Mar 18 1768
    Sureties: John Wallace, John Mayce.
    Distribution to: Representatives unknown to this Office.
    Administrator: Mr. Joseph Windsor.

Kirk Gunby   5.54   D   SO   £142.0.6   March 16 1768
    Sureties: John Crockett, William Woollen.
    Distribution to: Representatives unknown to this Office.
    Administratrix: Elisabeth Gunby.

William Stone   5.55   D   SM   £71.4.0   Jun 22 1767
    Sureties: William Stone, Jos. Stone.
    Legatees: Ann Grunwell (daughter), Joseph Stone (grandson), Henry Stone (son).
    Residue to: Ignatius (son).
    Executor: Ignatius Stone.

John Wilds   5.55   D   FR   £105.6.6   Aug 22 1767
    Sureties: Valentine Myers, John Richards.
    Distribution to: widow (unnamed).
    Executrix: Jane Wilds.

Thomas Speake   5.55   D   CH   £179.12.0   Jun 13 1767
    Legatees: Eleanor Young (granddaughter), Elisabeth Young (granddaughter), Sarah
        Ward (granddaughter), Sarah Stone (daughter), Alexander Smith Hawkins Speake
        (grandson), Cordelia Speake (granddaughter), Eleanor Ann Speake
        (granddaughter).
    Residue to: John (son).
    Executrix: Jane Moore, wife of Mathew Moore.

Robert Owens   5.56   D   FR   £80.15.9   Aug 2 1767
    Sureties: James Hook, John Simpson.
    Legatees (children): Robert, Margaret Clark, Lydia Pries, Rachel Harper.
    Distribution to: Rachel Owings (widow, 1/3). Residue to (equally): John Owings,
        James Owings, Owen Owings, David Owings, Thomas Owings, Jeremiah Owings Fobson
        (?).
    Administratrix: Rachel Owens.

William Weathered   5.56   D   AA   £127.18.2   Sep 2 1767
    Sureties: John Jacobs, Lewis Cheney.
    Legatees: Nancy Jacobs (daughter of John Jacobs (schoolmaster)).
    Residue to: Dorcas (widow).
    Executrix: Dorcas Weathered.

David Delauder   5.56   D   FR   £78.2.5   Mar 9 1768
    Legatees (children): George William, Maudelina Siler (wife of Mathias Siler).
    Distribution to: Widow (unnamed, 1/3). Residue to children (equally): Johannas,
        Catharine, Barbara.
    Executors: Jacob Brunner, John Brunner.

Unit Medford   5.56   D   KE   £226.5.7   Jul 28 1767
    Sureties: Rasin Gale, John Angier.
    Legatees: Sarah Angier.
    Residue to (equally): 3 children (unnamed, under age) of Anne Greenwood (sister).
    Executor: Macal Medford.

Samuel Wallis   5.57   D   KE   £753.6.0   Nov 4 1767
    Sureties: Thomas Wilkins, Henry Bodean.
    Legatees (children): Sarah, John, Henry, Samuel.
    Residue to children (unnamed, equally).
    Executor: Samuel Wallis.

Joseph Clements   5.57   D   CH   £72.4.11   Sep 1 1767
    Sureties: Richard B. Mitchell, Benjamin G. Smallwood.
    Legatees: Joseph, Jr. (son), Clement (son), Ann Clements (granddaughter), Mathew
        Sanders, (grandson).
    Residue to 7 children (equally): Leonard, Charity Delozier, Joseph, Clement,
        Walter, John, Elisabeth Wheeler.
    Executor: Leonard Clements.

Francis Yates   5.57   D   CH   £604.13.0   Aug 25 1767
    Legatees: Robert (brother), Ann Gwinn (niece, daughter of John Gwinn), Judith
        Bruce (niece), Theophilus (brother).
    Residue to: Theophilus (brother).
    Executor: Theophilus Yates.

James Sterling   5.58   D   KE   £2148.15.10   Nov 13 1767
    Sureties: Joseph Nicholson, John Scott.
    Legatees: Rebecca (daughter), widow (unnamed).
    Distribution to: Widow (unnamed, 1/3).
    Administratrix: Mary Binney, wife of Mr. Benjamin Binney.

Richard Bennett Boarman   5.58   D   CH   £1141.17.7   Jul 21 1767
    Sureties: Edward Edelin, Raphael Boarman.
    Legatees: Mary Ann (widow), Eleanor (daughter), Elisabeth (daughter), Raphael
        (son), Richard Bennett Boarman (son).
    Residue to 4 children (equally): Eleanor, Elisabeth, Raphael, Richard Bennett.
    Executrix: Mrs. Mary Ann Boarman.

John Williamson   5.58   D   KE   £1309.8.10   Aug 22 1767
    Sureties: Richard Lloyd, Dennis Dulany.
    Distribution to: widow (unnamed) during her natural life.
    Executrix: Elisabeth Williamson.

Thomas Elliott   5.59   D   CE   £379.5.3   1767
    Sureties: Slyter Baushell, Andrew Coulter.
    Legatees: Elisabeth Hedrick (daughter), Polly Palmer (daughter), Rebecca Palmer
        (daughter of Polly Palmer), Thomas Hedrick (grandson), George Hedrick
        (son-in-law).
    Distribution to: Widow (unnamed, 1/3).
    Executor: Thomas Palmer.

James Smallwood   5.59   D   CH   £407.4.1   Dec 5 1767
    Sureties: Thomas Smallwood, Samuel Smallwood.
    Legatees (children): Marbury, Samuel, Susannah, Frances Ann, James Bidon
        Smallwood.
    Executrix: Susannah Smallwood.

John Selby   5.59   D   PG   £459.11.0   Nov 24 1767
    Sureties: Allen Bowie, William Dorset.
    Legatees: Sarah (widow), Kenelm Groom Selby (son), John Smith Selby (son),
        Henrietta (daughter).
    Residue to (equally): Sarah (widow), John Smith Selby (son), Henrietta
        (daughter).
    Executrix: Sarah Selby.

William Jewett   5.60   D   SO   £1211.9.7   Mar 8 1768
    Sureties: Stephen Ward, Mathias Ward.
    Legatees: William Jewett (grandson, son of John Jewett), Martha (daughter), Betty
        Miles (daughter), Leah (daughter), Rhoda Leeke (daughter), Mary (daughter),
        Catharine Jewet (daughter), Nathaniel Jewet (son).
    Distribution to: Widow (unnamed, 1/3). Residue to 5 daughters (equally): Martha,
        Leah, Rhoda Leeke, Mary, Catharine.
    Executors: Mary Jewett, Nathaniel Jewett.

William Redgrave   5.60   D   KE   £190.1.1   Dec 1 1767
    Sureties: John Dier, James Kelley.
    Distribution to: widow (unnamed) during minority of children (unnamed, under 21);
        then to 2 children: Mary, William.
    Executrix: Elisabeth Dullahuntee, wife of William Dullahuntee.

John Emerson   5.60   D   QA   £125.2.7   Sep 17 1767
    Sureties: Peter Wrench, Henry Pratt.
    Executor: John Emerson.

Christian Smith   5.61   D PG   £409.10.8   Aug 31 1767
    Sureties: Alexander Seymour, David Crawford.
    Legatees: Thomas Lee (son), Sarah Brooke Lee (daughter), Mrs. Elisabeth Contee
        wife of Theodore Contee, Clement Smith (brother-in-law), Mrs. Catharine Simm
        (sister-in-law), Lucy Boteler, Barbara Smith (sister), Mrs. Ann Hollyday
        (friend), Mrs. Sarah Chitten, Joseph Walter Simm (brother).
    Residue to: Eleanor Addison Smith (daughter).
    Executor: Maj. Joseph Simm.

Philip Fose   5.61   D FR   £47.17.0   Mar 1 1768
    Sureties: Jacob Hummer, Henry Zoll.
    Legatees: William (son).
    Residue to daughters (unnamed, equally).
    Executors: Nicholas Stoltz, Eve Flaisper (formerly Eve Fose).

John Hoyle   5.62   D FR   £37.1.3   Mar 25 1768
    Legatees: Margaret (wife), Andrew (son), Christian Bodien (daughter), Conrad
        (son).
    Distribution to: Widow (unnamed, 1/3). Residue to 3 children (equally): Andrew,
        Christiana, Conrad.
    Executrix: Margaret Hoyle.

John Rigdon   5.62   D BA   £240.1.7   Feb 29 1768
    Sureties: Thomas Baker Rigdon, William Johnson.
    Legatees: Johannah Hitchcock (step-daughter).
    Distribution to: Widow (unnamed, 1/3). Residue to 6 children (unnamed, equally).
    Administratrix: Elisabeth Rigdon.

Tobias Stansbury   5.62   D BA   £657.1.0   Mar 29 1768
The amount of the accounts also included £45.9.6 sterling.
    Legatees: Tobias (son), George (son), Honor Gambrell (daughter), Sophia Robinson
        (daughter), Ellen Stansbury (granddaughter, under 16), Sarah Stansbury
        (granddaughter, under 16), Bowen (son).
    Distribution to 5 parts (equally): Tobias (son), George (son), Honour Gambrell
        (daughter), Sophia Robinson (daughter), Ellin Stansbury (granddaughter) &
        Sarah Stansbury (granddaughter).
    Executor: Tobias Stansbury.

Richard Wooderson   5.63   D KE   £606.8.10   Jun 1 1767
    Sureties: John Garland, James West.
    Distribution to: widow (unnamed) during widowhood; then to children (unnamed).
    Executors: Mrs. Sarah Wooderson, James Chiffin.

John Swann   5.63   D FR   £67.2.0   Mar 18 1768
The amount of the accounts also included #1851.
    Distribution to: Ann (daughter).
    Executors: Maddocks Dyson, James Dyson (formerly James Swann).

Note in overleaf: will of Edward Cole, Jr. recorded in Liber DD#1 (1760-1764) page
290; balance & distribution made in Liber EN#1 (1767) page 66.

Joseph Perkins   5.63   D KE   £220.8.10   Mar 3 1767
    Sureties: Thomas Ringgold.
    Legatees: Elisabeth Henry (housekeeper), Sarah (daughter).
    Residue to: Sarah Perkins.
    Executor: Mr. Richard Frisby.

Philip Ricketts   5.63   D KE   £330.10.4   Feb 26 1767
    Sureties: Nathaniel Ricketts, William Cowarden.
    Executrix: Charlotte Griffith, wife of Mr. Samuel Griffith.

Jonathon Ellis   5.64   D PG   £210.4.6   Nov 24 1767
    Sureties: Richard Estep, John Bowers.
    Legatees (sons): William, Elijah.
    Distribution to: Widow (unnamed, 1/3).
    Executrix: Elisabeth Ellis.

Isaac Williams   5.64   D DO   £620.13.7   Aug 17 1767
    Sureties: Thomas Cannon, Mathew Norwood.
    Legatees (children): Betty Williams, Stephen Williams, Sarah Richards.
    Distribution to 5 children (equally): Joshua, Spencer, Samuel, Stephen, Betty.
    Executor: Mr. Samuel Williams.

Mary Bussick   5.64   D DO   £83.15.1   Aug 12 1767
    Sureties: Benjamin Woodward, Levin Dorsey.
    Legatees (sons): Solomon, John, Joshua.
    Executor: Mr. Joshua Bussick.

Francis Harper   5.65   D   DO   £44.3.4   May 26 1767
    Sureties: Philemon Hays, John Murphy.
    Legatees: Rosannah Delaney (daughter), Elisabeth Shenton (daughter), Eleanor
        McGraw (daughter), James Murphy (son-in-law), Mary Murphy (daughter-in-law),
        Alley Murphy (daughter-in-law).
    Residue to: Mary (widow).
    Administratrix: Mrs. Mary Harper.

John Thompson   5.65   D   CH   £209.10.10   Sep 2 1767
    Sureties: Leonard Green, William Coombs.
    Legatees (daughters): Ann, Martha.
    Residue to (equally): Ann (widow), John (son), William (son), Thomas (son),
        Samuel (son).
    Executors: Ann Thompson, George Thompson.

Edward Ford   5.65   D   CH   £488.1.2   Jul 18 1767
    Sureties: Charles Allison Ford, John Wood.
    Legatees: John (son), Notley (son), Richard (son), Sarah Gwinn (granddaughter),
        Edward Gwinn (grandson), Charles Allison Ford (son), Allison (son).
    Distribution to: widow (unnamed) during lifetime; then to children (equally):
        John, Notley, Richard, Mary, Ann.
    Executrix: Elisabeth Ford.

Annastatia Crapper   5.66   D   CH   £206.5.3   Aug 5 1767
    Sureties: Thomas McPherson, George Clements.
    Distribution to: poor relations (unnamed) at discretion of priest of Pompret
        Chapple.
    Executor: Leonard Green.

Thomas Simpson   5.66   D   CH   £329.3.7   Aug 19 1767
    Sureties: Thomas Hussey Luckett, George Jenkins.
    Legatees (daughters): Elisabeth, Mary, Alanor, Ann.
    Residue to all children (unnamed, equally).
    Executrix: Elisabeth Simpson.

Mary Previn   5.66   D   CH   £49.2.11   Dec 2 1767
    Sureties: William Warden, James French.
    Legatees: Margaret (her share of her father's (unnamed) estate), Richard
        Robertson (son), Mary Robertson, Francis Robertson.
    Residue to children (unnamed, equally).
    Executor: Francis Robertson.

Edward Cole   5.66   D   CH   £2256.12.4   Dec 2 1767
    Sureties: Roger Smith, John Pye.
    Legatees: Sarah Tany (daughter-in-law).
    Executrix: Sarah Cole.

James McCatee   5.67   D   CH   £230.10.9   Dec 8 1767
    Sureties: William Coombs, Joseph Coombs.
    Legatees: James (son), Susannah (daughter), Eleanor (daughter), Elisabeth (one of
        youngest daughters), Monicka (one of youngest daughters), Anna Annason
        (daughter), James Atchason (grandson), Anna Atchason (daughter).
    Residue to son & 4 daughters (equally): James, Susannah, Elendor, Monicka,
        Elisabeth.
    Executors: James McCatee, Susannah McCatee.

William Dements   5.67   D   CH   £128.2.11   Dec 2 1767
    Sureties: John Cannington, Thomas Hyde Kellso.
    Legatees: Benajah Dement, George Dement, Martha Somerset (granddaughter).
    Residue to 2 sons & 2 daughters (equally): William, Walter, Dorcas, Lydia.
    Executor: Mr. William Robey.

William Neale   5.67   D   CH   £2098.4.3   Feb 22 1768
    Sureties: Roger Smith, William Mathews.
    Distribution to: Widow (unnamed, 1/3). Residue to children (unnamed, except
        Molly (daughter), equally).
    Executrix: Ann Neale.

Ignatius Hagan   5.68   D   CH   £279.14.0   Jan 8 1768
    Sureties: William Thompson, James Hagan.
    Legatees (children): James, Mary, Sarah, Elisabeth Speake, Eleanor Wheeler, Ann
        Blanford.
    Residue to: Magdalen (widow).
    Executrix: Magdalen Hagan.

John Swift   5.68   D   QA   £186.17.8   Aug 28 1767
    Sureties: Richard Swift, Gideon Swift.
    Distribution to (equally): Mable (wife), 6 children: John, Elisabeth, Thomas,
        James, Mary, Richard.
    Executor (acting): Mr. John Swift.

John Meekins   5.68   D DO   £71.7.7   Jun 10 1767
    Sureties: John Burn, Raymond Shenton.
    Legatees: John (son).
    Executrix: Catharine Meekins.

Robert Silo   5.68   D KE   £56.5.2   Mar 23 1767
    Distribution to: Representatives unknown to this Office.
    Administratrix: Hannah Sile.

John Loney   5.69   D BA   £391.13.10   Sep 7 1767
    Sureties: Andrew Landrum, John Henry.
    Distribution to: Mary (widow) during natural life or widowhood; then to 5
       children (equally): John, Stephen, William, Amos, Arabella.
    Executrix: Mary Loney.

Larkin Wilson   5.69   D DO   £79.17.11   1767
    Sureties: William Salsbury, James Cooper.
    Distribution to 2 daughters (equally): Sarah, Lucia.
    Executor: Jonathon Wilson.

Henry Fisher   5.69   D DO   £99.12.8   Nov 13 1767
    Sureties: David Todd, Thomas Ross.
    Distribution to: Mary (wife) during her lifetime; then to: Benjamin (son), Fisher
       Mezecks (grandson), Sarah Evans (granddaughter), Henry Fisher (son of John
       Pritchet Fisher), Betty Todd, Jane Hopkins.
    Executor: Benjamin Todd.

Edward Hadley   5.69   D QA   £330.18.0   Jan 22 1768
    Sureties: John Emory, John Rigdon Emory.
    Distribution to: Mary (wife) during life or widowhood; then to children
       (unnamed).
    Executrix: Mary Hadley.

John Williams   5.70   D FR   £227.8.8   Jul 27 1768
    Legatees: wife (unnamed), William (brother).
    Distribution to: Widow (unnamed, 1/3). Residue to 5 children (unnamed, equally).
    Executors: John Chrisman, Catharine Norris (formerly Catharine Williams).

John Harper   5.70   D CE   £288.1.2   Oct 23 1767
    Sureties: John Eliason, Benjamin Elsbury.
    Legatees: Martha (wife), Margaret (daughter), John (son).
    Distribution to: Widow (unnamed, 1/3). Residue to 5 children (equally):
       Margaret, John, Elisabeth, James, Thomas.
    Executrix (acting): Martha Harper.

William Hill   5.70   D BA   £143.2.8   Aug 11 1767
    Sureties: William Hill, Richard Hill.
    Legatees: Martha Junis (daughter).
    Distribution to: Martha (wife) during natural life or widowhood; then to 4 sons &
       daughter: James, Thomas, Moris, Aaron, Sarah.
    Executors: Martha Hill, James Hill.

John Covington   5.71   D QA   £86.8.4   Aug 27 1767
    Sureties: James Covington, Jr., William Price.
    Legatees (sons): James, John, Henry.
    Distribution to: Widow (unnamed, 1/3). Residue to 7 children (equally): Mary,
       Benjamin, Elisabeth, Rebeccah, Sarah, William, Simon.
    Executor: John Covington.

John Aaron   5.71   D DO   £131.19.1   Aug 20 1767
    Sureties: John Goutee, Jonathon Patridge.
    Legatees: Mary Aaron (cousin, daughter of John Aaron).
    Distribution to 2 cousins: Thomas Barnes, Mary Aaron (daughter of John Aaron).
    Executors: Thomas Barnes, Mary Aaron.

Archibald Jackson   5.71   D QA   £74.11.10   Jun 25 1767
    Sureties: James Sylvester, John Young.
    Legatees: son (unnamed) born of his wife (unnamed) in 1747, Hannah Forkham
       (daughter).
    Distribution to children (equally): Samuel, Abednego, James, Archibal, Tilghman,
       John, Ann, Rebeccah.
    Executor: Samuel Jackson.

John Jones   5.71   D KE   £19.18.3   May 9 1767
    Sureties: Stephen Kinney, Robert Meeke.
    Distribution to: Representatives unknown to this Office.
    Administratrix: Jane Jones.

Archibald McCullum   5.72   D   TA   £556.4.10   May 4 1768
    Sureties: William Tripe, Wolman Gibson.
    Distribution to: widow (unnamed) during natural life or widowhood; then to
        children: Alexander, William, Fanny.
    Executrix: Jane McCullum.

Patrick Hart   5.72   D   QA   £149.18.11   Sep 17 1767
    Sureties: Oneal Price, James Lane.
    Legatees (sons): Augustean, James, Patrick (under 18).
    Distribution to: Widow (unnamed, 1/3). Residue to 5 children (equally):
        Augustean, James, Patrick, Ann, Mary.
    Executors: Mary Hart, John Carty.

John Milburn   5.72   D   SM   £96.9.3   Jul 14 1767
    Distribution to: Widow (unnamed, 1/3). Residue to 5 children (equally): Ann,
        John, Sally, Susannah, Sophia.
    Executrix: Ann Milburn.

John Barnes   5.73   D   FR   £68.8.0   Aug 25 1767
The amount of the accounts also included #2400.
    Distribution to: Widow (unnamed, 1/3). Residue to: John Waters Barnes (son).
    Administratrix: Mary Mullican, wife of Bazil Mullican.

John Pringle   5.73   D   DO   £41.4.10   Jun 10 1767
    Sureties: Naboth Hart, Lewis Griffith.
    Distribution to (equally): wife (unnamed), Bete Ricketts (cousin).
    Executrix: Comfort Pringle.

Alice Lester   5.73   D   BA   £104.3.10   Feb 8 1768
    Sureties: Richard Garretson, Edward Garretson.
    Distribution to: Representatives unknown to this Office.
    Administrator: Robert McGay.

Francis Hollyday   5.73   D   KE   £380.12.10   Jun 3 1767
    Sureties: Luke Myers, Ebenezar Massey.
    Legatees (daughters): Mary, Sarah.
    Distribution to 6 children (the youngest): Hannah, Rachel, William, Benjamin,
        Ebenezar, John.
    Executors: Mary Brown (late Mary Hollyday), George Hollyday.

Richard Bond   5.74   D   BA   £235.7.6   1767
    Sureties: William Hammond (son of Benjamin Hammond), Joseph Osbourn.
    Legatees: Richard (son), Ruth Gott (daughter), other unmarried daughters
        (unnamed), Jemima Ensor (daughter), Mary (daughter), Anne Constanty
        (daughter), Philip & John & Eleanor Prindell (children of John Prindell & his
        wife Eleanor), Elisabeth Cole (daughter).
    Residue to 6 daughters (equally): Mary, Jemima Ensor, Phebe, Sarah, Helen,
        Margaret.
    Executors: Nichodomus Bond, Richard Gott.

Thomas Roberts   5.74   D   £655.0.0
See Folio 206.
    Mentions: one of the children (unnamed) since dead without issue.
    Distribution to: Widow (unnamed, 1/3). Residue to: Susannah Armstrong or her
        children (unnamed), Thomas, Mary, Elisabeth, John, Edward, 3 children
        (unnamed) of James Roberts, 3 children (unnamed) of Rebecca Blake.

Henry Covington   5.74   D   QA   £241.3.7   Nov 21 1767
    Sureties: John Roe, William Ratcliff.
    Legatees: Rachel (daughter), Esther Covington.
    Distribution to: Widow (unnamed, 1/3). Residue to 6 children (equally): Edward,
        Solomon, Samuel, Rebeccah, Rachel, Esther.
    Executrix: Rachel Covington.

Richard Besswick   5.75   D   TA   £179.13.11   May 27 1767
    Sureties: William Besswick, Simon Stephens Miller.
    Legatees: Mary Thomas (daughter), Thomas Thomas, Jr. (grandson), Thomas (son),
        Richard, Jr. (son), Susannah Besswick, Jr. (granddaughter, daughter of
        Richard), Nathan (son), Mary (wife), Denny Besswick, Jr. (grandson, son of
        Nathan), Eunice (daughter), Susannah, Sr. (daughter), Denny (son), Charles
        Sweat Miller (son of Simon Stephens Miller).
    Residue to 3 children (equally): Eunice, Susannah, Denne.
    Executor: Denny Besswick.

Ann Powell   5.75   D   TA   £548.14.8   Aug 18 1767
    Sureties: James Lloyd, Tristram Thomas.
    Distribution to 5 parts (equally): Henry Troth & Anne Troth & William Troth
        (grandchildren), Elisabeth Macmans (grandchild), Christopher Birkhead (child),
        Peter Sharpe (child), Harrison Brooke (child).
    Executor: Christopher Birkhead.

Levin Harris   5.75   D SO   £23.15.5   Mar 1 1768
    Sureties: Charles Hayman, John Harris.
    Distribution to: Representatives unknown to this Office.
    Administratrix: Eve Harris.

Joseph Cox Gray   5.76   D DO   £565.16.4   Mar 21 1768
This entry is marked "Wrong".
    Sureties: John Stewart, Levin Woolford.
    Distribution to: Representatives unknown to this Office.
    Administratrix: Rosannah Gray.

Catharine Johnson   5.76   D DO   £29.3.10   Jun 11 1767
    Sureties: James Johnson, John Murphy.
    Legatees: Philadelphia Johnson (mother).
    Administratrix: Philadelphia Johnson.

Samuel Weathered   5.76   D KE   £1027.16.7   1766
    Sureties: James Pearce, William Weathered.
    Legatees: Isabella Barkley, William Whetred.
    Distribution to: John Whetered.
    Executor: Mr. John Weathered.

William Corse   5.76   D KE   £338.12.3   Mar 18 1767
    Sureties: George Lamb, John Williams.
    Distribution to (equally): George Corse, Daniel Corse, James Corse, Ann Corse.
    Executrix: Elisabeth Everet, wife of Mr. Hales Everet.

Thomas Chandler   5.76   D KE   £162.18.2   Dec 23 1767
    Sureties: John Crew, Charles McCubbin.
    Legatees: Nathaniel, Hannah Chandler.
    Executor: Mr. Thomas Chandler.

Alexander Briscoe   5.77   D KE   £262.18.0   Feb 2 1767
    Sureties: John Maxwell, Robert Maxwell.
    Legatees: John (son), heirs (unnamed) of William (son).
    Distribution to children (equally): Joseph, Sarah March.
    Executor: Mr. Joseph Briscoe.

William Clark   5.77   D KE   £210.12.3   Jan 25 1767
    Sureties: John Woodall, John Clark.
    Legatees: widow (accountant), William Clark, Mary Woodall, Sarah Cloud, Mathew
      Clark, Rachel Clark.
    Distribution to (equally): widow (unnamed), 2 youngest children: Mathew, Rachel.
    Executrix: Mrs. Rachell Clark.

Jane Frisby   5.77   D KE   £570.1.5   Mar 23 1767
    Sureties: Thomas Smith.
    Legatees: William Frisby, James Frisby, Mary Granger.
    Residue to: Richard Frisby.
    Executor: Mr. Richard Frisby.

Nathaniel Hynson, Jr.   5.78   D KE   £462.16.3   Aug 20 1767
    Legatees: Nathaniel Hynson, Hannah Hollis, Rachel Pritchard, Mary Robinson,
      William Hynson (son of John Hynson), William (son), Benjamin Hynson.
    Residue to: widow (accountant).
    Executrix: Mrs. Mary Wickes (formerly Mary Hynson).

William Ralph   5.78   D KE   £189.12.3   Jun 3 1767
    Legatees: John Ralph, Nancy (daughter), Frances (daughter), Martha (sister).
    Residue to 3 children (unnamed, equally).
    Executor: Mr. John Ralph.

Roger Addams   5.78   D DO   £851.2.0   Sep 9 1766
Filed May 31, 1768.
    Sureties: William Cannon, James Addams.
    Legatees: Mary (daughter), Nisse (daughter), Nancy Sterling (daughter), Boze
      Adams (cousin), Mary Addams.
    Distribution to: Widow (unnamed, 1/3).
    Administrators: Richard Clarkson and his wife Betty Clarkson, Roger Addams,
      William Fountain.

John Hayman   5.79   D WO   £227.12.4   Jun 6 1762
    Legatees: widow (unnamed), James Hayman, Mathew Dorman Hayman, John Hayman, David
      Hayman.
    Distribution to: Widow (unnamed, 1/3). Residue to (equally): Sarah Hayman,
      Charity Hayman, Frances Hayman, Rachel Hayman, Mary Hayman, Elisabeth Hayman,
      Rebecca Hayman, Isaac Hayman, Nehemiah Hayman.
    Executrix: Mrs. Rachel Hayman.

Andrew Banning   5.79   D   TA   £44.16.1   Nov 18 1766
    Sureties: Thomas Loveday, Joshua Clarke.
    Distribution to: Representatives unknown to this Office.
    Mentions: William Carry.
    Administrator: William Banning.

Thomas Coale   5.79   D   BA   £176.18.9   Apr 23 1768
    Sureties: Samuel Coale, William Cole.
    Distribution to: Widow (unnamed, 1/3). Residue to 2 children (unnamed, equally).
    Administrator: Thomas Stockett.

Elisabeth Craig   5.80   D   WO   £430.1.5   Nov 18 1767
"Sent to Somerset County".
    Sureties: Ephraim Wilson, David Wilson.
    Distribution to: Nancy (daughter).
    Administrator (de bonis non): William Skirvin of Somerset County.

Philemon Charles Blake   5.80   D   QA   £3600.8.1   Oct 26 1768
The amount of the accounts also included #13409.
    Sureties: Peregrine Frisby, James Frisby.
    Distribution to: Widow (unnamed, 1/3). Residue to 4 children (equally):
        Henrietta Maria, Philemon Charles, Elisabeth, Charles.
    Administrator (de bonis non): Charles Blake, Jr.

James Trego   5.81   D   DO   £306.13.8   Dec 7 1768
    Sureties: William Trego, John Adams.
    Legatees: Levin Trego, Sarah Trego, Roger Trego, Bershaba Stevens.
    Distribution to: Widow (unnamed, 1/3). Residue to 5 children (equally): Roger,
        Levin, Priscell, Betsy, Sarah.
    Executors: Mary Trego, Levin Trego.

John Baptist Loveless   5.81   D   FR   £81.5.11   Jul 14 1767
The amount of the accounts also included #3750.
    Sureties: Charles Hardy, John Coxon.
    Distribution to: Widow (unnamed, 1/3). Residue to 4 children (equally): Vachell,
        Archibald, Mary Ann, Miliscent.
    Executrix: Eleanor Robey.

Folio 82 does not exist.

John Wilson   5.83   D   QA   £852.19.4   Aug 24 1768
    Sureties: Alexander Walters, Jones Goodhand.
    Legatees: widow (unnamed), William, (son), Mary Ann Goodhand (daughter), Sarah
        Wright (daughter), Elisabeth Earickson (daughter), John (son), Rachel Legg
        (daughter).
    Distribution to: Widow (unnamed, 1/3).
    Executors: Rebeccah Wilson, William Wilson.

Folio 84 does not exist.

Thomas Carradine   5.85   D   QA   £554.15.0   Aug 26 1768
    Sureties: Henry Costin, John Costin.
    Legatees: Richard Carradine, John Carradine, Eleanor Carradine, Hannah Carradine,
        Susannah Carradine.
    Distribution to: Widow (unnamed, 1/3).
    Executrix: Henrietta Roberts, wife of James Roberts.

Martha Little   5.85   D   QA   £77.19.11   Mar 10 1768
    Sureties: Timothy Meaner, James Meaner.
    Distribution to (equally): Robert Little, Mary Little, Thomas Little, Catharine
        Little, Margaret Little, Sarah Little.
    Administrator: Robert Little.

George Cole   5.86   D   KE   £348.9.4   Aug 11 1768
    Sureties: Ephraim Vansant, Joshua Redgrave.
    Distribution to: Representatives unknown to this Office.
    Administratrix: Jane Cole.

Thomas Manning   5.86   D   DO   £76.1.6   Feb 4 1768
    Sureties: John Steuart, James Cullen.
    Distribution to: Representatives unknown to this Office.
    Administrator (de bonis non): Stephen Garey Warner of Talbot County.

David Davis   5.86   D   FR   £163.10.9   Apr 22 1768
The amount of the accounts also included #5911.
    Sureties: James Gow, Clementine Gow.
    Distribution to (equally): Samuel, William, Ann, David, Charity.
    Administrator (de bonis non): Thomas Thompson.

Henry Eagle   5.86   D   QA   £178.17.10   Jul 1 1768
    Distribution to: Widow (unnamed, 1/3). Residue to: Sarah (only child).
    Administratrix: Mary Eagle.

Richard Robinett   5.87   D   KE   £61.1.2   Aug 26 1768
    Sureties: Sanders Bostock, Robert Napp Clothier.
    Distribution to: Representatives unknown to this Office.
    Administratrix: Mary Robinett.

William Smith   5.87   D   KE   £898.1.5   Aug 18 1768
    Sureties: Mathew Smith, George Piller.
    Distribution to: Representatives unknown to this Office.
    Administrator: William Smith.

John Fitzchew   5.87   D   DO   £32.6.9   Aug 6 176-
    Sureties: James Busick, William Madkin.
    Distribution to: Widow (unnamed, 1/3). Residue to 8 children (equally): John,
        Susannah, Mary, Priscilla, Nelley, Richard, Rebecca, Samuel.
    Administrators: Mary Fitzchew, John Fitzchew.

Ann Pearman   5.87   D   AA   £79.7.6   Apr 19 1768
    Sureties: Cornelius Garritson.
    Distribution to: Representatives unknown to this Office.
    Administrator: Thomas Hyde.

James Cann   5.87   D   KE   £211.12.0   Oct 8 1768
    Sureties: William Cowarden, James Millward.
    Distribution to: Representatives unknown to this Office.
    Administrators: Frances Cann, James Cann.

Joseph Smith   5.88   D   AA   £55.8.7   Jul 2 1768
    Distribution to: Representatives unknown to this Office.
    Administratrix: Charity Ward (late Charity Smith).

Jacob Linegar   5.88   D   KE   £38.14.0   Jun 15 1768
    Sureties: George Fountain, Jacob Hurlock.
    Distribution to: Representatives unknown to this Office.
    Administratrix: Grace Linegar.

Bartholomew Haydon   5.88   D   KE   £101.12.10   Jun 29 1767
    Sureties: David Shahon, John Crew.
    Distribution to: Representatives unknown to this Office.
    Administratrix: Mary Collins, wife of Bartholomew Collins.

Elisabeth Williams   5.88   D   KE   £315.3.5   Jun 15 1768
    Sureties: Thomas Browning, George Medford.
    Distribution to: Representatives unknown to this Office.
    Administrator (surviving): Sanders Bostock.

William Dunn   5.88   D   KE   £342.13.0   Jun 14 1768
    Distribution to: Representatives unknown to this Office.
    Administratrix: Ann Fitzgerrald, wife of John Fitzgerrald.

Henry Moore   5.89   D   KE   £330.15.0   Apr 8 1768
    Sureties: John Graham, Francis Rutter.
    Distribution to: Representatives unknown to this Office.
    Administrator: Rudolph Moore.

John Parrott   5.89   D   AA   £51.13.11   Jul 12 1768
    Sureties: George Vatts, Elijah Robinson.
    Distribution to: Representatives unknown to this Office.
    Administrator: Francis Shepherd.

William Day   5.89   D   CA   £185.1.6   May 26 1768
    Distribution to: Representatives unknown to this Office.
    Administratrix: Jane Day.

Thomas Gerrard Slye   5.89   D   CH   £360.17.1   Jul 15 1768
    Sureties: Richard Southern of St. Mary's County, John Southern.
    Distribution to: Widow (unnamed, 1/3). Residue to 2 children (equally): Mary
        Slye, John Southern Slye.
    Administratrix: Elisabeth Briscoe, wife of James Briscoe.

Samuel Moss   5.89   D   AA   £212.19.10   Aug 3 1768
    Sureties: Richard Moss, John Aires.
    Distribution to: Representatives unknown to this Office.
    Administratrix: Elisabeth Moss.

Richard Wright　　　　　　　　　5.90　　D　CH　£208.6.11　　Jul 15 1768
　　Sureties: George Grimes, Joseph Letchworth.
　　Distribution to: Widow (unnamed, 1/3). Residue to: Ann (only child).
　　Administratrix: Elisabeth Briscoe, wife of James Briscoe.

Michael Oden　　　　　　　　　　5.90　　D　CH　£160.19.4　　Jun 1 1768
　　Sureties: Francis Oden, John Biggs of Prince George's County.
　　Distribution to: Widow (unnamed, 1/3). Residue to 3 children (equally): Sarah,
　　　　Michael, Eleanor.
　　Administratrix: Elisabeth Oden.

Jacob Thoms　　　　　　　　　　5.90　　D　SO　£46.7.2　　Jun 16 1768
　　Sureties: Selathel Griffin, Evans Whinwright.
　　Distribution to: Widow (unnamed, 1/3). Residue to (equally): Stephen Thoms, Mary
　　　　Thoms.
　　Administratrix: Sarah Thoms.

William Robertson　　　　　　　5.90　　D　SO　£42.18.11　　May 4 1768
　　Sureties: Henry Newman, Isaac Newman.
　　Distribution to: Widow (unnamed, 1/3). Residue to (equally): Isaac Newman in
　　　　right of his wife (unnamed), Thomas Newman in right of his wife (unnamed),
　　　　other representatives (unnamed, probably 3 in number).
　　Administratrix: Rachel Robertson.

John Compton　　　　　　　　　　5.91　　D　CH　£249.2.3　　May 10 1768
　　Sureties: William Compton, Stephen Compton.
　　Distribution to: Widow (unnamed, 1/3). Residue to children (equally): William,
　　　　Mary Ann, Theo.
　　Administratrix: Margaret Compton.

Nathaniel Chapman　　　　　　　5.91　　D　CH　£2474.10.11　Apr 21 1768
　　Distribution to: Widow (unnamed, 1/3). Residue to 6 children (equally):
　　　　Elisabeth Hunter, Amelia Weems, Nathaniel, Louissa Washington, Pearson,
　　　　George.
　　Administratrix: Constant Chapman.

Jane Bruce　　　　　　　　　　　5.91　　D　CH　£888.17.6　　Apr 13 1768
　　Sureties: James Campbell, Theophilus Yates.
　　Distribution to children (equally): Judith, John, Elisabeth, Townley, Robert,
　　　　William, Walter, Jane, Jane Little Bruce.
　　Administrator: John Bruce.

Jesse Tull　　　　　　　　　　　5.91　　D　DO　£249.12.6　　Aug 1 1768
　　Sureties: Richard Clarkson, Jr., William Juett.
　　Distribution to: Widow (unnamed, 1/3). Residue to 8 children (equally): Levin,
　　　　Elijah, Celia, Noble, Sally, Jesse, Andrew, Jane.
　　Administratrix: Mary Tull.

Betty Rix　　　　　　　　　　　　5.92　　D　DO　£167.13.0　　Aug 11 1768
　　Sureties: Thomas Moore, William Kilman.
　　Distribution to (equally): Anne Rix, Nancy Rix, Sarah Melvill.
　　Administrators (de bonis non): Thomas Smith and his wife Rachel Smith.

Edmund Farrell　　　　　　　　　5.92　　D　TA　£683.7.7　　Sep 13 1768
　　Sureties: William Ratcliff, Isaac Falkner.
　　Distribution to: Representatives unknown to this Office.
　　Administrators: Philip Perkins and his wife Ann Perkins.

Emanuel Jenkins　　　　　　　　5.92　　D　TA　£256.14.0　　Aug 2 1768
　　Sureties: Pollard Edmondston, Powell Cox.
　　Distribution to: Widow (accountant, 1/3). Residue to 3 children (equally):
　　　　Sarah, John, Thomas.
　　Administratrix: Martha Jordan, wife of Thomas Jordan.

James Layton　　　　　　　　　　5.92　　D　DO　£36.18.11　　Aug 11 1768
　　Sureties: Solomon Hubbert, Elijah Standford.
　　Distribution to (equally): Rachel Smith, James Layton, Dina Wheeler, Mary
　　　　Elliott, Nancy Layton, Charles Layton.
　　Administrator: James Layton, Jr.

John Warren　　　　　　　　　　　5.93　　D　DO　£106.18.0　　Aug 25 1768
　　Sureties: Thomas Steuart, Charles Manship.
　　Distribution to: Widow (unnamed, 1/3). Residue to 5 children (equally): Mary
　　　　Ann, Agness, Alefare, William, John.
　　Administrator: John Brinnagan.

Sarah Phillips　　　　　　　　　5.93　　D　CE　£7.1.3　　Oct 19 1768
　　Sureties: William Reynolds, Alexander McDugging.
　　Distribution to: Representatives unknown to this Office.
　　Administrator: James Rock.

John Osbourne   5.93   D   CE   £41.12.3   Oct 19 1768
    Sureties: James Rock, Andrew Ryan.
    Distribution to: Widow (unnamed, 1/3). Other representatives unknown to this
        Office.
    Administratrix: Mary Osbourne.

Bartholomew Parsley   5.93   D   CE   £151.4.2   Jun 29 1768
    Sureties: Bartholomew Etherington, Richard Welsh.
    Distribution to: Widow (unnamed, 1/3). Residue to 6 children (equally): Thomas,
        Elisabeth, Ann, Rebeccah, Benjamin, Eleanor.
    Administratrix: Judith Mareer, wife of James Mareer.

Mary McGarvey   5.94   D   CE   £30.7.1   Jun 29 1768
    Sureties: James Wallis, Henry Baker.
    Distribution to: Representatives unknown to this Office.
    Administrator: Mr. Samuel Shepherd.

John Black   5.94   D   CE   £66.7.1   Apr 6 1768
    Sureties: Thomas Stewart.
    Distribution to: Representatives unknown to this Office.
    Administrator: John McWherton.

Benjamin Falkner   5.94   D   QA   £53.12.11   Jul 28 1768
    Sureties: James Stant, James Plowman.
    Distribution to (equally): Hannah Falkner, James Falkner, Margarett Falkner,
        Benjamin Falkner.
    Administrator: John Falkner of Talbot County.

William Godwin   5.94   D   QA   £91.6.9   Aug 10 1768
    Sureties: John Pickerine, Edward Godwin.
    Distribution to: Widow (unnamed, 1/3). Residue to children (equally): Edward,
        William, John, Allen, Thomas, Sarah, Rachel.
    Administratrix: Sarah Godwin.

Daniel Robinson   5.94   D   BA   £182.15.8   Jul 13 1768
    Sureties: Jacob Giles, Amos Garratt.
    Distribution to: Representatives unknown to this Office.
    Administratrix: Susannah Garretson.

Robert Maxwell   5.95   D   KE   £315.12.9   Sep 19 1768
    Sureties: Alexander Kelley, John Wallis.
    Distribution to: Widow (unnamed, 1/3). Residue to 4 children (equally): John,
        Robert, Rachel wife of James Camion, Ruth wife of William Steuart.
    Administrator: William Maxwell.

John Watts   5.95   D   BA   £556.11.1   Jun 21 1768
    Sureties: Solomon Bowing, Edward Sweeting.
    Distribution to: Widow (unnamed, 1/3). Residue to 9 children (unnamed, equally).
    Administratrix: Sarah Watts.

James Mathews   5.95   D   QA   £73.4.6   Mar 17 1768
    Sureties: Henry Wrench, William Mathews.
    Distribution to: Widow (accountant, 1/3). Residue to (equally): William Mathews,
        James Mathews.
    Administratrix: Hannah Dunbracco, wife of John Dunbracco.

James Devorix   5.96   D   QA   £75.9.8   May 2 1768
    Sureties: Valentine Thomas Honey, William Reed.
    Distribution to (equally): Valentine Devorix, Mary Bishop wife of Richard Bishop,
        Rachel Devorix, Margaret Devorix, Rebeccah Devorix, William Devorix, Hester
        Devorix, Thomas Devorix.
    Administrator: Valentine Devorix.

Basil Brooke   5.96   D   CH   £400.3.10   Jul 18 1768
    Sureties: John Wheatley, George Ross.
    Distribution to: Representatives unknown to this Office.
    Administratrix: Sarah Wheeler, wife of Edward Wheeler.

Joseph Wright   5.96   D   CH   £272.1.7   Jul 9 1768
    Sureties: Zacheus Davis, Richard Reeder.
    Distribution to: Widow (unnamed, 1/3). Residue to 6 children (equally): Mary
        Booker, Margarett, Chloe, Winifred, Gorey, Leonard.
    Administratrix: Anne Wright.

Robert Dines   5.96   D   DO   £77.17.1   Apr 12 1768
    Sureties: Thomas Moore, David Bramble.
    Distribution to: Widow (unnamed, 1/3). Residue to 3 children (equally):
        Jeremiah, Mary, Cleah.
    Administratrix: Elisabeth Dines.

Joshua Wall					5.97		D	DO	£123.19.5	May 2 1768
    Sureties: Raymond Stapleford, Charles Waters.
    Distribution to: Kesiah (widow, accountant, 1/3). Residue to 2 children
       (equally): Rispy, Joshua.
    Administratrix: Kesiah Lee, wife of William Lee.

Roger Hodson					5.97		D	DO	£80.15.3		May 24 1768
    Sureties: John Kirke.
    Distribution to: Widow (unnamed, 1/3). Residue to (equally): Thomas Hodson, Ann
       Hodson.
    Administratrix: Mary Lloyd, wife of Isaac Lloyd.

John Pearce					5.97		D	PG	£258.15.2	May 10 1768
    Sureties: William Pearce, Thomas Pearce.
    Distribution to: Representatives unknown to this Office.
    Administrator: John Pearce.

Susanna Richardson				5.97		D	PG	£177.18.10	May 11 1768
    Sureties: John Burgess, William Lux.
    Distribution to: Representatives unknown to this Office.
    Administrator: Henry Howard.

Lettice Woolen					5.98		D	DO	£13.1.9		Mar 24 1768
    Sureties: George Boaz, Uriah Dean.
    Legatees: Edmondson Stevens.
    Residue to: Nancy Woolen (sister).
    Administratrix: Mary Dean, wife of William Dean, Jr.

Lewis Griffith					5.98		D	DO	£996.1.9		Mar 1 1768
    Sureties: George Slacomb, Joseph Andrews.
    Legatees: Lewis Griffith Paul (son of Rachel Paul), Mary Paul (supposed daughter
       of Betty Paul).
    Residue to (equally): Lewis Griffith Paul, Sliter Griffith Paul, Desier Griffith
       Paul, Jane Griffith Paul.
    Executrix: Mary Keene.

William Shenton					5.98		D	DO	£220.15.11	Mar 21 1769
    Sureties: William Phillips, Ezekiel Johnson.
    Distribution to: Representatives unknown to this Office.
    Executor: Joseph Shenton.

William Oldfield				5.99		D	DO	£22.6.8		Mar 14 1768
    Sureties: Obed Dixon, Robert Dixon.
    Legatees: Margaret Ege.
    Residue to: Elisabeth Chance wife of William Chance (now in North Carolina).
    Executor: Aaron Chance.

Peter Rich					5.99		D	DO	£434.7.7		May 20 1769
    Sureties: Arthur Wheatly, Samuel Fountain.
    Legatees: Elisabeth Chanch (one of eldest daughters), Sydney Harrington (one of
       eldest daughters), Richey Heald (daughter, wife of John Heald).
    Distribution to: Widow (unnamed, 1/3). Residue to 4 children (equally): William,
       Cynthia, Susannah, Peter Nixon Rich.
    Executor: William Rich.

Roger Addams					5.99		D	DO	£851.2.0		Sep 9 1766
See Folio 78.
    Sureties: William Cannon, James Adams.
    Legatees: Mary (daughter), Misse (daughter), Charles (son), Nancy Sterling
       (daughter), Bose Addams (cousin), Mary Adams (cousin, daughter of William
       Adams).
    Administrators: Richard Clarkson and his wife Betty Clarkson, Roger Adams,
       William Fountain.

Dinah Bryan					5.100		D	QA	£118.18.4	Mar 31 1769
    Sureties: Benjamin Tanner, Dobbs Joyner.
    Legatees: James (son), Solomon Bryan, Stephen Bryan, Susannah Blunt, Sarah
       Collins, Elisabeth Hollingsworth, Mary Collier (daughter), Sarah Bryan
       (granddaughter), James Bryan (grandson, son of John Bryan), John Bryan
       (grandson), Rebeccah Bryan (widow of John Bryan), Dinah Bryan (granddaughter,
       daughter of John Bryan), John Bryan (grandson, son of John Bryan), John
       Collier (grandson, son of Mary Collier), John Bryan (grandson, son of Stephen
       Bryan), James Bryan (grandson, son of James Bryan), Stephen Bryan (grandson,
       son of Solomon Bryan), William Hampton (grandson), Mary Ann Hampton
       (granddaughter, daughter of William Hampton) and her sister Luirocy Hampton.
    Residue to 2 grandsons (equally): John Bryan (son of Solomon Bryan), John Bryan
       (son of Stephen Bryan).
    Executor (acting): Stephen Bryan.

James Preston   5.101   D   BA   £888.14.4   Aug 23 1769
    Sureties: Samuel Durham, Jr., James Moore, Jr.
    Legatees: Benjamin Preston (son of James Preston (son)), John Preston (son of
        James Preston (son)), Ann (daughter), Mary (daughter).
    Distribution to: Widow (unnamed, 1/3). Residue to children (equally): Sarah
        Maccomas, Elisabeth Gilbert, Ann, Martin, Mary, Bernard, children (unnamed) of
        Hannah Ruff (daughter).
    Executrix: Clemency Preston.

Robert Brierly   5.101   D   BA   £24.1.0   Jul 4 1768
son of John Brierly.
    Sureties: Robert Brierly, Thomas Brierly.
    Distribution to 2 sons (equally): John, Nathan.
    Executor: John Brierly.

John Meekins   5.101   D   DO   £69.14.10   Jun 14 1768
    Sureties: Raymond Shenton, Joshua Burn.
    Legatees: John (youngest son).
    Executrix: Catharine Meekins.

Laurence Everett   5.102   D   QA   £74.17.9   Sep 1 1768
    Sureties: Jonathon Culbreath, John Ewbanks.
    Legatees (children): Samuel Everet, Edward, Susannah, Lettitia, Corby.
    Residue to sons & daughters (equally): Edward, Joseph, Benjamin, Susannah, Mary,
        Lettitia, Corby.
    Executor: Laurence Everett.

Francis Harper   5.102   D   DO   £36.17.6   Jun 6 1768
    Sureties: Philemon Hays, John Murphey.
    Legatees: Rosannah Delaney (daughter), Elisabeth Shenton (daughter), Annastatia
        Summers (daughter), James Murphey (son-in-law), Mary Murphey
        (daughter-in-law), Alley Murphey (daughter-in-law).
    Residue to: Mary (wife).
    Administratrix: Mary Harper.

Henry Waggaman   5.103   D   SO   £5748.17.4   Aug 17 1767
    Sureties: Ephraim King, Levin Gale, Levin Wilson, Arnold Elzey, Ephraim Wilson,
        Samuel Wilson.
    Legatees: Mary (wife), John Elliot Waggaman (son), William Elliot Waggaman (son),
        Henry (son), George (son), Sarah (daughter), Elisabeth (daughter), Mary
        (daughter, since dead).
    Residue to children (unnamed, equally).
    Executrix: Mary Waggaman.

William Kirby   5.104   D   QA   £356.7.11   Sep 1 1768
    Sureties: Benjamin Walters, John Walters.
    Distribution to: Rachel (widow, 1/3). Residue to 3 children (equally): Walter,
        Elisabeth, Ann.
    Administratrix: Rachel Kirby.

John Perry   5.104   D   CH   £62.15.5   Sep 14 1768
    Sureties: Thomas Perrie, John Perrie.
    Legatees: Thomas (son), John (son), William (son), Elisabeth Warden (daughter),
        Ann Favell (daughter), Mary Posey (daughter), Rachel Ratcliff (daughter),
        Rachel (wife).
    Residue to 2 sons (equally): Hugh, Francis.
    Executors: Rebecca Perry, Hugh Perry.

Charles Ford   5.104   D   CE   £1347.9.1   Sep 7 1768
    Sureties: Robert Veazey, Thomas Wallace.
    Legatees: Cordelia (wife), William (son).
    Distribution to: Cordelia (wife, 1/3). Residue to 2 sons (equally): William,
        John.
    Executors: Cordelia Donnahoe wife of Joshua Donnahoe, John Veazy, Jr.

James Hughs   5.105   D   CE   £135.9.8   Aug 3 1768
    Sureties: Henry Pennington, James Coppin.
    Legatees: James (son).
    Residue to 2 daughters (equally): Sarah, Jemimah.
    Executor: James Hughs.

Daniel Nowland   5.105   D   CE   £42.5.3   Apr 9 1768
    Sureties: Hugh Mathews, William Savin.
    Legatees: Benjamin Nowland (grandson, son of Augustine Nowland), John Nowland
        (grandson, son of Augustine Nowland), Hannah (daughter).
    Residue to 2 sons (equally): Benjamin, Ephraim.
    Executor: Benjamin Nowland.

Frances Camperson   5.105   D   TA   £122.10.8   Sep 13 1768
     Sureties: Robert Kirby, Joshua Clark, Jr.
     Legatees: Sarah Hues, Benjamin Kirby (son of Robert Kirby), Daniel Clark, William
          Bryan (under 21), Henr. Clark.
     Residue to (equally): William Cooper, Sarah Hues, John Hues (son of Sarah Hues),
     Executor: Henry Clark.

William Owins   5.106   D   WO   £406.8.6   Jun 10 1768
     Sureties: David Owins, Robert Dunn.
     Legatees (children): Nancy Griffith (eldest daughter), Mary, Rebecca, Betty
          Dashiel Owin, Robert.
     Distribution to: Elisabeth (accountant, 1/3).
     Executrix: Elisabeth Owins.

Samuel Selby   5.106   D   FR   £264.4.2   Jul 23 1768
     Sureties: William Magruder Selby, William Mullikin.
     Legatees: Mary Ann (daughter).
     Distribution to: Amelia (widow, 1/3). Residue to (equally): Samuel Selby,
          William Harris Selby, Philip Selby, Cassandra Selby (daughter), Mary Ann Selby
          (daughter), Amelia Selby (daughter), Barbary Selby (daughter).
     Executor (surviving): Samuel Selby.

Nicholas Smith, Jr.   5.106   D   KE   £56.3.2   Aug 2 1768
     Sureties: Jonathon Smith, George Vansant.
     Legatees: George (eldest son).
     Distribution to: Widow (accountant, 1/3). Residue to rest of children (unnamed,
          equally).
     Executrix: Mary Welsh, wife of Lewis Welsh.

Henry Williams   5.107   D   QA   £184.1.3   May 21 1768
     Sureties: Christopher Cross Routh, William Satterfield, James Chairs.
     Legatees (sons): George, Nathan, James.
     Distribution to: Widow (unnamed, 1/3). Residue to son & daughters (equally):
          Henry, Margaret, Sarah, Mary, Elisabeth.
     Executrix: Mary Hurlock.

William Hickman   5.107   D   FR   £269.6.6   Mar 19 1768
The amount of the accounts also included #2400.
     Sureties: William Luckett, Sr., William Luckett, Jr.
     Legatees: Stephen (son), Elisabeth Burns (daughter), Betty Fletchall (daughter),
          Ann Lewis (daughter), John Baxter.
     Residue to 4 children (equally): Stephen, Elisabeth Burns, Betty Fletchall, Ann
          Lewis.
     Executors: Thomas Lewis, Stephen Hickman.

Thomas Mastin   5.108   D   KE   £163.4.2   Aug 16 1768
     Sureties: Thomas Mastin, William Kendall.
     Legatees: Thomas (son).
     Distribution to: Ann (widow, 1/3). Residue to sons (equally): Francis, Brittain,
          Samuel, John, William, Hamer.
     Executor: James Mastin.

Nathaniel Trueman Greenfield 5.108   D   SM   £1470.4.1   Jun 30 1768
     Sureties: Thomas Greenfield, Henry Jarnagon.
     Legatees: Rebeccah (accountant, widow), Thomas Trueman Greenfield (son).
     Distribution to (equally): wife, all his children (unnamed).
     Executrix: Rebeccah Greenfield.

Richard Linox   5.108   D   CH   £39.18.4   May 31 1768
     Sureties: Robert Buchanan, William Weathered.
     Distribution to 3 sons (equally): Richard, James, John.
     Executor: Charles Hynson.

William Kersey   5.109   D   KE   £328.5.8   Jun 28 1767
     Sureties: John Sutton, John Ralph.
     Legatees: Margaret (wife), Francis Kersey (cousin) of Talbot County, James Henley
          (son of James Henley).
     Residue to (equally): Margaret (wife), aforesaid Francis Kersey.
     Executrix (acting): Margaret Gibbons, wife of William Gibbons.

Henrietta Gamble   5.109   D   KE   £523.9.9   Feb 28 1768
     Sureties: William Apsley, John Ambrose, Jr.
     Legatees: Darius Gambrell (son), Bethier Gambrell (daughter), Sarah Gambrell
          (daughter), Lethisa Boone (daughter), Rebeckar Kennard (granddaughter),
          Stephen Kennard (son-in-law).
     Residue to: rest of children (unnamed).
     Executors: Stephen Kennard, Joseph Boone.

William Stoops   5.109   D   KE   £123.0.3   Jun 25 1768
    Sureties: Sanders Bostock, John Chrisfield.
    Legatees (3 daughters): Cornelia, Mary, Rachel.
    Residue to 2 sons (equally): Benjamin Townsend Stoops, William Stoops.
    Executor: John Stoops.

William Boyer   5.110   D   KE   £253.3.8   Aug 27 1768
    Sureties: Thomas Ellis, Robert Napp Clothier.
    Distribution to: Catharine (widow, accountant, 1/3). Residue to 2 daughters
        (equally): Rebeccah, Eleanor.
    Executrix: Catharine Boyer.

Thomas Sedgwicks   5.110   D   CA   £348.19.1   Aug 23 1768
    Sureties: John Kent, Thomas Freeman.
    Legatees: Thomas Sedgwick (son), John Segwick (son), William Sedgwick (son),
        Elisha Sedgwick (son), Mary Dorsey (daughter), Rebeccah Dorsey
        (granddaughter), Willa Dorsey & Sarah Dorsey & William Dorsey (grandchildren,
        children of Mary (daughter)).
    Distribution to: Catharine Sedgwick (widow, 1/3). Residue to 5 children
        (equally): Thomas, John, William, Elisha, Mary.
    Executors: Thomas Sedgwicks, John Sedgwicks.

Edward Clements   5.111   D   CH   £522.9.1   Jul 5 1768
    Sureties: Daniel McPherson, John Clements.
    Legatees: John (brother), Walter (brother), Ann Wheeler (niece), Charles
        (brother).
    Residue to siblings (equally): Jacob, Walter, Francis, John, Charles, Jean, Clare
        Sanders, Martha Dyer.
    Executor: Francis Clements.

Samuel Wickes   5.111   D   KE   £1078.4.11   May 31 1768
    Sureties: Alexander Calder, Nathaniel Hynson.
    Legatees: Mary (wife), children: Lambert, Richard, Joseph, Frances Dunn, Martha,
        Mary, Sarah.
    Distribution to: Widow (unnamed, 1/3). Residue to children (equally): Samuel,
        Lambert, Richard, Joseph, Martha, Mary, Sarah.
    Executrix: Mary Wickes.

Benjamin Colegate   5.112   D   BA   £191.11.0   Oct 28 1768
    Sureties: Daniel Preston, Thomas Johnson.
    Distribution to: Charity (widow) during widowhood; then to 6 children (equally):
        Thomas, Rebeccah, Elisabeth, Ann, Mary, Ruth.
    Administrator: Job Key.

William Fairbank   5.112   D   TA   £134.13.8   Oct 6 1768
    Sureties: Thomas Ray, Philip Horney.
    Legatees (children): John, James, Mary (her mother's (unnamed) saddle),
        Elisabeth, Bridget, Rachel.
    Executor: Richard Grason.

John Reardon   5.112   D   KE   £45.7.8   Aug 4 1768
    Sureties: Thomas Ringgold.
    Distribution to: Representatives unknown to this Office.
    Administratrix: Sarah Reardon.

Patrick Dennis   5.113   D   CE   £108.17.2   Jul 6 1768
    Sureties: James Smith, James Frazier.
    Legatees (daughters): Margaret Murphy, Elisabeth Leonard.
    Distribution to: Widow (accountant, 1/3). Residue to children: John (2/3), Mary
        (1/3).
    Executrix: Elisabeth Dennis.

Anthony Fatado   5.113   D   CE   £272.10.0   May 7 1768
    Sureties: James Smith, Andrew Crow.
    Legatees (children): Barbary, Joseph.
    Distribution to: Susannah (wife, 1/3). Residue to children (equally): Anthony,
        Barbary.
    Executors: Peter Rider, Susannah Roberts (late Susannah Fatado) wife of James
        Roberts.

James Hopkins   5.113   D   TA   £612.8.5   Jul 5 1768
    Sureties: Henry Banning, Hugh Owen.
    Distribution to: Sarah (widow) during widowhood; then to (equally): Sarah Bartlet
        (daughter), Mary Spry (daughter), Thomas Esgate (grandson), Jonathon Hopkins
        (grandson).
    Executor: Thomas Esgate.

John Coulbourn   5.114   D   WO   £50.16.5   Mar 18 1768
    Sureties: Jabey Riggen, John Townsend.
    Legatees: Margaret (widow), Sarah Redden (daughter of Charles Redden), James
        Worrel (son-in-law).
    Distribution to: Margaret (widow, 1/3). Residue to children (equally): William,
        Grace Brown.
    Executor: Andrew Brown.

John Lancaster   5.114   D   CH   £1988.8.8   Jun 1 1768
    Sureties: Dr. John Corry, Bennet Neale.
    Legatees: James Ashby, Mary (wife) to have services of Carpenter Harry and his
        wife (unnamed), Mary Bradford (daughter), John Holmes (grandson), Raphael
        (son), Anthony and his wife Jane and their 2 sons Anthony & Nasey.
    Residue to children: John, Joseph, Katharine Combs.
    Executors: John Lancaster, Joseph Lancaster.

Joseph Whaley   5.115   D   KE   £170.19.10   Jul 1 1768
    Sureties: William Spearman, James Webb.
    Distribution to: Esther (widow, accountant) during widowhood or lifetime; then to
        children (equally): Joseph, Daniel, Abraham, Mary Stewart, Esther Heath,
        Rachel Whittington, Sarah McDonnell, Hannah.
    Executrix: Esther Whaley.

Henry Hurt   5.115   D   KE   £790.19.2   Aug 17 1768
    Sureties: Josiah Ringgold, Charles Ringgold.
    Legatees (children): John, James, Joce, Martha, Sarah. Daughters are under age
        and unmarried.
    Executrix: Martha Ambrose, wife of John Ambrose.

Ignatius Mitchel   5.115   D   CH   £512.0.0   May 18 1768
    Sureties: Richard Bennett Mitchel, William Hambleton.
    Legatees: Rachel (wife, accountant), Samuel (son), Ignatius (son).
    Distribution to: Widow (unnamed, 1/3). Residue to children (equally): Richard,
        Winefred, Ann, Henrietta.
    Executrix: Rachel Mitchel.

Nathaniel Claggett   5.116   D   CA   £200.13.1   May 26 1768
    Sureties: William Day, Samuel Gray.
    Legatees (siblings): Sarah Dawkins wife of Joseph Dawkins, Mary Clagget, Charles
        Clagget, Jr., Martha Clagget, Rebeccah Clagget.
    Distribution to: Frances (widow, accountant, 1/3). Residue to: child/children
        "wife goes with".
    Executrix: Frances Clagett.

John Talbert   5.116   D   WO   £266.5.5   Nov 4 1767
    Sureties: Richard Miles, Isaac Shockley.
    Legatees (children): Betty, George, Prisse, Joshua, John.
    Executor: Joshua Hitch of Somerset County.

John Dunnington   5.117   D   CH   £80.18.10   May 29 1768
    Sureties: John Perrie, Patrick McDaniel.
    Legatees (children): John, Ann Rye, Sarah, Burditt, Mary, Cloe, Ezra.
    Distribution to: Widow (unnamed, 1/3). Residue to 3 youngest children (unnamed,
        equally).
    Executrix: Dorothy Dunnington.

Charles Flanagan   5.117   D   BA   £213.5.4   Jul 18 1768
    Sureties: John Craton, Arthur Cashery.
    Legatees: Edward (father), Edward (son), Mary (daughter).
    Distribution to: Ann (widow, 1/3).
    Administratrix: Ann Flanagan.

Mathew Smallwood   5.118   D   CH   £92.17.1   Sep 17 1768
    Sureties: James Griffin, Richard Robey.
    Legatees: Beane Smallwood, Priscilla Smallwood, Francis Green Smallwood, Martha
        (daughter), Benjamin Smallwood, Beane Smallwood & Priscilla Smallwood in trust
        for Philip Smallwood & James Smallwood as long as they remain unmarried.
    Distribution to children (beforementioned, equally).
    Executors: John Harris, Priscilla Smallwood.

William Phillips   5.118   D   DO   £121.19.11   Aug 1 1768
    Sureties: John Lecompte, Benjamin Woodward.
    Legatees: widow (unnamed), Elisabeth Siddle, Aquila Long.
    Distribution to: Widow (unnamed, 1/3). Residue to (equally): William Phillips,
        Joseph Phillips, Mary Phillips, Nancy Phillips, Rebeccah Phillips, Sarah
        Phillips.
    Executors: Mary Phillips, William Phillips.

Sarah Adams   5.119   D   SO   £387.11.1   Aug 6 1768
   Sureties: Isaac Costin, Stephen Mills.
   Legatees: Ann Adams, Catharine Harper, Mary Adams & Betty Adams (mentions negroes
      given them in their father's (unnamed) will), Philip Colin Adams, Sarah
      Harper.
   Residue to 4 daughters (equally): Catharine Harper, Ann, Mary, Betty.
   Executor: Samuel Adams.

Alexander Hutcheson   5.119   D   CE   £364.13.11   Feb 23 1768
   Sureties: John Roberts, John Moody.
   Executors: Samuel Hutchison, Mary Moody wife of Robert Moody.

Anne Edelin   5.120   D   CH   £176.15.8   Mar 24 1768
   Sureties: James Campbell, Theophilus Roach.
   Legatees: Ignatius Gardiner, Richard Gardiner, Mary Chunn, Henrietta Smith,
      Clement Smith, Mary Smith, Joseph Mudd, Richard Edelin, Jane Edelin.
   Residue to: Jane Edelin.
   Executor (acting): Richard Gardiner.

James Furnice   5.120   D   SO   £187.16.5   Jun 14 1768
   Sureties: Jesse King, Isaac Caustin.
   Legatees: Elisabeth Cordray (daughter).
   Mentions: widow (unnamed).
   Residue to (equally): Sarah Furnice, Judith Furnice, Jonathon Furnice, George
      Furnice.
   Executor: William Furnice.

Francis Linthicumb   5.121   D   AA   £46.19.9   Aug 16 1768
   Sureties: Richard Williams, Jr., Thomas Mayhew.
   Legatees: Eleanor Clark, 3 youngest children (unnamed).
   Executor: Francis Linthicumb.

John Wallis   5.121   D   KE   £497.0.8   Aug 2 1768
   Sureties: Henry Bodeen, John Gilbert.
   Legatees: widow (unnamed), Susannah Razin, Ann Wallis, John Wallis, Francis
      Wallis, Margaret Wallis, Hannah Wallis, Elisabeth Wallis.
   Distribution to: Widow (unnamed, 1/3).
   Executrix: Hannah Warner, wife of Philip Warner.

Benjamin Mackall   5.122   D   CA   £604.18.8   Sep 6 1768
   Sureties: Parker Young, Young Cox.
   Legatees: Ann Mackall, Thomas How Mackall (son of John Mackall), Mary Mackall &
      Rebecca Mackall & Ann Mackall (daughters of John Mackall), Ann Broome,
      Alexander Broome, Kesia Broome, Hanna Mackall (relict of James Mackall), John
      Mackall (son of Hannah Mackall).
   Residue to: John (brother).
   Executor: John Mackall.

James Smith   5.122   D   KE   £2077.7.10   Oct 29 1768
The amount of the accounts also included £306.8.8 sterling and #56032.
   Legatees: Ann Murray, William Nicholson (son of Josep Nicholson).
   Residue to (equally): Hannah Nicholson, Sarah Ringgold, James (son), Mary Wicks,
      Ann Murray, William (son), Mary Sterling (granddaughter).
   Executor: William Murray.

George Baynard   5.123   D   QA   £1397.17.7   Sep 22 1768
The amount of the accounts also included £58.11.3 sterling.
   Legatees: Rachel (daughter).
   Residue to (equally): Job Baynard, George Baynard, Sarah Baynard, Lydia Baynard,
      Rachel Baynard.
   Executor (surviving): John Tillotson.

Joseph Darden   5.123   D   TA   £1894.16.6   Jan 3 1769
   Sureties: Samuel Bowman, Benjamin Berry, Lodman Elbert.
   Distribution to: Widow (unnamed, 1/3). Residue to 8 children (unnamed, equally).
   Executrix: Mary Darden.

James Clayland   5.123   D   QA   £538.2.9   Jan 30 1769
   Sureties: Thomas Emory (son of Arthur Emory), Arthur Emory (son of Arthur Emory).
   Distribution to: Widow (unnamed, 1/3). Residue to 3 children (unnamed, equally).
   Administratrix: Ann Miller, wife of James Miller.

Ralph Elston   5.124   D   TA   £626.0.7   May 5 1769
   Sureties: Jeremiah Banning.
   Distribution to: Widow (unnamed, 1/3), now right of Thomas Hardcastle (son of
      Robert Hardcastle a former husband of Tamson). Residue to 3 children
      (equally): Rachel, Elisabeth, William. Rachel died an infant; her portion was
      distributed to the widow, the two other children, and to Henry Eubanks a son
      of the widow by a former husband (unnamed).
   Administrator (de bonis non): John Shannahan.

John Higgins   5.124   D KE   £144.7.0   Mar 1769
    Sureties: William Murray, John Kennard.
    Distribution to: Mary (wife) during here lifetime; then to Sarah Devorix
        (daughter-in-law).
    Executrix: Mary Kennard, wife of John Kennard.

Folios 125 through 134 do not exist.

Nicholas Boon   5.135   D AA   £441.18.11   Jun 4 1767
    Sureties: Joseph Jacobs, Richard Jacobs.
    Legatees (sons): John Boone, Richard Boone.
    Distribution to: Widow (unnamed, 1/3). Residue to 3 children (equally): John,
        Richard, Ann. Ann's portion was distributed to the remaining representatives.
    Executrix: Susannah Fowler, wife of Benjamin Fowler.

Ann Connerly   5.136   D DO   £24.16.7   Oct 28 1769
    Sureties: James Wright, Isaac Charles.
    Legatees (children): Thomas, Mary.
    Residue to (minors, equally): Ann Connerly, James Connerly, Margaret Connerly.
    Executor: Solomon Charles.

Elisha Hall   5.136   D CE   £1190.0.11   Oct 29 1765
    Sureties: Jos. Hopkins, Samuel Harriss.
    Legatees: Elisabeth Harrisson (daughter).
    Distribution to: Widow (unnamed, 1/3). Residue to (equally): Elihu Hall, Joseph
        Hall, Richard Hall, Elisha Hall, John Hall, Elisabeth Harrisson.
    Executors: Elihu Hall, Ruth Hunt wife of James Hunt.

Grove Thomlinson   5.137   D FR   #841   Aug 23 1758
The amount of the accounts also included £783.3.7 gold and £41.0.0 sterling.
    Sureties: James Gore, John Maddox.
    Legatees: William Mockbee, Mary Mockbee, Ann Mockbee, Lucy Mockbee, Lessue
        Mockbee.
    Distribution to: Widow (unnamed, 1/3). Residue to (equally): Ninian Mockbee,
        Mary Mockbee, Ann Mockbee, Lucia Mockbee.
    Executor: Ninian Tanahil.

Edmund Rutland   5.137   D AA   £516.3.11   Sep 15 1769
    Sureties: Richard Maccubin, Samuel Chase.
    Distribution to: Widow (unnamed, 1/3). Residue to 2 children (unnamed, equally).
    Administratrix: Mrs. Elisabeth Rutland.

Henry Richey   5.137   D FR   £77.0.6   Dec 16 1768
    Sureties: Peter Beard, John Mefford.
    Distribution to: Widow (unnamed, 1/3). Residue to 4 children (equally): Adam,
        Margaret, Daniel, William.
    Administrator: Isaac Richey.

Mathew Kennard   5.138   D KE   £104.3.7   Jan 25 1769
    Distribution to: Representatives unknown to this Office.
    Administratrix: Martha Kannard.

John Hall   5.138   D SO   £87.15.3   Feb 21 1769
    Distribution to: Widow, 4 children: Jesse, Betty, Martha, accountant. Residue to
        (equally): John, Ann, Ezekiel, Charles.
    Administrator: William Hall.

Richard Slowers   5.138   D SM   £101.8.1
    Sureties: James Beall, John Hour Abell.
    Distribution to: Representatives unknown to this Office.
    Administrator: Edward Abell, Sr.

Richard Forrest   5.138   D SM   £96.2.10   Apr 21 1769
    Distribution to: Representatives unknown to this Office.
    Administrator: William Hebb.

Thomas Baynard   5.138   D QA   £474.18.6   May 11 1769
    Distribution to: Widow (unnamed, 1/3). Residue to children (equally): Elisabeth
        wife of John Tillotson, Jr., Lydia (a daughter who is since dead), Margaret
        wife of Henry Downes, Jr.
    Administratrix: Hannah Thompson, wife of Henry Thompson.

Joseph Johnson   5.139   D QA   £11.14.6   May 4 1769
This entry is crossed out.
    Sureties: Valentine Bugess, James Burroughs.
    Distribution to: Widow (unnamed, 1/2). Residue to: Elisabeth (sister) wife of
        William Shepherd.
    Administratrix: Rebeccah Johnson.

Joseph Johnson   5.139   D QA   £11.14.6   May 4 1769
    Sureties: Valentine Burgess, James Burroughs.
    Distribution to: Widow (unnamed, 1/2). Residue to: Elisabeth (sister) wife of
        William Shepherd.
    Administratrix: Rebeccah Johnson.

James Truman Greenfield   5.139   D PG   £2202.12.0   Nov 26 1768
    Sureties: Nathaniel Truman Greenfield, Thomas Brooke (son of Walter Brooke).
    Distribution to: Widow (unnamed, 1/3). Residue to 5 children (equally): Ann
        Truman, Mary, William Truman, Sarah, Susannah Eve.
    Administratrix: Elisabeth Brook.

Ann Roberson   5.139   D CA   £60.0.11   Aug 23 1768
    Sureties: John Ogden, Ellis Slater.
    Distribution to: Representatives unknown to this Office.
    Administrator: Thomas Goslin Hutchins.

Joseph Ingram   5.140   D WO   £71.0.4   Feb 26 1768
    Sureties: William Spicer, Joseph Boyce.
    Distribution to: Widow (unnamed, 1/3). Residue to 8 children (unnamed, equally).
    Administratrix: Ann Ingram.

Paul Waples   5.140   D WO   £948.15.8   Jul 1 1768
    Sureties: William Tunnell, John Waples.
    Distribution to: Widow (unnamed, 1/3). Residue to 10 children (unnamed,
        equally).
    Administrator: William Waples.

John Shelton   5.140   D FR   £91.10.4   Sep 1 1768
The amount of the accounts also included #4765.
    Distribution to: Widow (unnamed, 1/3). Residue to 7 children (unnamed, equally).
    Administratrix (acting): Martha Shelton.

Thomas Wright   5.141   D CH   £124.8.6   Nov 7 1768
    Sureties: Booker Wright, John Wright, Jr.
    Distribution to: Representatives unknown to this Office.
    Administrator: John Wright.

William Waugh   5.141   D FR   £63.2.6   Mar 12 1769
    Sureties: John Carey.
    Distribution to: Widow (unnamed, 1/3). Residue to 4 children (unnamed, equally).
    Administratrix: Elisabeth Waugh.

Benjamin Burroughs   5.141   D SM   £511.17.7   Sep 22 1768
    Sureties: George Burroughs, Philemon Estop.
    Distribution to: Representatives unknown to this Office.
    Administrator: James Burroughs.

Michael Duskin   5.141   D BA   £153.18.6   Sep 4 1768
    Sureties: Luke Johnson, George Prickett.
    Distribution to: Representatives unknown to this Office.
    Administratrix: Sarah Duskin.

John Perkins   5.142   D PG   £81.8.3   May 21 1769
    Sureties: Thomas Askey, John Ulan.
    Distribution to: Representatives unknown to this Office.
    Administratrix: Ann Perkins.

Henry Moore   5.142   D KE   £206.8.4   Mar 10 1769
    Sureties: John Graham, Francis Rutter.
    Distribution to: Representatives unknown to this Office.
    Administrator: Rudolph Moore.

Thomas Miles   5.142   D FR   £248.9.8   Apr 8 1769
    Distribution to: Representatives unknown to this Office.
    Administratrix: Sarah Duvall, wife of Mareen Duvall.

Devalt Teter   5.142   D FR   £192.9.4   Mar 25 1769
    Sureties: Christopher Shull, Jacob Slarrum (?).
    Distribution to: Widow (unnamed, 1/3). Residue to 2 sons (equally): Jacob,
        Devalt.
    Administrator: Michael Waggoner.

Francis Gibson   5.143   D BA   £182.17.7   May 26 1769
    Distribution to: Representatives unknown to this Office.
    Administratrix: Catharine Gibson.

Jesse Costin   5.143   D WO   £70.6.6   Feb 3 1769
    Distribution to: Widow (unnamed, 1/3). Residue to 2 children (infants, equally): Levy, Stephen.
    Administrator: Edward Smullen.

Charles Riggin   5.143   D WO   £36.16.8   Jan 20 1769
    Sureties: William Boyce, John Swain.
    Distribution to: Widow (unnamed, 1/3). Residue to 2 children (unnamed, infants, equally).
    Administratrix: Rachel Benson, wife of George Benson.

Charles Mooney   5.143   D CH   £48.7.0   Apr 14 1769
    Sureties: William Salmon, John Waples.
    Distribution to: Widow (unnamed, 1/3). Residue to 5 children (unnamed, equally).
    Administratrix: Sarah Mooney.

William Wharton   5.144   D WO   £23.5.8   Apr 11 1769
    Distribution to: Widow (unnamed, 1/3). Residue to 8 children (unnamed, equally).
    Administrator: Charles Wharton.

John Preston   5.144   D KE   £37.16.5   Apr 5 1769
    Sureties: Thomas Smith, Thomas Kenny.
    Distribution to: Representatives unknown to this Office.
    Administratrices: Mary Preston, Elisabeth Preston.

Nathaniel Kennard   5.144   D KE   £27.12.6   Feb 25 1769
    Distribution to: Representatives unknown to this Office.
    Administratrix: Mary Kennard.

Holman Johnson   5.144   D KE   £496.2.5   Feb 29 1769
    Sureties: Jacob Comegys, William Spearman.
    Distribution to: Representatives unknown to this Office.
    Administratrix: Hannah Parsons, wife of Benjamin Parsons.

John Richardson   5.144   D BA   £99.3.2   Apr 15 1769
    Sureties: Robert Gillis, William Johnson.
    Distribution to: Representatives unknown to this Office.
    Administratrix: Isabell Richardson.

Elisabeth Gambra   5.145   D CH   £258.3.4   Apr 26 1769
    Sureties: William Penn, Jonathon Yates.
    Distribution to (equally): Elisabeth Joy (mother), siblings: Joseph Joy, William Joy, Ann Joy, Mary Joy.
    Administrator: Joseph Joy.

Joseph King   5.145   D CH   £261.13.0   Feb 9 1769
    Sureties: Joseph Joy, Charles Brandt.
    Distribution to (equally): Joseph King, Jane King, Assa King.
    Administrator: Joseph King.

James McDowell   5.145   D CE   £378.8.8   Nov 16 1768
    Sureties: William Rutter, Moses Rutter.
    Distribution to: Widow (unnamed, 1/3). Residue to 3 children (equally): James, Daniel, Thomas.
    Administratrix: Levina McDowell.

George Simpson   5.145   D CH   £102.12.8   May 2 1769
    Sureties: John Gwinn, Richard Ford.
    Distribution to: Widow (unnamed, 1/3). Residue to: William (accountant, only son).
    Administrator: William Simpson.

Peter Hickson   5.146   D TA   £86.7.3   May 13 1769
    Sureties: John Mullikin, Henry Jenkins.
    Distribution to: Widow (unnamed, 1/3). Residue to 2 children (equally): Ann, Mary Ann.
    Administratrix: Mary Ann Hickson.

Greenwood Gaskin   5.146   D TA   £117.11.2   May 13 1769
    Sureties: Thomas Powell, Howell Powell.
    Distribution to: Widow (unnamed, 1/3). Residue to: Deborah (only child).
    Administrator: Thomas Dudley.

John Milbourn   5.146   D SO   £219.17.0   Apr 18 1769
    Sureties: John Collins, William Hall.
    Distribution to: Widow (unnamed), John Houston who married a daughter (unnamed), Grace Flavill (daughter). Residue to other representatives (unnamed).
    Administrator: Caleb Milbourn.

Jesse Cooper   5.146   D CH   £155.7.6   Feb 17 1769
    Sureties: Richard Price, Ignatius Ratliff.
    Distribution to 3 children (equally): Karon Hapuck, Zopera, Eliab.
    Administrator: Joseph Ratliff.

Rosannah Cole   5.147   D DO   £75.8.2   Mar 15 1769
    Sureties: Joseph Hurst, Richard Woodland.
    Distribution to (equally): Charles Cole (accountant), John Cole, Hezekiah Cole.
    Administrator: Charles Cole.

Samuel Birkhead   5.147   D AA   £60.0.0   Nov 9 1768
    Sureties: Richard Randall, Philip Richardson.
    Distribution to: Representatives unknown to this Office.
    Administrator (acting): Nehemiah Birkhead.

Mary Birkhead   5.147   D AA   £58.0.0   Nov 9 1768
    Sureties: Richard Randall, Philip Richarson.
    Distribution to: Representatives unknown to this Office.
    Administrator (acting): Nehemiah Birkhead.

William White   5.147   D QA   £229.16.0   Nov 26 1768
    Sureties: Thomas Price, John Logg.
    Distribution to: Prudence (widow, since dead, wife of the accountant, 1/3).
        Residue to 5 children (equally): Mary wife of William Chambers, Elisabeth,
        Henrietta, Prudence, Samuel.
    Administratrix: Prudence Derochbrune (widow), wife of Lewis Derochbrune.

James Grennage   5.148   D QA   £13.7.9   Nov 24 1768
    Sureties: Samuel Blunt, Thomas Price, Jr.
    Distribution to: Elisabeth (widow, 1/3) now wife of Peter Bently. Residue to:
        Ann (only child).
    Administrator: Sherry Grennage.

Mary Smoot   5.148   D CH   £541.18.4   Oct 11 1768
    Sureties: William Courts, James Maddox.
    Distribution to 5 parts (equally): Ignatius Middleton, William Stone, Charles
        Sewell, Frances Goodrick, children (unnamed) of Edward Goodrick.
    Administrator: Charles Smoot.

Thomas Evans   5.148   D QA   £68.17.2   Nov 10 1768
    Sureties: Jonathon Wooters, William Yoe.
    Distribution to: Widow (accountant, 1/3). Residue to 3 children (equally):
        James, Henrietta, Mary.
    Administratrix: Sarah Evans, wife of Jonathon Evans.

Thomas Williams   5.149   D DO   £275.19.7   Nov 5 1768
    Sureties: Jacob Charles, Edward Thompson.
    Distribution to: Widow (unnamed, 1/3). Residue to: Eleanor (only child).
    Administratrix: Joanna Williams.

Hugh Wilson   5.149   D DO   £51.16.7   Dec 19 1768
    Sureties: Daniel Willson, John Hughey.
    Distribution to: Widow (unnamed, 1/3). Residue to 4 children (equally): William,
        Ann, Jonathon, Caty.
    Administratrix: Mary Kirkman, wife of James Kirkman.

Stephen Dean   5.149   D QA   £120.14.1   Mar 13 1769
    Sureties: Valentine Burrows, Stephen Myers.
    Representatives: Sarah Skinner (only one, former administratrix). Children of
        said Sarah are: Sarah Skinner (accountant), Rhoda wife of Stephen Myers, Mary
        wife of Peter Bailey.
    Administratrix (de bonis non): Sarah Skinner.

William Earle   5.149   D QA   £94.10.0   May 4 1769
    Sureties: James Earle, Benjamin Earle.
    Distribution to: Representatives unknown to this Office.
    Administrator (de bonis non): John Earle.

Thomas Jackson   5.150   D QA   £58.16.5   Feb 6 1769
    Sureties: William Kirley, James Jones.
    Distribution to: Widow (unnamed, 1/3). Residue to 8 children (equally): Thomas,
        John, William, Lambert, Susannah wife of Robert Cope, Mary, Jane, Sarah.
    Administrators: Judith Jackson, Thomas Jackson.

Esther Cooper   5.150   D CH   £58.4.2   Feb 17 1769
    Sureties: Thomas Price, Richard Price.
    Distribution to (equally): Karen Hepuch Cooper, Zeporah Cooper, Eliab Cooper.
    Administrator: Joseph Ratliff.

William Wrench						5.150	D	QA	£585.6.9		Dec 6 1768
    Sureties: Richard Costin, John Costin.
    Distribution to: Margaret (only daughter).
    Administrator (de bonis non): Peter Wrench.

James Blake						5.150	D	TA	£50.13.0		Feb 23 1769
    Sureties: John Bracco, Richard Grason.
    Distribution to: Widow (unnamed, 1/3). Residue to 2 children (equally):
       Margaret, James.
    Administratrix: Sarah Mansfield, wife of Richard Mansfield.

Charles Baker						5.151	D	QA	£41.14.10		Ma. 2 1769
    Sureties: John Walker, Jonathon Evans.
    Distribution to: Widow (unnamed, 1/3). Residue to 5 children (equally):
       Jonathon, Eliza, Ann, Nathan, Charles.
    Administrators: Sarah Baker, Jonathon Baker.

James Williams						5.151	D	QA	£34.18.6		Mar 9 1769
    Sureties: Henry Wright Pratt, John Costin.
    Distribution to: Representatives unknown to this Office.
    Administratrix: Ann Williams.

Alexander Lee						5.151	D	QA	£32.9.7		Ma. 9 1769
    Sureties: Thomas Greaves, Mathew Greaves.
    Distribution to: Widow (unnamed, 1/3). Residue to 10 children (equally):
       Elisabeth wife of John Dailey, William, Vincent, David, Solomon, Rachel, Ruth,
       Joshua, Frances, Amos.
    Administratrix: Rachel Lee.

Thomas Devorix						5.151	D	QA	£55.8.5		Ma. 9 1769
    Sureties: Thomas Graves, William Gregory.
    Distribution to: Widow (accountant, 1/3). Residue to 3 children (equally): Mary
       wife of William Jackson, Sarah, Hannah wife of Lambert Jackson.
    Administratrix: Susannah Devorix.

John Preston						5.152	D	QA	£124.19.10		Apr 6 1769
    Sureties: Charles Warren, James Horsley.
    Distribution to: Widow (unnamed, 1/3). Residue to 5 children (equally): Mary,
       John, Eliza, David, Alexander.
    Administrators: David Preston and his wife Elisabeth Preston (late Elisabeth
       Preston).

Joseph Nelson						5.152	D	QA	£37.13.1		Ma. 11 1769
    Sureties: Vincent Clements, John Foster.
    Distribution to: Widow (unnamed, 1/3). Residue to 2 children (equally): Mary,
       John.
    Administratrix: Ann Clements, wife of Vincent Clements.

Mary Robey						5.152	D	CH	£74.18.2		Jan 11 1769
    Sureties: William Robey (son of John Robey), Thomas Robey, Jr.
    Distribution to (equally): William Robey (accountant), Eleanor Robey, Victoria
       Adamson wife of Jeremiah Adamson.
    Administrator: William Robey.

Thomas Cook						5.152	D	QA	£123.17.0		Mar 23 1769
    Sureties: William Green, Benjamin Elliott.
    Distribution to: Widow (unnamed, 1/3). Residue to 7 children (equally): Thomas,
       Charles, Martha wife of Job Baynard, Joseph, James, Rachel, John.
    Administrators: Mary Ann Cook, Thomas Cook.

William Robey						5.153	D	CH	£48.17.3		Feb 1 1769
    Sureties: Thomas Hyde Hollow, Thomas Robey (son of Michael Robey).
    Distribution to: Widow (unnamed, 1/3). Residue to 6 children (equally):
       Elisabeth, Mary, Cloe, Mildred, Annan, Linda.
    Administratrix: Mary Robey.

Benjamin Covington					5.153	D	QA	£105.12.7		Oct 20 1768
    Sureties: Nathaniel Covington, John Legar.
    Distribution to: Widow (unnamed, 1/3). Residue to 6 daughters (equally):
       Rebeccah wife of Vincent Benton, Jr., Elisabeth, Ann, Sarah, Mary, Rachel.
    Executrix: Elisabeth Sands, wife of Thomas Sands.

Arthur Emory						5.153	D	QA	£345.10.10		Sep 8 1768
    Sureties: Gideon Emory, Arthur Emory, Jr.
    Legatees: Thomas (son), Arthur (son), Ann (daughter) wife of James Clayland,
       Margaret Downes (daughter), Arthur Emory (grandson), Elisabeth Emory
       (granddaughter), James Clayland (grandson), Solomon Wright (grandson), Coursey
       Wright (grandson), Sarah Wright (granddaughter).
    Residue to 4 children (equally): Thomas, Arthur, Ann, Margaret.
    Executors: Thomas Emory, Arthur Emory, Jr.

Lewis Griffith   5.154   D   DO   £972.2.0   Mar 11 1769
    Sureties: George Slacomb, Joseph Andrews.
    Legatees: Lewis Griffith Paul (son of Rachel Paul), Mary Paul (supposed daughter
        of Betty Paul).
    Mentions: John Munroe.
    Residue to (equally): Lewis Griffith Paul, Slater Griffith Paul, Desier Griffith
        Paul, Jane Griffith Paul.
    Executrix: Mary Keene.

Thomas Collins   5.154   D   WO   £346.4.5   Nov 9 1767
    Sureties: Andrew Gibb, John Massey.
    Legatees (daughters): Sarah, Betty.
    Distribution to: Elisabeth (widow, 1/3). Residue to 8 children (equally): Levy,
        Mary, Sarah, Eli, Betty, Noah, Tobiah, Hannah.
    Executrix: Elisabeth Collins.

William Turpin   5.154   D   SO   £779.6.4   Nov 1768
    Sureties: Thomas Williams, Nehemiah Turpin.
    Distribution to: Widow (unnamed, 1/3). Residue to (equally): John Turpin, Joshua
        Turpin, William Turpin, Betty Turpin.
    Executor: John Turpin.

Thomas Bennett   5.155   D   BA   £272.8.6   Nov 9 1768
    Sureties: Nathaniel Tevis, Anthony Lindsey.
    Legatees (children): Thomas, Ann.
    Distribution to: Widow (unnamed, 1/3). Residue to 9 children (equally): William,
        John, Samuel, Benjamin, Elisha, Mary, Eleanor, Elisabeth, Lydia.
    Administrator: Thomas Bennett.

Elisabeth Butler   5.155   D   SO   £28.4.4   Nov 1 1768
    Sureties: Joshua Hall, John Hall.
    Residue to: Ann Maddox.
    Executor: Samuel Tull.

William Neale   5.155   D   CH   £707.10.4   Apr 19 1769
    Sureties: Richard Neale, Thomas Wheeler.
    Legatees: William Francis Neale.
    Residue to (equally): John Neale, Joseph Neale, William Francis Neale, Elisabeth
        Neale, Mary Neale, Ann Neale, Mildred Neale, Catharine Neale, Sally Neale.
    Executor: John Neale.

Richard Meekins   5.156   D   DO   £44.7.5   Nov 9 1768
    Sureties: Thomas Wroughton, Daniel Liddell.
    Legatees: Henry (son), Joshua (son), Mary Johnson (daughter), Sarah Ruark
        (daughter), Ann Phillips (daughter), Mathew (son), Benedict (son), Ezekiel
        (son), Henry Holton Meekins (grandson), Elisabeth Meekins (granddaughter).
    Distribution to: Widow (unnamed, 1/3). Residue to: John Dennard Meekins (son).
    Executrix: Hannah Meekins.

John Brown   5.156   D   DO   £571.7.6   Nov 9 1768
    Sureties: Daniel Sullivane, Anderton Brown.
    Legatees: Anderton (son), Francis (son), Ezekiel (son), Charles (son), Mary
        (daughter), Sarah (daughter), Betty (daughter), Mary Brown (granddaughter).
    Distribution to: Mary (wife).
    Executrix: Mary Brown.

William Insley   5.157   D   DO   £70.5.5   Nov 9 1768
    Sureties: Andrew Insley, Jacob Insley.
    Distribution to: Widow (unnamed, 1/3).
    Executor: William Insley.

Edward Garratt   5.157   D   DO   £98.0.11   Dec 16 1768
    Sureties: Obid Dixon, Robert Dixon.
    Legatees (children): Sarah (eldest daughter), son (unnamed), Rebeccah, Ann,
        Thomas.
    Distribution to: Widow (unnamed, 1/3).
    Executor: Thomas Garratt.

John Dorsey   5.157   D   AA   £3023.11.2   Nov 9 1768
son of Edward Dorsey. This entry is crossed out.
    Sureties: Ely Dorsey.
    Executors: Michael Dorsey, Vachel Dorsey.

John Dorsey   5.158   D   AA   £3023.11.2   Nov 9 1768
son of Edward Dorsey.
    Sureties: Ely Dorsey, Cornelius Howard.
    Legatees (grandchildren): John Barnes (son of Edam Barnes), John Elder, John
        Laurence, John Howard (son of Henry Howard), John Dorsey (son of Nathan
        Dorsey), Honour Elder, Honour Warfield, Honour Elder (daughter Michael
        Dorsey), Sarah Berry.
    Legatees (daughters): Hannah Barnes, Ruth Ramney, Sarah Howard, Susannah
        Laurence, Jemima Hobbs.
    Residue to 4 sons (equally): Michael, Vachel, Edward, Nathan.
    Executors: Michael Dorsey, Vachel Dorsey.

Jacob Lockerman, Jr.   5.159   D   DO   £99.7.7   May 1 1767
    Sureties: Thomas Hewett, James Woolford Steuart.
    Distribution to 6 parts (equally): Rosannah Gray (mother), siblings (half-blood):
        Rosalinda Gray, James Woolford Gray, Joseph Cox Gray, John Gray.
    Administratrix: Rosannah Gray.

William Pritchett   5.159   D   DO   £109.11.0   Dec 10 1768
    Sureties: Henry Lake, Thomas Whiteley.
    Legatees: Josebet (daughter), William (son), Levin (son), Elijah (son), Edward
        (son), Jabez (son), Sarah (wife).
    Mentions: Eleanor Hall.
    Executrix: Sarah Pritchet.

------ Reynolds   5.160   D   DO   £152.2.8   Jan 19 1769
First name is not cited.
    Sureties: James Busick, Thomas Phillips.
    Distribution to: Mary (wife).
    Executrix: Mary McGhuire (widow), now wife of Hugh McGhuire.

James Griffin   5.160   D   CH   £343.9.11   Mar 1 1769
    Sureties: Edward Miles, Robey Wornall.
    Distribution to: Widow (unnamed).
    Executrix: Sarah Griffith.

Robert Steel Clark   5.160   D   BA   £123.3.4   May 15 1769
    Sureties: Robert Clark, Aquilla Clark.
    Legatees: eldest daughter (unnamed).
    Distribution to: widow (unnamed) during widowhood; then to children: Daniel,
        Elisabeth, Mary, Charity.
    Executrix: Elisabeth Clark.

Edward Burch   5.161   D   CH   £659.11.2   Dec 19 1768
See Folio 164 for distribution.
    Sureties: John Thomas, Robert Gladding.
    Administrators: Mary Burch, Jesse Burch.

Thomas Ryland   5.161   D   CE   £148.14.10   Jan 18 1769
    Sureties: Henry Hays, Alphonse Cosdin.
    Legatees: Thomas Byland (son).
    Distribution to: Alriches (son, 1/2). Residue to 5 children (equally): Frodus,
        Stephen, John, Mary, Rebeccah.
    Executor: John Ryland, Jr.

Sarah Vincent   5.161   D   CH   £153.1.8   Apr 26 1769
    Sureties: William Penn, Bowles Tyer Balthrop.
    Legatees: Eleanor Joy (granddaughter), Sarah Ford (daughter), William Vincent
        (son).
    Mentions: father (unnamed) of William Vincent (son).
    Residue to children (unnamed, equally).
    Executor: John Vincent.

Benjamin Wood   5.162   D   CH   £1011.8.6   May 17 1769
    Sureties: William Posten, John Dent (son of Hatch Dent).
    Distribution to: Widow (unnamed, 1/3). Residue to children: Benjamin (1/6),
        Druscilla (1/6), John (1/12), Leonard (1/12), Helena (1/12), Elisabeth (1/12).
    Executors: Ann Wood, Benjamin Wood.

John Stoddert   5.162   D   CH   £1095.8.3   Apr 24 1769
    Sureties: John Hanson, Jr., Benjamin Ward.
    Legatees (children): William Trueman Stoddert, Kenelm Trueman Stoddert, Richard
        Trueman Stoddert, Walter Trueman Stoddert, Mary Trueman Fendal, Maryanne
        Trueman Alexander.
    Residue to 6 children (equally): William Trueman Stoddert, Kenelm Trueman
        Stoddert, Richard Trueman Stoddert, Walter Trueman Stoddert, Mary Trueman
        Fendal, Maryanne Trueman Alexander.
    Executors: William Trueman Stoddert, Kenelm Trueman Stoddert.

James Callaghane   5.163   D   TA   £163.10.10   May 3 1769
    Sureties: William Besswicke, James Morton.
    Legatees: Catharine Callaghane.
    Distribution to: Widow (unnamed, 1/3). Residue to children (unnamed, equally).
    Executors: Sarah Callaghane, Ferdinando Callaghane.

John Auld   5.163   D   TA   £248.19.4   Mar 9 1769
    Sureties: Joseph Harrison, John Auld.
    Distribution to: Widow (unnamed, 1/3). Residue to children (unnamed, equally).
      Portion of Mary Hamilton to be paid to Margaret Hamilton (daughter of said
      Mary).
    Executrix: Mary Auld.

Cornelius Dickerson   5.164   D   WO   £921.10.2   Oct 16 1767
    Sureties: William Barkley Townsend, Solomon Townsend.
    Legatees: Cornelius Dickerson, Josiah Dickerson, Joshua Dickerson, Grace
      Dickerson, Lucuia Dickerson.
    Administrator: Josiah Dickerson.

Edward Burch   5.164   D
See Folio 161.
    Legatees: Elisabeth Burch, Catharine Burch, Jam Burch, Edward Burch, Ann Burch.
    Distribution to: Widow (unnamed, 1/3). Residue to children (unnamed, equally).

Esther Keiron   5.166   D   QA   £39.1.5   Jan 9 1769
Cites payment in Pennsylvania money.
    Sureties: Nathaniel Scott, Jeremiah Barnulo.
    Legatees: James Keiron (son of John Keiron (brother)), Mary Keiron (daughter of
      Richard Keiron (brother)), Henry Council, (cousin) to help discharge debt of
      William Keiron (brother) to Charles Brown.
    Distribution to (equally): James Keiron (aforesaid), children (unnamed) of
      Richard Keiron (brother).
    Executor: John Davis, Jr.

William Barkhust   5.166   D   QA   £75.0.9   Mar 13 1769
    Sureties: James Sparks, Nathan Sparks.
    Legatees (children): Elisabeth, Anne, John, William, James.
    Residue to (equally): widow (unnamed), Thomas (son), George (son), Solomon (son),
      Joseph (son), Nathaniel (son), 5 daughters (unnamed).
    Executors: Susannah Barkhust, George Barkhust.

David Melvill   5.167   D   DO   £254.1.2   Dec 16 1768
    Sureties: Thomas Smith, Thomas Smith, Jr.
    Distribution to: Rachel (widow, 1/3). Residue to sisters (equally): Mary Smith,
      Frances Smith, Sarah Melvill.
    Executrix: Rachel Smith, wife of Thomas Smith.

James Chaires   5.167   D   QA   £89.9.7   Feb 2 1769
    Sureties: Thomas Chaires, Abraham Sherlock.
    Legatees: Jeanne Roe, John (brother), William (brother), Nathan (brother).
    Distribution to: Widow (unnamed, 1/3). Residue to: Thomas (son).
    Executor (acting): William Chairs.

William Juett   5.168   D   SO   £1211.9.7   Mar 7 1769
    Sureties: Stephen Ward, Mathias Ward.
    Legatees: William Juett (son of John Juett), Nathan Juett, Martha Juett, Betty
      Miles, Leah Juett, Rebeccah Leek, Mary Juett, Catharine Juett.
    Distribution to: Widow (unnamed, 1/3). Residue to (equally): Martha Juett, Leah
      Juett, Rhoda Juett.
    Executor: Nathan Juett.

David Evans   5.168   D   BA   £129.9.7   Feb 27 1769
    Sureties: Thomas Street, Hugh Brierly.
    Distribution to: Widow (unnamed, 1/3). Residue to children (equally): David,
      Margaret.
    Executrix: Margaret Evans.

John Cotrall   5.169   D   BA   £137.9.0   Oct 4 1768
    Sureties: Luke Raven, Benjamin Buck.
    Legatees: widow (unnamed), Martha (daughter), Thomas (brother), Luke Raven
      (son-in-law).
    Executor: John Buck.

William Roach   5.170   D   WO   £475.4.0   Nov 3 1768
    Sureties: James Roach, George Smith.
    Legatees: widow (unnamed), Mary (daughter), Elisabeth (daughter).
    Distribution to: Widow (unnamed, 1/3). Residue to 5 children (equally): Sarah
      Fook, Levin, Mary Boazman Roach, Stephen, James.
    Administrator (de bonis non): Stephen Roach.

Thomas Davis   5.170   D CE   £1206.18.2   Nov 16 1768
    Sureties: John Veazy, John Ward.
    Distribution to: Widow (unnamed, 1/3). Residue to children (unnamed, equally).
    Executors: Rebeccah Davis, William Davis.

Jacob Shingletaker   5.171   D FR   £125.18.8   Mar 13 1768
    Sureties: John Carr, Peter Mossner.
    Distribution to: Widow (unnamed, 1/3). Residue to children (8 parts): Jacob (2
        parts), George, Andrew, Michel, Elisabeth, Catharine, Margaret.
    Executors: Jacob Shingletaker, Elisabeth Shingletaker.

William Thompson   5.171   D CH   £319.7.7   Mar 1 1769
    Sureties: Joseph Coombs, Raphael Green.
    Residue to children (equally): Leonard, James, Elisabeth, Appelonia, Mary,
        Susannah.
    Executors: Leonard Thompson, Elisabeth Thompson.

Thomas Cooper   5.172   D SO   £48.16.2   Jun 6 1769
    Sureties: William Smith, Jr., Thomas Bunt.
    Legatees (children): Abraham (eldest son), Thomas.
    Distribution to: Widow (unnamed, 1/3). Residue to 4 children (unnamed, equally).
    Administratrix: Isabell Cooper.

William Andrews   5.172   D FR   £144.9.8   Jul 12 1768
    Sureties: Samuel McFarren, Martin Adams.
    Legatees (children): John, Jane, Mary.
    Distribution to: Widow (unnamed, 1/3).
    Executor: Samuel Andrews.

Edward Welsh   5.173   D SM   £388.12.2   Feb 14 1769
    Sureties: James Burroughs, Leonard Lyer.
    Legatees: Sarah (daughter), Elisabeth Waters, John Welsh (grandson, under 21),
        Mary Welsh (granddaughter, under 16), Birgin Mitchel (under 21), Mary (wife).
    Executrix: Mary Welsh.

Philip Selby   5.173   D WO   £656.8.5   Oct 14 1768
    Sureties: John Selby, Daniel Selby.
    Legatees: Daniel (son), Philip (son), Mary (widow).
    Residue to (equally): Mary (widow), Daniel (son), Philip (son).
    Executrix: Mary Wallace, wife of Hugh Wallace.

James Elliott   5.174   D AA   £265.1.10   Jan 31 1769
    Sureties: Joseph Lowell, Cornelius Barry.
    Legatees: Elisabeth Cavell (daughter).
    Residue to: Sarah (widow, accountant).
    Executrix: Sarah Elliott.

David Cathell   5.174   D WO   £234.8.7   Mar 8 1769
    Sureties: Jonathon Cathell, George Toadvine.
    Distribution to: Elisabeth (widow, accountant, 1/3).
    Executrix: Elisabeth Cathell.

Peter Ford, Sr.   5.174   D SM   £674.6.4   Apr 4 1769
    Sureties: Anthony Roberts, John Ford (son of Peter Ford).
    Legatees: Mary (widow), Richard (son), Peter Ford (grandson, son of Bennett
        Ford), John Javett Ford (grandson, son of Bennett Ford).
    Distribution to: Mary (widow, accountant, 1/3). Residue to 3 children (equally):
        Peter, John, Priscilla.
    Executrix: Mary Ford.

William Smith   5.175   D WO   £86.3.8   Apr 4 1769
    Sureties: Joseph Jones, John Smith.
    Distribution to: widow (unnamed) during lifetime.
    Executrix (acting): Rebeccah Smith.

Capt. Adam Spence   5.175   D WO   £1757.6.4   Jul 4 1768
    Sureties: John Irving, Samuel Purnel.
    Distribution to: Mary (widow, 1/3). Residue to 8 children (equally): Margaret,
        Betty, Adam, John, Mary, George, Anne, Sarah.
    Executor: Adam Spence.

Arthur Christfield   5.175   D KE   £47.19.1   Mar 18 1769
    Sureties: John Ambrose, Jr., Edward Worrell.
    Distribution to: widow (unnamed).
    Executors: Hans Blackiston and his wife Anne Blackiston.

Stonile Booker   5.176   D   FR   £455.11.11   Feb 14 1769
    Sureties: Adam Fisher, Christian Bringle.
    Legatees: John Bugar (son).
    Distribution to: Linora (widow, 1/3). Residue to children (equally): John Bugar,
        Chatharine Bugar, Jacob Bugar, Eleanor Bugar, Frederick Bugar, Charlotte
        Bugar, child "wife is now pregnant with".
    Executor (acting): Valentine Rape.

William Holland   5.176   D   CA   £565.1.10   Nov 29 1768
    Sureties: John Hamilton, John Smith.
    Legatees (daughters): Margaret Cole (one of eldest), Sarah Spring (one of
        eldest).
    Distribution to: Ann (widow, accountant, 1/3). Residue to daughters (equally):
        Wilhelmina, Mary.
    Executrix: Ann Holland.

Thomas Glann   5.177   D   FR   £82.1.10   Feb 9 1769
    Sureties: Mathew Gault, Patrick Watson.
    Distribution to: Jean Glan (widow, 1/3). Residue to: Robert (son).
    Executor: Robert Brown.

George Booth   5.177   D   SM   £104.9.4   Oct 25 1768
    Sureties: Francis Thompson, Ignatius Wheeler.
    Legatees (children): daughter (unnamed), George, John, Thomas, Richard, James,
        Basil.
    Distribution to: Widow (unnamed, 1/3). Residue to 3 sons (equally): Richard,
        James, Basil.
    Executrix: Monica Booth.

Thomas Lewis   5.178   D   KE   £184.0.9   Mar 20 1769
    Sureties: William Ringgold, Thomas Ringgold, Jr.
    Executor: Thomas Ringgold.

John Soper   5.178   D   PG   £369.19.10   Dec 10 1768
See Folio 365.
    Sureties: Ignatius Hardy, John Hardy.
    Legatees: Mary Ellis, Susannah (daughter), Sarah (daughter).
    Distribution to: Widow (unnamed, 1/3). Residue to (equally): John Soper, Charles
        Soper, Thomas Soper, James Soper, Nathan Soper, Basil Soper, Rachel Soper.
    Executor: Charles Soper.

Richard Brown   5.178   D   SM   £34.17.5   Oct 10 1768
    Sureties: Peter Brown, Nicholas Brown, Jr. Legatees: Richard (son).
    Distribution to: Widow (unnamed, 1/3). Residue to children (unnamed, equally).
    Executrix: Annastatia Brown.

Zephaniah Plummer   5.179   D   FR   £57.14.7   Mar 4 1769
    Sureties: James Manning Gore, Jacob Clive.
    Legatees: Jeremiah (brother), Dorichlar (sister), mother (unnamed).
    Executor: Daniel Veach.

Thomas Powel   5.179   D   QA   £77.10.2   Jan 10 1769
    Distribution to: accountant (only representative).
    Administrator: John Powell.

Archibald Akin   5.179   D   BA   £229.9.0   Feb 20 1769
    Sureties: John Byarly, Patrick Roach.
    Legatees: Margaret Kelley (step-daughter).
    Distribution to: Margaret (widow, accountant, 1/3). Residue to: Eleanor Aikins
        (daughter).
    Executrix: Margaret Akin.

John Irving   5.180   D   WO   £348.7.4   Aug 16 1768
    Sureties: Adam Spence, James Martin.
    Distribution to: Widow (unnamed, 1/3). Residue to 4 children (equally): Mary,
        Sarah, Betty, John.
    Administratrix: Margaret Irving.

William Purkins   5.180   D   WO   £107.1.9   Sep 2 1768
    Sureties: Daniel Cox, John Chambers Crapper.
    Legatees: Tabitha (widow, accountant), Mary Harrison (daughter), Thomas Perkins
        (son), Sarah Perkins (daughter).
    Residue to 6 children (equally): Thomas Perkins, Tabitha Perkins, Comfort
        Perkins, Sarah Perkins, Zeporah Perkins, Betty Perkins.
    Executors: Tabitha Purkins, Thomas Purkins.

Stephen Roach   5.181   D   WO   £118.9.3   Nov 3 1768
    Sureties: Joshua Sturgis, James Roach.
    Distribution to: Deborah (widow, accountant, 1/3).
    Executrix: Deborah Roach.

Moses Tennant   5.181   D   KE   £199.14.3   Feb 4 1769
    Sureties: Abell Chanler, Francis Rutter.
    Legatees (sons): John, Moses, William, James.
    Residue to 4 daughters (equally): Elisabeth, Sarah, Susannah, Hannah.
    Administrators: Moses Tennant, William Tennant.

William Herbison   5.182   D   KE   £49.13.3   Feb 27 1769
    Sureties: Jonathon Smith, William Woodall.
    Distribution to: wife (unnamed) during widowhood.
    Executor (acting): David Falls.

Augustine Boyer   5.182   D   KE   £471.8.10   Mar 22 1769
    Sureties: Gustavia Hanson, Andrew Hynson.
    Legatees: all his grandchildren (unnamed).
    Residue to: Augustine (son).
    Administrator: Augustine Boyer.

Thomas Walter   5.182   D   WO   £71.8.9   Feb 24 1769
    Sureties: Joseph Melson, William Melson.
    Legatees (brothers): Peleg, John.
    Residue to: Peter Dolby (friend).
    Executor: Peter Dolby.

John Oneal   5.183   D   WO   £48.8.11   Feb 24 1769
    Sureties: Thomas Oneal, George Benson.
    Legatees: Elisabeth (daughter).
    Residue to children (unnamed, equally).
    Executor: Samuel Oneal.

Archibald Dale   5.183   D   WO   £58.18.3   Feb 18 1769
    Sureties: John Givan, John Laurence.
    Legatees: Margaret (wife).
    Residue to: Samuel (son).
    Executor: Samuel Dale.

Thomas Morriss   5.183   D   WO   £30.18.5   May 8 1769
    Sureties: Luke Bowen, James Selby.
    Legatees: Thomas (son).
    Residue to children (equally): William, Sarah, Lissa, John, Jethro, Cornelius,
        Leah.
    Administratrix: Comfort Morriss.

George Wilson   5.184   D   SO   £139.17.3   Apr 4 1769
    Sureties: Thomas Tripe, Jos. Wilson.
    Legatees: Abraham (son), William (son), Jesse (son), Levin (son), David (son),
        Rhody (wife).
    Mentions: Samuel (brother).
    Distribution to: Rhody (widow, accountant, 1/3). Residue to 10 children
        (equally): William, Jesse, Sophia, Levin, Sarah, Hannah, Ann, Abraham, Mary,
        David.
    Executrix: Rodey Wilson.

Isaac Callaway   5.184   D   WO   £93.9.5   Mar 3 1769
    Sureties: Andrew Spear, William Price.
    Distribution to: wife (unnamed) until all children raised to maturity; then to
        children (unnamed, equally, except Patience Low).
    Executrix: Mary Callaway.

Michael Godwin   5.185   D   WO   £237.9.10   Feb 6 1769
    Sureties: Annanias Hudson, Peter Robinson.
    Legatees: William (son), Elisabeth (daughter), Hannah (daughter), Thomas Godwin,
        Mary Huron, Catharine (wife), Rhoda Robinson (daughter).
    Residue to children (equally): William, Rhoda, Mary, Elisabeth, Naomi, Ruth,
        Thomas, Hannah.
    Executors: William Holland, Elisabeth Godwin.

Samuel Lamberson   5.185   D   WO   £47.14.0   Jan 20 1769
    Sureties: James Smith, John Stockley.
    Legatees (children): Smith, Elisabeth.
    Residue to 6 children (equally): Casiah, Sinah, Saley, Samuel, Lucy, Smith.
    Executor: Jonathon West Watson.

James Hickman   5.186   D   WO   £57.18.11   Feb 24 1769
The entry is crossed out. See Folio 188.
    Sureties: Elia Henry, James Baker.
    Legatees (daughters): Leah, Nehemiah, Comfort, Levin, Rachel.
    Residue to 4 children (equally): Joshua, Thomas, Rachel, Levin.
    Executor (acting): Thomas Hickman.

William Evans   5.186   D WO   £114.7.5   Feb 24 1769
    Sureties: John Miller, John Morgan.
    Legatees: Catharine (wife), William Evans (grandson, son of Joshua Evans), Rachel
        Johnson, Comfort Justice, Martha (daughter).
    Distribution to: Catharine (wife, 1/3). Residue to (equally): Mary Hudson,
        Martha Evans.
    Executor: Elisha Evans.

Basil Dorsey   5.187   D AA   £5135.11.2   Dec 14 1768
    Sureties: John Dorsey (son of Caleb Dorsey), Joshua Dorsey,
    Legatees: Thomas Dorsey, Dennis Dorsey, Sarah Burgess (daughter), Achsah Burgess,
        Sarah Burgess (granddaughter), Basil Burgess, Ariana Dorsey, Eleanor Dorsey.
    Distribution to: Widow (unnamed, 1/3). Residue to (equally): Thomas Dorsey,
        Dennis Dorsey, Ariana Dorsey, Eleanor Dorsey, Elisabeth Dorsey.
    Executor: Thomas Dorsey.

Ann Trueman   5.188   D PG   £1186.9.3   Aug 24 1768
    Sureties: John Stone Hawkins, James Brisco.
    Legatees (children): Thomas, James, Leonard, Cloe, Clara, Sarah, Henry, Jane,
        Alexander, Edward.
    Executor: Thomas Trueman.

James Hickman   5.188   D WO   £57.18.11   Feb 25 1769
    Sureties: Elias Henry, James Baker.
    Legatees (children): Leah, Nehemiah, Comfort.
    Residue to 4 children (equally): Joshua, Thomas, Rachel, Levin.
    Executor (acting): Thomas Hickman.

James Walters   5.189   D QA   £155.19.4   Sep 7 1769
    Sureties: Solomon Clayton, Charles Clayton.
    Distribution to (equally): Ann (mother), Robert (accountant, brother), Ann
        (sister) wife of John Seeders, Frances (sister), Sarah (sister) wife of John
        Hackett, representatives (unnamed) of Mary Tanner (half-sister) late wife of
        Benjamin Tanner, Elisabeth Gardiner (half-sister) wife of John Gardiner.
    Administrator: Mr. Robert Walters.

Burgess Nelson   5.189   D FR   £581.0.3   Jun 23 1769
    Legatees: Henry (son).
    Distribution to: Widow (unnamed, 1/3). Residue to children (equally): Rachel,
        Benjamin, Sarah.
    Administrator: Mr. Henry Howard.

Mitchel Walter   5.190   D WO   £191.12.6   Sep 18 1766
    Distribution to: widow (unnamed) during lifetime; then to (equally): Ann Walter,
        Smith Walter, John Walter, Mary Walter.
    Executrix: Ann Walter.

John Sullivane   5.190   D QA   Oct 6 1769
    Administratrix: Mrs. Sarah Sullivane.

William Smith   5.191   D CE   £584.8.4   Nov 24 1769
    Sureties: Samuel Sliawil (?), John Scott.
    Distribution to: Widow (unnamed), 5 children: Mary, James, John, Robert, William.
    Administrators (de bonis non): Robert Smith, John McWhorter.

William Commegys   5.191   D KE   £130.0.0   Nov 14 1769
    Sureties: Cornelius Vansant, John Commegys.
    Distribution to: Jesse Cosden (1/3) in right of his wife Ann widow of Edward
        Commegys. Residue to: William St. Clair (1/3) in right of his wife Mary
        (widow), Mary (daughter).
    Administrator (de bonis non): Jesse Cosden.

James Walters, Sr.   5.192   D QA   £155.19.4   Sep 7 1769
See Folio 189.
    Sureties: Solomon Clayton, Charles Clayton.

Jacob Hufman   5.192   D FR   £126.11.0   Oct 5 1767
    Distribution to: Widow (unnamed, 1/3). Residue to 6 children (unnamed, equally).
    Administrator: Mr. Charles Beatty.

William Dunn   5.192   D QA   £150.17.9   Jun 22 1769
    Sureties: Nathan Hatcheson, Stephen Glanvill.
    Distribution to: Representatives unknown to this Office.
    Administratrix: Ann Dunn by her sureties Nathan Hatcheson & Stephen Glanvill.

Ann Pearman   5.193   D AA   £73.4.6   Mar 7 1770
    Sureties: Cornelius Garretson.
    Administrator: Thomas Hyde.

Hugh Merrikin　　　　　　　　5.193　　D　AA　£340.10.3　　May 24 1770
    Sureties: Lloyd Johnson, Thomas Mayo.
    Distribution to: Representatives unknown to this Office.
    Administrator: Hugh Merrikin.

Benjamin Start　　　　　　　　5.193　　D　TA　£186.11.0　　Oct 19 1769
    Sureties: William Kemp, Joseph Bewley.
    Distribution to: Widow (unnamed, 1/3). Residue to 10 children (equally): Elisabeth, John, Benjamin, Rebecca, Martha, Sarah, Mary, Moses, Alice, Ann.
    Administratrix: Martha Start.

Joseph Manning　　　　　　　　5.194　　D　CA　£319.16.10　　Jan 12 1770
    Sureties: Richard Speake, Walter McPherson.
    Distribution to: Widow (unnamed, 1/3). Residue to 3 children (equally): Anne Gardiner, Mary Ann Manning, Francis Speak Manning.
    Administratrix: Elisabeth Manning.

Stephen Hammel　　　　　　　　5.194　　D　CH　£23.0.4　　Nov 10 1769
    Sureties: Edward Wheeler, William Hammel.
    Distribution to: Widow (unnamed, 1/3). Residue to 2 children (equally): John, Sarah.
    Administratrix: Arsenah Shaw, wife of John Shaw.

Andrew Buchannan　　　　　　　5.194　　D　CH　£132.4.8　　Aug 7 1769
    Sureties: Robert Hendley Courts, William Courts.
    Distribution to: Representatives unknown to this Office.
    Administrator: Hugh McBride.

Samuel Parsons　　　　　　　　5.195　　D　QA　£54.5.6　　Oct 17 1769
    Sureties: William Henwock, John Tauton.
    Distribution to: Widow (unnamed, 1/3). Residue to 4 children (unnamed, equally).
    Administratrix: Michel Parsons.

Constant Lomax　　　　　　　　5.195　　D　CH　£58.8.11　　Jun 7 1769
    Sureties: Joseph Gray, Robert Covert.
    Distribution to 6 children (equally): Seth, Margaret, Brazilla, Thomas Anderson (or Thomas Anderson Lomax), Rebecca, Mark.
    Administrator: Seth Lomax.

Jacob Jacobs　　　　　　　　　5.195　　D　QA　£58.11.8　　Aug 26 1769
    Sureties: John Seth, William Mason.
    Distribution to: Representatives unknown to this Office.
    Administrator: Thomas Baker.

Thomas MacDaniel　　　　　　　5.196　　D　CH　£75.1.5　　Jun 7 1769
    Sureties: Thomas Darnall, William Darnall.
    Distribution to: Widow (unnamed, 1/3). Residue to 11 children (unnamed, equally).
    Administratrix: Rebecca McDaniel.

Thomas Dennaho　　　　　　　　5.196　　D　QA　£45.7.8　　Aug 17 1769
    Sureties: John Atkinson, Richard Costin.
    Distribution to: Catherine (widow, 1/3) now wife of Thomas Norris. Residue to: William (only child).
    Administrator: William Meredith.

William Garey　　　　　　　　5.196　　D　TA　£147.19.4　　Oct 5 1769
    Sureties: Rev. John Gordon, John Garey.
    Distribution to: Widow (unnamed, 1/3). Residue to 9 children (equally): Ann wife of Nicholas Benson, Jr., John, William, Henry, George, Elisabeth, Frances, Solomon, Samuel.
    Administratrix: Mary Ann Garey.

Samuel Beck　　　　　　　　　　5.197　　D　BA　£155.19.9　　Jul 24 1769
    Sureties: Spencer Legor, Benjamin Debruller.
    Distribution to: Representatives unknown to this Office.
    Administratrix: Mary Beck.

Isaac Raven　　　　　　　　　　5.197　　D　BA　£265.4.4　　Jul 17 1769
    Sureties: Luke Raven, Christopher Duke.
    Distribution to: Representatives unknown to this Office.
    Administratrix: Lettice Raven.

Abraham Cole　　　　　　　　　5.197　　D　DO　£49.5.6　　Nov 15 1769
    Sureties: William Walker, Richard Parish.
    Distribution to: Widow (unnamed, 1/3). Residue to: only child (unnamed).
    Administratrix: Jenny Hughs, wife of Levin Hughs.

John Wheeler the elder   5.197   D   BA   £104.16.7   Oct 9 1769
    Sureties: Thomas Collings, John Forster.
    Distribution to: Representatives unknown to this Office.
    Administratrix: Elisabeth Wheeler.

Thomas Cooper   5.198   D   DO   £35.4.7   Oct 11 1769
    Sureties: William Smith, Thomas Bunt.
    Distribution to: Widow (unnamed, 1/3). Residue to 10 children (equally): James,
        Thomas, John, Betty, Priscilla, Catharine, Rhody, Owen, Mary, Stephen.
    Administratrix: Rebecca Cooper.

Thomas Ginn   5.198   D   DO   £200.9.10   Sep 5 1769
    Sureties: Elial Vinson, Thomas Smith (son of William Smith).
    Distribution to: Widow (unnamed, 1/3). Residue to 7 children (equally): James,
        Josiah, Samuel, Anne, Sarah, Thomas, Mary.
    Administratrix: Sicily Ginn.

James Jarrard   5.198   D   DO   £109.3.7   Oct 2 1769
    Sureties: Patrick Beshawn, Samuel Busick.
    Distribution to: Representatives unknown to this Office.
    Administrator (de bonis non): Mr. Leek Robinson.

Samuel Gray   5.199   D   CH   £837.2.0   Oct 28 1769
    Sureties: John Speake, Jr., John Martin.
    Distribution to: Widow (unnamed, 1/3). Residue to: only daughter (unnamed) now
        wife of John Maddocks.
    Administratrix: Mrs. Jane Gray.

William McKemmy   5.199   D   DO   £23.3.9   Nov 15 1769
    Sureties: Ralph Smith, Thomas Smith.
    Distribution to: Widow (unnamed, 1/3). Residue to 6 children (equally): Sarah,
        Gideon, William, Nathan, Nathaniel, Mary.
    Administratrix: Mrs. Rachel McKemmy.

John Casson   5.199   D   DO   £381.11.11   Nov 23 1769
    Sureties: John White, Joseph Foster.
    Distribution to: Widow (unnamed, 1/3). Residue to 5 children (equally): Robert,
        John, Fardinando, Myers. (Only 4 names given.)
    Administratrix: Margaret Driver, wife of Mr. Mathew Driver, Jr.

Mathew Heneker   5.200   D   CH   £41.3.4   Jul 27 1769
    Sureties: Belain Posey, Mark Brayfield.
    Distribution to: Widow (unnamed, 1/3). Residue to 3 children (equally): John,
        Sally, Henrietta.
    Administratrix: Elisabeth Heneker.

John Turner   5.200   D   DO   £240.6.8   Aug 15 1769
    Sureties: John Greenwood, John Hayward.
    Distribution to: Widow (unnamed, 1/3). Residue to 6 children (equally): John,
        Mary, Ann, Henry, George, William, Richard. (Note: There should only be 6
        names; I don't know which pair to combine.)
    Administratrix: Mrs. Anne Turner.

William Bordley   5.200   D   CE   £693.2.11   Oct 27 1769
    Sureties: John Ward, Edward Mitchel.
    Distribution to: Widow (unnamed, 1/3). Residue to 2 children (equally): Stephen,
        Mary.
    Administrator: Mr. Andrew Pearce.

Anthony Lynch   5.201   D   CE   £814.15.9   Sep 13 1769
    Sureties: John Ward, Jr., Nathaniel Ward.
    Distribution to: Widow (unnamed, 1/3). Residue to 5 children (equally): William,
        George, Anthony, James, & Elisabeth & Anthony Lynch son of Alice (daughter).
    Administrators: Elisabeth Lynch, William Lynch.

Emanuel Swift   5.201   D   QA   £59.9.10   Sep 7 1769
    Sureties: Robert Brody, Frances Stevens.
    Distribution to: Rachel (widow, accountant, 1/3). Residue to 6 children
        (equally): Vincent, Rebecca, Mary, Rachel, Martha, Sarah.
    Administratrix: Mrs. Rachel Swift.

Edward Goodrick   5.201   D   TA   £594.2.3   Oct 13 1769
    Sureties: Hugh Mitchel, Joseph Thompson.
    Distribution to: Representatives unknown to this Office.
    Administratrix: Sarah Maddock, wife of Mr. James Maddock.

John Vanderford (Chester)   5.202   D   QA   £34.14.5   Oct 12 1769
   Sureties: Daniel Ford, Robert Dunkin.
   Distribution to: Widow (unnamed, 1/3). Residue to 2 children (equally): John,
     James.
   Administrators: Mr. William Gregory and his wife Ruth Gregory.

Thomas Moody   5.202   D   CE   £80.6.10   Sep 20 1769
   Sureties: Samuel Hutchison, David Moody.
   Distribution to: Widow (unnamed, 1/3). Residue to 2 children (equally):
     Alexander, John.
   Administrator (de bonis non): Mr. Robert Moody.

Thomas Colson   5.202   D   DO   £13.17.7   Jun 19 1769
   Sureties: Edmund Mace, John Mace.
   Administratrix: Mrs. Elisabeth Colson.

Susannah Jobson   5.203   D   AA   £432.13.11   Aug 17 1769
   Sureties: Allen Gwynn, Jacob Franklin.
   Distribution to: Widow (unnamed, 1/3). Residue to 4 children (equally): Benjamin
     Allen, William Allen, Joseph Allen, Prindowell Allen.
   Administrators: MM Joseph Allen, Prindowell Allen.

Elisabeth Wootton   5.203   D   AA   £61.4.11   Aug 8 1769
   Sureties: Alexander Ferguson, Nicholas Brewer.
   Distribution to children (equally): Rachel Brewer (wife of accountant), Samuel
     Wootton.
   Administrator: Mr. Joseph Brewer.

William Chiffin   5.203   D   AA   £41.11.3   Jul 27 1769
   Sureties: Robert Welsh, Edward Lee.
   Distribution to (equally): Margaret Stockett (half-sister), Rachel Covington
     (half-sister), Eleanor Read (whole sister).
   Administrator: Mr. John Read.

William Wilson   5.204   D   TA   £165.5.9   May 25 1769
   Sureties: Charles Gardiner, John Young.
   Distribution to: Widow (unnamed, 1/3). Residue to: Deborah (only child).
   Administratrix: Mary Gibson, wife of Mr. James Gibson.

Patrick Mullikin   5.204   D   TA   £130.10.8   Jul 3 1769
   Sureties: Edward Harrison, John Eason.
   Distribution to: Widow (unnamed, 1/3). Residue to 5 children (equally): Patrick,
     Rachel, Mary, Elisabeth, Joseph.
   Administratrix: Ann Edmondson, wife of Mr. William Edmondson.

Ralph Elston   5.204   D   TA   £626.0.7   May 5 1769
   Sureties: Jeremiah Banning.
   Distribution to: Representatives unknown to this Office.
   Administrator (de bonis non): Mr. John Shanahan.

Thomas Hamer   5.205   D   QA   £291.11.10   Mar 16 1769
   "New balance in E. V. #2" (Liber 6). (No folio number given.)
   Sureties: Thomas Hackett, James Hackett.
   Distribution to: Widow (unnamed, 1/3). Residue to 4 children (equally): Mary,
     Hannah, Thomas, Elisabeth.
   Administrator (surviving): Mr. James Benson.

Hannah Earle   5.205   D   QA   £102.12.9   May 25 1769
   Sureties: James Earle, Benjamin Earle.
   Distribution to: Ann (only daughter).
   Administrator: Mr. John Earle.

Robert Kent   5.205   D   QA   £248.2.8   Jun 6 1769
   Sureties: John Kent, William Dames.
   Distribution to: Susannah (widow, accountant, 1/3). Residue to 4 children
     (unnamed, equally).
   Administratrix: Mrs. Susannah Kent.

Thomas Roberts   5.206   D   TA   £721.13.0   Feb 28 1770
   Sureties: Joseph Bewley, William Parrott.
   Legatees: Susannah Armstrong (daughter), Thomas Roberts & Rebeccah Roberts & Ann
     Roberts (grandchildren, children of James Roberts (son)), Nancy (daughter).
   Distribution to: Rebecca (accountant, 1/3). Residue to 7 parts (7 children,
     equally): Thomas, Mary Besswicks, Elisabeth Kirby, John, Edward, Nancy, Peter
     Blake & John Blake & Mary Blake (grandchildren, children of Rebeccah Blake
     (daughter)).
   Executors: Rebecca Roberts, John Roberts.

William Finnicum   5.206   D QA   £90.17.3   Jun 14 1769
    Sureties: Richard Heathers, Edward Burroughs.
    Distribution to: Isabella (widow, accountant, 1/3). Residue to 4 children
        (equally): Ann, Margaret, Stephen, William.
    Administratrix: Isabella Barkhust, wife of James Barkhust.

Maj. Nathan Wright   5.207   D QA   £909.4.4   Jan 5 1770
    Sureties: Edward Chetham, James Chetham.
    Distribution to: accountant (widow) until Robert (son) comes to age 21 or
        marries.
    Executrix: Mary Wright.

Philemon Hamilton   5.207   D TA   £1150.4.11   Mar 3 1770
    Sureties: Feddeman Rolle, John Berry.
    Legatees: Sarah (wife), Margaret (daughter).
    Distribution to: Sarah (wife, 1/3). Residue to 3 children (equally): William,
        Philemon, Margaret.
    Executrix: Sarah Trippe, wife of Edward Trippe.

Rebeccah Tippins   5.207   D QA   £20.1.2   Jun 29 1769
    Sureties: John Sparks (joiner), Allen Hollinsworth.
    Distribution to: Representatives unknown to this Office.
    Administrator: Mr. Joseph Sparks.

William Courts   5.208   D CH   £1299.6.7   Aug 23 1769
    Sureties: Charles Courts, John Fendall.
    Legatees: Elisabeth (wife), John (son), Richard Hendley Courts (son).
    Distribution to: Elisabeth (wife, 1/3). Residue to 3 sons (equally): John,
        William, Richard Hendley Courts.
    Executors: Samuel Love, Jr. and his wife Elisabeth Love, Richard Hendley Courts.

Nathaniel Reed   5.208   D QA   £365.5.10   Sep 6 1769
    Sureties: Turbutt Betton, John Kent.
    Distribution to: Sarah (wife).
    Executrix: Sarah Reed.

Frances Gould   5.209   D QA   £639.14.0   Jun 13 1769
    Sureties: Mathew Hawkins, William Pryor.
    Legatees: Richard (son), Elisabeth Primrose (daughter), James (son), Benjamin
        (son), Frances Hawkings (daughter), Margaret Hackett (granddaughter), Mirimy
        Gould (granddaughter), Frances Hawkins (granddaughter), Frances Gould
        (granddaughter).
    Residue to 4 children (equally): Elisabeth Primrose, James, Benjamin, Frances
        Hawkins.
    Executor: Mr. Benjamin Gould.

Joseph Milburn Semmes   5.209   D CH   £685.11.3   Oct 2 1769
    Sureties: Robert Mundell, Raphael Neale.
    Legatees (children): Eleanor Adams, Joseph, Rachel, Elisabeth, Catharine, Clare.
    Residue to 3 daughters (equally): Mary Ann, Martha, Teresa.
    Administrator (de bonis non): Mr. Marmaduke Semmes.

Richard Gibson   5.210   D TA   £1187.0.3   May 31 1769
    Sureties: John Gibson, Richard Grason.
    Legatees (children): Rachel, James.
    Distribution to: Sarah (widow, 1/3). Residue to 2 children (equally): Rachel,
        James.
    Executor (surviving): Mr. James Gibson.

Thomas Warfield   5.211   D AA   £590.16.3   Nov 5 1769
    Sureties: Caleb Dorsey, Jr., Henry Griffith.
    Legatees: mother (unnamed), Aney Simpon & Tomsey Simpon & Nancy Simpon & Sally
        Simpon (sisters-in-law), Basil Simpson (brother-in-law), Francis Simpson
        (father-in-law).
    Residue to siblings (equally): John, Brice, Alexander, Elisabeth, Ruth, Deborah.
    Executor: Mr. Francis Simpson.

Thomas Mooth   5.211   D QA   £141.0.9   May 25 1769
    Sureties: George Webb, William Ridgeway.
    Legatees: Margaret (daughter), Mary Hammond (daughter), Mary (wife).
    Executor (one of them): Mr. James Mooth.

James Gough   5.212   D SM   £717.16.6   Nov 4 1769
    Sureties: Luke Heard, Matthew Heard.
    Legatees (children): Stephen, James, Ignatius, Eleanor Greenwell, Susannah, Mary,
        Elisabeth Jenkins.
    Distribution to: Widow (unnamed, 1/3). Residue to children (equally): Eleanor
        Greenwell, Mary, Susannah, Stephen, James, Ignatius.
    Executor (surviving): Mr. Stephen Gough.

John Barkhust   5.212   D   QA   £80.6.4   Jun 14 1769
    Sureties: Edward Burroughs, Thomas Walker.
    Legatees: Elisabeth (wife), James (son), Elisabeth (daughter).
    Distribution to: Elisabeth (wife, 1/3). Residue to 7 children (unnamed,
        equally). Only Stephen (son) is cited.
    Executors: Elisabeth Barkhust, Stephen Barkhust.

John Clayland   5.213   D   QA   £793.7.2   Oct 12 1769
See new balance in "E. V. #2" (Liber 6). No folio cited.
    Sureties: Christopher Thomas, Tristram Thomas.
    Legatees: Thomas (son), John Clayland (grandson), John (son), Elisabeth Taylor
        (daughter), William (son), Sarah Clayland (granddaughter, daughter of Thomas
        (son)), Thomas Clayland (grandson, son of Thomas (son)).
    Residue to: John (son), Thomas (son), William (son), Elisabeth (daughter),
        children (unnamed) of James (son).
    Executor: John Clayland.

Elisabeth Hamer   5.213   D   QA   £132.6.0   May 16 1769
See new balance in "E. V. #2" (Liber 6). No folio is cited.
    Sureties: Thomas Hackett, James Hackett.
    Legatees (3 daughters, equally): Mary Hamar, Hannah Hamar, Elisabeth Hamar.
    Executor (surviving): Mr. James Benson.

Edward Barwick   5.214   D   DO   £249.12.10   Aug 31 1769
    Sureties: James Lecompte, Edward White.
    Legatees: John (son), Alice (wife), William (son), James (son), Edward (son),
        Nathan (son), Joshua (son), Solomon (son).
    Distribution to (equally): Alice (wife), 4 youngest children: Edward, Nathan,
        Joshua, Solomon.
    Executrix: Alice Edmunds, wife of Mr. Robert Edmunds.

John Bully   5.214   D   CE   £56.5.3   Aug 16 1769
    Sureties: Samuel Biddle, Alphanso Cosdon.
    Legatees: wife (unnamed), Mary (sister).
    Residue to (equally): wife (unnamed), sister (unnamed).
    Administratrix: Rebecca Sutton (late Rebecca Bully), wife of Mr. Ashberry
        Sutton.

John Twyford   5.215   D   DO   £350.14.4   Aug 9 1769
    Sureties: John Merine, James Smith.
    Legatees: Elisabeth Harper.
    Residue to: John Twyford (grandson).
    Executor: John Twyford.

James Hamilton   5.215   D   QA   £241.11.8   May 25 1769
    Sureties: Morgan Brown, John Watson.
    Distribution to (equally): James (son), John Hamilton, Sarah Hamilton, Ann
        Hamilton, Mary Ann Hamilton.
    Executors: MM John Hamilton, Thomas Bourne.

John Boyer   5.215   D   QA   £44.16.6   Jun 14 1769
    Sureties: Valentine Burroughs, James Burroughs.
    Distribution to: widow (unnamed).
    Executrix: Mary Watson, wife of Mr. Pryor Watson.

Thomas Morton   5.216   D   TA   £87.13.0   Jun 6 1769
    Sureties: Thomas Beall, James Morton.
    Legatees (children): John, James, Thomas, Margaret Vincent, Henry, Jonathon,
        Elisabeth, Mary Ann.
    Residue to: Mary (widow, accountant).
    Executrix: Mrs. Mary Morton.

William Meek   5.216   D   CE   £36.8.4   May 31 1769
    Sureties: Robert Williams, Patrick McGarrity.
    Legatees: James (son).
    Distribution to: Ann (widow, accountant, 1/3). Residue to (equally): William,
        Jane.
    Administratrix: Mrs. Ann Meek.

Jacob Evertson   5.217   D   CE   £765.0.10   May 31 1769
    Sureties: Charles Heath, James Heath.
    Legatees: Esther (widow, accountant), Elisabeth (daughter), Rebecca Alfree
        (daughter).
    Distribution to: Esther (widow, accountant, 1/3). Residue to children (equally):
        Elisabeth, Rachel, Jacob, Evert, Easther, Barnet, Frederick.
    Executrix: Mrs. Easter Evertson.

Mary Hyland   5.217   D CE   £471.12.2   Jun 27 1769
See also Folio 130, Liber E. V. #2 (Liber 6).
    Sureties: Edward Mitchell, John Read.
    Legatees (children): Rachel, Edward, Jacob, Elisabeth, Sampson, Mary.
    Residue to: the same.
    Executor: Mr. Nicholas Hyland.

Thomas Wingate   5.218   D DO   £193.8.9   Jun 2 1769
    Sureties: James Busick, James Moore.
    Legatees (granddaughters): Delilah Adams, Sarah Adams.
    Executor: Philip Wingate.

David Evans   5.218   D BA   £129.9.7   Oct 16 1769
Some legacies in Pensilvania currency.
    Sureties: Thomas Strat (?), Hugh Brierly.
    Legatees: daughter (unnamed).
    Distribution to: Margaret (widow, 1/3). Residue to children (equally): David
        (under 21), Margaret.
    Executrix: Margaret Evans.

Charles Drury   5.219   D AA   £2334.19.7   Jul 15 1769
    Sureties: Samuel Lane, Thomas Stockett.
    Legatees (daughters): Sarah, Elisabeth, Margaret, Mary, Ann, Easter.
    Distribution to: Mary (widow, accountant, 1/3). Residue to 3 sons & 6 daughters
        (equally): William, Samuel, Charles, Sarah, Elisabeth, Margaret, Mary, Ann,
        Easter.
    Administratrix: Mrs. Mary Drury.

Christopher Green   5.219   D QA   £286.1.8   Feb 1 1770
    Sureties: Robert Walters, John Seeders.
    Distribution to: Widow (unnamed, 1/3). Residue to sons (equally): Philemon, John
        (since dead, redistributed to the others).
    Administratrix: Sarah Hackett, wife of John Hackett.

Thomas Odell   5.220   D FR   £202.0.10   Sep 16 1769
    Sureties: William Offutt, James Offutt.
    Distribution to: Widow (unnamed, 1/3). Residue to 3 children (equally): Baruch,
        Eleaner, Sarah.
    Administratrix: Kesiah Beall, wife of Zephaniah Beall.

Adam Hiltibrand   5.220   D FR   £82.9.0   Sep 23 1769
    Sureties: Jacob Staley, John Stull.
    Distribution to: Widow (unnamed, 1/3). Residue to 4 children (equally): Jacob,
        Joseph, Mary, Philipina.
    Administrators: Christopher Stull, Ann Maria Hiltibrand.

George Fenwick   5.220   D SM   £253.5.7   Jul 18 1769
    Sureties: Enoch Fenwick, Cornelius Wildman.
    Distribution to: Representatives unknown to this Office.
    Administratrix: Belinda Fenwick, wife of Robert Fenwick.

Joshua Burton   5.221   D WO   £1030.7.10   Aug 12 1769
    Sureties: Levin Derrickson, John Waples.
    Distribution to: accountant in right of his wife (unnamed, widow, 1/3). Residue
        to 4 children (unnamed, equally).
    Administrator (de bonis non): William Tunnell.

Joseph Dirickson   5.221   D WO   £761.3.8   Feb 3 1770
    Sureties: George Spencer, Abraham Davis.
    Legatees: Mary (wife), Levin (son), Betty Vaughan (daughter), Mitchel (son),
        Joseph (son), Molly (daughter), Nancy Miller (daughter), Samuel (son).
    Distribution to: Widow (unnamed, 1/3). Residue to 7 children (abovenamed,
        equally).
    Executor: Levin Dirickson.

James Elder   5.222   D AA   £360.6.4   Nov 15 1769
    Sureties: Caleb Davis, Samuel Riggs.
    Distribution to: Rachel (widow, 1/3). Residue to 8 children (unnamed, equally).
    Administrator: Mr. John Elder.

Jacob Brunner   5.222   D FR   £117.9.8   Jul 28 1768
    Sureties: John Brunner, Jacob Brunner.
    Distribution to: Widow (unnamed, 1/3). Residue to 4 children (unnamed, equally).
    Administrator: Mr. Stephen Ransberg.

John Ridgley   5.222   D AA   £72.8.8   Jun 26 1769
    Sureties: Benjamin Yieldhall, John Frazier.
    Distribution to: Widow (unnamed, 1/3). Residue to 5 children (unnamed, equally).
    Administratrix: Mrs. Elisabeth Ridgley.

```
Robert Wilson                  5.223    D   TA   £253.7.5     Oct 12 1769
Updated 23 August 1773.
    Sureties: Daniel Killiam.
    Legatees: Robert Pickering (son-in-law), John (son), Robert (son), Catharine
        (daughter), Deborah Wilson (granddaughter).
    Residue to (equally): Robert Pickering (son-in-law), John Wilson, Robert Wilson,
        Catharine Wilson, Deborah Wilson.
    Executor: Mr. Robert Pickering.

Ann Bishop                     5.223    D   QA   £171.18.5    Jun 1 1769
    Sureties: Edward Clayton, Robert Walters.
    Distribution to 5 children (equally): William, Elijah, Risdon, Richard, Smyth.
    Administrator: Mr. Elijah Bishop.

John Webster                   5.224    D   BA   £31.19.8     Oct 16 1769
    Sureties: Abraham Andrews, Asael Gittings.
    Distribution to: Widow (unnamed, 1/3).
    Executrix: Mary Lynch, wife of John Lynch.

Thomas Lewis                   5.224    D   KE   £63.15.9     Nov 1 1769
    Sureties: William Ringgold, Thomas Ringgold, Jr.
    Executor: Thomas Ringgold.

Daniel Killey                  5.224    D   WO   £239.19.4    Jan 23 1770
    Sureties: John Newbold, Charles Polk.
    Legatees: Elisabeth (accountant), George Kelley, John Kelley, Daniel Kelley (son
        of John Kelley), William Kelley, Barsheba Williams.
    Distribution to: Widow (unnamed, 1/3). Residue to (equally): George Kelley,
        William Kelley, Worrington Volk.
    Executrix: Elisabeth Killey.

John Graham                    5.225    D   KE   £1398.16.2   Nov 16 1769
    Sureties: Isaac Spencer, John Commegys.
    Legatees: widow (unnamed), Andrew (son), James (son), John (son), Elisabeth
        (daughter), Mary (daughter), William (son), Robert (son), Sarah Cooper.
    Distribution to: Widow (unnamed, 1/3). Residue to 7 children (equally): Andrew,
        John, Elisabeth, Mary, William, Robert, Ann.
    Executor: William St. Clair and his wife Mary, Andrew Graham.

Daniel Clocker                 5.225    D   SM   £64.4.3      Dec 24 1769
    Sureties: John Simmons, Charles Smith.
    Distribution to: wife (unnamed) during widowhood; then to 6 children: Benjamin,
        Mary, Elisabeth, Daniel, William, Ann.
    Executrix: Rebecca Clocker.

Jeremiah Collins               5.225    D   KE   £48.18.4     Nov 28 1769
    Sureties: Thomas Ringgold.
    Legatees: Mary Colsley, John Collins.
    Residue to (equally): Mary Colsley, Nancy Colsley, Elisabeth Collings, Martha
        Collings, Sarah Collings.
    Executor: Nathaniel Hynson.

Mary Brown                     5.226    D   BA   £37.10.9     Sep 4 1769
    Sureties: Benjamin Guyton.
    Distribution to: Robert Dutton (brother).
    Executor: Robert Dutton.

William Pritchett              5.226    D   FR   £572.2.3     Sep 16 1769
    Sureties: James Doull, Alexander Offutt.
    Legatees: wife (unnamed), Mary (daughter).
    Distribution to: Widow (unnamed, 1/3). Residue to children (equally): 2 sons
        (unnamed), Jane.
    Executrix: Kesiah Beall, wife of Zephaniah Beall.

Richard Conner                 5.226    D   WO   £43.8.2      Dec 15 1769
    Sureties: Thomas Davis, Isaac Pain.
    Distribution to: Representatives unknown to this Office.
    Administratrix: Elisabeth Bishop, wife of Jos. Bishop.

Thomas Miller                  5.227    D   KE   £603.2.1     Jun 10 1769
    Sureties: Charles Groome, Richard Hozier.
    Distribution to: Widow (unnamed, 1/3). Residue to children (unnamed, equally).
    Executrix: Jane Miller.

Roger Bishop                   5.227    D   BA   £154.5.4     Aug 22 1769
    Sureties: Gilbert Crockett, Roger Bishop.
    Distribution to: Avis (widow, accountant) during her lifetime; then to children
        (unnamed).
    Executrix: Avis Bishop.
```

Vincent Blackiston   5.227   D KE   £540.7.8   Aug 17 1769
    Sureties: George Copper, John Gearly.
    Distribution to: Susannah (accountant) during natural life or widowhood.
    Executrix: Susannah Blackiston.

Henry Goldsberry   5.227   D SM   £98.13.11   Dec 24 1769
    Sureties: Justinian Mills, Mathew Clark.
    Distribution to: Representatives unknown to this Office.
    Administratrix: Jane Raley, wife of Henry Raley.

John Tennison   5.228   D SM   £328.9.1   Oct 25 1769
    Sureties: John Cole, Francis Swale.
    Distribution to: Abraham (father).
    Executor (surviving): Jesse Tennison.

John Mairman   5.228   D SM   £724.7.8   Jun 7 1769
    Sureties: Cyrus Vowles, John Johnson.
    Distribution to: Ann (widow, accountant) during her lifetime.
    Executrix: Ann Mairman.

Henry Shiercliff   5.228   D SM   £36.0.6   May 7 1769
    Sureties: Thomas Shanks, Ignatius Fenwick.
    Distribution to: Widow (unnamed) during her lifetime; then to children: Joseph,
        Thomas, Mary.
    Executrix: Mary Shiercliff.

Thomas Dyar   5.229   D PG   £756.12.8   Nov 28 1769
    Sureties: James Marshall, Richard Henderson.
    Legatees (children): Edward, Elisabeth.
    Distribution to: Widow (unnamed, 1/3). Residue to children (unnamed, except
        Edward (son), equally).
    Executors: Henrietta Dyer, Thomas Clement Dyer.

Christopher Spry   5.229   D QA   £156.13.4   Nov 6 1769
    Sureties: William Ridgaway, James Hammond.
    Legatees: Mary (widow, accountant), Christopher (son), George (son), Humphry
        (son).
    Distribution to: Mary (widow, accountant, 1/3). Residue to 5 children (equally):
        Rebecca, Humphry, Mary, John, Abraham.
    Executors: Mary Spry, George Spry, Humphry Spry.

Ann Haley   5.229   D KE   £93.10.0   Oct 12 1769
    Sureties: William Merritt, Thomas Boyer.
    Distribution to: Representatives unknown to this Office.
    Administrator (de bonis non): Christopher Hall.

Daniel Page   5.230   D PG   £576.1.5   Aug 23 1769
    Sureties: Charles Butler, Thomas Contee.
    Legatees (daughters): Elisabeth Morris, Lucy Hodgkin, Mary Boone, Susannah
        Lanham, Rachel Hodgkin, Mildred Berry.
    Distribution to: Widow (unnamed, 1/3). Residue to 3 sons (equally): Daniel,
        George, Anthony Deane Page.
    Executor: Daniel Page.

Mr. Samuel Chew (Wells)   5.230   D AA   £3119.12.10   Dec 6 1769
    Sureties: David Weems, William Lock.
    Legatees: Elisabeth (daughter).
    Distribution to: Sarah (widow, accountant, 1/3). Residue to 4 children
        (equally): Samuel, John, William, Elisabeth.
    Executrix: Mrs. Sarah Chew.

William Commegys   5.230   D KE   £265.0.1   Jul 26 1769
    Sureties: Bartus Comegys, Philemon Pratt.
    Distribution to: Representatives unknown to this Office.
    Administratrix: Aleatha Vansant, wife of Peter Vansant.

Francis Pickering   5.231   D TA   £470.3.4   Oct 12 1769
New balance on Folio 261 (actually folio 361).
    Sureties: James Gibson, Daniel Killam.
    Legatees (children): Robert, Mary Wilson.
    Distribution to: Margaret (widow, 1/3). Residue to children (unnamed, equally).
    Executors (one of them): Mr. Robert Pickering.

Thomas Stansbury   5.231   D BA   £867.8.11   Jun 27 1769
The amount of the accounts also included £32.11.9 sterling.
    Sureties: Henry Stevenson (Brittain Ridge), William Stansbury.
    Legatees: Edmund (son).
    Distribution to: Widow (unnamed, 1/3). Residue to children (equally): John,
        Thomas, Daniel, Dickson, Edmund, Jemima Lynch.
    Executor: Mr. John Stansbury.

Richard Robinett   5.231   D KE   £52.9.10   Aug 19 1769
    Sureties: Sanders Bostock, Robert Nap Choir.
    Distribution to: Representatives unknown to this Office.
    Administratrix: Mary Robinett.

John Everet   5.232   D BA   £296.2.0   Jun 19 1769
    Sureties: James Osborn, William Osborn.
    Legatees (children): Ann, James (under 18), John (under 18). Some legacies to be
        paid in 1775.
    Distribution to: Widow (unnamed, 1/3).
    Executrix: Martha Hollis, wife of Mr. Amos Hollis.

John Graham   5.232   D SO   £381.11.5   Jun 29 1769
    Sureties: Robert Collier, Robert Dashiell.
    Distribution to: Philip (brother).
    Administrator: Mr. Philip Graham.

John Cave   5.232   D SO   £30.9.8   Jul 12 1769
    Sureties: Hezekiah Reed, James Read.
    Distribution to: Ann (accountant).
    Administratrix: Mrs. Ann Cave.

Daniel Walter   5.233   D FR   £81.14.3   Jun 24 1769
    Sureties: James Fyffe, Arthur Hickman.
    Legatees: John (son), Clement (son), William (son), Levi (son), Sarah (daughter),
        David Osborn (grandson), Mary Osborn (granddaughter).
    Distribution to: Widow (unnamed, 1/3). Residue to children (equally): John,
        Samuel, George, Clement, William, Levi, Ann Osborn, Sarah.
    Executor: John Walter.

James Pelly   5.233   D FR   £122.19.11   Jun 24 1769
    Sureties: William Thompson, John Fletchall.
    Distribution to: Widow (unnamed, 1/3). Residue to 2 daughters (equally): Mary,
        Ann.
    Executor (surviving): Mr. Harrison Pelly.

Benjamin Foreman   5.233   D KE   £56.8.2   Jul 31 1769
    Sureties: Nathaniel Kennard, John Buck.
    Distribution to: Representatives unknown to this Office.
    Administrator: Abraham Cannell.

Stevens White   5.234   D SO   £551.14.7   Jun 6 1769
    Sureties: Jacob Adams, Jr., John Collins.
    Legatees: Betty (wife).
    Residue to (equally): wife (unnamed), William Stevens White (son).
    Executor: Mr. Elias White.

William Trew   5.234   D KE   £362.3.8   Jun 2 1769
    Sureties: John Sutton, Pearce Lamb.
    Legatees: Mary (wife), children: Elisabeth, Sarah, Mary, William, John.
    Distribution to: Widow (unnamed, 1/3). Residue to children (unnamed, equally).
    Executrix: Mary Hastings, wife of Mr. George Hastings.

Thomas Noble   5.234   D PG   £764.4.7   Mar 18 1769
Lives in Frederick. (This is a note in the margin, but I am not sure for whom.)
    Sureties: Enoch Magruder, Robert Wade.
    Distribution to: Representatives unknown to this Office.
    Administratrix: Mary An Gilbert, wife of Francis Gilbert.

John Hufman   5.235   D FR   £918.6.6   Jul 2 1769
    Sureties: Elias Brummer, Conrod Grosh.
    Distribution to: widow (unnamed) during natural life or widowhood.
    Executors: Mr. George Hufman, Barbara Cart (formerly Barbara Hufman).

Dr. Edward Wakeman   5.235   D BA   £1483.17.8   Mar 31 1769
    Legatees: Elisabeth (daughter), Sarah (daughter), Mary (daughter), James
        Pritchard (son-in-law), Thomas Tredway, John Atkinson.
    Executor: Mr. John Hall of Cranbury.

Isaac Redgrave   5.235   D KE   £168.9.0   Jun 14 1769
    Sureties: Joseph Stavely, James Stavely.
    Distribution to (equally): wife (unnamed), unmarried children (unnamed).
    Executors: MM Isaac Redgrave, William Redgrave.

Richard Hendon   5.236   D BA   £43.13.0   Apr 5 1769
    Sureties: George Crudgington, George Consilman.
    Legatees: Sarah (wife), Lydia (daughter), Benjamin Hendon & Dinah Hendon
        (children of Joseph Hendon (son)).
    Distribution to (equally): wife (unnamed), children (unnamed).
    Executors: Richard Hendon, Henry Hendon.

Thomas Dudley   5.236   D   TA   £286.1.7   Aug 15 1769
    Sureties: Edward Clark, Jr., Caleb Clark.
    Legatees: Jane (daughter).
    Distribution to: Accountant (widow, 1/3). Residue to (equally): Jane Dudley,
        William Dudley, Richard Dudley.
    Executrix: Mary Dudley.

William Seal   5.236   D   BA   £429.1.11   Jun 26 1769
    Sureties: Martin Brice, John Bacon.
    Distribution to: Priscilla (wife) during natural life or widowhood.
    Executor: William Horton.

Abraham Collins   5.237   D   DO   £236.12.10   Aug 9 1769
    Sureties: Samuel Andrew, John Andrew.
    Legatees: Ann (wife), Abraham Collings (son), Isaac Collings (son), Ann Harris
        (daughter), Wilfred (daughter).
    Distribution to: Ann (wife, 1/3).
    Executor: Mr. Abraham Collins.

Summer Adams   5.237   D   DO   £32.15.4   Aug 9 1769
    Sureties: McNemarra Adams, John Woodland.
    Legatees: Nancy (daughter), Sarah (wife), heirs (unnamed) of Rose Hurley
        (daughter).
    Residue to (equally): Sarah (wife), Nancy (daughter), Rachel (daughter).
    Executors: Sarah Adams, John Woodland and his wife Nancy Woodland.

Susannah Boult   5.237   D   SM   £109.10.0   Sep 16 1769
    Sureties: John Tarlton, Jesse Tennison.
    Distribution to: Representatives unknown to this Office.
    Administrators: Mrs. Mary Boult, John Parlton (son of James Parlton).

Roger Smith   5.238   D   CH   £1340.7.4   Nov 6 1769
    Sureties: James Crack, Henry Hagan.
    Distribution to: Henrietta (wife).
    Executrix: Henrietta Wheeler, wife of Ignatius Wheeler, Jr.

Valentine Green   5.238   D   QA   £410.16.5   Aug 10 1769
    Sureties: Thomas Hardcastle, Robert Hardcastle.
    Legatees: Sarah (wife), children: Valentine (eldest), John, Ann, Rachel.
    Distribution to: Sarah (wife, 1/3). Residue to 4 children (equally): Valentine,
        John, Ann, Rachel.
    Executrix: Sarah Casson, wife of John Casson.

Rev. Alexander Adams   5.238   D   AA   £1426.9.9   Aug 14 1769
    Sureties: Abraham Simmonds, Richard Wells.
    Distribution to: Representatives unknown to this Office.
    Administratrix: Mrs. Sarah Adams of Somerset County.

Jane Penn   5.239   D   CH   £161.2.7   Jul 3 1769
    Sureties: Stephen Compton, Wilson Cage.
    Legatees: Jane Bateman (granddaughter), Joseph King (grandson).
    Residue to (equally): Elisabeth Bateman (daughter), Benjamin Bateman (grandson).
    Executor: Benjamin Bateman, Jr.

Isaiah Cheney   5.239   D   AA   £39.16.9   Jun 14 1769
    Sureties: Joseph Leek, Philip Chambers.
    Distribution to: Rachel (accountant, 1/3). Residue to children (unnamed,
        equally).
    Executrix: Mrs. Rachel Cheney.

Ford Barnes   5.240   D   BA   £199.1.4   Jul 5 1769
    Sureties: Joseph Smith, Amos Garrett.
    Distribution to: Ruth (widow, accountant, 1/3). Residue to 4 children (equally):
        Bennett, Richard, Arrabella, Amos.
    Executrix: Mrs. Ruth Barnes.

William Insley   5.240   D   DO   £66.16.8   Jun 2 1769
    Sureties: Andrew Insley, Jacob Insley.
    Distribution to: Betty (widow, 1/3).
    Executor: William Insley.

Thomas Bunt   5.240   D   DO   £38.5.11   Nov 15 1769
    Sureties: Benjamin Woodard, Henry Brannock.
    Distribution to: Elisabeth (widow).
    Administratrix: Elisabeth Blunt.

Richard Dove   5.241   D DO   £109.14.5   Aug 28 1769
    Sureties: James Edmondson, Lawrence James.
    Legatees: Isaac Dove (son of Isaac Dove).
    Residue to: Hannah (widow).
    Executrix: Hannah Falkner, wife of Thomas Falkner, Jr.

Richard Simmonds   5.241   D KE   £314.11.0   May 30 1769
    Sureties: Charles Baker, Robert George.
    Legatees: Sarah (widow, accountant).
    Executrix: Mrs. Sarah Simmonds.

John Selby   5.241   D AA   £226.13.4   Apr 7 1769
    Sureties: Elijah Green, John Ducker.
    Distribution to: accountant (widow) during her lifetime.
    Executrix: Mrs. Jemima Selby.

William Davis   5.242   D WO   £93.4.9   Jul 1 1769
    Sureties: Stephen Atkins, Levin Disharoon.
    Distribution to: Widow (unnamed) during lifetime.
    Executrix: Mrs. Patience Davis.

Zachariah Lanham   5.242   D PG   £448.4.7   Jul 20 1769
    Sureties: Thomas Blacklock, John Smith.
    Distribution to: Representatives unknown to this Office.
    Administratrix: Mary Lanham.

Nathaniel Hynson   5.242   D QA   £23.15.3   Oct 7 1769
    Sureties: William Meridith, Benjamin Meridith.
    Distribution to: Representatives unknown to this Office.
    Administrator: Mr. Richard Hynson.

Clement Christopher   5.242   D SO   £35.4.7   Jul 13 1769
    Sureties: John Christopher, Thomas Collins.
    Distribution to: Representatives unknown to this Office.
    Administrator: Mr. Sarah Christopher.

John Cleaver   5.243   D KE   £145.5.9   May 31 1769
    Sureties: Joseph Cox Thomas, William Cleaver.
    Distribution to: Representatives unknown to this Office.
    Administratrix: Mrs. Mary Cleaver.

Joseph Parsons   5.243   D KE   £351.5.3   May 31 1769
    Sureties: John Myers, James Welch.
    Distribution to: Representatives unknown to this Office.
    Administratrix: Margaret Pratt, wife of Mr. Thomas Pratt.

John Woodard   5.243   D KE   £9.0.6   Jun 26 1769
    Sureties: Kirvin Wroth, William Copper.
    Distribution to: Representatives unknown to this Office.
    Administrator: Mr. John Meeks.

Samuel Groome   5.243   D KE   £1189.3.1   Jun 7 1769
    Sureties: William Cowarden.
    Distribution to: Representatives unknown to this Office.
    Administrators: Mr. Charles Groome, John Waltham.

Thomas Trussell   5.244   D BA   £15.14.9   May 22 1769
    Sureties: Jacob Giles.
    Distribution to: Representatives unknown to this Office.
    Administrator: Mr. Amos Garrett.

John Gale, Jr.   5.244   D KE   £152.8.7   Jun 3 1769
    Sureties: Andrew Tolson, Marmaduke Medford.
    Distribution to: Representatives unknown to this Office.
    Administratrix: Mrs. Phebe Gale.

Richard Scrivener   5.244   D AA   £303.4.6   May 23 1769
    Sureties: Morgan Jones, John Batson.
    Distribution to: Representatives unknown to this Office.
    Administratrix: Mary Scrivener.

Thomas Jefferies   5.244   D BA   £164.11.4   Jun 26 1769
    Sureties: James Armstrong, Andrew Cunningham.
    Distribution to: Representatives unknown to this Office.
    Administratrix: Mrs. Martha Jeferies.

Catharine Vannetson   5.245   D WO   £47.19.10   Jun 10 1769
    Sureties: Joseph Brotherer, John Wingate.
    Distribution to: Representatives unknown to this Office.
    Administratrix: Mrs. Catharine Jester.

Robert Yeats   5.245   D KE   £179.8.3   May 29 1769
    Sureties: Cooler Griffith, John Kennard.
    Distribution to: Representatives unknown to this Office.
    Administratrix: Jane Yeats.

Henry Hozier   5.245   D KE   £763.11.10   Aug 15 1769
    Sureties: Thomas Smith, Richard Hozier.
    Distribution to: Representatives unknown to this Office.
    Administratrix: Rebecca Hozier.

William Billingsley   5.245   D SM   £297.5.2   1769
    Sureties: Benjamin Stevens, William Pruce.
    Distribution to: Representatives unknown to this Office.
    Administratrix: Jane Billingsley.

Folios 246 through 345 do not exist.

William Saunders   5.346   D FR   £110.3.6   Aug 24 1769
The amount of the accounts also included #3737.
    Sureties: Thomas Gore, John Wood.
    Distribution to: Representatives unknown to this Office.
    Administrator: William Saunders.

Isaac Horrell   5.346   D SM   £48.3.10   Nov 24 1769
    Sureties: John Mills, William Rapeur.
    Distribution to: Representatives unknown to this Office.
    Administrator: John Baptist Greaves.

Moses Goodwin   5.346   D BA   £782.3.2   Aug 3 1769
    Distribution to: Representatives unknown to this Office.
    Administratrix: Rachel Goodwin.

James Robertson   5.346   D SO   £103.14.10   Apr 4 1769
    Sureties: William Badley, James Taylor.
    Residue to: James (son).
    Administrator: John Robertson.

John Woodward   5.347   D CH   £112.11.8   May 8 1769
    Sureties: William Dunnington, William Mathews.
    Legatees: Mary Risen (daughter), Violetta (daughter), Sarah Macpherson
        (granddaughter).
    Distribution to: wife (unnamed) during her lifetime; then to children: Sarah
        Harrison, Lovereta Young.
    Administrators: William Risen, Joseph Macpherson.

Edward Short   5.347   D WO   £228.3.2   Aug 2 1769
    Sureties: John Weavers, George Hopkins.
    Legatees: Shadrack Short, Philip Short, Jacob Short, Elisabeth Tindal, Edward
        Short, Isaac Short (under 19), William Short, John Short.
    Distribution to: Widow (unnamed, 1/3). Residue to children (unnamed, equally).
    Executors: Elisabeth Short, Edward Short.

Thomas Buswell   5.348   D KE   £111.0.6   Mar 24 1769
Cites a bond due in Baltimore County.
    Sureties: Stephen Bordley, Arthur Miller.
    Legatees: George Chambly (son-in-law), Bridget Agin, Thomas Allum, Joseph
        Jackson.
    Mentions: Joseph Jackson (servant), John Carvill, John Andrews, George Daws, John
        Bolton, John Rolph, Mr. Arthur Miller.
    Executor: Mr. Arthur Miller.

Leonard Snavely   5.348   D FR   £122.2.1   Jun 23 1769
    Sureties: Martin Casner, John Flanner.
    Legatees: widow (unnamed), Elisabeth (daughter) books of 1st wife (unnamed).
    Residue to (equally): widow (unnamed), children (unnamed).
    Executor: Mr. Henry Snavely.

Jonathon Cottingham   5.349   D WO   £39.12.0   Jun 23 1769
    Sureties: John McCuddy, Rowland Beavins.
    Legatees: Jonathon (son, has items in Kent on Delaware), William (son), Daniel
        (son), Mary Nicholson (daughter).
    Residue to: Margaret (wife) during her lifetime; then to children: Sarah Laws
        (1/6), Elisha Cottingham (5/12), Thomas Cottingham (5/12).
    Executor (surviving): Mr. William Cottingham.

Joshua Merrill   5.349   D   WO   £492.15.10   Jun 3 1769
The amount of the accounts also included #117.
    Sureties: Littleton Dennis, Isaac Layfield.
    Legatees: widow (unnamed), children: William, Joshua, Sarah, Betty, Leah.
    Distribution to: Widow (unnamed, 1/3). Residue to 8 children (equally): William,
        Sarah, Betty, Leah, Nancy, Elenor, Joshua, Anne.
    Executrix: Mrs. Mary Merrill.

Esther Crapper   5.350   D   WO   £66.16.0   May 23 1769
    Sureties: Hezekiah Purnell, Samuel Hopkins.
    Legatees: Sarah Ardis, Sarah Wolton (granddaughter), Mary Jones, Esther Jennet.
    Residue to (equally): issue of Sarah Ardis (daughter), issue of Mary Jones
        (daughter), Sarah Wolton (granddaughter).
    Executor: Benjamin Aydelott.

Richard Meekins   5.350   D   DO   £39.8.2   Nov 9 1769
    Sureties: Thomas Wroughton, David Liddell.
    Legatees: Henry (son), Joshua (son), Mary Johnson (daughter), Sarah Ruark
        (daughter), Ann Phillips (daughter), Mathew (son), Benedict (son), Ezekiel
        (son), Henry Holten Meekins (grandson), Elisabeth Meekins (granddaughter).
    Distribution to: Widow (unnamed, 1/3). Residue to: Denwood (youngest son).
    Executrix: Hannah Ruark, wife of Mr. Robert Ruark.

Thomas Andrews   5.351   D   DO   £322.18.0   Oct 19 1769
    Sureties: William Cannon, Charles Brown.
    Legatees: Betsy (daughter) wife of Anderton Brown, Thomas (son), Rebecca
        (daughter).
    Distribution to: widow (unnamed) during lifetime; then to children: Thomas,
        Rebecca.
    Executrix: Mrs. Elisabeth Andrews.

William Husband   5.352   D   CE   £1252.17.6   Jun 12 1769
    Sureties: Benjamin Rumsey, James Hart.
    Legatees: Thomas (son), William Porter (grandson), Hannah (daughter), Margery
        (daughter), Ann (daughter), Sarah (daughter).
    Residue to 5 daughters (equally): Hannah, Mary, Margery, Ann, Sarah.
    Executor: Mr. William Husband.

James Hendley   5.352   D   QA   £334.4.0   Oct 5 1769
    Sureties: Edward Wright, William Brown.
    Legatees: widow (unnamed), James (son), William (son), Elisabeth (daughter).
    Distribution to: Widow (unnamed, 1/3).
    Executrix: Mrs. Eve Hendley.

Absalom Tennison   5.353   D   SM   £63.16.3   Nov 16 1769
    Sureties: John Cole, Francis Swabb.
    Legatees: Christian (daughter), Sarah Doxey, Sebo Corror, Thomas Tennison, Ann
        (daughter), Elisabeth Tennison, Absalom Tennison.
    Distribution to: Widow (unnamed, 1/3).
    Executor: Jesse Tennison.

Theophilus Randal   5.353   D   KE   £636.16.8   Oct 7 1769
    Sureties: John Ecleston, Philip Warner.
    Distribution to: Widow (unnamed, 1/3). Residue to children & grandchildren
        (unnamed, equally).
    Executor: Mr. Samuel Wallis.

John Houston   5.354   D   WO   £638.1.1   Aug 21 1769
    Sureties: John Collins, Robert Mitchell.
    Legatees: John (son).
    Distribution to: Widow (unnamed, 1/3). Residue to: Robert (son).
    Executor: Robert Houston.

John Ryan   5.354   D   AA   £784.6.2   Oct 10 1769
    Sureties: Henry Griffith, Edward Norwood.
    Legatees (children): Benjamin, William, John, Ruth Shanks, Mary Penn, Rachel
        Elder, Rebeccah, Robert, Joseph.
    Distribution to: Widow (unnamed, 1/3). Residue to (equally): Jacob Ryan,
        Susannah Ryan, Rachel Ryan, Charity Ryan, Rebeccah Ryan, Ann Ryan.
    Executrix: Mary Warfield, wife of Vachel Warfield.

Elisabeth Davis   5.355   D TA   £688.2.2   Aug 15 1769
    Sureties: Pewter Comerford, Joseph Bewley.
    Legatees: Ann Oldham (cousin, daughter of Edward Oldham), Mary Markland (cousin,
        daughter of Edward Oldham), Elisabeth Oldham (cousin, daughter of Edward
        Oldham), Peter Eaton, Jane Trotter (cousin), Hannah Harding (cousin, daughter
        of Edward Harding), Ann Harding (cousin, daughter of Edward Harding), Martha
        Harding (cousin, daughter of Edward Harding), Rachel Harding (cousin, daughter
        of Edward Harding).
    Residue to 3 cousins: ------ (name not given, daughter of Edward Harding), Ann
        Oldham & Elisabeth Oldham (daughters of Edward Oldham).
    Administrator: Joshua Clark.

Solomon Yewell   5.355   D QA   £83.3.7   Mar 8 1770
    Sureties: Solomon Slaughter Yewell, Christopher Yewell.
    Distribution to: Widow (unnamed, 1/3). Residue to: William Seeder (son of widow,
        his share of his father's (unnamed) estate), Isaac Yewell (his share of his
        father's (unnamed) estate), all children (unnamed) by both marriages.
    Executrix: Margaret Yewell.

Dr. John Jackson   5.356   D QA   £2093.16.7   Mar 13 1770
The amount of the accounts also included £117.8.6 sterling. Amended 3 September 1771.
    Sureties: James Hollyday, James Earle.
    Legatees: Edward (son, died before testator).
    Distribution to: Widow (unnamed, 1/3). Residue to 7 children (equally):
        Elisabeth, Rachel, Catharine, Christopher, William Finny Jackson, John,
        Walter.
    Executrix: Catharine Jackson.

Alexander Robertson   5.356   D QA   £298.9.2   Aug 17 1769
    Sureties: Francis Stevens, Joseph Tarboten.
    Legatees: Daniel (son).
    Distribution to: Widow (unnamed, 1/3). Residue to 2 children (equally).
    Executrix: Catha West, wife of John West.

Justinian Burch   5.357   D CH   £160.13.1   Feb 19 1770
    Sureties: Bennett Dyson, John Noe.
    Legatees: widow (unnamed) then to Susannah Maddox, widow (unnamed) then to
        Leonard Burch, Leonard Burch, Justinian Thomas Burch, Benjamin Burch, widow
        (unnamed) then to Sarah Burch, Sarah Burch, Ann Burch.
    Executrix: Ann Burch.

Edward Northcraft   5.358   D FR   £454.9.1   Apr 28 1768
The amount of the accounts also included #2826.
    Sureties: John Seger, John Fryor.
    Legatees: Elisabeth (widow), children: Richard, Susannah Cullom, Frances, Ann,
        Mary Ann.
    Distribution to: Elisabeth (widow, 1/3). Residue to 6 children (equally):
        Richard, Edward, Susannah, Frances, Ann, Mary Ann.
    Executrix: Elisabeth Hook (formerly Elisabeth Northcraft).

Benjamin Brown   5.358   D AA   £242.7.0   Apr 18 1770
    Sureties: John Frost, Aquilla Randall.
    Legatees: Benjamin Brown, Rachel Todd, Ruth Todd.
    Distribution to: Widow (unnamed, 1/3). Residue to (equally): Joshua Brown,
        Vachel Brown, Susannah Brown, Richard Brown, Charles Brown, Ephraim Brown,
        Rebeccah Brown, Benjamin Brown.
    Executors: Susannah Brown, Samuel Brown.

Oneal Price   5.359   D QA   £817.8.6   Jun 22 1770
    Sureties: James Miller, Charles Downes, Jr.
    Distribution to: Hester (widow, accountant, 1/3). Residue to 7 children
        (equally): Neal, James, Mary, Ann, Edward, John, William.
    Administrators: Mr. John Meeds and his wife Hester Meeds, Charles Price.

John Merrill   5.360   D WO   £116.7.7   Aug 2 1768
    Legatees: William (son).
    Residue to children (unnamed, equally).
    Executor: John Merrill.

Everhart Apler   5.360   D FR   £237.11.6   May 2 1770
    Sureties: Michael Ramer, John Horse.
    Legatees: Roshall (widow) then to Jacob (son), Easter (daughter), Elisabeth
        (daughter), Rosura (daughter).
    Executors: Balser Lambert, Ulrick Misler.

```
Francis Pickering              5.361    D  TA    £305.0.5     Aug 21 1770
Balance passed on 12 October 1769 is hereby annulled.
    Sureties: James Gibson, Daniel Killam.
    Legatees: Robert Pickering, Mary Wilson.
    Distribution to: Margaret (widow, 1/3).  Residue to children (unnamed, equally).
    Executor: Robert Pickering.

Sarah Roberts                  5.361    D  WO    £66.11.5     Sep 6 1766
    Legatees: Harriet (daughter).
    Residue to children (equally): Harriet, John.
    Administrator: Joseph Massey.

Samuel Brown                   5.362    D  TA    £137.13.1    Mar 11 1769
    Sureties: William Hayward, William Nicolls.
    Distribution to (equally): Cassandra (daughter by his last wife (unnamed)),
        surviving child (unnamed) by his former wife (unnamed).
    Administrator (de bonis non): Mr. John Stevens during the minority of William
        Brown (son).

Adam Meek                      5.362    D  CE    £463.6.8     Jun 27 1770
    Sureties: James Carson, Joseph Rutherford.
    Distribution to: Jane (one of accountants, 1/3).  Residue to children (equally):
        Rebecca, Mary, Jane, Margaret, Moses, Nancy, James, Adam.
    Executors: Jane Meek, Andrew Meek.

John Shepherd                  5.363    D  FR    £345.15.11   Aug 28 1770
Some legacies in Pensylvania money.
    Sureties: James Smith, Christopher Grinder.
    Legatees: widow (accountant), children: Thomas, William, Margaret, Druzilla
        (under age, unmarried), Sarah, Mary & Rebecca (twins, born since death of
        testator).
    Distribution to: Widow (unnamed, 1/3).
    Executrix: Sarah Burroughs, wife of John Burroughs.

John Disharoon                 5.364    D  WO    £366.10.9    May 6 1768
    Sureties: William Disharoon, Samuel Ingelsel.
    Legatees: Mary Disharoon, Elisabeth Disharoon.
    Mentions: wife (unnamed, died prior to deceased), Stephen (son, died prior to
        deceased), Samuel (son, infant, died 2 months after deceased), Ebe (daughter,
        born after making of will but prior to death of deceased).
    Residue to 7 children (equally): Obadiah, Thomas, George, Francis, Mary,
        Elisabeth, Ebe.
    Administrator: Obediah Disharoon.

James Offutt                   5.365    D  FR    £209.19.1    Aug 25 1769
    Distribution to: Widow (accountant, 1/3).  Residue to (equally): William Offutt,
        Rebeccah Offutt, Rachel Offutt, Hannah Offutt, Thomas Offutt.
    Executrix: Mrs. Sarah Offutt.

John Soper                     5.365    D  PG    £352.19.4    Nov 22 1770
    Sureties: John Hardy, Ignatius Hardy.
    Legatees (daughters): Mary, Susannah, Sarah.
    Distribution to: Widow (unnamed, 1/3).  Residue to (equally): John Soper, Charles
        Soper, Thomas Soper, James Soper, Nathan Soper, Basil Soper, Rachel Soper.
    Executor: Charles Soper.

Margaret Page                  5.366    D  AA    £269.6.7     Dec 3 1770
Executrix and residuary legatee of husband George Page.  Legatees of George Page: Mary
Evitts, George Pecker, Henry Todd, Richard Todd.
    Sureties: John Campbell, Phil. Hammond.
    Legatees: Mary Evitts (daughter), Henry Todd.
    Distribution to: Mary Evitts (1/2) held in trust by the executors.  Residue to
        (equally): George Pecker (under 21), Henry Todd (under 21), Richard Todd
        (under 21).
    Executors: Nathan Hammond, John Merriken.

Joseph Scrivener               5.367    D  QA    £255.17.1
    Sureties: John Meredith, William Wrench.
    Legatees: brother (unnamed).
    Distribution to: Widow (unnamed, 1/3).  Residue to 2 children (equally): William,
        Robert.
    Administrator: Mr. Isaac Scrivener.
```

Philip Key, Esq.   5.367   D SM   £1389.0.0   Dec 9 1769
The amount of the accounts also include £2112.16.11 sterling, #60857, and £3617.19.4 gold.
    Sureties: William Jordan, Jeremiah Jordan.
    Legatees: widow (unnamed), Thomas Key (accountant), Richard Ward Key, Philip Key, Susannah Gardiner, Francis Key, John Ross Key, Philip Barton Key, Elisabeth Scott, Susannah Gardiner Bruce, Elisabeth Mills, Roger Copocy, Norman Bruce.
    Residue to: Richard Ward Key (1/16), Susannah Gardiner Bruce (1/16), Philip Key (1/8), Susannah Gardiner Key (1/8), Edmund Key (1/8), Thomas Key (1/4), Francis Key (1/4).
    Executor (surviving): Mr. Thomas Key.

John Richardson   5.368   D AA   £236.0.6   Mar 3 1770
    Sureties: Capt. John Ijams, William Ijams.
    Distribution to: Representatives unknown to this Office.
    Administrator: Mr. Phillip Richardson.

Charles Hopkins   5.368   D DO   £75.14.1   Sep 11 1770
    Sureties: Joseph Brown, Richard Clarkson.
    Distribution to: Representatives unknown to this Office.
    Administrator: Mr. Charles Brown (son of Jos. Brown).

Thomas Ginn   5.369   D DO   £121.14.3   Jul 12 1770
    Sureties: Eliab Vinson, Thomas Smith (son of William Smith).
    Distribution to: Widow (unnamed, 1/3). Residue to 7 children (equally): James, Josiah, Anne, Samuel, Sarah, Thomas, Mary.
    Administratrix: Sicilly Ginn.

Ralp Holmes   5.369   D CH   £62.19.4   Aug 21 1770
    Sureties: William Nicholls, James Dickenson, Jr.
    Distribution to: Representatives unknown to this Office.
    Administrator: Mr. Ralph Holmes, Sr.

John Burch   5.369   D CH   £411.7.1   Jul 18 1770
    Sureties: Bennett Dyson, Thomas Reeves.
    Distribution to: Widow (unnamed, 1/3). Residue to 2 children (equally): Orpah, Martha.
    Administratrix: Mrs. Ann Burch.

John Smith   5.369   D SO   £93.2.7   Aug 24 1770
    Sureties: Charles Leatherbury, James Trehearn.
    Distribution to: Representatives unknown to this Office.
    Administratrix: Mary Wright, wife of Mr. Stephen Wright.

Robert Richardson   5.370   D BA   £37.19.7   Apr 17 1770
    Distribution to: Representatives unknown to this Office.
    Administrators: Mrs. Ann Richardson, James Richardson.

Charles Bond   5.370   D BA   £347.4.2   May 10 1770
    Sureties: Edward Bond, Charles Bond.
    Distribution to: Representatives unknown to this Office.
    Administratrix: Mrs. Eleanor Bond.

John Morris   5.370   D BA   £72.8.8   May 15 1770
son of Thomas Morris.
    Sureties: Thomas Morris, Acquila Law.
    Distribution to: Representatives unknown to this Office.
    Administratrix: Mrs. Mary Morris.

John Furlong   5.370   D SO   £920.6.6   Jul 23 1770
    Sureties: Henry Newman, Isaac Newman.
    Distribution to: Widow (unnamed, 1/3). Residue to: John (only son).
    Administratrix: Mrs. Martha Furlong.

James Meeks   5.370   D KE   £278.5.4   May 1 1770
    Sureties: Richard Willis, William Copper.
    Distribution to: Representatives unknown to this Office.
    Administrators: Mrs. Mary Meeks, John Meeks.

Joseph Morgan   5.371   D BA   £312.10.1   Jun 26 1770
    Sureties: Job Barnes, Darby Lux.
    Distribution to: only accountant.
    Administrator: Mr. Joseph Morgan.

Joseph King   5.371   D CH   £402.2.9   May 24 1770
    Sureties: Baker Howard, Benjamin Lattimore.
    Distribution to: Widow (unnamed, 1/3). Residue to: Ann Pen King (only child).
    Administratrix: Mrs. Rebeccah King.

John Bailey, Jr.   5.371   D   QA   £157.11.0   Jul 7 1770
    Sureties: John Atkinson, William Ridgaway.
    Distribution to: Juliana (widow, accountant, 1/3). Residue to 3 children
        (equally): Sarah, Elisabeth, James.
    Administratrix: Juliana Scrivener, wife of Mr. Robert Scrivener.

Elisabeth Richardson   5.371   D   QA   £15.17.0   Jul 9 1770
    Sureties: Daniel Richardson, John Wright.
    Distribution to: Representatives unknown to this Office.
    Administrator: William Richardson.

William Meeds, Jr.   5.372   D   QA   £146.0.10   Jul 26 1770
    Sureties: Amos Jermon, Jonathon Evans.
    Distribution to 2 children (equally): Walter, Sarah.
    Administrator (de bonis non): Mr. John Meeds, Jr.

Abraham Everett   5.372   D   QA   £378.2.11   Jul 13 1770
    Sureties: Henry Trulock, William Cowarden.
    Distribution to 3 children (equally): Martha, Margaret, Mary.
    Administrator: Mr. St. Leger Everett.

Richard Hawkins   5.372   D   QA   £40.2.9   Jun 7 1770
    Sureties: William Bell, Lambert Clements.
    Distribution to: Widow (accountant, 1/3). Residue to 3 children (equally):
        James, William, Elisabeth.
    Administratrix: Mrs. Elisabeth Hawkins.

David Henry   5.372   D   CE   £178.7.11   Dec 6 1769
    Sureties: Sand. Sheppard, William Foster.
    Distribution to: Widow (unnamed, 1/3). Residue to 2 children (equally): Mary,
        Stephen.
    Administratrix: Mrs. Catharine Henry.

Josias Causin   5.373   D   CH   £642.16.10   Mar 10 1770
    Sureties: Phillip Richard Fendall, John Barnes.
    Distribution to siblings: Gerrard Causin, Thomas Vowles, Richard Vowles, Matthew
        Vowles, Rebeccah Berryman.
    Administrator: Mr. Gerrard Causin.

Edward Gray   5.373   D   CH   £58.18.2   Apr 6 1770
    Sureties: William Hargis Gray, Henry Gray.
    Legatees: accountant, Henrietta Gray, Randolph Gray (died before testator), Sarah
        Appleby (died before testator), Constant Lemar (died before testator).
    Residue to (equally): accountant, Abigal Shelton, Rebeccah Davis.
    Executor: Mr. Moses Gray.

Thomas Jones   5.373   D   SO   £319.15.3   Mar 6 1770
    Sureties: Arnold Elzey, Thomas Sloss.
    Distribution to: Representatives unknown to this Office.
    Administrator: Mr. Denwood Wilson.

Isaac McCrady   5.374   D   SO   £54.8.5   Mar 21 1770
    Sureties: Thomas Tull, Caleb Milburn.
    Distribution to: Widow (unnamed, 1/3). Residue to 6 children (equally): Rachel,
        Stephen, Mary, Andrew, Sarah, Edey.
    Administratrix: Mrs. Eleanor McCrady.

John Carey   5.374   D   BA   £155.1.9   Mar 7 1770
    Sureties: John Stinchcomb, Elijah Owings.
    Distribution to: Representatives unknown to this Office.
    Administratrix: Mrs. Dorothy Carey.

Jane McDonald   5.374   D   TA   £276.15.0   Dec 11 1769
    Sureties: William Besswick, Joseph Turner.
    Distribution to (equally): Mary Millington wife of Allemby Millington, Jane
        Burgess wife of George Burgess, Sarah McDonald, Rachel McDonald.
    Administratrix: Mary Millington, wife of Allemby Millington.

Solomon Bryan   5.374   D   QA   £180.4.9   Jun 9 1769
    Sureties: John Tillotson, James Roe.
    Distribution to: Martha (widow, accountant, 1/3). Residue to: unknown.
    Administratrix: Martha Copper, wife of Mr. Samuel Copper.

Andrew Miffin   5.375   D   DO   £237.6.1   Jul 14 1770
    Sureties: Jacob Rumbly, Edward Rumbly.
    Distribution to: Widow (unnamed, 1/3). Residue to children (equally): Eleanor,
        Catharine, Mathias, Andrew, William.
    Administratrix: Eleanor Hinds, wife of David Hinds.

Cornelia Ally   5.375   D QA   £11.16.0   Oct 16 1769
   Sureties: Absalom Sparks, James Dowling.
   Distribution to 2 children (equally): Sarah Alley, John Alley.
   Administrator: Mr. Caleb Sparks.

John Sullivane   5.375   D QA   £331.8.4   Oct 6 1769
See Liber "E. V. #2" (Liber 6) Folio 12.
   Sureties: Robert Walters, Walter Ruth.
   Distribution to: Widow (accountant, 1/3). Residue to (equally): Moses Floyd (son
     of Eleanor Floyd (sister)), Susannah Dolern & Elisabeth Purney & Charles
     Higgins & Sarah Higgins (children of Barbara Higgins (sister)).
   Administratrix: Sarah Sullivane.

James Brown   5.376   D QA   £246.8.11   Nov 9 1769
   Sureties: Samuel Whiting, Joel Brown (?).
   Distribution to: Ann (widow, accountant, 1/3). Residue to 6 children (equally):
     Sarah, Esther, Mary, James, John, Francis.
   Administratrix: Ann Brown.

Charles Seth   5.376   D QA   £195.11.4   Nov 9 1769
   Sureties: Dennis Carey, Jacob Seth.
   Distribution to: Rachel (widow, accountant, 1/3). Residue to 7 children
     (equally): Elisabeth, Jacob, Charles, William, Susannah, Sarah, Rachel.
   Administratrix: Mrs. Rachel Seth.

Margaret Pickering   5.376   D TA   £69.4.3   Aug 22 1770
   Sureties: Henry Henricks, Elbert Downes.
   Distribution to: Representatives unknown to this Office.
   Administrator: Mr. Robert Pickering.

William Meredith   5.376   D QA   £215.8.11   Jun 26 1770
   Sureties: John Meredith, Samuel Thomas.
   Distribution to: Representatives unknown to this Office.
   Administratrix: Sarah Ferrill, wife of Mr. William Ferrill.

Thomas Jones   5.377   D SO   £322.2.3   Oct 9 1770
   Sureties: Thomas Dashiel, James Robertson.
   Distribution to: Widow (unnamed, 1/3). Residue to 5 children (equally): Ann,
     Britain, Margaret, Richard, Joshua.
   Administratrix: Elisabeth Dorman, wife of Mr. Josiah Dorman.

William Willis   5.377   D SO   £33.14.1   Oct 9 1770
   Sureties: James Willis, John Willis.
   Distribution to: Widow (unnamed, 1/3). Residue to children (equally): Jabus,
     William, James, Sarah, Tabitha, Elijah, Grace.
   Administratrix: Mrs. Tabitha Willis.

William Bateman   5.377   D CE   £131.5.4   Jul 2 1770
   Sureties: James Porter, Richard Savin.
   Distribution to: Widow (unnamed, 1/3). Residue to 6 children (equally): John,
     Elisabeth, William, Sarah, Mary, Michael.
   Administrator (de bonis non): Mr. John Sterling.

John Lawson   5.377   D BA   £508.4.3   Jun 18 1770
   Sureties: Joseph Sutton, Joseph Grover.
   Distribution to: Representatives unknown to this Office.
   Administrator: Mr. John Lawson.

Richard Simpers   5.378   D CE   £197.18.1   Jun 27 1770
   Sureties: John Simpers, William Howell.
   Distribution to: Widow (unnamed, 1/3). Residue to 7 children (equally): George,
     Thomas, James, Jacob, Mary, Richard, William Howell Simpers.
   Administrators: Mrs. Catharine Simpers, Thomas Simpers.

David Hagur   5.378   D FR   £93.5.4   Sep 18 1770
   Sureties: Nathaniel Nesbitt, Thomas Smith.
   Distribution to: Representatives unknown to this Office.
   Administrator: Mr. Jonathon Hagur.

Nathaniel Simpers   5.378   D CE   £592.7.8   Jun 27 1770
   Sureties: John Read, John Simpers.
   Distribution to: Widow (unnamed, 1/3). Residue to 4 children (equally): Anna,
     Richard, Thomas, Nathaniel.
   Administrators: Mr. Francis Simpers, William Beaks and his wife Ann Beaks.

Henry Eubanks   5.379   D TA   £131.3.8   Jul 24 1770
   Sureties: James Benson, Phillip Horney.
   Distribution to: Widow (unnamed, 1/2). Residue to: William Hardcastle
     (half-brother).
   Administratrix: Sarah Kinnimont, wife of Francis Kinnimont.

Peter Hopkins   5.379   D TA   £110.16.2   Jul 3 1770
    Sureties: Charles Bullen, Thomas Delehay.
    Distribution to: Widow (accountant, 1/3). Residue to 2 children (equally):
        James, Richard.
    Administratrix: Mrs. Sarah Hopkins.

Richard Gatton   5.379   D FR   £357.6.10   Apr 2 1770
    Sureties: Henry Claggett, James Smith.
    Distribution to: Widow (unnamed, 1/3). Residue to 8 of children (equally):
        James, Zachariah, Richard, Ann, Eleanor, William, Mary Gatton, Mary Wheat.
    Executor (acting): Mr. Zachariah Gatton.

Thomas Miles the younger   5.380   D BA   £241.9.2   Jun 25 1770
    Sureties: William Robinson, Aquila Thompson.
    Distribution to: Representatives unknown to this Office.
    Administratrix: Mrs. Margaret Miles.

Charles Stainton   5.380   D DO   £82.14.3   Feb 17 1770
    Sureties: Daniel Payne, William Snow.
    Distribution to: Widow (accountant, 1/3). Residue to 2 children (equally):
        William, Major.
    Administratrix: Mrs. Jemima Stainton.

Joshua Hewitt   5.380   D TA   £101.1.1   May 8 1770
    Sureties: Powell Cox, Samuel Dickinson.
    Distribution to: Sarah (widow, one of accountants, 1/3). Residue to 2 children
        (equally): Mary, Joshua.
    Administratrix: Sarah Kirby, wife of Mr. Matthew Kirby.

Daniel Flynn   5.380   D KE   £101.15.0   Mar 21 1770
    Sureties: Edward Comegys, Abraham Mitton.
    Distribution to: Representatives unknown to this Office.
    Administratrix: Mrs. Lydia Flynn.

Mary Jones   5.381   D TA   £41.9.8   May 8 1770
    Sureties: Phillip Perkins, Thomas Roberts, Jr.
    Distribution to: Isaac Palmer (accountant), Vincent Jones, Mary Jones, Sarah
        Jones.
    Administrator: Mr. Isaac Palmer.

Thomas Ijams   5.381   D AA   £103.6.7   Jun 13 1770
    Sureties: John Ijams, Plummer Ijams.
    Legatees: heirs (unnamed) of Thomas Shemparis.
    Residue to 7 children (unnamed, equally).
    Executor: Thomas Ijams (son of Thomas Ijams).

Daniel Whaley   5.381   D KE   £60.13.9   Mar 20 1770
    Sureties: John Whittington, Daniel Stanley.
    Distribution to: Representatives unknown to this Office.
    Administratrix: Mrs. Elisabeth Whaley.

Nicholas Smith   5.381   D FR   £138.16.0   Jun 7 1770
    Sureties: Henry Ridenour, Martin Harry.
    Distribution to: Widow (unnamed, 1/3). Residue to 5 children (unnamed, equally).
    Administrator: Mr. Nicholas Smith.

Jacob Wirtz   5.382   D FR   £283.15.7   May 14 1770
    Sureties: Lodowick Byaly, Frederick Hoffner.
    Distribution to: Widow (unnamed, 1/3). Residue to 2 children (unknown, equally).
    Administrators: Mrs. Mary Wirtz, John Stover.

Jacob Kellor   5.382   D FR   £164.13.0   May 17 1770
    Sureties: Melcher Lighter, Casper Mentz.
    Distribution to: Widow (unnamed, 1/3). Residue to 7 children (unnamed, equally).
    Administrators: Mrs. Elisabeth Kellor, Jacob Kellor.

William Philson   5.382   D FR   £313.8.5   Jun 1 1770
    Sureties: Phillip Greenwall, Abraham Hayter.
    Distribution to: 10 children (unnamed).
    Administrator (surviving): Mr. John Philson.

Abraham Vaughan   5.382   D BA   £277.12.9   Jun 4 1770
    Sureties: Abraham Coles, Abraham Vaughan.
    Distribution to: Representatives unknown to this Office.
    Administrator (de bonis non): Mr. Gist Vaughan.

Jacob Crouse   5.383   D FR   £70.14.6   May 25 1770
    Sureties: Phillip Bemmer, Abraham Hayter.
    Distribution to: Widow (unnamed, 1/3). Residue to 7 children (unknown, equally).
    Administrators: MM Jacob Crouse, Valentine Null.

Obediah Dawson					5.383		D	DO	£48.2.9		Jan 15 1770
   Sureties: William Gray, Charles Scott.
   Distribution to: Widow (unnamed, 1/3). Residue to 5 children (equally): Joseph,
      William, Willis, Louisinia, Ann.
   Administratrix: Mrs. Emilia Dawson.

Joseph Ogle					5.383		D	FR	£630.0.3	Apr 19 1770
   Legatees: Mary Butler, Judith Butler (daughter of Mary Butler), Mary Ogle
      (daughter of Benjamin Ogle), Susanna Ogle & Joanna Ogle (his other 2
      children).
   Distribution to: Sarah Henry (accountant, 2/9). Residue to (equally): Sarah,
      Eleanor, Joseph, Benjamin, Thomas, William, James.
   Administratrix: Mrs. Sarah Henry (formerly Sarah Ogle).

John Coode					5.384		D	SM	£142.13.7	Feb 18 1770
   Sureties: James Jordan, John Naitton.
   Distribution to: Representatives unknown to this Office.
   Administratrix: Mrs. Susanna Coode.

John Standfield					5.384		D	SM	£453.18.2	Apr 24 1770
   Distribution to: Representatives unknown to this Office.
   Administrator: Mr. Richard Standfield.

William Kenner					5.384		D	SM	£391.5.7	Jul 1 1770
   Sureties: Thomas Allison, John Cole.
   Distribution to: Representatives unknown to this Office.
   Administrator: Francis Kenner by his sureties Thomas Allison & John Cole.

Thomas Sappington				5.384		D	KE	£502.9.5	May 14 1770
   Sureties: William Merrit, John Hurt.
   Distribution to: Representatives unknown to this Office.
   Administrators: Mr. James Welch, Milcah Welch.

Edward Reeves					5.384		D	SM	£163.0.1	Jul 11 1770
   Sureties: William Fowler, Ignatius Mattingly.
   Distribution to: Representatives unknown to this Office.
   Administratrix: Jane Cusack, wife of Mr. Michael Cusack.

William Johnson					5.385		D	WO	£119.1.9	May 1 1770
   Sureties: Charlton Smith, William Benton.
   Distribution to 5 children (equally): Susannah, Snead, Southy, Edmund, Nelly.
   Administrator: Mr. Snead Johnson.

Richard Collins					5.385		D	KE	£13.14.7	Jun 21 1770
   Distribution to: Representatives unknown to this Office.
   Administratrix: Mrs. Unice Dunn.

Edward Hammond					5.385		D	WO	£68.16.10	Apr 7 1770
   Sureties: Elisha Purnell, Jethro Bowen.
   Distribution to: Widow (accountant, 1/3). Residue to 4 children (equally):
      Sarah, Mary, Alice, Leah.
   Administratrix: Mrs. Leah Hammond.

Capt. John Randall				5.385		D	BA	£120.10.9	Jun 22 1770
   Distribution to: Widow (unnamed, 1/3). Residue to 1 daughter (unnamed).
   Administrator: Mr. Joseph Ensor.

Mary Spence					5.386		D	WO	£344.6.2	Jun 9 1770
   Sureties: Adam Spence, George Spence.
   Distribution to: 8 children (unnamed).
   Administrator: Mr. John Spence.

James Downes					5.386		D	QA	£283.19.10	Jul 9 1770
   Administratrix: Mrs. Rebeccah Downes.

Henry Hozier					5.386		D	KE	£621.2.11	Oct 31 1770
   Sureties: Thomas Smith, Richard Hozier.
   Distribution to: Representatives unknown to this Office.
   Administratrix: Mrs. Rebecca Ozier.

Peter Peake					5.386		D	SM	£61.7.10	Jul 9 1770
   Sureties: Mark Norris, Thomas Norris.
   Distribution to: Representatives unknown to this Office.
   Administratrix: Mrs. Mary Peake.

Robert Hagur					5.386		D	SM	£103.10.2	Jul 8 1770
   Distribution to: Representatives unknown to this Office.
   Administratrix: Mildred Hilton, wife of Mr. William Hilton.

John Biggs						5.387	D SM	£103.13.1	Sep 3 1770
   Sureties: Joseph Nevitt, Thomas Green Martin.
   Distribution to: Representatives unknown to this Office.
   Administrator: John Harrel assigned to Mrs. Ann Biggs.

Thomas Briscoe					5.387	D SM	£178.18.9	Sep 10 1770
   Distribution to: Representatives unknown to this Office.
   Administratrix: Mary Langley, wife of Mr. William Langley.

John Smith						5.387	D SM	£382.3.3	Sep 10 1770
   Sureties: James Jordan, William Jordan.
   Distribution to: Representatives unknown to this Office.
   Administratrix: Mrs. Elisabeth Smith.

John Langley					5.387	D SM	£316.17.0	Sep 10 1770
   Sureties: Robert Hilton, John Withrington.
   Distribution to: Representatives unknown to this Office.
   Administratrix: Mary Langley.

Thomas Wood						5.387	D KE	£18.6.2		Sep 18 1770
   Sureties: Joseph Nicholson, Jr., Charles Gordon.
   Distribution to: Representatives unknown to this Office.
   Administrator: Joseph Nicholson, Sr., Esq.

Thomas Little					5.388	D BA	£400.3.10	Nov 1 1770
   Legatees: Thomas Little.
   Residue to 4 children (equally): William, George, Mary, Thomas.
   Administrator (de bonis non): Mr. George Little.

George Noble					5.388	D PG	£859.6.9	Aug 27 1770
   Distribution to: Representatives unknown to this Office.
   Administratrix: Elisabeth Hawkins, wife of Mr. James Hawkins.

James Wood						5.388	D PG	£233.11.7	Jul 24 1769
   Sureties: John Tyler, Benjamin Hidgdon.
   Distribution to: Representatives unknown to this Office.
   Administratrix: Elisabeth Hilton, wife of Mr. James Hilton.

James Fullerton					5.388	D SO	£22.1.8		Nov 7 1769
   Sureties: William Willis, Nehemiah Crockett.
   Distribution to: Peggy Fullerton.
   Administrator: Mr. Joshua Fullerton.

John Johnston					5.389	D PG	£266.16.0	Sep 22 1769
   Sureties: THomas Letchworth, Robert Dove Cook.
   Distribution to: Representatives unknown to this Office.
   Administrator: Mr. James Johnson.

Ezekiel Hilman					5.389	D SO	£46.15.11	Oct 31 1769
   Sureties: John Hilman, William Disharoon.
   Distribution to: Widow (unnamed, 1/3). Residue to children (equally): Unice, Nancy, William, John, Betty.
   Administratrix: Mrs. Sarah Hilman.

George Gale						5.389	D SO	£879.18.11	Oct 30 1769
   Sureties: Alexander Robertson, John Day Scott.
   Distribution to: Widow (unnamed, 1/3). Residue to children (equally): Milcah, John, George, Elisabeth, Leah.
   Administrators: Mrs. Elisabeth Gale, Henry Gale.

Frederick Stoner				5.389	D FR	£32.3.0		Feb 8 1770
   Sureties: Philip Kefalker.
   Distribution to: Widow (unnamed, 1/3). Residue to 4 children (equally): Michael, Peter, Susanna, Rosanna.
   Administrator: Mr. Michael Boyer.

Daniel Wales					5.390	D SO	£923.18.4	Aug 23 1769
   Sureties: Day George Scott, William Stewart.
   Distribution to: Widow (unnamed, 1/3). Residue to children (equally): Joseph Wailes, Helany Wailes, Sarah Wailes, Elisabeth Wailes, Ann Wailes.
   Administratrix: Mrs. Elisabeth Wales.

Nicholas Evans					5.390	D SO	£1045.14.1	Sep 4 1769
   Sureties: Thomas Irving, Levin Gilliss.
   Distribution to: Widow (unnamed, 1/3). Residue to children (equally): John, Thomas, Priscilla, Jean, James, William.
   Administratrix: Mrs. Prissey Evans.

Benjamin Hobbs   5.390   D SO   £92.13.2   Sep 5 1769
    Sureties: Isaac Mitchell, John Howard.
    Distribution to: Widow (unnamed, 1/3). Residue to children (equally): Ephraim,
        Assenah.
    Administratrix: Mrs. Christian Hobbs.

Thomas Pantain   5.390   D QA   £86.3.7   Nov 11 1769
    Sureties: Vinson Benton, Charles Downes.
    Distribution to: 2 children (unnamed).
    Administrator: John Conikin.

Christian Creagier   5.391   D FR   £117.7.0   Aug 10 1770
    Sureties: John Cooper, Martin Smith.
    Distribution to: Widow (unnamed, 1/3). Residue to children (unnamed).
    Executors: MM Valentine Creagier, Conrad Creagier.

James Edelin   5.391   D PG   £1559.16.5   Jan 4 1770
    Sureties: John Barnes, Nathaniel Newton.
    Legatees (children): Elisabeth, Mary, Char Solome, Martha, Sarah, Joseph, Samuel,
        James.
    Distribution to: Widow (unnamed, 1/3). Residue to (equally): Edward, Joseph,
        Samuel, James, Elisabeth, Mary, Catharine, Solome, Margaret, Sarah.
    Executor: Mr. James Edelin, Jr.

William Dyall   5.392   D FR   £86.17.6   Feb 2 1770
    Sureties: Stephen Hickman, Valentine Shroiner.
    Legatees (children): James Dyel, Leonard Dyel, Ann Dyer wife of James Dyer,
        Tabitha Dyel.
    Residue to: widow (unnamed), William George Josias Dyel, Rebecca Dyel, Lettis
        Dyel, Stacy Dyel, Sarah Dyel.
    Executor: Joseph Stevens.

George Owler   5.392   D FR   £58.8.1   Jun 1 1770
    Sureties: Jonathon Hays, John Marker.
    Legatees: Elisabeth (daughter), Susannah (wife).
    Distribution to: Susannah (wife, 1/3). Residue to: Elisabeth (daughter).
    Executors: Andrew Owler, Mathias Zacharias.

John Bateman   5.392   D PG   £512.11.9   Nov 2 1770
    Sureties: Thomas Pratt, Jacob Green.
    Distribution to: widow (unnamed).
    Executrix: Mrs. Sarah Bateman.

Henry Glassford   5.393   D KE   £466.6.11   Oct 27 1770
A new balance made out in 1772.
    Sureties: John Maxwell, James Graham.
    Legatees: widow (unnamed), Mary Page, Elisabeth Cry.
    Residue to: Jane Black.
    Executor: Mr. James Black.

David Register   5.393   D QA   £510.4.1   Oct 15 1770
    Sureties: Thomas Emory (son of Charles Emory), John Ruth.
    Legatees: Ann (no surname, daughter of the widow (unnamed)), Sarah (no surname,
        daughter of the widow (unnamed)), Ann Jacob, John Register, Arnold Register,
        Mary Register.
    Distribution to: Widow (unnamed, 1/3). Residue to (equally): John Register,
        Arnault Register, Elisabeth Register, Mary Register.
    Executor: Mr. John Register Emory.

Jonathon Dreddon   5.393   D SO   £91.2.4   Aug 23 1770
    Sureties: Jonathon Tull, David Dreadon.
    Distribution to: Widow (unnamed, 1/3). Residue to children (unnamed, equally).
    Executrix: Mrs. Rachel Dreddon.

Mary Ann Harris   5.394   D BA   £86.9.9   Jul 30 1770
    Sureties: William Fitz, Conjudnn Gash.
    Distribution to grandchildren (equally): Joseph Langdon, Mary Howlett wife of
        John Howlett.
    Executor: Mr. John Howlett.

Thomas West   5.394   D BA   £61.6.11   Mar 12 1770
    Sureties: Nicodemus Bond, Richard Gott.
    Distribution to: Mary Price (wife).
    Executor: Mr. Mordecai Price.

Mary Dawkins   5.394   D CA   £291.17.1   Oct 2 1770
    Sureties: Alexander Somervill, Samuel Gray.
    Distribution to: children (unnamed).
    Administrators: MM James Dawkins, William Dawkins.

George Wells 5.394 D QA £173.12.9 Nov 9 1769
    Distribution to: Representatives unknown to this Office.
    Administratrix: Hannah Irons, wife of Mr. George Irons.

Elisabeth Skiles 5.395 D FR £36.2.0 Nov 20 1770
    Sureties: Tobias Risenour, Henry Wehaw.
    Legatees: Ephraim Skiles, Owen Davis, George Davis, Henry Stiles, Daniel Davis, Elisabeth Obenhiser.
    Residue to: Ephraim Skiles, Owen Davis, John Limbenstone, George Davis, Daniel Davis.
    Executor: Mr. John Lewiston.

Joseph Leonard 5.395 D SO £277.10.9 Sep 7 1770
    Sureties: Thomas Cox, John Tatom.
    Legatees: Joseph Leonard, John Leonard.
    Distribution to: Widow (unnamed, 1/3). Residue to (equally): children (unnamed) of Michael (son), Eleanor Gordy, Joseph Leonard, John Leonard.
    Executor: Mr. Joseph Leonard.

Uriah Davis 5.395 D BA £122.12.10 Oct 12 1770
    Sureties: Jacob Spindler, Martin Howk.
    Legatees (4 children): Solomon, William, Uriah, Deaner.
    Distribution to: Widow (unnamed, 1/3).
    Executrix: Margaret Brown, wife of Mr. John Brown.

John Dorman 5.396 D SO £77.13.9 Sep 4 1769
    Sureties: Michael Cluff, Gideon Tilghman.
    Legatees (children): John, Zadock, Mathias, Mary.
    Distribution to: Widow (unnamed, 1/3). Residue to 3 youngest children (unnamed, equally).
    Executrix: Mrs. Catharine Dorman.

Athanius Nottingham 5.396 D SM £72.4.1 Oct 20 1770
    Sureties: Zachariah Forrest, George Greenwell.
    Legatees: Philip (son).
    Distribution to: Widow (unnamed, 1/3). Residue to 9 children (equally): Basil, Catharine, Eleanor, Bennett, Barbara, Elisabeth, Mary Ann, Ann, Enoch.
    Executors: Mr. Clement Medley (Shorts), Mary Nottingham.

William Townsend 5.396 D WO £272.3.11 Jul 2 1770
    Sureties: Isaac Bozman Schoolfield, Thomas Barnes.
    Distribution to: widow (unnamed).
    Executrix: Mrs. Sarah Townsend.

Priscilla Gough 5.397 D SM £283.6.3 Aug 15 1770
    Sureties: Bennett Raley, John Fenwick.
    Legatees: Eleanor Greenwell (daughter).
    Residue to (equally): Elisabeth Jenkins, Mary Roads, James Gough, Ignatius Gough, Susanna Dante.
    Executor: Mr. James Gough.

John Matthews 5.397 D FR £80.5.8 May 1 1770
    Sureties: Samuel Swearington.
    Distribution to: Rachel (daughter).
    Executor: Mr. Charles Hodges.

Beavins Morris 5.397 D WO £121.14.9 Mar 30 1770
    Sureties: Benjamin Schoolfield, John Lockwood.
    Legatees: Lewisa Morris, Bevan Morris, Sarah Staten, Rebeccah Lockwood, Elisabeth Morris, Mary Wharton, Sidney Rikard.
    Distribution to: widow (unnamed).
    Executor: Mr. Beavins Morris.

George Jewill 5.398 D FR £99.3.4 May 10 1770
    Sureties: George Walter, Arthur Kirkman.
    Legatees: Moses Jewill.
    Distribution to: Widow (unnamed, 1/3). Residue to (equally): David Jewell, Sarah Waters, Moses Jewel, Precious Jewel, Elisabeth Jewel.
    Executor: Mr. Moses Jewill.

Esaw Boston 5.398 D SO £240.3.7 Aug 23 1770
    Sureties: Jacob Adams, Ephraim Adams.
    Legatees: Elijah Boston (grandson, son of Mathew (son)), Isaac Boston (grandson, son of Mathew Boston (son)), Jacob (son), Mary Cottingham (daughter), Betty Boston (granddaughter), Lazarus (son), Jacob Boston (grandson, son of Esaw (son)), Elijah Boston (grandson), Isaac Boston (grandson), Ephraim Boston (grandson), David Boston (grandson).
    Administrator: Mr. Elijah Matthews.

Benjamin Gray   5.398   D CA   £51.5.5   Dec 21 1769
    Sureties: David Slater, William Ireland.
    Distribution to: Representatives unknown to this Office.
    Administrator: James Somerville.

Benedict Fenwick   5.399   D SM   £269.14.3   Aug 30 1770
    Sureties: Enoch Fenwick, Henry Sewell.
    Legatees: George Fenwick, Jane Fenwick, St. Alevigis Chapel, William King,
        Jestener Moore, John Lucas.
    Residue to (equally): William Fenwick, George Fenwick, Jane Fenwick.
    Executor: Mr. William Fenwick.

Thomas Latchum   5.399   D WO   £166.7.0   Jun 30 1770
    Sureties: Thomas Bumbage, Peter Latchum.
    Legatees (children): Rusiner Davis, Thomas.
    Distribution to: Dinah (widow, accountant, 1/3). Residue to 8 children
        (equally): Rusiner Davis, Nehemiah, Peter, John Randall Latchum, George,
        Isaiah, Joseph, Thomas.
    Executrix: Mrs. Dinah Latchum.

James Dale   5.399   D CA   £240.4.1   Sep 28 1769
    Sureties: James Gibson, John Gibson.
    Distribution to: Representatives unknown to this Office.
    Administratrix: Mrs. Lydia Dale.

Francis Pickering   5.400   D TA   £305.0.5   Aug 21 1770
    Sureties: James Gibson, Daniel Killum.
    Legatees: Robert Pickering, Mary Wilson.
    Distribution to: Widow (unnamed, 1/3). Residue to: children (unnamed) & their
        representatives (unnamed).
    Executor (one of): Mr. Robert Pickering.

Jesse Ford   5.400   D SM   £122.9.5   Jun 9 1770
    Sureties: George Booth, John Ford (son of Peter Ford).
    Legatees: John Kinnelin Madcalf (nephew), Sarah Medcalf (sister), Ignatius
        (brother).
    Executrix: Sarah Wheatley, wife of Mr. Silvester Wheatley.

William Bradey   5.401   D CA   £75.4.0   Aug 10 1769
    Sureties: William Gray, James Brinkley.
    Distribution to: Representatives unknown to this Office.
    Administratrix: Margaret Cox, wife of Jeremiah Cox.

David Haines   5.401   D SO   £52.8.11   Apr 20 1770
    Sureties: Levin Callaway, John Callaway.
    Distribution to: Widow (unnamed, 1/3). Residue to 4 children (equally):
        Constant, Ephraim, Oratio, James.
    Administratrix: Mrs. Elisabeth Haines (also Elisabeth Unge).

John Caldwell   5.401   D CE   £179.13.11   Dec 20 1769
    Distribution to: Representatives unknown to this Office.
    Administrator: Mr. Samuel Caldwell.

William Sappington   5.401   D AA   £162.8.1   Jul 3 1770
    Distribution to: Ann (widow, accountant, 1/3). Residue to children (equally):
        child (unnamed, died since testator), James.
    Administratrix: Ann Brashears, wife of Nathaniel Brashears.

George Howard   5.402   D BA   £13.1.4   May 17 1770
    Sureties: Nicholas Jones, Joshua Howard.
    Distribution to: Representatives unknown to this Office.
    Administrator: Mr. Cornelius Howard.

Samuel Osborn   5.402   D QA   £241.11.10   Jun 22 1770
    Sureties: John Legg, John OBrien.
    Legatees: Sarah Osborn, John Osborne, Sarah Osborne.
    Distribution to: Widow (accountant, 1/3). Residue to children (unnamed,
        equally).
    Executrix: Mrs. Violetta Osborn.

Edward Thorpe   5.402   D BA   £1135.13.2   Jul 30 1770
    Sureties: John Wilmott, Benjamin Amos.
    Distribution to: Representatives unknown to this Office.
    Administratrix: Mrs. Rachel Thorpe.

Robert Hunter   5.402   D   TA   £57.17.7   May 1 1770
    Sureties: Phillip Perkins, Solomon Perkins.
    Legatees: Robert (son), James Hunter (grandson).
    Distribution to (4 parts): Rebecca Eubanks, Elisabeth Newman, Robert, heirs
        (unnamed) of Mary (daughter).
    Executor: Mr. Robert Hunter.

Benjamin Denny   5.403   D   QA   £125.11.10   Nov 9 1769
    Sureties: Stephen Yoe, Samuel Everett.
    Legatees: Susanna (widow), Nancy (daughter).
    Distribution to: Susanna (widow, 1/3).
    Executrix: Mrs. Susanna Denny.

William Prior   5.403   D   QA   £207.14.11   Nov 10 1769
The amount of the accounts also included #487.
    Sureties: Benjamin Harris, John Commegys.
    Legatees: Rebecca Swift, William Prior, Joseph Prior.
    Distribution to 7 children (equally): Thomas, Ann, Rosiller, James, Emory,
        Catharine, Joseph.
    Executor: Mr. William Prior.

Patrick Lynch   5.403   D   BA   £821.18.0   Nov 15 1770
    Sureties: Abraham Eggleston, Tobias Stansbury.
    Distribution to children (4 daughters, equally): Martha Cretin, Ann Flanagan,
        Flora Smith, Mary Gray. They have a total of 11 children (unnamed).
    Executors: MM Robuck Lynch, Daniel Smith.

This section appears at the back of Liber 5. "Papers returned to the Prerogative Court beginning 20 February 1767." the Prerogative Court in 1767.)

Folio 1

Returned from Somerset County by Mr. Thomas Holbrook, March 20, 1767.

- Bonds: William Hitch, William Shephard, Samuel Fleuellin, Charles Tulley.
- Wills: William Shephard, Samuel Fleuellin.
- Accounts: Joseph Ward, John Phillip.

From Baltimore County, April 1, 1767

- Bonds: William Wheeler, Charles March, Lewis Potee, Avarilla Lynch, Daniel Sanders, Joseph Frost, John Robston, Joseph Paulson, Samuel Howel, Jacob Scott, Thomas Shea.
- Wills: Samuel Howell, James Steuart, William Wheeler, William Seal, Avarilla Lynch, James Shephard, Thomas Shea, Jacob Scott.
- Inventories: Thomas Browire, Francis Gibson, Edward Tull, David Evans, Edward Talbot, Thomas Miles, Thomas Hammond, John Clarks, William Elliot, Susannah Harrot.
- Accounts: Thomas Brown, William Elliot, James Brice.

From Somerset County, April 1.

- Inventories & Accounts: Anthony Sarley.

From Dorchester County, April 1.

- Inventories & Accounts: Henry Traverse.

From Baltimore County, April 1.

- Inventories: David McCulloch.

Folio 2

From Kent County, April 1.

- Bonds: William Smith, Hannah George, William Sloops, William Comegys, Robert Maxwell, Mary St. Clair.
- Wills: Joseph Whaley, Hannah George, William Sloops.
- Inventories: Sarah Pearce, James Fields, James McCawans, John Williamson, Daniel Smith, Mary Philips, Peter Cole, William Corse, John Williamson, Thomas Mills, John Williamson.
- Accounts: Peter Cole, William Corse, Robert Sils, Jane Frisby, William Bruffit.

From Somerset County, April 8.

- Inventories & Accounts: William Nelson.

From Somerset County, April 14.

- Bonds: William Juett, Jesse Covington.
- Wills: William Juett, Jesse Covington.
- Inventories: William Evans, Benjamin Hugens, Joseph Allen, Thomas Wilson, Alexander Fullerton.

From Worcester County, April 21.

- Bonds: William Gillett, Richard Blizard, James Hickman, William Dunlap, Samuel Lamberson, John Coulbourn, Archibald Dales, Lucretia Claywell, John Short, John Oneal, William Roach, Philip Selby, John Bowins, Thomas Walters, Valentine Dennis, James Cambell, Whittington Johnson, Paul Waples, William McClanahan, Isaac Bells, Michael Leonard, Major Townsend, John Bessicks, Joseph Schoolfeild, Thomas Holland, William Figgs, John Fenecy, Valentine Dennis.

Folio 3

- Wills: William Gillett, John Short, Archibald Dale, James Campbell, John Bowins, James Hickman, Philip Selby, Samuel Lamberson, William Dunlap, John Colbourn, John Oneal, William Roach, Lucretia Claywell, Thomas Morris, Thomas Walters.
- Inventories: Paul Waples, William Harrisson, William Perkins, Stephen Roach, John Davis, Samuel Donaldson, Whittington Johnson, Micajah Selby, Major Hitchins, Henry Selby, William Benson, William Evans, Thomas Cade, Valentine Dennis (will).
- Accounts: Ann Sheil, Nicholas Warren, Samuel Donaldson, Samuel Betts, John Donohoe, William Gray, Richard Walton, Richard Gostee.
- Renunciation: William Maclanachan, Valentine Dennis, John Bowin, Samuel Lamberson, William Roach, James Hickman, John Short, William Figgs.

From Frederick County, April 22.

- Bonds: Frederick Stoner, William Gibson, Benjamin Machall, Henry Conrod, John Swann, Jacob Shingeltaker, Thomas Windom.
- Wills: Drusilla Plumer, Josias Holland, Benjamin Mackall, Daniel Neare, William Wheat, John Swann, Jacob Shingeltaker, Thomas Windom.
- Inventories: Leonard Johnson, John Hoyle, Spicer Owin.
- Accounts: Edward Mathews, Thomas Pain.

Folio 4

From Anne Arundel County, May 11, 1767.

- Inventories: James Mouat.
- Accounts: Richard Dorsey, Samuel Gaither, Stephen Pickering.

From Baltimore County, May 11.

- Accounts: William Hamilton, William Nicholson.

From Charles County, May 11.

- Wills: Edward Burch.
- Bonds: Edward Burch.

From Frederick County.

- Bonds: Stephen Gatrell.

From Queen Anne's County.

- Accounts: Thomas Harriss.

From Anne Arundel County, May 11.

- Bonds: John Ridgley, Samuel Howard, Henry Wall, Thomas John Hammond, Joseph Foard, James Elder, Jonas Green, William Weathered, James Dixon, Caleb Conner, Samuel Chapman, Thomas Warfield.
- Wills: Susannah Anderson, Samuel Chapman, William Weathered, Joseph Evitt, Samuel Howard, Thomas Warfield, Elisabeth Burgess, James Dixon.
- Renunciation: Michael Stanly, Achsah Conner.
- Inventories: Joseph Hawkins, Charles Small, George Payne, Charles Drury, Samuel Howard, John Dorsey, Sr., William Kirkland, James Dixon, John Ashpaw, Ann Searman.
- Accounts: Ann Cooke, Thomas Bear, Sarah Crandal, Elisabeth Selman, Valentine Meek, James Cummings, John Cheney.

From Dorchester County, May 11.

- Bonds: William Insley, William Covey.
- Wills: William Insley, Richard Meekins.
- Inventories & Accounts: Bethulia Wallace.
- Accounts: Mary Crutcher, William Button.
- Renunciation: Sarah Garrott.

Folio 5

From Somerset County, May 11.

- Bonds: William Robertson, Clement Christopher, Joseph Tilghman.
- Wills: Joseph Tilghman.
- Inventories: Elisabeth Shiles, Sarah Vinson.

From Talbot County, May 11.

- Bonds: Jane McDonald, Mary Jones, James Callaghane, Capt. Adam Hill.
- Wills: Adam Hill, James Millard, James Callaghane, John Roe, Arthur Rigby.
- Inventories: Jacob Hindman, Jonathon Gibson, William Geary, William Harvey.

From Queen Anne's County, May 27.

- Bonds: William Kelley, John Campbell, Stephen Dear, John Humphries, John Boyer, Joseph Johnston, Thomas Walker, Ann Bishop, Christopher Spry, John Bailey, John Emory, Robert Kent, Christopher Green, Joseph Nelson, James Walker, Martha Emory, William Wrench.
- Inventories: John Doherty, Thomas Carradine, James Chambers, Henry Covington, Samuel Mosh, Joseph Jerman, Thomas Fisher, Benjamin Roberts, Charles Browne, Abraham Everet, Dinah Bryan, James Slaughter, Thomas Mooth, William Lyon, Mary Thomas, Edward Crapper, John Preston, Alexander Lee, Dennis McGlachlan.
- Wills: Chr. Spry, William Cannon, John Boyer.
- Renunciation: Dinah Bryan.
- Accounts: Thomas Fisher, Joseph Jerman, John Doherty, Edward Burk, John Bryan, Nathaniel Wright, James Cassey, Thomas Carradine.

Folio 6

From Prince George's County, May 27.

- Bonds: Charles Clark, Joseph Brooke, Thomas Clarke, Esq., William Fowler, John Selby, James Thorn, Thomas Hollyday, Zachariah Lanham, John Perkins, Hugh Glasford, John Beall (son of Robert Beall), Sabritt Clagett.
- Wills: Charles Clarke, Joseph Brooke, James Thorn, John Beall (son of Robert Beall), John Selby, Sabrit Clagett, Thomas Hollyday.
- Inventories: Thomas Hollyday, John McClean, John Beall, Samuel Butt, Thomas Soaper, William Jenkins, Jeremiah Evans, John Orme, Hugh Glassford.
- Accounts: Benjamin Brookes, Annanias Gears, Edward Lanham, Thomas Soapers, Charles Robinson, Samuel Butt.

From St. Mary's County, May 27.

- Bonds: Augustine Meekins, John Riswick, Charles Dillion, John Gibbands, John Johnson, M. A. McGill, Luke Morris, Stephen Cawood, John Guyther.
- Wills: Augustine Meekin, John Riswick, John Guyther, Luke Morris, John Johnson, Stephen Cawood.
- Inventories: Elenor Bailey, Richard Cooper, James Dreeden, Elisabeth Syffert (executor Stephen (no surname)), Stephen Syffert, John Coode, Stourton Edwards, John Stanfield, Richard Millars, Richard Brown, Peter Gough, Meverell Loch, Robert Thompson.
- Accounts: William Spalding, John Foord, John Newton, Henry Bacon Smith, Richard Millard, Ann Norris, Thomas Doxey, Henry Bryon, James Armstrong, John Mansfield.

Folio 7

From Cecil County, May 27.

- Bonds: John Sutton, Thomas Hannah, John Carnan, James Vance, William Abbott, Bartholomew Parsly, Joseph Chisel.
- Wills: William Foster, John Carnan, William Abbott.
- Inventories: Robert Mercer, Samuel Galt, Alexander Hutcheson, Robert William, Johannas Arrants, Martha Hyland, Thomas Ryland, William Ellis, Richard Smith, John Osburn, Cardiff Tagart, John Bully, James Veazey, John Brown, William Smith.
- Accounts: John Brown, Sampson George, James Veazey.

From Somerset County, May 27.

- Bonds: Richard Stevens, David Dorman, Joseph Lenard.
- Wills: David Dorman, Joseph Leonard.
- Inventories: Zabulon Wright, James Furnace, Col. Robert Jenkins Henry.

From Charles County, May 27.

- Bonds: Henry Coffe, Alden Clayton, Francis Adams.
- Wills: Mary Ching, William Pisson, Edward Brawner.
- Accounts: John Crain.
- Inventories: Thomas McDaniel, Lut. Jameson, Joseph King, Francis Montgomery, Ann Edelen.

From Frederick County, May 27.

- Bonds: Jacob Bonds, John McKinley.
- Wills: John McKinley.
- Inventories: Caleb Litton, Samuel Sand. Welder.
- Accounts: John Weaver, Moses Chapline, Samuel Stan. Welder, Caleb Litton.

Folio 8

From Kent County, May 27.

- Bonds: Southy Mifflin, Joseph Whaley, Samuel Wicks, Joseph Parsons, Laurance Stainer, John Arnold, James Humphrey.
- Wills: Samuel Wicks, John Arnold, Laurance Stainer.
- Renunciation: Mary Wicks, Rebecca Arnold.
- Inventories: William Boyer, Meridith Walton, Henry Thomas, Joseph Busil, Thomas Hadley, John Tilden, Mathew Zuille.
- Accounts: Joseph Basil, John Jones, Thomas Honor, Amos Hollingsworth, John Tilden, Joseph Basil, Mathew Zuille, Peter Cole.

From Baltimore County, June 1.

- Bonds: Samuel Hopkins, William Seals, Ephraim Joy, William Johnson, Daniel Thorn, Joseph Fling, Peter Carroll, Thomas Tolson, Jacob Rock, John Watts, Thomas Trussell.
- Wills: Joseph Fling, Jacob Combest, John Rorer, William Johnson, Samuel Hopkins.
- Inventories: William Wheeler, William Cox, Joseph Aulton, Lewis Potee, Jr., Charles Bond, William Jenkins, John Cotrall, Samuel Ricketts of Edward Mead, John Hannah (executor of Alexander Hanna), Ruth Cox (administrator of William Cox), Mark Alexander, J. R. Couper, Jacob Hanson.

From Charles County, June 2, by Samuel Briscoe.

- Bonds: Samuel Briscoe, James Marten, John Stoddert, Mary Provin, John Johnston, James Provin, George Venebles, Jesse Cooper, Thomas Cawood, William Boarman, Jane Bruce, John Tyler.

Folio 9

- Wills: John Stoddert, Richard Tubman, James Smallwood, Jr., Mary Provin, William Boarman.
- Inventories: William Blackey, Alexander Semmes, Elisabeth Thompson, Jane Doyne, Michael Eden.
- Accounts: Jacob Andrew Minotree, Joseph Clements, William Dement, Ignatius Milched, Robert Jackson, Justinian Burch, Daniel Wright, Robert Franklin, Alexander Semmes, Bennett Posey.

From Anne Arundel County, June 22.

- Bonds: Thomas Bastford, Joseph Pumphrey.
- Renunciation: Joseph Pumphrey.
- Wills: Thomas Bastford, William Barrett.
- Inventories: Richard Franklin, William Chapman, Jr., George Harden John James, Sibella Crandall, Thomas Warfield, William Hayne, Caleb Conner, Samuel Moss.
- Accounts: John Thompson, Sybella Crandall, Thomas Lusby, Jr., George Harden John James, William Tucker.

From Anne Arundel County, June 22.

- Accounts: Samuel Moss, William Chapman, Sr., Nicholas Boone, William Chapman, Jr., Henry Woodward.

From Dorchester County, June 22.

- Bonds: John Anderson.
- Accounts: Peter Rich, Lewis Griffith, Peter Rich.

From Queen Anne's County, June 22.

- Accounts: George Wells, Edward Neale, Edward Brown.

From Frederick County, June 22.

- Accounts: Samuel Rogers, Elier Burton.
- Inventories: Burgess Nelson.

From Cecil County, June 22.

- Wills: John Rigbie.
- Bonds: John Rigbie.

From Talbot County, June 22.

- Accounts: John Robins, Rebecca Clarke.

From Charles County.

- Inventories: Benjamin Huntt.

From Prince George's County.

- Accounts: Robert Marsh. Waring.

From Kent County.

- Accounts: William Comegys.

From Baltimore County.

- Accounts: John Wilmot.

Folio 10

From Calvert County, June 23.

- Bonds: Ann Taylor, William Bradey, Ann Robinson, Jacob Stallinges.
- Wills: Joseph Isaackes, Mary Stallinges.
- Accounts: Thomas Morgan, John Stone, Jacob Freeman, Alexander Wallace, John griffith.
- Inventories: Jos. Fowles.

From Dorchester County, June 23.

- Bonds: John Brown, Jonathon Stevens.
- Wills: John Brown, John Anderton.
- Accounts: David Campbell, Thomas Hackett, John Nunam, Joseph Loit, Jacob Goutee, Jr., Thomas Cooper, Mary Evans, Lewis Griffith.
- Inventories: William Philipps, Richard Pearson, John Nunam, Richard Dose, William Hill, William Hill, Richard Dose, Thomas Cooper.

From Dorchester County, June 23.

- Bonds: James Branklin, Thomas Wingate, Thomas Bending, Roger Gordon, Levin Pritchet, Richard Cole, Summer Adams, Charles Stainton, John Granger, Rosannah Cole, Henry Hooper, David Shehawn, John Low, John Clarage, Thomas Manning, James Cannon, Thomas Dent, Mary Jarrard, James Jarret, John Aaron.
- Wills: John Aaron, John Low, Mary Jarrard, Summer Addams, Henry Hooper.
- Accounts: Thomas Airey, Patrick Reed, James Pritchet, Richard Dose, John Woolen.
- Inventories: Ann Paulson,

Folio 11

John Wooters, Thomas Airey, Alexander Frazier, David Murray, Jos. Cox Gray, James Pritchet.

From Kent County, June 30.

- Bonds: John Haley, Ann Haley, Richard Lenox, Nathan Simcock, Jacob Linegar, Arthur Christfield, Richard Robinett.
- Wills: Richard Lenox, Arthur Christfield.
- Inventories: Richard Wooderson, Isaac Redgrave, Augustin Boyer, Samuel Wallis, John Sewell, Nicholas Lynch, John Gamble, Patrick Maccatee, William Comegys, Thomas Mastin, William Meeks, Robert Maxwell, Abraham Falconar, James Calder, George Cole, William Smith, Francis Hollyday, William Cry, Richard Wooderson, Jane Medford, William Rasin, Sutton Burgin, John Cleaver, George Cole.
- Accounts: John Cleaver, William Rasin, John Gamble, George Cole, Sutton Burgin, Elisabeth Falconar, Abraham Falconar, Jane Medford, William Rolph, Francis Holladay, Richard Wooderson.

From Anne Arundel County, July 20.

- Inventories: John Brice, Joseph Ford, Edmond Key.
- Accounts: Andrew Beard, William Haynes.

From Baltimore County, July 20.

- Inventories: Patrick Lynch, James Sollers.

From Dorchester County, July 20.

- Wills: John Caile.
- Bonds: John Caile.
- Renunciation: John Caile.

Here ends Mr. Goldsborough proceedings.

Folio 12

Returned by Daniel Jenifer, Esq.

From Charles County, July 20.

- Accounts: John Philpot, Richard White, John Davis.

From Somerset County, July 20.

- Bonds: Sarah Adams.
- Renunciation: John Graham.
- Wills: John Graham, Sarah Adams.
- Inventories: William Hitch, Samuel Handy, Jesse Covington, George Gale, Jr.

From Talbot County, July 20.

- Bonds: Peter Cox, Handley Robins, George Thompson, William Henesy, James Millard.
- Wills: Christopher Spry, Ann Noble, George Thompson, Handley Robins.
- Inventories: John Harrison, Emanuel Jenkinson, George Brinsfield, Archibald McCallum, Joseph Darden.
- Accounts: Richard Besswick, Hannah Alexander.

From Baltimore County, July 27.

- Bonds: James Heath, William Gough, Charles Bond, John Rorer, Richard Williams, Jacob Combest, Richard Miller Cole, James Stewart, Esther Whisler, Charles Jones.
- Wills: Richard Williams, George Cole, Thomas Rycraft.
- Inventories: Jacob Scott, George Simmons, Robert Brierly, Charles Flanagan, Robert Fisher, Thomas Shhea, Adam Burchfield, James Reed, John Loney.
- Accounts: Nathan Wheeler, Jeremiah Croney, Hannah Fisher.

From Somerset County, July 27.

- (Bonds): Thomas Wright, Jacob Airs, John Milbourn, Jacob Thoms, Christopher Piper.
- Wills: Henry Lowes.

Folio 13

- Inventories: Levin Harris, Robert Lafeld, William Juett, William Robertson, Levin Powell, Jean Dashiel, Hezekiah Darmon, Isaac Surman, William Shephard.
- Accounts: Jean Dashiel, John Stapleford, Benjamin Flowers, Thomas Martain, Edward Bennett, John Williams, D. Stone, Alexander Fullerton, Levin Powell, John Crouch, William Shephard.

From Queen Anne's County, August 9.

- Bonds: Jonathon Barrett, Benjamin Endsworth, Joseph Broadaway, James Andrew, John Massey, John Covington, James Hamilton, Thomas Jackson, Mary May, Samuel Wright, William Barkhust, Mathew Bryan, William Finnicum, William Bankes.
- Wills: James Hamilton, John Covington, Mathew Bryan, Nathan Wright, William Barkhust, Jonathon Barrett, Jonathon Endsworth, Samuel Wright.
- Inventories: Henry Costin, Thomas Evans, Solomon Obryan, Thomas Cook, Hannah Earle, Jonathon Newton, John Dickson, Martha Little, James Browne, John Emerson, Archibald Jackson.
- Accounts: Archibald Jackson, Thomas Barnett, Jonathon Newton.

From Cecil County, August 10.

- Wills: Bryan Conally.

From Charles County, August 10.

- Bonds: Walter Hanson.

From Baltimore County, August 10.

- Bonds: William Young.

Folio 14

From Kent County, August 26.

- Bonds: Bedd. Hands, Holman Johnson, Darius Dunn, John Ashley, John Higgins, Daniel Whaley, George Bennett.
- Wills: John Ashley, George Bennett.
- Accounts: John Williamson, Sarah Pearce, William Pearce, Robert Dollace, William True, James Whittington, Uriel Medford.
- Inventories: William Kersey, Richard Robinett, William Sloops, James Whittington, Samuel Wilkes, Edward Mason, John Williamson, William Kersey, Robert Dollace, Robert Dollace, James Whittington, Stephen Kendall, John Williamson.

From Dorchester County, August 26.

- Bonds: Richard Meekins, Stephen Sherwin, Thomas Colson.
- Wills: Lettice Woollen, Stephen Sherwin, Thomas Wingate, Richard Cole, John Granger, Thomas Bending.
- Inventories: Mary Jarrard, Edward Garratt, John Aaron, James Banning, John Broughton, Jonathon Stevens, Robert Medford, James Edget, Joshua Wall, William Insley, John Paul.
- Accounts: Isaac Williams, James Layton, William Abbot, John Hurley, John Pringel, John Meekins, John Broughton, Catharine Johnson, Mary Fisher, Joseph Whiteley, Charles Lowd, John Woolen, John Jones, Francis Harper, Alexander Frazier, David Murray, John Phillips, Thomas Rottin, Thomas Howell, John Clarkson, Jos. Cox Gray, Jacob Lookerman, James Trego.

Folio 15

From Somerset County, September --.

- Bonds: Thomas Holbrook, Alexander Pooler, Kirk Gunby, Jr., William Turpin.
- Wills: William Turpin.
- Inventories: Richard Stevens Bounds, Clement Christopher, Joseph Leonard.

From Talbot County, September --.

- Bonds: Richard Gibson, William Thomas.
- Wills: William Thomas, Richard Gibson.
- Inventories: Ann Powell.
- Accounts: Ann Powell.

From Charles County, September 5.

- Bonds: Thomas Monroe, Mary Askins.
- Wills: Mary Askins.
- Inventories: Joseph Wright, John Johnson, Eleanor Gambra, James Provin, Richard Marloe, Joseph Joy, Nathan Harriss, Mary Provin, Robert Mastin, John Stoddert.
- Accounts: Jacob Andrew Minet, Thomas McDaniel, Annastasius Crapper, Richard Marloe, Thomas Simpson, James Bowling, John Carpenter.

From Cecil County, September 5.

- Bonds: John Kirk, John Hart, Joshua Thompson.

- Wills: Samuel Tagart.
- Inventories: Hannah Johnson, Bartholomew Parsley, John Sutton, Abigail Hollings.
- Accounts: Nicholas Price, Thomas Price.

From Queen Anne's County, September 7.

- Accounts: Edward Neale.

From Baltimore County, September 7.

- Accounts: Anthony Addison, Capt. John Errington.
- Inventories: Anthony Addison.

From Frederick County, September 7.

- Inventories: Stephen Gabrill, Nicholas Baker.
- Accounts: Nicholas Baker.
- Bonds: William Talbot.

From Talbot County, September 7.

- Accounts: John Graham.

Folio 16

From Anne Arundel County, September 7.

- Accounts: Richard Warfield, John Dorsey (son of Edward Dorsey), John Golder, William Disney, Humphrey Boone, Basil Dorsey, Caleb Dorsey.
- Inventories: William Disney, John Golder, John Dorsey, Humphrey Boone.
- Bonds: William Barrett, John New, Samuel Birkhead, Nathaniel Sappington, John Sappington, Sr.
- Inventories: William Weathered, John Ridgley, William Barrett, John Kent.
- Accounts: John Kent, Jr., Sarah Kent, John Kent, Sr., William Weathered, Peter Hardesty, Andrew Beard.

From Queen Anne's County, September 11.

- Bonds: Thomas Wright, John Wilson, Cornelia Alley, Thomas Pantain, William Hand, Isaac Boon, William Bright, William Kirby, Nathan Wright.
- Wills: Mary Dyre, John Wilson, Isaac Boon.
- Inventories: William Wrench, Arthur Emory, Richard Hynson, Charles Baker, Joseph Barnett, William Finnicum, John Covington, Christopher Spry, Joseph Sinners, Emanuel Swift, James Brown, Robert Yewell, Thomas Hamer, Joseph Councel, Thomas Jackson, William Barkhust, William Kelley, Joseph Johnson, John Boyer, Thomas Walker, Solomon Seney.
- Accounts: John Connikin, John Swift, Thomas Carradine, Joseph Barnett, Robert Yewell, Thomas Harris, John Covington, Thomas Walker, John Rochester, Jr.

Folio 17

From Charles County, September 14, from Samuel Briscoe.

- Bonds: William Sissan, Basil Brook, Charles Venables, Thomas Hussy, Joseph Wright, James Smalwood, John Maddox.
- Wills: Basil Brooke.
- Inventories: Benjamin Thorn, Thomas Wright, Henry Coffer, Jonathon Davis, Mary Philpot, Olden Claten, John Hamill, Sr., Thomas Cawood, Francis Adams, Jesse Cooper, George Venables, William Boarman, William Neale, James Martin.
- Accounts: Richard Bennett Boarman, William Sanders Ginan Slye, John Kinsman, Edward Ford, John Thompson, Philip Edelen, Thomas Gerarld, William Neale, Thomas Green, Thomas Speake, John Hammill, Jr. Elisabeth Hungerford, Charles Willett, Mary Roby, William Cawood.

From Frederick County, September 14.

- Bonds: Thomas Bowles, Chr. Smith, Henry Bichey, John Chilton, William Waugh, George Cost.
- Wills: Christian Smith.
- Inventories: John Swann, Charles Pell, John Barns, Zephaniah Plumer, Hugh Campbell, Jacob Shingeltaker, Rachel Veach, James Petty, Jacob Grouse, James Dickson, James Dickson, Bartholomew Jessarang, Daniel Davis.
- Accounts: John Wiles, Peter Foxall, Robert Owins, Hugh Campbel, John Bapt. Loveless, John Barnes, Bartholomew Jessarang, Daniel Davis.

From Dorchester County, September 14.

- Wills: Charles Goldsborough.

Folio 18

From Worcester County, October 28, by Benton Harris.

- Bonds: Teagle Taylor, George Layfield, Andrew Gibb, Joseph Cord, Thomas Milbourn, John Crawford, Christopher Glass, Esther Crapper, Thomas Larsham, Joshua Caldwell, Joshua Merrill, Benjamin Bishop, Elisha Purnell, Samuel Atkinson, Michael Godwin, Avery Morgan, David Cathell, Alexander Linch, John Blades, Joseph Collins.
- Wills: Joshua Caldwell, Thomas Latchum, George Layfield, Avery Morgan, John Blades, Alexander Linch, Joshua Merrill, David Cathell, Naomi Godwin, Ester Crapper, Timothy Carey, Comfort Turner, Michael Godwin, Joseph Collins, Christopher Glass, Benjamin Bishop, Elisha Purnell, Samuel Atkinson.
- Renunciation: George Layfield, Benjamin Bishop.
- Inventories: Daniel Hull, Solomon Bevans, Joshua Fleming, William

Nelson, Henry Selby, Peter Corbin, William Smith, Isaac Bell, Charles Riggen, John Bowen, Philip Selby, Lebin Dickinson, John Crawford, George Layfield, Alexander Linch, Archibald Dale, Thomas Holland, Richard Blizard, Michael Lenard, John Colbourn, William Gillett, Joseph Cord, Michael Godwin, Andrew Gibb, Thomas Walter, Samuel Lamberson, Elijah Brittingham, Ebenezar Jones.
- Accounts: Joshua Dale, Ebenezar Jones, William Harrison, Nathaniel Brumbley, John Allen, Abraham Outten, William Nelson, William Robinson, Peter Lindall, Henry Selby, Martha Truitt, John Morris, Joseph Davis, John Philips, Angelo Atkinson,

Folio 19

Joshua Fleming.

From Charles County, October 28.

- Bonds: Joseph Melbourn Semmes, Katharine Woodward, William Thompson, John Woodward.
- Wills: Katherine Woodward, William Thompson, John Woodward.
- Inventories: Edward Burch, Elisabeth Hunt, Jane Brice, John Tyler, Mary Smoot, Charles Venables.
- Accounts: Francis Yates, Robert Mastin, John Lancaster, Joseph Clements, Jeremiah Linch, John Thompson, Elisabeth Hungerford, Benjamin Adams, Jr., Thomas Gilpin, Francis Meeks.

From Kent County, October 8.

- Bonds: Darby Shawn, John Robinson, John Morris Burgin, Sutton Burgin, William Hynson, Darby Shawn, Sarah Kelley, Richard Porter.
- Wills: William Hynson, John Robinson, John Morris Burgin.
- Inventories: Benjamin Howard, Jacob Linegar, Richard Linox, Arthur Christfield, Holman Johnson, Ann Haley.
- Accounts: Nathaniel Hynson, Jr., James Kelley, Stephen Kendal, Thomas Sewell.

From St. Mary's County, October 28.

- Bonds: Samuel Mahoney, Francis Thompson, Edward Welsh, Henry Shirtcliffe, Henry Tippett, Richard Simsatt, John Allimand.
- Wills: Edward Welsh, John Gibbons, Henry Goldsberry, Leonard Greenwell, John Hendley, Henry Neale, Joseph Hebb, Augustine Meekins, John Riswick.

Folio 20

- Inventories: Ignatius Goldsberry, Thomas Coode, Aaron Haskins.
- Accounts: John Raley, William Stone, Thomas Asquith, Meverel Lock, John Milburn, Jane Hill.

From Calvert County, October 29.

- Bonds: Benedict Spalding, Elisha Skinner, Thomas Sedgwick, Elisabeth Griffin.
- Wills: Elisabeth Smith, Eleanor Bourne.

From Cecil County, October 28.

- Bonds: Samuel Baker, John Rigbie, Richard Sedgwick, Thomas Husband.
- Accounts: Thomas Elliot.
- Wills: Richard Sedgwick.

From Prince George's County.

- Inventories: James Wardrop, James Wardrop.
- Bonds: George Scott.
- Accounts: Christ. Smith.

From Calvert County.

- Bonds: Benjamin Makal, Clement Smith.
- Wills: Benjamin Mackal, Thomas Sedgwick.

From Charles County, October 29.

- Inventories: Peter Wood.
- Accounts: John Douglass.
- Wills: Richard Molineux.

From Worcester County.

- Accounts: Cornelius Dickenson.
- Inventories: Cornelius Dickenson.

From Queen Anne's County.

- Accounts: Edward Neale.
- Wills: Robert Pratt.

From St. Mary's County.

- Accounts: James Gough.

From Frederick County.

- Accounts: Samuel Selby.

From Talbot County.

- Accounts: Ralph Elston.

From Somerset County.

- Accounts: Edward Killum.

From Baltimore County.

- Wills: Thomas Miles.

From Dorchester County.

- Bonds: John Goldsborough.

From Anne Arundel County.

- Accounts: John Rait.

From Anne Arundel County, October 29.

- Bonds: Robert Franklin, Susannah Hoxton, Jonathon McGlachlin, Thomas Sparrow, Thomas Barber, Hezekiah Linthicumb, Mary Kirckhead, John Parrott.
- Wills: Susannah Hoxton.

- Inventories: Jones Green, Joseph Heard.
- Accounts: John Sappington, Thomas Bear.

Folio 21

From Baltimore County, October 29.

- Bonds: Moses Goodwin, Jacob Tasner, Michael Deskins, Absalom Brown, Jr.
- Inventories: Daniel Sanders, William Johnson, Enoch Baily, Joseph Polson, Samuel Hopkins.
- Accounts: William Hill, Richard Bond, Adam Burchfield, Jr., Mary Loney, Moses Hill, John Clark, John Wisler (cordwainer), Joseph Paulson.

From Somerset County, October 29.

- Bonds: Samuel Roach, William Eason.
- Inventories: Jacob Airs, David Dorman, Sarah Addams.
- Accounts: Roger Train, Mary Benson, Isaac Sirman, Hezekiah Dorman.

From Dorchester County, November 11.

- Wills: James Bright.
- Bonds: James Bright, John Warren, Andrew Russel, Isaac Cannon.
- Inventories: William Oldfield, Thomas Wingate, Thomas Swan, James Branklin, Abraham Cole, Summer Addams, John Clarage, William Arnett, John Low, David Shehawn, Rosannah Cole, Charles Stainton, John Grainger, Isaac Williams, Abraham Cole, Col. Henry Hooper, John Follin, Richard Meekins.
- Accounts: William Insley, Jonathon Stevens, Mary Bussick, Abraham Cole, Henry Ennalls, Jr., Rosannah Cole, Richard Dove, James Burn, Ayres Newman, John Follin, Isaac Williams, George Boaz, Jr.

Folio 22

From Somerset County, November 11.

- Inventories: John Graham, Thomas Wright, David Hopkins, Samuel Flewelling.

From Talbot County, November 26.

- Bonds: Daniel Sherwood, Jos. Coleman, Robert Wilson, James Chapman, William Sales, William Wilson.
- Wills: James Chapman, Daniel Sherwood, Robert Wilson, Joseph Coleman, John Coxman, James Loyd.
- Inventories: Sarah Small.
- Accounts: John Register.

From Worcester County, November 26.

- Bonds: Charles Mooney, Thomas Morris.
- Wills: Betty Roach, Reach Hickman.
- Inventories: Joseph Collins, Catharine Rounds, John Oneal, Avery Morgan, John Blades, David Cathell, James Hickman, Benjamin Bishop, Christopher Glass, Joshua Merrill, John Short.
- Accounts: William Robins, Henry Benson, Richard Crocket, James Smyley.

From Charles County, November 17.

- Bonds: Justinian Burch, Jane Whitticoe, James Griffin.
- Wills: Jane Whitticoe, James Griffin, Justinian Burch.
- Inventories: William Jisson, Thomas Munroe, Mary Askins, Basil Brooks, Anne Fowkes, John Maddox.
- Accounts: Ignatius Semmes, John Cole, William Smallwood Taylor, John Gwyn, Richard Thompson, Elisabeth Jameson, James Skinner, Joseph Joy, Alexander McDaniel, Daniel Wright, Theophilus Swift, John Philpot, Ann Fowkes.

Folio 23

From Kent County, December 1.

- Bonds: Christian Whittington, Robert Hodges, Rebecca Boyer, Marly McDaniel, John Greenwood, Rhoda Kingsley, John Greenwood.
- Wills: John Greenwood.
- Inventories: John Ashley, John Higgins, James Cann, John Rawlinson, Moses Tennant, James Duffy, Joseph Whaley, David Whaley, James Calder, Nicholas Lynch, Samuel Wallis.
- Accounts: Mary Phillips, Samuel Wallis, Nicholas Lynch, James Sterling, James Cawan, James Calder.

From St. Mary's County, December 5.

- Bonds: George Booth, Athanasius Nottingham, Elisabeth Fowler, William Price, Priscilla Gough, Mathias Nottingham, Charles Carroll, Owen Allen.
- Wills: Athanasius Nottingham, George Booth, Sr., William Price, Priscilla Gough, Arnold Livers, Mathias Nottingham, James Ashby.
- Inventories: Henry Shincliffe, George Booth, Sr., Richard Wimsatt, Luke Norris, John Heard, Henry Tippett, Mathew Herbert, Samuel Mahoney.

From Baltimore County, December 5.

- Bonds & Wills: Martha Garretson, William Grafton, Thomas McCool, Malcolm Adams, Simon Friends, John Tipton, John Lawson, Francis Gibson.
- Wills: Deborah Smith, Thomas Johnson.
- Inventories: Hozier Johns, John Watts, Thomas Nisbit, Charles March, Joseph Frost, Charles Jones, Lewis Peter, Absolom Brown, William Bond, Sr., James Preston.
- Accounts: William Hamilton, Richard Johns (administrator of Richard Johns), William Fisher, Jr. (administrator of James Beal), Sarah Watts (administrator

of John Watts), Joseph Alton.

Folio 24

From Somerset County, December 8.

- Bonds: Ann Fowler.
- Bonds & Wills: Robert Geddes, John Dennis.
- Inventories: Thomas Jones, Alexander Porter, Robert Jenkins Henry, John Milbourn.
- Accounts: Joshua Whittington, William Evans, Joseph Rawle, Elisabeth Craig, Henry White, Robert Jenkins Henry, John Hitch, Roger Nicholson.

From Dorchester County, December 8.

- Bonds & Wills: Robert Creighton, Richard Reynolds, William Pritchet, John Brown, Hewit Nutter.
- Bonds: Robert Dines, Ann Sullivane, Thomas Brown, Lettice Woollen, Thomas Bramble.
- Inventories: Thomas Dent, Andrew Russell, Thomas Colson, John Brown, Thomas Bending, Roger Gordon, James Bright, Levin Pritchet, Philip Tall.
- Accounts: James Banning, William Oldfield, Charles Lowd, Thomas Swann, Henry Sworden, John Wootters, John Aaron, Larkin Wilson, Thomas Manning, Henry Fisher, Roger Gordon, Summer Adams, John Paul, Jos. Cox Gray, Betty Rawley, John Staples, William Phillips, James Layton, Thomas Ayrey, Jesse Tull.

From Queen Anne's County, December 8.

- Bonds & Wills: Benjamin Covington, Henry Wrench, John Clayland.
- Bonds: James Grenage, Jr., Ph. Charles Blake, Samuel Rice, Stephen Barnes, Franc. Spry, Jr., Robert Camper, Jr., Solomon Scott, Richard Cook.
- Inventories: John Humphreys, Robert Kent, James Williams, John Wilson, James Hamilton, Richard Gould, Michael Flower, George Dodd, James Clayland, James Bailey, Cornelia Albey, Charles Green,

Folio 25

- Inventories (cont): Stephen Dear, James Pratt, William Honey, John Campbell, Nathaniel Hynson, Charles Seth, James Grenage, Jr.
- Accounts: John Campbell, William Briley, Patrick Hart, John Emerson, William Burton Carsman, Richard Gould, James Pratt, Charles Greeer, Henry Covington, Michael Flower.

From Prince George's County, December 10.

- Bonds & Wills: Elisabeth Evans, Henry Grear, Robert Dove Cooke.
- Bonds: Eleazar Lanham, Rev. John Everfield, Paul Rawlings.
- Inventories: Zachariah Lanham, John Perkins, Paul Rawlings, John Ball, Jr., Robert Dove Cooke, Mary Wade, John Eversfield, Eleazar Lanham, John Selbey.
- Accounts: Colmore Beanes, John Selbey, Paul Rawlings, John Smith Prather, William Jenkins, Mary Wade, John Deal, Jonathon Ellis.

From Anne Arundel County, December 11.

- Bonds: Dorcas Hill, Margaret Moor, Charles Cross, Samuel Battee, Elisabeth Wootton, Mary Lusby, Edward Dorsey.
- Wills: Samuel Battee, Absalom Warfield, Josiah Darby, Charles Cross, Edward Dorsey, Rezin Warfield.
- Inventories: Samuel Birkhead, Mary Birkhead, Joseph Pumphrey, Susanna Jobson.
- Accounts: Susannah Jobson, Sarah Kent.

From Frederick County, December 11.

- Bonds: Honicle Booker, Notley Thomas, Nicholas Haymond.
- Wills: John Veach, Nicholas Haymond, Honicle Booker, Thomas Johnson, Sr., Ninian Taneyhill, Sr.

Folio 26

- Inventories: Jacob Bonte, Henry Conrod, Thomas Kelly, notley Thomas, William Waugh, Jacob Loy, John Middagh, William Waugh.
- Accounts: Peter Beard (administrator of Jacob Siderman), Samuel Norris, Charles Pell, Joseph Hardman, Jacob Crouse, John Ripley, Jacob Loy, Daniel Thomas, Jacob Hofner.

From Queen Anne's County, December 12.

- Bonds & Wills: John Falconar, Thomas Bailey, William Pryor, Nathaniel Read.
- Bonds: Samuel Osburne.
- Inventories: Thomas Mooth, James Andrew, William Meridith, John Emory.
- Accounts: James Lane, John Emory, William Meredith.

From Charles County, December 30.

- Bonds: William Robey, John Wood.
- Inventories: William Thompson, Thomas Hussey Luckett, James Smalwood, Jos. Milb. Semmes, Francis Parnham.
- Accounts: William Deck, James Maddox, Samuel Perkins, Eleanor Gambra, James Provin, Edward Cole, William Dement, Mary Proin, James Smalwood.

From St. Mary's County, December 18.

- Inventories: Kenelm Truman Greenfield, Aaron Hawkins, Henry Neale, Thomas Hatton Combs, Henry Shiercliffe, Mathew Herbert.
- Accounts: Kenelm Truman

Greenfield, Henry Goldsborough, John Stevens, Robert Thompson, Robert Hagar, Elisabeth Bailey, Thomas Hatton Combs, John Taney, Leonard Greenwall, Reuben Cheseldine, Augustine Meekins, Joseph Kelley, John Reed, John Barton Miles, James Gough.

Folio 27

From Talbot County, December 19.

- Bonds: John Sherwood, John Bozman, Henry Pritchard, William Henry.
- Wills: Henry Pritchard.
- Inventories: Frances Camperson.

From Calvert County, December 23.

- Bonds: Mary Dawkins, Ann Cockshut Johnson, Samuel Robertson.
- Wills: Ann Griffin, John Dowell, Samuel Robertson, Mary Dawkins, Sarah King.
- Inventories: Ann Robinson, William Bradey, Edward Blackburn.
- Accounts: Susannah Hoverton, William Hamilton Smith, William Holland.

From Kent County, December 31.

- Bonds: John Graham, Philip Davis, Rebecca Ashley, Charles McDermot, Joseph Worrell, Robert Yeates, Henry Hosier.
- Wills: Philip Davis, John Graham, James Ringgold.
- Inventories: John Preston, John Morris Burgin, Joseph Parsons, Bartholomew Haydon, Nathan Simcocks.
- Accounts: William Redgrave, John Welsh, John Tilden.

From Cecil County, December 31.

- Bonds: Jacob Evertson, Robert Veazey, Adam Mock, Henrietta Rigbie, Thomas O'Neil, Charles Carty, James Brookes, Michael Manycousins, Mary Hyland, Bryan Connally, Samuel Tagart, Mary Brooks.
- Wills: Adam Mock, Jacob Evertson, Mary Hyland, Robert Veazey.
- Accounts: Mary Ricketts, John Osburn.
- Inventories: William Abbot, Richard Sedgwick, John Kirk, John Parnon, James Vance, Peter Bayard, John Hart, James Hughes.

INDEX

Companies
  Free School of Cecil
    County 17
  Pompret Chapple 53
  Poor 65
  St. Alevigis Chapel 102

Aarden
  Mary 5
Aaron
  Ambrous 29
  John 29, 54, 107, 108, 112
  Mary 29, 47, 54
  Nancy 29
  Sally 29
Abbot
  William 108, 113
Abbott
  William 106
Abel
  Samuel 6
Abell
  Edward 67
  John 49
  John Hour 67
  Samuel 6
Acre
  Abraham 8
  Thomas 8
Adair
  Robert 15, 19, 24
Adams
  Alexander 88
  Ann 66
  Benjamin 46, 110
  Betty 26, 66
  Boze 56
  Delilah 84
  Eleanor 82
  Ephraim 3, 101
  Francis 106, 109
  Hopewell 30
  Isaac 3
  Jacob 13, 87, 101
  James 9, 36, 61
  John 12, 57
  Malcolm 111
  Martin 75
  Mary 26, 61, 66
  McNemarra 88
  Nancy 88
  Philip 13
  Philip Colin 66
  Philip Collins 26
  Rachel 88
  Richard 12
  Roger 9, 61
  Samuel 12, 26, 66
  Sarah 13, 26, 66, 84, 88, 107
  Summer 88, 107, 112
  Thomas 46
  William 61
Adamson
  Jeremiah 71
  Victoria 71
Addams
  Ann 34
  Bose 61
  Charles 61
  George 34
  Henry 32

  James 56
  Mary 56, 61
  Misse 61
  Nisse 56
  Priscila 47
  Richard 47
  Roger 36, 56, 61
  Sarah 111
  Summer 107, 111
  Valentine 34
  William 22
Addison
  Anthony 109
Agin
  Bridget 90
Aikins
  Eleanor 76
Aires
  John 58
Airey
  John Pitt 46
  Leah Hicks 46
  Louisa 46
  Mary 46
  Milcah 46
  Richard Hill 46
  Thomas 46, 107
  Thomas Hill 46
Airs
  Jacob 108, 111
Akin
  Archibald 76
  Margaret 76
Albey
  Cornelia 112
Alder
  James 28
Alexander
  Hannah 32, 107
  Mark 106
  Maryanne Trueman 73
  William 32
Alfree
  Rebecca 83
All
  Mary 26
  Robert 26
Allen
  Benjamin 81
  John 110
  Joseph 81, 104
  Owen 46, 111
  Prindowell 81
  William 17, 81
Alley
  Cornelia 109
  John 96
  Sarah 96
Allimand
  John 110
Allison
  Thomas 98
Allum
  Thomas 90
Allwell
  Sarah 4
Ally
  Cornelia 96
Allyn
  Benjamin 27
Allynn
  Thomas 27
Alridge
  Nicholas 43
  William 43
Alton

  Joseph 112
Alwell
  Elisabeth 4
  Jacob 4
  John 4
  Mary 4
  Nathan 4
  Sarah 4
  Stephen 4
  Thomas 4
  William 4
Ambrose
  John 50, 63, 65, 75
  Martha 65
Ames
  Mordecai 5
  William 5
Amos
  Benjamin 102
Anderson
  Agness 33
  Elisabeth 33
  James 11, 33, 35
  John 35, 106
  Mary 11
  Robert 11, 33
  Samuel 33
  Susannah 105
  Thomas 79
  William 15
Anderton
  John 107
Andrew
  James 10, 108, 112
  John 10, 88
  Joseph 10
  Nehamiah 47
  Samuel 88
  Thomas 10
  William 10
Andrews
  Abraham 85
  Agnes 17
  Betsy 91
  Elisabeth 91
  James 3, 17
  Jane 75
  John 44, 75, 90
  Joseph 3, 61, 72
  Mary 3, 75
  Rebecca 91
  Samuel 75
  Stephen 48
  Thomas 91
  William 75
Angier
  John 16, 50
  Sarah 50
Annason
  Anna 53
Apler
  Easter 92
  Elisabeth 92
  Everhart 92
  Jacob 92
  Roshall 92
  Rosura 92
Appleby
  Sarah 95
Apsley
  William 63
Arbunkill
  James 12
Ardis
  Sarah 91
Armstrong

Dinah 39
Edward 34
George 39
Hellen 39
James 39, 89, 105
John 34, 39
Rebecca 34
Robert 39
Susannah 55, 81
Arnett
  William 111
Arnold
  John 8, 106
  Rebecca 106
Arrants
  Johannas 11, 106
Ashby
  James 65, 111
Ashley
  John 108, 111
  Rebecca 113
Ashpaw
  John 105
Askey
  Thomas 68
Askins
  Mary 108, 111
Asquith
  Thomas 110
Atchason
  Anna 53
  James 53
Atkins
  Stephen 89
Atkinson
  Angelo 110
  John 1, 79, 87, 95
  Mary 1
  Samuel 109
Atkison
  Betty 43
  Isaac 43
  Joshua 43
  William 43
Augustin
  Julius 36
Auld
  John 74
  Mary 74
Aulton
  Joseph 106
Aydelott
  Benjamin 91
Ayres
  Harrison 4
Ayrey
  Thomas 112

Baden
  Eleanor 19
  John 19
  Letice 19
  Letitia 19
  Martha 19
  Thomas 19
Bacon
  John 88
Badley
  William 90
Bailey
  Clement 36
  Elenor 105
  Elisabeth 95, 113
  James 95, 112
  John 95, 105
  Juliana 95
  Peter 70
  Sarah 95
  Thomas 112

Baily
  Enoch 111
  Henry 34
Baine
  Adam 38
Baker
  Ann 71
  Cassandra 40
  Charles 45, 71, 89, 109
  Christopher 17
  Dorcas 17
  Eleanor 40
  Eliza 71
  Francis 8
  Henry 16, 60
  Ignatius 40
  Isaac 17
  Jacob 17
  James 77, 78
  Jesse 17
  John 40
  Jonathon 71
  Margret 40
  Nathan 71
  Nicholas 40, 109
  Rachel 40
  Samuel 110
  Sarah 71
  Thomas 79
  Walter 40
  William 40
Ball
  John 112
  William 49
Balthrop
  Bowles Tyer 73
Bankes
  William 108
Banning
  Andrew 57
  Henry 64
  James 108, 112
  Jeremiah 66, 81
  Thomas 34
  William 57
Barber
  Edward 26
  Elisabeth 26
  John Mevert 26
  John Miphert 26
  Mary 26
  Sarah 26
  Thomas 26, 110
Barcos
  Rebecca 18
Barkhust
  Anne 74
  Elisabeth 74, 83
  George 74
  Isabella 82
  James 74, 82, 83
  John 74, 83
  Joseph 74
  Nathaniel 74
  Solomon 74
  Stephen 83
  Susannah 74
  Thomas 74
  William 74, 108, 109
Barklet
  Abraham 13
  Rachel 13
Barkley
  Isabella 56
Barnes
  Amos 88
  Ann 2
  Arrabella 88
  Bennett 88
  Burr 2

  Catherine 2
  Edam 73
  Ford 88
  Hannah 73
  James 2
  Jane 2
  Job 94
  John 1, 17, 55, 73, 95, 100, 109
  John Waters 55
  Katherine 2
  Mary Ann 2
  Mathew 2
  Richard 2, 88
  Ruth 88
  Stephen 112
  Thomas 54, 101
  Violetta 2
Barnett
  Joseph 48, 109
  Rebecca 48
  Thomas 47, 108
Barnhouse
  Elisabeth 29
  Richard 29
  Timothy 29
Barnwell
  James 34
Barns
  John 109
Barnulo
  Jeremiah 74
Barrett
  Jonathon 108
  William 106, 109
Barry
  Basil 34
  Cornelius 38, 75
  Jacob 34
  Mordecai 34
  Sarah 34
Bartlet
  Sarah 64
Barwick
  Alice 83
  Edward 12, 83
  Eleanor 12
  James 83
  Jane 12
  John 12, 83
  Joshua 83
  Nathan 83
  Solomon 83
  William 12, 83
Basil
  Joseph 106
Basill
  Joseph 49
Bastford
  Thomas 106
Bateman
  Benjamin 88
  Elisabeth 42, 88, 96
  Jane 88
  John 42, 50, 96, 100
  Mary 96
  Michael 96
  Sarah 96, 100
  William 96
Batson
  John 89
  Susannah 35
Battee
  Samuel 112
Baushell
  Slyter 51
Baxter
  John 63
Bay
  John 30

Thomas 30
Bayard
  Peter 113
Baynard
  Elisabeth 67
  George 66
  Job 66, 71
  Lydia 66, 67
  Margaret 67
  Rachel 66
  Sarah 66
  Thomas 9, 67
Bayne
  Lydia 49
  William 20, 32, 49
Baynes
  Walmsly 32
Beaks
  Ann 96
  William 96
Beal
  James 111
Beale
  Thomas 28
Beall
  Benjamin 25
  Elisabeth 2
  James 67
  John 2, 105
  Kesiah 84, 85
  Robert 105
  Thomas 36, 83
  Zephaniah 84, 85
Bean
  Thomas 18
Beanes
  Colmore 112
Beans
  Elisabeth 32
Bear
  Thomas 105, 111
Beard
  Andrew 107, 109
  Chloe 30
  John 30
  Nicholas 30
  Peter 67, 112
Beaston
  George 31
Beatty
  Charles 78
  Edward 22
  Elijah 22
  Ezekiel 22
  Ezra 22
  Thomas 22
Beavin
  Charles 22
  Edward 22
  Rebecca 22
  Richard 22
Beavins
  Ann 21, 22
  Rowland 90
Beck
  Edward 4
  Mary 79
  Samuel 79
  Sarah 24
  William 24
Beckwith
  Charles 20, 25
Beddah
  Absalom 4
Beech
  Lydia 28
  Thomas 28
Beedle
  John 36
  Noble 34

William 14, 15
Belgrave
  Andrew 27
Bell
  Isaac 110
  William 95
Bellican
  Christopher 28
Bells
  Isaac 104
Bemmer
  Phillip 97
Bending
  Thomas 107, 108, 112
Bennett
  Ann 72
  Benjamin 72
  Edward 108
  Eleanor 72
  Elisabeth 72
  Elisha 72
  George 108
  John 39, 72
  Lydia 72
  Mary 72
  Samuel 72
  Thomas 72
  William 72
Benny
  James 32
  Thomas 7
Benson
  George 69, 77
  Henry 111
  James 26, 43, 81, 83, 96
  Mary 111
  Nicholas 79
  Rachel 69
  William 104
Benston
  Mary 10
Bently
  Peter 70
Benton
  Elisabeth 44
  John 44
  Vincent 71
  Vinson 100
  William 98
Bergman
  Solomon Turner 35
Berry
  Benjamin 66
  James 8, 34
  John 82
  Mildred 86
  Robert 32
  Sarah 73
  Susannah 32
Berryman
  Rebeccah 95
Beshawn
  Patrick 80
Bessicks
  John 104
Besswick
  Denne 55
  Denny 55
  Eunice 55
  Mary 34, 55
  Nathan 55
  Richard 55, 107
  Susannah 55
  Thomas 34, 55
  William 55, 95
Besswicke
  William 74
Besswicks
  Mary 81
Betton

Turbutt 82
Betts
  Hezekiah 19
  Samuel 104
Beuly
  John 12
Bevans
  Solomon 109
Bewley
  Joseph 79, 81, 92
Bichey
  Henry 109
Biddle
  Samuel 83
Biggs
  Ann 99
  John 59, 99
Billican
  Christopher 35
Billingsley
  Jane 90
  William 90
Binney
  Benjamin 51
  Mary 51
Birkhead
  Christopher 55
  Elisabeth 13, 35
  Francis 35
  John 35
  Joseph 35
  Mary 35, 70, 112
  Nehemiah 13, 35, 70
  Samuel 13, 35, 70, 109, 112
Birstall
  John 32
Birster
  John 33
Biscoe
  George 29
Bishop
  Ann 85, 105
  Avis 85
  Benjamin 109, 111
  Elijah 85
  Elisabeth 85
  Jos. 20, 85
  Joseph 24
  Mary 60
  Richard 60, 85
  Risdon 85
  Rizden 5
  Roger 85
  Smyth 85
  William 20, 24, 85
Black
  James 100
  Jane 100
  John 60
Blackburn
  Edward 113
Blackey
  William 106
Blackiston
  Ann 5
  Anne 75
  Ebenezar 8
  George 37
  Hans 75
  Henrietta 8
  John 2, 17, 37
  Sarah 37
  Susannah 86
  Vincent 86
  William 37
Blacklock
  Thomas 18, 89
Blackmore
  Charles 35

Mary 35
Blackston
  Benjamin 16
  George 16
  John 16
  Priscilla 16
  Sarah 16
  William 16
Blackwood
  John 45
Blades
  Ann 24
  Elisabeth 24
  Isabella 24
  James 24
  John 109, 111
  Mary 24
  Samuel 24
Blake
  Barbara 46
  Charles 57
  Elisabeth 57
  Henrietta Maria 57
  James 71
  John 81
  Margaret 71
  Mary 81
  Peter 81
  Ph. Charles 112
  Philemon Charles 57
  Rebecca 55
  Rebeccah 81
  Thomas 46
Blanford
  Ann 53
Blizard
  Richard 104, 110
Blunt
  Elisabeth 88
  Laban 27
  Rebecca 27
  Samuel 70
  Susannah 61
Boarman
  Ann 26
  Eleanor 51
  Elisabeth 51
  Mary 26
  Mary Ann 51
  Raphael 51
  Richard 26
  Richard Bennett 51, 109
  William 106, 109
Boaz
  Bridget 33, 47
  George 33, 47, 61, 111
  Henry 33
  James 33
  John 33
  Joseph 33
  Mary 33
  Nancy 33
  William 33
Bodean
  Henry 50
Bodeen
  Henry 66
Bodein
  Henry 6
Bodien
  Christian 52
Bolton
  John 90
  Rachel 3
  William 3
Bond
  Benjamin 37
  Charles 94, 106, 108
  Christopher 37
  Daniel 18
  Edward 37, 94
  Eleanor 94
  Elisabeth 37
  Helen 55
  Henry 37
  Jacob 35
  Joshua 5, 35, 37
  Luke Jacob 18
  Margaret 55
  Mary 55
  Nichodomus 55
  Nicodemus 100
  Peter 37
  Phebe 55
  Richard 12, 46, 55, 111
  Samuel 37
  Sarah 55
  Susanna 37
  Thomas 48
  William 5, 111
Bonds
  Jacob 106
Bonte
  Jacob 112
Booker
  Honicle 112
  Linora 76
  Mary 60
  Stonile 76
Boon
  Ann 67
  Isaac 109
  Jacob 37
  Jemimah 37
  Jemmima 37
  John 67
  Nicholas 67
  Rachel 37
  Richard 43, 67
  William 37
Boone
  Charles 25
  Elisabeth 25
  Humphrey 25, 109
  Jemima 3
  John 25, 43, 67
  John Kandell 35
  Joseph 63
  Lethisa 63
  Mary 86
  Nicholas 16, 35, 43, 106
  Richard 67
  Thomas 25
Boor
  Elisabeth 49
Booth
  Basil 76
  George 42, 76, 102, 111
  James 76
  John 7, 42, 76
  Monica 76
  Richard 76
  Thomas 76
Bordley
  Mary 80
  Stephen 12, 80, 90
  William 80
Bostick
  John 38
  Sanders 16, 27, 28
Bostock
  Sanders 58, 64, 87
Boston
  Betty 101
  David 101
  Elijah 101
  Ephraim 101
  Esaw 101
  Isaac 101
  Jacob 101
  Lazarus 101
  Mathew 101
Botelar
  Ann 29
Boteler
  Henry 39
  Lucy 52
Botts
  George 26
Boulding
  William 34
Boult
  Mary 88
  Susannah 88
Bounds
  Richard Stevens 108
Bourk
  Edward 42
  James 42
  Thomas 10
Bourn
  Esther 1
  Jacob 1
Bourne
  Eleanor 110
  Thomas 83
Bouston
  Joseph 17
Bowden
  James 7
Bowen
  Abraham 8
  Edmond 22
  Edward 17
  Jethro 98
  John 110
  Jonas 22
  Luke 77
  Samuel 17, 22
Bower
  Peter 2
Bowers
  John 52
Bowie
  Allen 51
Bowin
  John 104
Bowing
  Solomon 60
Bowins
  John 104
Bowland
  William 30
Bowles
  Thomas 109
Bowling
  James 47, 108
  Mary Ann 47
Bowman
  Samuel 66
Box
  Arraminta 49
Boyce
  Ann 34
  John 34
  Joseph 34, 68
  William 30, 34, 69
Boyer
  Augustin 107
  Augustine 77
  Catharine 64
  Eleanor 64
  Elisabeth 7
  John 83, 105, 109
  Michael 99
  Rebecca 111
  Rebeccah 64
  Thomas 86
  William 64, 106
Boyle

Bozel (cont.)
    James 21
Bozley
    Elisabeth 18
    James 18
    Prud 18
    William 18
Bozman
    John 113
Bracco
    John 71
Bradey
    William 102, 107, 113
Bradford
    Catherine 15
    Mary 65
    William 15
Brafield
    Mark 12, 15
Bramble
    David 60
    John 48
    Mary 37
    Thomas 112
Brand
    James 48
Brandt
    Charles 69
    Elisabeth 11
    Randolph 22
    Richard 22
Branklin
    James 21, 107, 111
Brannock
    Henry 88
    Margaret 20, 25
Brashears
    Ann 102
    Nathaniel 102
Brawhawn
    Patrick 45
Brawner
    Edward 106
    Jos. 11
Brayfield
    Mark 80
Breakenbridge
    Barbara 12
    Robert 12
Bredon
    James 42
Brewer
    Joseph 81
    Nicholas 81
    Rachel 81
Brice
    James 42, 104
    Jane 110
    John 107
    Martin 88
    Mary 42
    Samuel 42
Brierly
    Hugh 74, 84
    John 62
    Nathan 62
    Robert 62, 108
    Thomas 62
Bright
    Francis 17
    James 111, 112
    William 109
Brightwell
    John 19
Briley
    Lucretia 44
    William 44, 112
Bringle
    Christian 76
Brinkley
    James 102
Brinnagan
    John 59
Brinsfield
    George 107
Brisco
    James 78
Briscoe
    Alexander 56
    Elisabeth 58, 59
    James 58, 59
    John 56
    Joseph 12, 38, 56
    Mary Ann 7
    Philip 44
    Samuel 106, 109
    Thomas 99
    William 7, 56
Brite
    James 40
Brittingham
    Elijah 110
    Levi 27
    Sarah 27
Broadaway
    Isaac 30
    James 4, 9
    Joseph 108
    Mary 4, 9, 30
    Samuel 30
    Sarah 4, 9
Brody
    Robert 80
Brome
    Ann 15
    Henry 15
    John 15
    Mary 15
    Thomas 15
    William 15
Brook
    Basil 109
    Benjamin 40
    Elisabeth 68
    Mary 40
Brooke
    Basil 60, 109
    Charity 41
    Chloe 41
    Elisabeth 26
    Francis 26
    Harrison 55
    John 41
    Joseph 105
    Sarah 41
    Thomas 68
    Walter 41, 68
    William 41
Brookes
    Benjamin 105
    James 113
    John 11
    Philip 5
Brooks
    Basil 111
    Henry 6
    John 44
    Mary 113
Broom
    Alexander 15
    Elisabeth 6
    Hooper 6
    Mary 6
    Nancy 6
    Sarah 6
    Thomas 6
Broome
    Alexander 66
    Ann 66
    Dorcas 6
    John Hooper 6
    Kesia 66
Brotherer
    Joseph 89
Broughton
    John 29, 108
Browire
    Thomas 104
Brown
    Absalom 111
    Absolom 111
    Anderton 72, 91
    Andrew 65
    Ann 96
    Annastatia 76
    Benjamin 92
    Betty 72
    Capt. 43
    Cassandra 93
    Charles 72, 74, 91, 92, 94
    Edward 38, 106
    Elisabeth 38
    Ephraim 92
    Esther 96
    Ezekiel 72
    Francis 72, 96
    George 25, 48
    Grace 65
    Hannah 43
    James 15, 27, 46, 96, 109
    Jane 14
    Joel 9, 96
    John 4, 38, 39, 46, 72, 96, 101, 106, 107, 112
    Jos. 94
    Joseph 94
    Joshua 92
    Margaret 101
    Mary 25, 55, 72, 85, 96
    Morgan 38, 83
    Nicholas 76
    Peter 76
    Rebeccah 92
    Richard 76, 92, 105
    Robert 76
    Samuel 92, 93
    Sarah 72, 96
    Susannah 92
    Thomas 104, 112
    Vachel 92
    William 46, 91, 93
Browne
    Charles 105
    James 108
Browning
    Cornelia 28
    George 17, 28
    Nicholas 28
    Thomas 29, 58
    Wilson 28
Bruce
    Elisabeth 59
    Jane 59, 106
    Jane Little 59
    John 59
    Judith 51, 59
    Norman 94
    Robert 59
    Susannah Gardiner 94
    Townley 59
    Walter 59
    William 59
Bruff
    Lucy 26
    Mary 26
    Rachel 26
    Rebecca 26
    Richard 26

William 26
Bruffit
  William 104
Bruffitt
  William 49
Brumbley
  Nathaniel 110
Brummer
  Elias 87
Brunner
  Jacob 50, 84
  John 50, 84
Brust
  Conrad 38
Bryan
  Charles 24
  Dinah 61, 105
  James 61
  John 42, 61, 105
  Martha 95
  Mathew 108
  Rebeccah 61
  Sarah 61
  Solomon 20, 25, 61, 95
  Stephen 61
  William 63
Bryon
  Eleanor 41
  Henry 41, 105
Bryson
  James 14
Buchanan
  Nathaniel 17
  Robert 63
Buchannan
  Andrew 79
Buck
  Benjamin 5, 74
  John 5, 74, 87
  Susannah 16
Bugar
  Charlotte 76
  Chatharine 76
  Eleanor 76
  Frederick 76
  Jacob 76
  John 76
Bugess
  Valentine 67
Bull
  Abraham 18
  Elisabeth 24, 35
  Hannah 18
  John 24, 35
  Martha 18
  Rachel 18
Bullen
  Charles 97
  Elisabeth 22
  Henry 22
  Mary 22
  Sarah 22
  Thomas 22
Bullock
  Francis 9
  Joseph 9
Bully
  John 83, 106
  Mary 83
  Rebecca 83
Bumbage
  Thomas 102
Bunt
  Elisabeth 88
  Thomas 75, 80, 88
Burch
  Ann 18, 74, 92, 94
  Benjamin 92
  Catharine 74
  Edward 18, 73, 74, 105, 110
  Elisabeth 74
  Jam 74
  Jesse 73
  John 94
  Justinian 18, 92, 106, 111
  Justinian Thomas 92
  Leonard 92
  Margaret 12
  Martha 94
  Mary 18, 73
  Orpah 94
  Sarah 92
  Stacy 18
  Thomas 45
  Winifred 18
Burchfield
  Adam 108, 111
Burgain
  Sutter 21
Burgess
  Achsah 78
  Basil 78
  Elisabeth 105
  George 95
  Jane 95
  John 46, 61
  Sarah 78
  Valentine 68
Burgin
  John Morris 110, 113
  Sutton 107, 110
Burk
  Edward 105
  John 5, 9
Burn
  James 34, 111
  John 37, 54
  Joshua 62
  Swetnam 33
  William 34
Burns
  Elisabeth 63
Burris
  Mary 7
Burroughs
  Benjamin 68
  Edward 82, 83
  Elisabeth 28
  George 68
  James 67, 68, 75, 83
  John 93
  Joseph 28
  Sarah 93
  Valentine 83
Burrows
  Valentine 70
Burton
  Elier 106
  Joshua 84
  Leah 20
  William 20
Bush
  Elisabeth 16
  Isaac 16
Busick
  James 58, 73, 84
  Samuel 80
Busil
  Joseph 106
Bussey
  Edward 16
Bussick
  John 52
  Joshua 52
  Mary 52, 111
  Solomon 52
Buswell
  Thomas 12, 90
Butler
  Charles 86
  Elisabeth 72
  John 11
  Judith 98
  Mary 98
Butt
  Samuel 105
Button
  Roger 40
  William 14, 40, 105
Byaly
  Lodowick 97
Byarly
  John 76
Byland
  Thomas 73
Byrd
  William 18
Byrn
  James 44
Byus
  William 9

Cade
  Thomas 104
Cage
  Wilson 88
Caile
  Hall 7
  John 107
Calder
  Alexander 64
  James 107, 111
Caldkins
  Henry 19
Caldwell
  John 102
  Joshua 109
  Samuel 102
  Thomas 50
Callaghane
  Catharine 74
  Ferdinando 74
  James 74, 105
  Sarah 74
Callaway
  Elisabeth 13
  Isaac 77
  John 102
  Levin 102
  Mary 77
  Peter 13
Cambell
  James 104
Camion
  James 60
Campbel
  Hugh 109
Campbell
  Daniel 35, 41
  David 107
  Hugh 109
  James 59, 66, 104
  John 24, 39, 44, 93, 105, 112
  William 24
Camper
  Robert 112
Camperson
  Frances 63, 113
Camplin
  Henry 22
Canaday
  Thomas 30
Cann
  Frances 58
  James 58, 111
Cannell

Cannington
  Abraham 87
  John 53
Cannon
  Alethea 36
  Ann 36
  Cartis 36
  Charity 36
  Constant 36
  Isaac 111
  Jacob 36
  James 107
  Jane 10
  Jesse 36
  John 36
  Levin 36
  Lucretia 36
  Mary 36
  Thomas 36, 52
  Whittington 36
  William 9, 36, 56, 61, 91, 105
Caradine
  Henrietta 48
Carey
  Dennis 27, 96
  Dorothy 95
  John 48, 68, 95
  Timothy 109
  William 43
Carman
  Henry Cully 3
  John 3
  William Burton 3
Carnan
  Christopher 44
  John 44, 106
Carpenter
  John 47, 108
Carr
  Benjamin 41
  John 75
Carradine
  Eleanor 48, 57
  Hannah 48, 57
  John 48, 57
  Richard 48, 57
  Susannah 48, 57
  Thomas 48, 57, 105, 109
  William 48
Carroll
  Charles 111
  Peter 106
Carry
  William 57
Carslake
  Mary 1
Carsman
  William Burton 112
Carson
  James 31, 93
  Mary 31
Cart
  Barbara 87
Carter
  Edward 10
  James 44
  William 10
Carty
  Charles 113
  John 55
Carvill
  John 90
Cashery
  Arthur 65
Casner
  Martin 90
Cassaway
  Thomas 11
Cassey
  Elisabeth 25
  James 25, 105
  Othaniel 25
Casson
  Fardinando 80
  John 80, 88
  Myers 80
  Robert 80
  Sarah 88
Cathell
  David 75, 109, 111
  Elisabeth 75
  Jonathon 75
Caton
  Henry 43
Catrop
  Elisabeth 3
  John 3
  Mary Ann 3
  William Marsh 3
Catterton
  Dilah 1
  Jeremiah 1
  Susannah 1
Causin
  Gerrard 95
  Josias 95
Caustin
  Isaac 66
Cave
  Ann 87
  John 87
Cavell
  Elisabeth 75
Cavender
  Ezekiel 31
Cawan
  James 111
Cawood
  Stephen 105
  Thomas 106, 109
  William 109
Cedar
  Ann 24
  John 24
Chaires
  James 74
  John 74
  Nathan 74
  Thomas 74
  William 74
Chairs
  James 63
  William 74
Chake
  Elisabeth 39
  John 39
  Margaret 39
  Martha 39
  Mary 39
  Priscilla 39
  Sarah 39
Chambers
  Charles 27
  James 105
  Philip 88
  William 70
Chambly
  George 90
Chance
  Aaron 61
  Daniel 34
  Elisabeth 61
  Martha 34
  Richard 34
  William 61
Chanch
  Elisabeth 61
Chandler
  Hannah 56
  Nathaniel 56
  Thomas 49, 56
Chanler
  Abell 77
Chap
  Elisabeth 1
Chaplain
  Ann 36
  Bridget 36
  Solomon 36
Chapline
  Agness 39
  Elisabeth 39
  Ester 39
  Jennet 39
  Joseph 39
  Josias 39
  Levica 39
  Lydia 39
  Mary 39
  Moses 39, 106
  William 39
Chapman
  Constant 59
  George 59
  James 111
  John 24
  Nathaniel 59
  Pearson 59
  Samuel 105
  William 106
Charles
  Isaac 67
  Jacob 70
  Solomon 67
Chase
  Samuel 67
Cheeke
  Mary 39
Cheney
  Isaiah 88
  John 105
  Lewis 50
  Rachel 88
Cheseldine
  Cyranius 6
  Kenelum 46
  Knelem 6
  Reuben 113
  Rubin 46
Chetham
  Edward 82
  James 82
Chew
  Elisabeth 86
  John 86
  Samuel 13, 35, 86
  Sarah 86
  William 86
Chezum
  Joseph 10
Chick
  William 21
Chiffin
  James 52
  William 81
Chilton
  John 109
Ching
  Mary 44, 106
Chipley
  Rebecca 10
Chisel
  Joseph 106
Chiswell
  Stephen Newton 29
Chittam
  Thomas 48
Chitten
  Sarah 52

Chittum
  Isaac 44
Choir
  Robert Nap 87
Chrisfield
  John 64
Chrisman
  John 54
Christfield
  Arthur 75, 107, 110
Christopher
  Clement 89, 105, 108
  John 89
  Sarah 89
Chun
  Lancelot 48
Chunn
  Catherine 26
  Joseph 26
  Mary 66
Clagett
  Frances 65
  John 22
  Sabrit 105
  Sabritt 105
Clagget
  Charles 65
  Martha 65
  Mary 65
  Rebeccah 65
Claggett
  Frances 65
  Henry 97
  Nathaniel 65
Clarage
  John 107, 111
Clare
  Christian 1
  Edmond 1
  Elisabeth 1
  Hannah 1
  Isaac 1
  James 1
  John 1
  Sarah 1
Clark
  Aquilla 73
  Caleb 88
  Charity 73
  Charles 17, 105
  Daniel 63, 73
  David 23
  Edward 88
  Eleanor 66
  Elisabeth 73
  George 5, 8
  Henr. 63
  Henry 30, 31, 63
  John 17, 48, 56, 111
  Joshua 63, 92
  Margaret 50
  Mary 5, 73
  Mathew 56, 86
  Rachel 17, 56
  Rachell 56
  Richard 13
  Robert 73
  Robert Steel 73
  William 56
Clarke
  Charles 105
  Jos. 19
  Joshua 57
  Mary 8
  Rebecca 107
  Thomas 105
Clarks
  John 104
Clarkson
  Bariah 36
  Betty 36, 56, 61
  John 47, 108
  Joseph 47
  Richard 9, 36, 56, 59, 61, 94
Claten
  Olden 109
Clay
  Daniel 41
Clayland
  Elisabeth 83
  James 66, 71, 83, 112
  John 83, 112
  Sarah 83
  Thomas 83
  William 83
Clayton
  Alden 106
  Charles 38, 39, 78
  Edward 43, 85
  Solomon 78
  William 43
Claywell
  Lucretia 104
  Shadrack 5
Cleaver
  John 89, 107
  Mary 89
  William 89
Clem
  George 37
Clements
  Ann 51, 71
  Charles 64
  Clement 51
  Edward 64
  Francis 64
  George 53
  Jacob 64
  Jean 64
  John 51, 64
  Joseph 51, 106, 110
  Lambert 95
  Leonard 51
  Vincent 71
  Walter 51, 64
  William 10
Clift
  Mary 37
Clim
  George 37
Clive
  Jacob 76
Clocker
  Ann 85
  Benjamin 85
  Daniel 85
  Elisabeth 85
  Mary 85
  Rebecca 85
  William 85
Clothier
  Robert Napp 58, 64
Cloud
  Sarah 56
Cluff
  Michael 29, 101
Coale
  Samuel 57
  Thomas 57
  William 42, 43
Coatney
  John 8
Cockran
  Joseph 35
Coe
  John 28
  Mary 28
Coffe
  Henry 106
Coffer
  Henry 109
Colbourn
  Elisabeth 21
  John 104, 110
  William 21
Cole
  Abraham 79, 111
  Ann 26, 36
  Benjamin 36
  Charles 70
  Edward 26, 52, 53, 112
  Elisabeth 36, 55
  Francis 36
  George 36, 40, 49, 57, 107, 108
  Hezekiah 70
  Jane 49, 57
  John 36, 70, 86, 91, 98, 111
  Joseph 26
  Margaret 76
  Martha 49
  Mary 36
  Peter 36, 49, 104, 106
  Rebecca 36
  Richard 107, 108
  Richard Miller 108
  Robert 26
  Rosannah 70, 107, 111
  Sarah 53
  William 57
Colegate
  Ann 64
  Benjamin 64
  Charity 64
  Elisabeth 64
  Mary 64
  Rebeccah 64
  Ruth 64
  Thomas 64
Coleman
  Jos. 111
  Joseph 111
  Richard 40
Coles
  Abraham 97
Collier
  Doubty 13
  George 22
  John 61
  Mary 61
  Robert 87
  Thomas 34
Collings
  Abraham 88
  Elisabeth 85
  Isaac 88
  John 6
  Martha 85
  Sarah 85
  Thomas 80
Collins
  Abraham 88
  Ann 88
  Bartholomew 58
  Betty 72
  Eli 72
  Elisabeth 13, 72
  Hannah 72
  Jeremiah 85
  John 18, 69, 85, 87, 91
  Joseph 109, 111
  Levy 72
  Mary 58, 72
  Nathan 13
  Noah 72
  Patrick 13
  Richard 98
  Sarah 61, 72

Solomon 13
Thomas 72, 89
Tobiah 72
Wilfred 88
William 6
Collison
  Benjamin 1
  Edward 1
  Frances 1
  George 1
  James 1
  Mary 1
  Sarah 1
Colret
  John 20
Colsley
  Mary 85
  Nancy 85
Colson
  Elisabeth 81
  Thomas 81, 108, 112
Combest
  Jacob 106, 108
Combs
  Katharine 65
  Thomas Hatton 112, 113
  William 30
Comeford
  Peter 5
Comegys
  Alethea 42
  Alphon 42
  Ann 42
  Bartus 86
  Cornelius 42
  Edward 42, 97
  Esther 3
  Isaac 26
  Jacob 69
  Jesse 42
  John 28, 42
  Jonathon 42
  Nathaniel 42
  Sarah 5, 37
  William 28, 42, 104, 107
Comerford
  Pewter 92
Commegys
  Ann 78
  Edward 78
  John 78, 85, 103
  Mary 78
  William 78, 86
Compton
  John 59
  Margaret 59
  Mary Ann 59
  Stephen 59, 88
  Theo 59
  William 59
Conally
  Bryan 108
Coniken
  John 47
Conikin
  John 100
Conn
  Jesse 33
  Martha 12
  Mary 14
  Samuel 33
  Thomas 12
Connally
  Bryan 113
Connell
  Elisabeth 38, 43
Conner
  Achsah 105
  Caleb 105, 106
  Richard 85
Connerly
  Ann 67
  James 67
  Margaret 67
  Mary 67
  Thomas 28, 67
Connikin
  John 109
Conrod
  Henry 104, 112
Consilman
  George 87
Constanty
  Anne 55
Contee
  Elisabeth 52
  Theodore 52
  Thomas 46, 86
Conway
  Susanna 36
Coode
  John 98, 105
  Susanna 98
  Thomas 110
Cook
  Andrew 33
  Ann 33
  Babbington 33
  Charles 71
  James 71
  John 71
  Joseph 71
  Martha 71
  Mary Ann 71
  Rachel 71
  Richard 112
  Robert Dove 99
  Sarah 33
  Thomas 33, 71, 108
Cooke
  Ann 105
  Robert Dove 112
  John 40
  Joshua 3
  Samuel 3
  William 3
Cooksey
  Thomas 2
  Thomas Reid 2
Coombs
  Joseph 53, 75
  William 53
Cooper
  Abraham 75
  Benjamin 1
  Betty 80
  Catharine 80
  Catherine 48
  Eliab 70
  Esther 70
  George 12
  Isabell 75
  James 12, 54, 80
  Jesse 70, 106, 109
  John 12, 80, 100
  Karen Hepuch 70
  Karon Hapuck 70
  Mary 80
  Owen 80
  Priscilla 80
  Rebecca 80
  Rhody 80
  Richard 12, 105
  Sarah 85
  Stephen 80
  Thomas 12, 75, 75, 80, 107
  William 9, 63
  Zeporah 70
  Zopera 70
Cope
  Robert 70
Copeland
  Barbara 47
  Joseph 48
  Lawrence 47
Coper
  Jane 18
Copocy
  Roger 94
Copper
  George 6, 86
  Joseph 12
  Martha 95
  Samuel 95
  William 6, 89, 94
Coppin
  James 62
Corbin
  Peter 110
Cord
  Joseph 109, 110
  Rachel 36
  William 36
Cordray
  Elisabeth 66
Corkran
  Elisabeth 22
  James 22
  Peter 22
  Timothy 22
Cornelius
  Eve 17
  Mary 17
  Mary Ann 17
  Peter 17
  Rebecca 17
Cornish
  Ann 10
  John 10
Corror
  Sebo 91
Corry
  George 12
  John 65
Corse
  Ann 56
  Daniel 56
  George 56
  James 56
  Michael 49
  William 56, 104
Cosden
  Jesse 28, 78
Cosdin
  Alphonse 73
Cosdon
  Alphanso 83
Cost
  George 109
Costen
  Abigail 14
  Ahab 14
  Jacob 14
  Matthias 14
Costin
  Henry 48, 57, 108
  Isaac 66
  Jesse 69
  John 48, 57, 71
  Levy 69
  Richard 71, 79
  Sarah 45
  Stephen 69
Cotrall
  John 74, 106
  Martha 74
  Thomas 74
Cottingham
  Daniel 90

Elisha 90
Jonathon 90
Margaret 90
Mary 101
Thomas 90
William 90
Coulbourn
   Elisabeth 30
   John 65, 104
   Margaret 65
   William 30, 65
Coulter
   Andrew 51
Councel
   Joseph 109
Council
   Henry 23, 74
Couper
   J. R. 106
Course
   James 2
Courts
   Charles 82
   Elisabeth 82
   John 82
   Richard Hendley 82
   Robert Hendley 79
   William 70, 79, 82
Covey
   Noble 22
Covert
   Robert 79
Covey
   William 105
Covington
   Ann 71
   Benjamin 54, 71, 112
   Edward 55
   Elisabeth 54, 71
   Esther 55
   Henry 54, 55, 105, 112
   James 54
   Jesse 104, 107
   John 54, 108, 109
   Mary 54, 71
   Nathaniel 71
   Nehemiah 16
   Philip 16
   Rachel 16, 55, 71, 81
   Rebeccah 54, 55, 71
   Samuel 55
   Sarah 54, 71
   Simon 54
   Solomon 55
   William 54
Cowarden
   William 29, 44, 52, 58,
      89, 95
Cowman
   Joseph 10
Cox
   Ann 31
   Christopher 29, 31
   Daniel 76
   Jacob 40
   James 31
   Jeremiah 102
   John 23, 31
   Lucy 31
   Margaret 31, 102
   Martha 31
   Mary 21
   Peter 107
   Powel 29
   Powell 22, 59, 97
   Ruth 40, 106
   Samuel 21
   Thomas 31, 101
   William 22, 40, 106
   Young 66
Coxman
   John 111
Coxon
   John 57
Crabb
   Christian 39
Crack
   James 88
Craig
   Elisabeth 57, 112
   Nancy 57
Crain
   Bateman 42
   Brafield 42
   John 42, 106
   Mark 42
Crandal
   Sarah 41, 105
Crandell
   Abell 4
   Esther 4
   Francis 4
   John 4
   Joseph 4
   Margaret 4
   Sibella 106
   Sybella 106
Crane
   Catherine 39
Crapper
   Annastatia 53
   Annastasius 108
   Edward 105
   Ester 109
   Esther 91, 109
   John Chambers 76
Craton
   John 65
Craw
   Andrew 31
Crawford
   Ann 11, 31
   David 11, 31, 52
   John 109, 110
   Rachel 1
Creag
   Sarah 35
Creagier
   Christian 100
   Conrad 100
   Valentine 100
Creighton
   Robert 112
Creswall
   David 31
   Isaac 31
   James 31
   John 31
   Margaret 31
   Robert 31
Cretin
   Martha 103
Crew
   John 56, 58
Crim
   Mason 19
Crock
   Hannah 16
Crocker
   Andrew 23
   Mary 23
   Thomas 23
   William 23
Crocket
   Gilbert 35
   Richard 111
Crockett
   Benjamin 35
   Gilbert 85
   John 50
   Nehemiah 99
Cromwell
   Eleanor 1
Croneen
   Daniel 21
   Rebecca 21
Croney
   Jeremiah 40, 108
   Mary 40
Cross
   Charles 112
Crouch
   John 108
   Nicholas 6
Crouse
   Jacob 97, 112
Crow
   Andrew 64
Crudgington
   George 87
Crutcher
   Mary 105
Crute
   Francis 17
   Rebecca 17
   Richard 17
   Robert 17
Cry
   Elisabeth 100
   William 107
Culbreath
   Jonathon 38, 62
Cullen
   James 57
   John 34
Cullens
   James 34
   John 34
Cullom
   Susannah 92
Cumming
   John 39
Cummings
   James 105
Cunningham
   Andrew 89
Cusack
   Jane 98
   Michael 98

Daffer
   Peter 27
Dailey
   John 71
Dale
   Archibald 77, 104, 110
   James 102
   Joshua 110
   Lydia 102
   Margaret 77
   Samuel 77
Dales
   Archibald 104
Daley
   Francis 43
Dallam
   Josias 15
   Richard 15
Dames
   William 81
Dante
   Susanna 101
Darby
   Josiah 112
Darden
   Joseph 66, 107
   Mary 66
Dare
   Ann 33, 36

Gideon 36
Nathaniel 36
Richard 36
Sebastian 37
Thomas Cleverly 6
Darmon
  Hezekiah 108
Darnall
  John 35
  Thomas 79
  William 79
Dashiel
  Ann 34
  Arthur 34
  Jean 108
  Louther 34
  Mathias 34
  Thomas 34, 96
  William 34
Dashiell
  George 13
  Robert 87
Davies
  Christopher 20
  Sarah 20
Davis
  Abraham 84
  Absalom 11
  Ann 57
  Caleb 84
  Charity 57
  Daniel 101, 109
  David 57
  Deaner 101
  Elisabeth 92
  George 101
  Henry 28
  James 9, 16
  John 21, 74, 104, 107
  Jonathon 109
  Joseph 110
  Owen 101
  Patience 89
  Philip 113
  Rebeccah 75, 95
  Rusiner 102
  Samuel 29, 57
  Solomon 101
  Thomas 7, 27, 75, 85
  Uriah 101
  William 9, 16, 57, 75, 89, 101
  Zacheus 60
Dawkins
  Allin 25
  Ann 25
  James 25, 100
  Joseph 65
  Mary 8, 25, 100, 113
  Sarah 65
  William 8, 100
Daws
  George 90
Dawson
  Ann 98
  Emilia 98
  Joseph 36, 98
  Louisinia 98
  Mary 36
  Obediah 98
  Rebecca 36
  William 98
  Willis 98
Day
  Araminta 12
  Jane 58
  John 12
  William 58, 65
Deakins
  Elisabeth 48

William 48
Deal
  John 112
Deale
  James 46
Dean
  Charles 20
  Mary 61
  Sarah 20
  Stephen 70
  Uriah 61
  William 61
Dear
  Stephen 105, 112
Deavers
  John 8
Debruler
  William 8
Debruller
  Benjamin 79
Deck
  William 112
Deford
  John 44
Delahay
  Henry 41
Delaney
  Rosannah 53, 62
Delauder
  Barbara 50
  Catharine 50
  David 50
  George William 50
  Johannas 50
Delehay
  Thomas 97
Delozier
  Charity 51
Dement
  Benajah 53
  George 53
  William 106, 112
Dements
  Dorcas 53
  Lydia 53
  Walter 53
  William 53
Dennaho
  Catherine 79
  Thomas 79
  William 79
Denning
  James 32
Dennis
  Elisabeth 64
  John 64, 112
  Littleton 91
  Mary 64
  Patrick 64
  Valentine 104
Denny
  Benjamin 103
  Nancy 103
  Peter 1
  Susanna 103
Dent
  Hatch 73
  John 73
  Thomas 107, 112
Denton
  John 30
  Rachel 30
Denwood
  Mary 28
  Thomas 28
Derochbrune
  Ann 26
  John 26
  Lewis 26, 70
  Prudence 70

Derrickson
  Levin 84
Deskins
  Michael 111
Devawn
  Michael 1
Devinport
  Abram 30
Devorix
  Ann 18
  Cornelius 18
  Hannah 71
  Hester 60
  James 60
  Margaret 60
  Mary 71
  Rachel 60
  Rebeccah 60
  Sarah 67, 71
  Susannah 71
  Thomas 60, 71
  Valentine 60
  William 60
Diamont
  John 42
Dick
  James 39, 43
Dickenson
  Cornelius 44, 110
  Daniel 4
  Grace 44
  James 94
  John 4
  Joshua 44
  Josiah 44
  Rachel 4
  Rebecca 4
  Sophia 44
  William 4
Dickerson
  Cornelius 74
  Grace 74
  Joshua 74
  Josiah 74
  Lucuia 74
Dickinson
  Lebin 110
  Samuel 97
Dickson
  James 109
  John 108
Dier
  John 51
Dillion
  Charles 105
Dines
  Cleah 60
  Elisabeth 60
  Jeremiah 60
  Mary 60
  Robert 60, 112
Dingle
  Edward 30
  William 21
Dirickson
  Joseph 84
  Levin 84
  Mary 84
  Mitchel 84
  Molly 84
  Samuel 84
Disharoon
  Ebe 93
  Elisabeth 93
  Francis 93
  George 93
  John 93
  Levin 89
  Mary 93
  Obadiah 93

Obediah 93
Samuel 93
Stephen 93
Thomas 93
William 93, 99
Disney
    William 109
Divers
    Christopher 20
Dixon
    Ellis 17
    James 105
    Obed 47, 61
    Obid 72
    Robert 61, 72
Dobson
    John 3
Dockery
    Mathew 32
Dodd
    Elisabeth 27
    George 112
Doherty
    John 105
Dolbee
    Isaac 30
    John 30
    Mary 30
    Susannah 30
Dolby
    Peter 77
Dolern
    Susannah 96
Dollace
    Robert 108
Dolvin
    Daniel 11
    Frances 11
    John 11
    Mary 11
    Richard 11
Donaldson
    Samuel 104
Donnahoe
    Cordelia 62
    Joshua 62
Donohoe
    John 34, 104
    Rachel 22
Dorman
    Catharine 101
    David 106, 111
    Elisabeth 96
    Hezekiah 111
    John 101
    Josiah 96
    Mary 101
    Mathias 101
    Rachel 34
    Samuel 34
    Zadock 101
Dorrumple
    Ann 9
    John 9
    William 15
Dorset
    William 51
Dorsey
    Ariana 78
    Basil 40, 78, 109
    Caleb 10, 46, 78, 82, 109
    Dennis 78
    Edward 72, 73, 109, 112
    Eleanor 78
    Elisabeth 40, 78
    Ely 72, 73
    John 40, 72, 73, 78, 105, 109
    John Hammond 48

Joshua 78
Levin 52
Mary 64
Michael 72, 73
Nathan 73
Rebeccah 64
Richard 40, 104
Samuel 10
Sarah 64
Thomas 46, 78
Vachel 13, 72, 73
Willa 64
William 64
Dose
    Richard 107
Dossey
    James 4
    John 4
Douglas
    Valentine 4
Douglass
    John 110
    William 10
Doull
    James 85
Dove
    Hannah 89
    Isaac 89
    Richard 89, 111
Dowell
    John 113
    Peter 16
Dowling
    James 96
Downes
    Charles 92, 100
    Elbert 96
    Henry 67
    James 98
    Margaret 71
    Rebeccah 98
Downie
    Elisabeth 29
Doxey
    Sarah 91
    Thomas 105
Doyne
    Jane 106
Dreadon
    David 100
Dreddon
    Jonathon 100
    Rachel 100
Dreeden
    James 105
Drew
    Anthony 25
Driver
    Margaret 80
    Mathew 80
Drury
    Ann 84
    Charles 84, 105
    Easter 84
    Elisabeth 84
    Margaret 84
    Mary 84
    Samuel 84
    Sarah 84
    William 84
Dubberly
    Esther 11
    Thomas 11
Ducker
    John 89
Ducket
    John 44
Duckett
    Jacob 29
    Sarah 29

Thomas 29
Dudley
    Jane 88
    Mary 88
    Richard 88
    Thomas 69, 88
    William 88
Duffler
    Peter 31
Duffy
    James 111
Duke
    Christopher 79
    James 1
    John 1
    Mary 1
Dulany
    Ann 16
    Dennis 51
Dullahuntee
    Elisabeth 51
    William 51
Dunbracco
    Hannah 60
    John 60
Dunkin
    Robert 81
Dunlap
    William 104
Dunlop
    William 35, 37
Dunn
    Ann 78
    Darius 26, 108
    Frances 64
    Robert 15, 63
    Unice 98
    William 58, 78
Dunnington
    Burditt 65
    Cloe 65
    Dorothy 65
    Ezra 65
    John 65
    Mary 65
    Sarah 65
    William 90
Durding
    William 44
Durham
    Jacob 16
    Samuel 62
    Sarah 16
Duskin
    Michael 68
    Sarah 68
Dutton
    Robert 85
Duvall
    John 19
    Joseph 3
    Mareen 68
    Mark Mareen 19
    Sarah 68
Dwiggens
    Ann 23, 39
    James 23, 39
Dyall
    William 100
Dyar
    Edward 86
    Elisabeth 86
    Thomas 86
Dye
    Avery 28
Dyel
    James 100
    Leonard 100
    Lettis 100
    Rebecca 100

Dyer
  Sarah 100
  Stacy 100
  Tabitha 100
  William George Josias 100
Dyer
  Ann 100
  Henrietta 86
  James 100
  Martha 64
  Mary 37
  Thomas Clement 86
Dyre
  Mary 109
Dyson
  Bennett 45, 92, 94
  James 52
  Joseph 45
  Maddocks 52

Eagle
  Henry 58
  Mary 58
  Sarah 58
Earickson
  Elisabeth 57
Earle
  Ann 81
  Benjamin 70, 81
  Hannah 81, 108
  James 70, 81, 92
  John 70, 81
  William 70
Eason
  John 81
  William 111
Eaton
  Peter 92
Eccleston
  Charles 21
  Hugh 7
  John 7, 49
  Margaret 49
Ecleston
  John 91
Edelen
  Ann 106
  Philip 109
Edelin
  Anne 66
  Catharine 100
  Char Solome 100
  Edward 51, 100
  Elisabeth 100
  James 19, 100
  Jane 44, 66
  Joseph 100
  Margaret 100
  Martha 100
  Mary 100
  Philip 13, 44
  Richard 66
  Samuel 100
  Sarah 100
  Solome 100
Eden
  John 35
  Michael 106
Edger
  William 47
Edget
  James 108
Edmondson
  Ann 81
  James 89
  William 81
Edmondston
  Pollard 59
Edmunds
  Alice 83
  Robert 83
Edwards
  Elisabeth 6, 40
  Jeremiah 30
  John 6
  Jonathon 28
  Joseph 44
  Stourton 28, 105
Ege
  Margaret 61
Eggleston
  Abraham 103
Eilbeck
  William 30
Elbert
  Ann 5
  Lodman 66
Elder
  Charles 9, 13
  Eli 9
  Elijah 9, 13
  Elisabeth 9
  Ely 13
  Honor 9, 13
  Honour 73
  James 13, 84, 105
  Jemima 9, 13
  John 9, 13, 73, 84
  Owen 9, 13
  Rachel 84, 91
Elias
  Zachariah 19
Eliason
  John 54
Elliot
  Thomas 110
  William 104
Elliott
  Benjamin 23, 71
  Elisabeth 23
  Henry 23
  James 75
  John 21, 23
  Mary 59
  Rachel 5
  Samuel 23
  Sarah 75
  Susannah 23
  Thomas 51
Ellis
  Elijah 52
  Elisabeth 52
  Jonathon 52, 112
  Mary 76
  Thomas 64
  William 52, 106
Elsbury
  Benjamin 54
Elsey
  Arnold 28
Elston
  Elisabeth 1, 66
  Rachel 1, 66
  Ralph 66, 81, 110
  William 66
Elton
  Dorothy 38, 43
Elzey
  Arnold 62, 95
Emerson
  John 51, 108, 112
Emory
  Ann 71
  Arthur 31, 38, 66, 71, 109
  Charles 100
  Deborah 12
  Elisabeth 71
  Gideon 24, 71
  John 54, 105, 112
  John Register 100
  John Rigdon 54
  Margaret 71
  Martha 105
  Philemon 31
  Thomas 24, 66, 71, 100
Endsworth
  Benjamin 108
  Jonathon 108
England
  Elisabeth 5
  George 5
  Hannah 5
  John 5
  Jos. 5
  Joseph 5
  Robert 5
  Samuel 5
Enimice
  Eliza 8
  Philip 8
Ennalls
  Bartholomew 41
  Henry 7, 34, 111
  Thomas 34, 46
Ensor
  Jemima 55
  John 1
  Joseph 98
Errington
  John 109
Esgate
  Thomas 64
Estep
  Richard 52
Estop
  Philemon 68
Etherington
  Bartholomew 60
  Robert 1
  Thomas 1
Eubanks
  Henry 66, 96
  Rebecca 103
Evans
  Bathsheba 20
  Caleb 20, 23
  Catharine 78
  David 74, 84, 104
  Elisabeth 20, 23, 112
  Elisha 78
  Esther 20, 23
  Francis 40
  Henrietta 70
  James 70, 99
  Jean 99
  Jeremiah 105
  John 18, 23, 99
  Jonathon 70, 71, 95
  Joshua 11, 78
  Margaret 74, 84
  Martha 78
  Mary 20, 40, 70, 107
  Nicholas 99
  Priscilla 99
  Prissey 99
  Sally 20, 23
  Sarah 54, 70
  Thomas 70, 99, 108
  Walter 20, 23
  William 20, 23, 78, 99, 104, 112
Everet
  Abraham 105
  Ann 87
  Elisabeth 56
  Hales 56
  James 87
  John 87

Samuel 62
Everett
    Abraham 95
    Benjamin 62
    Corby 62
    Edward 62
    Joseph 62
    Laurence 62
    Lettitia 62
    Margaret 95
    Martha 95
    Mary 62, 95
    Samuel 103
    St. Leger 95
    Susannah 62
Everfield
    John 112
    Mathew 40
    William 40
Everhart
    Barbara 34
    Christopher 34
Everit
    Ann 12
Eversfield
    John 112
Everte
    Esther 8
    Jacob 8
Evertson
    Barnet 83
    Easter 83
    Easther 83
    Elisabeth 83
    Esther 83
    Evert 83
    Frederick 83
    Jacob 13, 83, 113
    Rachel 83
Evitt
    Joseph 105
Evitts
    Mary 93
Ewbanks
    John 62
Ewen
    James 10
    John 10
Ewing
    Robert 38
    William 2

Fagg
    John 11
Faglor
    William Smallwood 45
Fairbank
    Bridget 64
    Elisabeth 64
    James 64
    John 64
    Mary 64
    Rachel 64
    William 64
Falconar
    Abraham 107
    Elisabeth 107
    John 112
Falconer
    John 17
Falkner
    Benjamin 60
    Hannah 60, 89
    Isaac 59
    James 23, 60
    John 60
    Margarett 60
    Thomas 89
    William 23

Falls
    David 77
Faris
    Peter 4
Farmer
    Jane 32, 33
Farrell
    Edmund 59
Fassit
    William 31
Fatado
    Anthony 64
    Barbary 64
    Joseph 64
    Susannah 64
Favell
    Ann 62
Fenby
    Charles 20
Fendal
    Mary Trueman 73
Fendall
    John 82
    Phillip Richard 95
Fenecy
    John 104
Fenwick
    Ann Elisabeth 38
    Belinda 84
    Benedict 102
    Bennett 6, 40
    Cornelius 38
    Cuthbert 6
    Edward 26
    Enoch 26, 46, 84, 102
    George 28, 40, 84, 102
    Ignatius 26, 86
    Jane 102
    John 101
    Joseph 4, 7
    Mary 26
    Richard 28
    Robert 4, 7, 38, 84
    William 102
Ferguson
    Alexander 81
Ferril
    Daniel 17
Ferrill
    Edward 17
    Sarah 96
    William 96
Few
    Daniel 6
Fiddeman
    Barthol. 11
    Bartholomew 23
Fidleman
    Bartholomew 39
Fields
    James 104
Figgs
    William 104
Finnicum
    Ann 82
    Isabella 82
    Margaret 82
    Stephen 82
    William 82, 108, 109
Fisher
    Abraham 36
    Adam 76
    Benjamin 54
    Hannah 40, 108
    Henry 54, 112
    John 42
    John Pritchet 54
    Mary 54, 108
    Robert 40, 108
    Thomas 42, 105

William 42, 46, 111
Fitz
    William 100
Fitzchew
    John 58
    Mary 58
    Nelley 58
    Priscilla 58
    Rebecca 58
    Richard 58
    Samuel 58
    Susannah 58
Fitzgerrald
    Ann 58
    John 58
Flaisper
    Eve 52
Flanagan
    Ann 65, 103
    Charles 65, 108
    Edward 65
    Mary 65
Flanner
    John 90
Flavill
    Grace 69
Fleaharty
    Ann 10
    John 10
    Mary 10
    Rebecca 10
    Stephen 10
Fleming
    Joshua 109, 110
Flemming
    Elisabeth 11
    Isaac 11
    John 21
    Sarah 21
Fletchall
    Betty 63
    John 87
Fleuellin
    Samuel 104
Flewelling
    Samuel 21, 111
Fling
    Joseph 106
Flower
    Michael 112
    Sarah 38
Flowers
    Benjamin 108
Floyd
    Eleanor 96
    Moses 96
    Susannah 39
    Thomas 25, 39
Flynn
    Daniel 97
    Lydia 97
Foard
    Joseph 105
Fobson
    Jeremiah Owings 50
Follin
    John 111
Fook
    Sarah 74
Fookes
    Ezekiel 35
Fooks
    Joseph 38
Foord
    John 42, 105
Ford
    Allison 53
    Ann 53
    Athanatius 26
    Bennett 75

Charles 35, 62
Charles Allison 45, 53
Cordelia 62
Cornelia 35
Daniel 81
Edward 33, 53, 109
Elisabeth 53
Ignatius 102
Jesse 42, 102
John 53, 62, 75, 102
John Javett 75
Joseph 107
Mary 38, 53, 75
Notley 53
Peter 38, 75, 102
Priscilla 75
Richard 53, 69, 75
Sarah 73
William 62

Foreman
  Benjamin 87
Forkham
  Hannah 54
Forrest
  Richard 67
  Zachariah 101
Forster
  John 80
Forwood
  Samuel 5
Fose
  Eve 52
  Philip 52
  William 52
Foster
  Hannah 25
  John 71
  Joseph 80
  William 95, 106
Fountain
  George 58
  Samuel 61
  William 9, 36, 56, 61
Fourd
  William 24
Fowkes
  Ann 111
  Anne 111
Fowler
  Abraham 29
  Ann 112
  Arthur 6
  Benjamin 43, 67
  Elisabeth 111
  Jacob 29
  John 20, 29
  Jonathon 29
  Josiah 29
  Keziah 6
  Mary 29
  Susannah 43, 67
  William 98, 105
Fowles
  Jos. 107
Foxall
  Peter 109
Foxon
  George 12
  Martha 12
Franklin
  Jacob 81
  Richard 106
  Robert 106, 110
  William 10
Frazer
  Thomas 41
Frazier
  Alexander 10, 35, 107, 108
  James 7, 64

John 84
Joseph 10
Mary 7
Sarah 35
Freeland
  Benjamin 15
  Elisabeth 15
  Francis 15
  Frisby 15
  Jacob 15
  Peregrine 15
  Rebecca 15
  Robert 15
  Sarah 15
Freeman
  Ann 18
  Isaac 10, 16
  Jacob 107
  Joseph 39
  Mary 39
  Thomas 64
French
  James 47, 53
  Zorababel 32
Friends
  Simon 111
Frisby
  James 56, 57
  Jane 56, 104
  Peregrine 57
  Richard 49, 52, 56
  William 56
Frost
  John 92
  Joseph 45, 104, 111
  Mary 45
Fryor
  John 92
Fullerton
  Alexander 104, 108
  James 99
  Joshua 99
  Peggy 99
Fulton
  Alexander 2
  Francis 2
  John 2
  Samuel 2
Furlong
  John 94
  Martha 94
Furnace
  James 106
Furnice
  George 66
  James 66
  Jonathon 66
  Judith 66
  Sarah 66
  William 30, 66
Furnis
  William 14
Fyffe
  James 87

Gabrill
  Stephen 109
Gaither
  Edward 12
  Margaret 12
  Samuel 104
Gale
  Elisabeth 46, 99
  George 99, 107
  Henry 99
  John 89, 99
  Leah 99
  Levin 62
  Milcah 99

Phebe 89
Rasin 50
Razin 10
Galt
  Samuel 106
Galwith
  Elisabeth 4
  Ignatius 4
  John 4
  Jonas 4
Gamble
  Henrietta 63
  John 107
Gambra
  Eleanor 108, 112
  Elisabeth 69
Gambrell
  Bethier 63
  Darius 63
  Honor 52
  Honour 52
  Sarah 63
Gantt
  Ann 24
  George 24
Gardiner
  Anne 79
  Charles 81
  Eleanor 26
  Elisabeth 78
  Ignatius 2, 66
  Jean 26
  John 78
  Richard 2, 66
  Sarah 26
  Susannah 94
Gardner
  John 44
Garey
  Ann 79
  Elisabeth 79
  Frances 79
  George 79
  Henry 79
  John 79
  Mary Ann 79
  Samuel 79
  Solomon 79
  William 79
Garland
  John 52
Garnett
  Bartus 8
  George 43
Garratt
  Amos 60
  Ann 72
  Edward 72, 108
  Rebeccah 72
  Sarah 72
  Thomas 72
Garretson
  Bennett 15
  Catharine 15
  Cornelius 78
  Edward 15, 55
  Elisabeth 15
  Frances 15
  Garret 15
  George 15
  George Goldsmith 15
  Goldsmith 15
  James 15
  Martha 15, 111
  Mary 15
  Pheneta 15
  Richard 55
  Susannah 60
Garrett
  Amos 88, 89

Garrison
   Frederick 27
Garritson
   Cornelius 58
Garrott
   Sarah 105
Gash
   Conjudnn 100
Gaskin
   Deborah 69
   Greenwood 69
Gassaway
   Benjamin 25
   James 25
   Mary 25
   Nicholas 25
   Rachel 25
   Richard 25
   Robert 25
   Sarah 25
   Thomas 25
Gatrell
   Stephen 105
Gatton
   Ann 97
   Eleanor 97
   James 97
   Mary 97
   Richard 97
   William 97
   Zachariah 97
Gault
   Mathew 76
Gearly
   John 86
Gears
   Annanias 105
Geary
   William 105
Geddes
   Robert 112
George
   Hannah 104
   Robert 89
   Sampson 106
   Sidney 14
Gerarld
   Thomas 109
Getty
   John 14, 15
Gibb
   Andrew 72, 109, 110
Gibbands
   John 105
Gibbens
   Amey 29
Gibbins
   Elisabeth 30
   John 30
Gibbons
   John 110
   Margaret 63
   William 63
Gibbs
   Ann 20
   Isaac 23
   James 20
   William 20
Gibson
   Ann 11
   Catharine 68
   Elisabeth 11
   Francis 68, 104, 111
   James 81, 82, 86, 93, 102
   John 1, 11, 82, 102
   Jonathon 105
   Mary 11, 81
   Peter 1
   Rachel 11, 82
   Richard 16, 82, 108
   Robert 11
   Sarah 82
   William 104
   Wolman 55
Gilbert
   Elisabeth 62
   Francis 18, 87
   Jervis 5
   John 66
   Mary An 87
   Mary Ann 18
   Ruth 5
Giles
   Jacob 46, 60, 89
Gillet
   Samuel 24
   Sarah 24
   William 24
Gillett
   William 104, 110
Gillis
   Robert 69
Gilliss
   Levin 99
Gilpin
   James 46
   Joseph 14
   Thomas 46, 110
Ginn
   Anne 80, 94
   James 37, 80, 94
   Josiah 80, 94
   Mary 80, 94
   Samuel 80, 94
   Sarah 80, 94
   Sicilly 94
   Sicily 80
   Thomas 80, 94
Gittings
   Asael 85
   Thomas 32
Givan
   John 77
Gladding
   Robert 73
Glan
   Jean 76
Glanding
   Robert 11
Glann
   Robert 76
   Thomas 76
Glanvill
   Stephen 78
Glasford
   Hugh 105
Glass
   Christopher 109, 111
Glassford
   Henry 100
   Hugh 105
Glenn
   Jane 15
   Johannus 32
   Mary 32
   Samuel 15
Glover
   Richard 21
Goddart
   Jane 32
   John 32
Godwin
   Allen 60
   Catharine 77
   Edward 60
   Elisabeth 77
   Hannah 77
   John 60
   Mary 77
   Michael 77, 109, 110
   Naomi 77, 109
   Rachel 60
   Rhoda 77
   Ruth 77
   Sarah 60
   Thomas 60, 77
   William 60, 77
Goe
   Elisabeth 1
   John 1
   Mary 1
   William 1
Golder
   John 39, 109
Goldsberry
   Henry 86, 110
   Ignatius 110
Goldsborough
   Charles 109
   Henry 113
   John 41, 110
   Mr. 107
   Nicholas 30
   William 7
Good
   James 37
Goodhand
   Jones 57
   Mary Ann 57
Goodman
   Richard 35
   Sarah 35
Goodrick
   Edward 70, 80
   Frances 70
Goodwin
   Moses 90, 111
   Rachel 90
Goodwine
   Naher 48
Gordon
   Alexander 49
   Charles 99
   John 43, 79
   Robert 10
   Roger 107, 112
Gordy
   Eleanor 101
Gore
   Elisabeth 30
   Jacob 30
   James 67
   James Manning 76
   Thomas 90
Gorsuch
   David 35
Gosh
   Elisabeth 8
   Mary 8
Goslin
   Waitman 18
Gosling
   Ezekiel 27
Gostee
   Richard 104
Gott
   Elisabeth 39
   Ezekiel 39
   John 39
   Richard 55, 100
   Robert 39
   Ruth 55
   Samuel 39
   Walter 4, 39, 41
Gough
   Ignatius 82, 101
   James 82, 101, 110, 113
   Mary 82
   Peter 105

Priscilla 101, 111
Stephen 82
Susannah 42, 82
William 108
Gould
   Benjamin 9, 82
   Frances 9, 82
   James 9, 82
   Mary 21
   Mirimy 82
   Richard 82, 112
Goutee
   Jacob 40, 107
   John 40, 54
Goutte
   Jacob 47
Gouttee
   Jacob 33
   John 47
Gow
   Clementine 57
   James 57
Grace
   William 32
Grafton
   William 111
Graham
   Andrew 85
   Ann 85
   Catrin 12
   David 27
   Elisabeth 85
   James 85, 100
   John 58, 68, 85, 87, 107, 109, 111, 113
   Mary 12, 85
   Philip 87
   Robert 12, 85
   William 12, 85
Grainger
   John 111
Granger
   John 107, 108
   Mary 56
Grant
   Elisabeth 6
   John 6
Grason
   Joshua 1
   Richard 64, 71, 82
Graves
   Thomas 71
Gray
   Benjamin 102
   Edward 95
   Henrietta 95
   Henry 18, 95
   James Woolford 73
   Jane 80
   John 18, 19, 73
   Jos. Cox 107, 108, 112
   Joseph 30, 79
   Joseph Cox 47, 56, 73
   Mary 103
   Moses 95
   Randolph 95
   Rosalinda 73
   Rosannah 47, 56, 73
   Samuel 65, 80, 100
   Susannah 19
   Thomas 10, 18
   William 10, 18, 98, 102, 104
   William Hargis 95
   Zachariah 45
Grear
   Annanias 40
   Benjamin 40
   Elisabeth 40
   Henry 112
   Hezekiah 40
   James 40
   Margret 40
Greaves
   John Baptist 90
   Mathew 71
   Thomas 71
Greeer
   Charles 112
Green
   Alexander 10
   Ann 88
   Charles 112
   Christopher 84, 105
   Elijah 89
   Elisabeth 24
   Francis 10
   George 24
   Jacob 100
   John 4, 84, 88
   Jonas 105
   Jones 111
   Leonard 10, 53
   Martha 12
   Mary 22
   Peter 10
   Philemon 24, 84
   Rachel 88
   Raphael 75
   Sarah 88
   Thomas 109
   Valentine 88
   William 71
Greenfield
   Ann Truman 68
   Elisabeth 8
   James 8, 42
   James Truman 68
   Kenelm Truman 112, 113
   Mary 68
   Micajah 8, 42
   Nanny 29
   Nathaniel Trueman 63
   Nathaniel Truman 29, 68
   Rebecca 29
   Rebeccah 63
   Sarah 68
   Susannah Eve 68
   Thomas 29, 63
   Thomas Trueman 63
   Thomas Truman 29
   William 8
   William Truman 68
Greenwall
   Leonard 113
   Phillip 97
Greenwell
   Eleanor 13, 82, 101
   George 101
   James 13
   John 38
   John Basil 13
   Joshua 13
   Leonard 110
Greenwood
   Anne 50
   James 32
   John 80, 111
   Rebecca 32
Greggory
   Ann 32
   Anthony 32
   Elisabeth 32
   Esther 32
   Grace 32
   Lidia 32
   Mary 32
Gregory
   John 32
   Ruth 81
   William 71, 81
Grenage
   James 112
Grennage
   Ann 70
   Elisabeth 70
   James 70
   Sherry 70
Griffin
   Ann 113
   Elisabeth 110
   James 24, 65, 73, 111
   Selathel 59
Griffith
   Charlotte 43, 52
   Cooler 90
   Daniel 7
   Henry 82, 91
   John 10, 41, 107
   Joshua 42, 43
   Lewis 55, 61, 72, 106, 107
   Martha 43
   Mary 10
   Mathew 9
   Nancy 63
   Samuel 15, 28, 43, 52
   Sarah 73
Grimes
   George 59
Grindage
   Charles 16
Grinder
   Christopher 93
Groome
   Charles 44, 85, 89
   Samuel 44, 89
Grosh
   Conrod 87
Grouse
   Jacob 109
Grover
   Joseph 96
Grunwell
   Ann 50
Gunby
   Elisabeth 50
   Kirk 50, 108
Guthry
   Caleb 11
Guybert
   John 11
Guyther
   John 105
Guyton
   Benjamin 85
Gwinn
   Ann 51
   Edward 53
   John 19, 51, 69
   Sarah 53
Gwyn
   Ann 33
   John 111
Gwynn
   Allen 81
   Benjamin 33
   John 33

Hacket
   James 25
Hackett
   James 9, 25, 81, 83
   John 78, 84
   Margaret 82
   Oliver 41
   Rebeccah 41
   Sarah 84
   Thomas 24, 41, 81, 83,

107
  William 24
Hadaway
  Elisabeth 2
  Mary 2
  Thomas Lambden 2
  William 2
Haddon
  Elisabeth 37
  Jannet 37
  John 37
  William 37
Hadley
  Edward 54
  Mary 54
  Thomas 106
Hagan
  Henry 88
  Ignatius 53
  James 53
  Magdalen 53
  Mary 53
  Sarah 53
Hagar
  Robert 113
Hagur
  David 96
  Jonathon 96
  Robert 98
Haines
  Constant 102
  David 102
  Elisabeth 102
  Ephraim 102
  James 102
  Oratio 102
Hale
  Edward 18
  John 18
Haley
  Ann 86, 107, 110
  John 107
Hall
  Ann 42, 67
  Betty 67
  Charles 67
  Christopher 2, 16, 86
  Edward 42
  Eleanor 73
  Elihu 67
  Elisabeth 38
  Elisha 38, 43, 67
  Ezekiel 67
  George 2
  Isaac 19
  Jesse 67
  Johannah 41
  John 2, 15, 67, 72, 87
  Joseph 42, 43, 67
  Joshua 43, 72
  Martha 67
  Mary 10, 38, 43
  Philip 10
  Richard 67
  Ruth 19
  Sarah 42
  Sophia 42
  Thomas 9
  William 25, 67, 69
Halmsley
  Jasper 38
Hamar
  Elisabeth 83
  Hannah 83
  Mary 83
Hambleton
  William 65
Hamer
  Elisabeth 81, 83
  Hannah 81

Mary 81
Thomas 81, 109
Hamill
  John 109
Hamilton
  Ann 83
  James 83, 108, 112
  John 46, 76, 83
  Margaret 74, 82
  Mary 74
  Mary Ann 83
  Philemon 82
  Sarah 82, 83
  William 21, 47, 82, 105, 111
Hammel
  John 79
  Sarah 79
  Stephen 79
  William 79
Hammersley
  William 11
Hammett
  William 39
Hammill
  John 109
Hammilton
  William 31
Hammond
  Alice 98
  Ann 44
  Benjamin 55
  Edward 98
  James 39, 86
  John 39
  Leah 98
  Mary 39, 82, 98
  Nathan 33, 44, 93
  Phil. 93
  Rachel 39
  Rezin 33
  Sarah 1, 98
  Thomas 104
  Thomas John 105
  William 24, 45, 55
Hampton
  Luirocy 61
  Mary Ann 61
  William 61
Hand
  William 109
Hands
  Bedd. 108
Handy
  Samuel 107
  Thomas 21
Hanna
  Alexander 106
Hannah
  John 106
  Thomas 106
Hanson
  Gustavia 77
  Gustavus 44
  Jacob 42, 106
  John 73
  Joseph 45
  Walter 36, 108
Hardcastle
  Robert 66, 88
  Thomas 66, 88
  William 96
Harden
  George 106
Hardesty
  Henry 43
  James 43
  Peter 109
Harding
  Ann 92

Edward 92
Hannah 92
John 29
Joseph 41
Martha 92
Rachel 92
Hardman
  Joseph 112
Hardwick
  James 38
Hardy
  Charles 57
  Ignatius 76, 93
  John 76, 93
  Susanna 7
Harkins
  Cornelius 17
Harper
  Catharine 66
  David 41
  Elisabeth 54, 83
  Francis 53, 62, 108
  Jacob 8, 22
  James 54
  John 22, 54
  Margaret 54
  Martha 54
  Mary 53, 62
  Rachel 50
  Sarah 66
  Thomas 54
Harrel
  John 99
Harrington
  Anthony 42
  Sydney 61
Harris
  Ann 13, 88
  Benjamin 103
  Benton 109
  Bloys 13
  Eve 56
  John 56, 65
  Levin 56, 108
  Mary Ann 100
  Thomas 109
  William 16
Harrison
  Ann 25
  Charlotte 25
  Edward 81
  Henry 15, 29
  James 15
  John 25, 107
  Joseph 2, 74
  Joseph Hanson 28, 29
  Mary 25, 41, 76
  Richard 25
  Richard Everingham 25
  Sarah 90
  Thomas 1
  William 15, 25, 110
Harriss
  Ann 22
  Edward 43
  Elisabeth 43
  John 24
  Margaret 43
  Mary 43
  Nathan 22, 108
  Samuel 67
  Sarah 43
  Thomas 43, 105
  William 43
Harrisson
  Elisabeth 67
  William 104
Harrot
  Susannah 104
Harry

Hart
- Carpenter 65
- Martin 97

Hart
- Ann 55
- Augustean 55
- James 55, 91
- John 16, 108, 113
- Mary 31, 55
- Morgan 31
- Naboth 55
- Patrick 11, 55, 112

Harvey
- William 105

Haskins
- Aaron 110
- Sarah 46
- William 46

Hastings
- George 87
- Mary 87

Hatchenson
- Nathan 31

Hatcheson
- Nathan 26, 78

Hatchison
- John 17

Hatton
- Margaret 1
- Mary 1
- Richard 1

Hawkings
- Frances 82

Hawkins
- Aaron 112
- Elisabeth 9, 95, 99
- Ernault 9
- Frances 9, 82
- James 9, 95, 99
- John 9
- John Stone 12, 40, 78
- Joseph 105
- Mary Brown 38
- Mathew 9, 82
- Richard 95
- William 95

Haycraft
- Mary 45

Haydon
- Bartholomew 58, 113

Hayman
- Charity 56
- Charles 56
- David 56
- Elisabeth 56
- Frances 56
- Isaac 56
- James 56
- John 56
- Mary 56
- Mathew Dorman 56
- Nehemiah 56
- Rachel 56
- Rebecca 56
- Sarah 56

Haymond
- Nicholas 112

Hayne
- William 106

Haynes
- William 107

Hays
- Henry 73
- John 44
- Jonathon 39, 100
- Philemon 53, 62

Hayter
- Abraham 97

Hayward
- George 48
- John 80

- William 31, 93

Heald
- John 61
- Richey 61

Heard
- John 111
- Joseph 111
- Luke 82
- Mark 29
- Matthew 82

Hearn
- Ann 14
- Betty Day 13
- Ebenezar 14
- Elisha 13, 14
- George 14
- Jemima 14
- John 14
- Joshua 13, 14
- Mary 13
- Nehemiah 13, 14
- Sarah 14
- Thomas 13, 14
- William 13, 14

Heath
- Charles 13, 83
- Esther 65
- James 83, 108
- Sarah 3
- William 3

Heathers
- Richard 82

Hebb
- Joseph 110
- William 67

Hebbron
- Thomas 7

Hedge
- Charles 35

Hedrick
- Elisabeth 51
- George 51
- Thomas 51

Heighe
- Barbara 24
- Betty 24
- James 24
- Mary 24
- Thomas Holdsworth 24

Hellen
- Charles 1
- Jesse 1
- John 1
- Mary 1
- Nicholas 1
- Penelope 1
- Rebecca 1
- Richard 1
- Walter 1

Helms
- Joseph 39

Henderson
- Mary 19
- Mathias 23
- Richard 86

Hendley
- Elisabeth 91
- Eve 91
- James 91
- John 110
- William 91

Hendon
- Benjamin 87
- Dinah 87
- Henry 87
- Joseph 87
- Lydia 87
- Richard 87
- Sarah 87

Hendricks
- James 30

Hendrickson
- John 28, 30
- Matthias 23

Heneker
- Elisabeth 80
- Henrietta 80
- John 80
- Mathew 80
- Sally 80

Henesy
- William 107

Heniken
- Elisabeth 15
- Mathew 15

Henikin
- Mathew 12

Henkin
- Elisabeth 12

Henley
- James 63

Henricks
- Henry 96

Henry
- Catharine 95
- David 95
- Elia 77
- Elias 78
- Elisabeth 52
- John 54
- Mary 95
- Robert Jenkins 106, 112
- Sarah 98
- Stephen 95
- William 113

Henslough
- John 17

Henwock
- William 79

Herbert
- Mary 46
- Mathew 111, 112

Herbison
- William 77

Herring
- Elisabeth 18
- Sarah 18

Hew
- Patrick 21

Hewes
- Henry 15

Hewett
- Thomas 73

Hewitt
- Joshua 97
- Mary 97
- Sarah 97

Hews
- James 1

Hickman
- Arthur 87
- Betty 27
- Bety 27
- Comfort 77, 78
- David 27
- Director 27
- Henry 27
- James 77, 78, 104, 111
- Joshua 27, 77, 78
- Leah 77, 78
- Levin 77, 78
- Nehemiah 77, 78
- Rachel 77, 78
- Reach 111
- Solomon 27
- Stephen 63, 100
- Thomas 77, 78
- William 63

Hicks
- John 48

Hill (cont.)
  Joseph 19, 29
  Levin 31
  Mary 31
Hickson
  Ann 69
  Mary Ann 69
  Peter 69
Hidgdon
  Benjamin 99
Higdon
  Ann 24
  Benjamin 24
Higgins
  Barbara 96
  Charles 96
  Elisabeth 11
  John 67, 108, 111
  Mary 67
  Sarah 96
  William 11
Hill
  Aaron 54
  Adam 105
  Dorcas 112
  Elisabeth 44
  James 54
  Jane 110
  Jean 44
  Levin 5
  Martha 54
  Moses 111
  Moris 54
  Richard 54
  Sarah 54
  Thomas 54
  William 54, 107, 111
Hillary
  Henry 48
Hilman
  Betty 99
  Ezekiel 99
  John 99
  Nancy 99
  Sarah 99
  Unice 99
  William 99
Hiltibrand
  Adam 84
  Ann Maria 84
  Jacob 84
  Joseph 84
  Mary 84
  Philipina 84
Hilton
  Elisabeth 99
  James 99
  Mildred 98
  Robert 99
  William 98
Hindman
  Jacob 105
Hinds
  David 95
  Eleanor 95
  Elisabeth 44
Hitch
  Elisabeth 14
  James 18
  John 14, 112
  Joshua 18, 65
  Risdon 14
  Solomon 14
  Susannah 14
  William 104, 107
Hitchcock
  Johannah 52
Hitchins
  Major 104
Hobbs
  Assenah 100
  Benjamin 100
  Christian 100
  Ephraim 100
  Jemima 9, 73
  Joseph 9
  Marthillas 13
Hodges
  Charles 101
  Robert 111
Hodgkin
  Lucy 86
  Rachel 86
Hodson
  Ann 48, 61
  Mary 48
  Roger 48, 61
  Thomas 48, 61
Hoffner
  Frederick 97
Hofman
  Peter 37
Hofner
  Jacob 112
Holbrook
  Thomas 104, 108
Holbrooke
  Thomas 43
Holladay
  Francis 107
Holland
  Ann 76
  John 35
  Josias 104
  Mary 76
  Thomas 29, 104, 110
  Wilhelmina 76
  William 34, 76, 77, 113
Hollings
  Abigail 109
Hollingsworth
  Amos 49, 106
  Elisabeth 61
  Henry 14
  Jacob 14
  Jesse 14
  John 14
  Levy 14
  Lydia 14
  Mary 14
  Samuel 14
  Stephen 14
  Thomas 14
  William 49
  Zebulon 14
Hollinsworth
  Allen 82
Hollis
  Amos 87
  Ann 19
  Catherine 19
  Hannah 56
  Jemima 13
  Joseph 13
  Martha 87
  William 19
Hollow
  Thomas Hyde 71
Hollyday
  Ann 52
  Benjamin 55
  Ebenezar 55
  Francis 55, 107
  George 55
  Hannah 55
  James 25, 92
  John 55
  Mary 55
  Rachel 55
  Sarah 55
  Thomas 105
  William 55
Holmes
  John 65
  Ralp 94
  Ralph 94
Homwood
  Hamutal 38
Honey
  Valentine Thomas 60
  William 112
Honor
  Thomas 106
Hooe
  Robert 29
Hook
  Elisabeth 49, 92
  James 50
Hooper
  Henry 107, 111
  Jacob 45
  John 2
  John Ashcomb 2
  May 2
  Nicy 36
  Roger Ashcomb 2
  Samuel Ashcomb 2
  Thomas 2
Hoopman
  Barbara 26
  Jacob 26
Hopewell
  Bennett 28
  Thomas 44, 46
Hopkins
  Charles 20, 94
  David 111
  George 90
  James 22, 64, 97
  Jane 54
  Jonathon 64
  Jos. 67
  Moses 22
  Penelope 22
  Peter 97
  Richard 22, 97
  Samuel 91, 106, 111
  Sarah 64, 97
Horn
  William 35
Horney
  Philip 64, 96
Horrell
  Isaac 90
Horse
  John 92
Horsey
  John 3
  Revell 3
  Stephen 3
Horsley
  James 71
  Mary 47
  Thomas 47
Horton
  William 88
Hosier
  Henry 4, 113
Hoskinson
  Charles 37
Houston
  John 30, 69, 91
  Robert 91
Hoverton
  Susannah 113
How
  Robert 41
Howard
  Baker 94
  Benjamin 12, 110
  Cornelius 73, 102

George 102
Henry 12, 61, 73, 78
John 73, 100
Joseph 12
Joshua 102
Lemuel 5
Margaret 12
Margery 12
Robert 31
Samuel 105
Sarah 73

Howe
    Elisabeth 42
Howel
    Samuel 104
Howell
    Samuel 104
    Thomas 47, 108
    William 96
Howk
    Martin 101
Howlett
    John 100
    Mary 100
Hoxton
    Susannah 110
Hoyle
    Andrew 52
    Christiana 52
    Conrad 52
    John 52, 104
    Margaret 52
Hozier
    Henry 90, 98
    Rebecca 90
    Richard 85, 90, 98
Hubbert
    Edward 41
    Mary 33
    Nehemiah 29
    Peter 19
    Solomon 59
    William 33
Hudson
    Annanias 77
    Elisabeth 46
    Esther Ann 36
    John 4, 36
    Mary 78
    Rachel 4
    William 46
Hues
    John 63
    Sarah 63
Huffington
    Elisabeth 48
Hufman
    Barbara 87
    George 87
    Jacob 78
    John 87
Hufnagle
    Eve 35
    Valentin 35
Hugens
    Benjamin 104
Hughes
    James 113
Hughey
    John 70
Hughs
    James 62
    Jemimah 62
    Jenny 79
    Levin 79
    Sarah 62
Hukill
    Guilder 15
    Hester 14, 15
Hull
    Daniel 109
Hummer
    Jacob 52
Humphrey
    James 106
Humphreys
    John 112
Humphries
    John 105
    Martha 25
Humphris
    Thomas 14
Humphrys
    Philis 18
    Thomas 18
Hungerford
    Elisabeth 46, 109, 110
    John 6
Hunt
    Elisabeth 110
    James 67
    Mary 15
    Ruth 67
Hunter
    Elisabeth 59
    Ezekiel 7
    James 103
    Mary 103
    Robert 30, 103
Huntt
    Benjamin 107
Hurley
    John 108
    Rose 88
Hurlock
    Jacob 58
    Mary 63
Huron
    Mary 77
Hurry
    George 11
Hurst
    Joseph 70
Hurt
    Cornelius 17
    Hannah 17
    Henry 65
    James 65
    Joce 65
    John 26, 65, 98
    Martha 65
    Sarah 65
Husband
    Ann 91
    Hannah 91
    Margery 91
    Mary 91
    Sarah 91
    Thomas 91, 110
    William 91
Husey
    Thomas 9
Hussy
    Thomas 109
Hutcheson
    Alexander 66, 106
Hutchings
    James 7
    William 7
Hutchins
    Aquila 32
    Thomas Goslin 68
Hutchinson
    Mary 8
Hutchison
    Ann 11
    Samuel 66, 81
Hutton
    George 22
    Margaret 19

Richard 19, 46
Hyde
    Thomas 58, 78
Hyland
    Edward 84
    Elisabeth 14, 84
    Jacob 84
    John 26, 35
    Martha 106
    Mary 26, 35, 84, 113
    Nicholas 26, 84
    Rachel 84
    Sampson 84
Hynson
    Andrew 9, 10, 77
    Benjamin 56
    Charles 63
    James 9, 10
    John 56
    Mary 56
    Nathaniel 56, 64, 85, 89, 110, 112
    Richard 89, 109
    William 56, 110

Ijams
    John 34, 40, 94, 97
    Plummer 97
    Thomas 97
    William 4, 34, 94
Ingelsel
    Samuel 93
Ingram
    Ann 68
    Joseph 68
    Mary 34
    Paul 34
Insley
    Andrew 72, 88
    Betty 88
    Jacob 72, 88
    William 72, 88, 105, 108, 111
Ireland
    George 8
    Gideon 8
    John John 8
    Mary 8
    Richard 8
    Thomas 8
    William 102
Irons
    George 101
    Hannah 101
Irving
    Betty 76
    James 22
    John 75, 76
    Margaret 76
    Mary 76
    Sarah 76
    Thomas 99
Isaac
    Jos. 20
Isaackes
    Joseph 107

Jackson
    Abednego 54
    Ann 54
    Archibal 54
    Archibald 54, 108
    Catharine 92
    Christopher 92
    Edward 92
    Elihu 22
    Elisabeth 92
    George 22, 42

James 22, 54
Jane 70
John 22, 25, 54, 70, 92
Joseph 90
Joshua 22
Judith 70
Lambert 70, 71
Mary 70
Rachel 92
Rebeccah 42, 54
Robert 106
Samuel 22, 54
Sarah 22, 70
Sophia 22
Susannah 70
Thomas 18, 27, 70, 108, 109
Tilghman 54
Walter 92
William 22, 70, 71
William Finny 92

Jacob
  Ann 100
  Luke 18

Jacobs
  Ann 13
  Bartholomew 38
  Jacob 79
  John 50
  Joseph 43, 67
  Nancy 50
  Richard 43, 67
  Winder 13

James
  Charles 23
  George Hardon John 41
  Hannah 6
  Jane 6
  John 6, 106
  Lawrence 89
  Margaret 6
  Thomas 39
  Walter 39

Jameson
  Elisabeth 111
  Henrietta 3
  Henry 3
  Lut. 106

Jarish
  James 37

Jarman
  Rachel 6
  Solomon 6
  William 6

Jarnagon
  Henry 63

Jarrard
  James 80
  Mary 107, 108

Jarret
  James 107

Jarvis
  Hannah 7

Jeferies
  Martha 89

Jefferies
  Thomas 89

Jeffers
  Bazil 11
  Jacob 11
  John 11
  Mary 11
  Peter 11
  Reuben 11
  William 11

Jefferson
  John 48
  Rachel 48

Jenifer
  Daniel 107
  Daniel of St. Thomas 49

Jenings
  Edmund 46

Jenison
  Thomas 38

Jenkins
  Edward 37
  Elisabeth 82, 101
  Emanuel 59
  George 43, 53
  Henry 30, 69
  John 59
  Josiah 37
  Lewis 30
  Margaret 30
  Mathew 8, 43
  Matthew 30
  Michael 16
  Phillip 37
  Sarah 30, 59
  Thomas 8, 30, 59
  Walter 30
  William 105, 106, 112

Jenkinson
  Emanuel 1, 107
  John 1

Jennet
  Esther 91

Jerman
  Joseph 105

Jermon
  Amos 95

Jernagan
  Henry 29

Jessarang
  Bartholomew 109
  Michael 17

Jesserang
  Bartholomew 48
  Catharine 48
  Daniel 48
  George Michael 48
  Lewis 48
  Michael 48
  Peter 48

Jester
  Catharine 89

Jewel
  Elisabeth 101
  Moses 101
  Precious 101

Jewell
  David 101

Jewet
  Catharine 51
  Nathaniel 51

Jewett
  Catharine 51
  John 51
  Leah 51
  Martha 51
  Mary 51
  Nathaniel 51
  William 51

Jewill
  George 101
  Moses 101

Jisson
  William 111

Jobson
  Susanna 112
  Susannah 81, 112

Johns
  Ann 49
  Elisabeth 2
  Hozier 111
  Richard 17, 27, 46, 49, 111
  Thomas 2, 24

Johnson
  Amos 49
  Ann Cockshut 113
  Archibald 23, 46
  Barnet 42
  Benjamin 41
  Catharine 56, 108
  Edmund 98
  Elisabeth 67, 68
  Ezekiel 45, 47, 61
  Hannah 109
  Holman 69, 108, 110
  James 56, 99
  John 17, 86, 105, 108
  Joseph 67, 68, 109
  Leonard 104
  Lloyd 79
  Luke 68
  Mary 2, 72, 91
  Nathan 40
  Nelly 98
  Philadelphia 56
  Rachel 78
  Rebeccah 67, 68
  Sarah 8
  Snead 98
  Southy 98
  Susannah 98
  Thomas 17, 42, 64, 111, 112
  Whittington 104
  William 40, 52, 69, 98, 106, 111

Johnston
  John 99, 106
  Joseph 105

Joiner
  Elisabeth 11
  William 11

Jones
  Ann 28, 96
  Britain 96
  Charles 40, 108, 111
  Daniel 16
  David 46
  Ebenezar 110
  Elisha 24
  Griffith 16
  Jacob 23
  James 18, 70
  Jane 54
  John 16, 46, 54, 106, 108
  Joseph 75
  Joshua 96
  Margaret 96
  Mary 46, 91, 97, 105
  Morgan 89
  Nicholas 102
  Precious 24
  Richard 28, 96
  Rosannah 46
  Samuel 24
  Sarah 18, 97
  Solomon 46
  Thomas 18, 95, 96, 112
  Vincent 97
  William 21, 22, 24, 28

Jordan
  James 98, 99
  Jeremiah 94
  Martha 59
  Thomas 59
  William 94, 99

Joy
  Ann 69
  Eleanor 73
  Elisabeth 45, 69
  Ephraim 106
  Joseph 45, 69, 108, 111
  Mary 69

William 69
Joyce
  Joseph 47
Joyner
  Dobbs 61
Jubbs
  Susannah 49
Juett
  Catharine 74
  John 74
  Leah 74
  Martha 74
  Mary 74
  Nathan 74
  Rhoda 74
  William 59, 74, 104, 108
Junis
  Martha 54
Justice
  Comfort 78

Kane
  Elisabeth 43
Kannard
  Martha 67
Karenhappuch
  Sophia 37
Keene
  Capewell 29
  Francis 7
  Margaret 7
  Mary 61, 72
  Philip 21
  Sarah 29
  Shadrack 21
  Zebulon 21
Kefalker
  Philip 99
Keiron
  Esther 74
  James 74
  John 74
  Mary 74
  Richard 74
  William 74
Kelley
  Alexander 60
  Daniel 85
  George 85
  James 51, 110
  John 85
  Joseph 113
  Margaret 76
  Sarah 110
  William 85, 105, 109
Kellim
  Elisabeth 37
Kellor
  Elisabeth 97
  Jacob 97
Kellso
  Thomas Hyde 53
Kelly
  Thomas 112
Kemp
  William 79
Kendal
  Stephen 110
Kendall
  Stephen 50, 108
  William 63
Kennard
  John 32, 67, 90
  Mary 67, 69
  Mathew 67
  Nathaniel 69, 87
  Rebeckar 63
  Stephen 63
Kenner
  Francis 98
  William 98
Kennett
  John 20
Kenny
  Thomas 69
Kent
  John 6, 7, 47, 64, 81, 82, 109
  Robert 81, 105, 112
  Sarah 46, 109, 112
  Susannah 81
  William 7
Kenton
  Solomon 11, 12
Keplinger
  Eve 28
  George 28
  Martin 35, 37
Kerby
  Mary 31
Kersey
  Anna 41
  Eleanor 41
  Elisabeth 41
  Francis 41, 63
  John 41
  Margaret 41, 63
  Mary 41
  Sarah 41
  William 63, 108
Kershaw
  Francis 39
Kersley
  William 18
Key
  Edmond 107
  Edmund 94
  Francis 94
  Job 64
  John Ross 94
  Philip 94
  Philip Barton 94
  Richard Ward 94
  Susannah Gardiner 94
  Thomas 94
Keybert
  John 9
  Thomas 9
Kibble
  William 49
Kilgore
  Thomas 36
Killam
  Daniel 86, 93
Killey
  Daniel 85
  Elisabeth 85
Killiam
  Daniel 85
Killium
  Edward 48
  John 48
Killman
  Thomas 40
  William 21
Killum
  Daniel 102
  Edward 48, 110
  John 48
Kilman
  William 59
Kimble
  Frances 19
  Martha 19
  Richard 19
  Samuel 19
  William 19
Kimbol
  John 22

King
  Ann Pen 94
  Assa 69
  Betty 31
  Catherine 31
  Ephraim 62
  James 30
  Jane 69
  Jenny 31
  Jesse 14, 66
  John 14
  Joseph 69, 88, 94, 106
  Rachel 31
  Rebeccah 94
  Sarah 113
  Southy 13
  Thomas 31
  Whittington 14
  William 102
Kingsley
  Rhoda 111
Kinnard
  John 49
Kinnemont
  Elisabeth 43
  John 43
  Susannah 43
Kinney
  Stephen 54
Kinnimont
  Ambrose 32
  Francis 96
  Lidia 32
  Sarah 96
Kinsman
  John 9, 109
Kirby
  Ann 62
  Benjamin 63
  Elisabeth 62, 81
  Matthew 97
  Rachel 62
  Robert 63
  Sarah 97
  Walter 62
  William 62, 109
Kirckhead
  Mary 110
Kirk
  John 108, 113
Kirke
  John 61
Kirkland
  William 105
Kirkman
  Arthur 101
  James 70
  Mary 70
Kirley
  William 70
Kitely
  Elisabeth 19
  Rachel 19
  William 19
Kittinger
  John 26
Knock
  Benjamin 2, 16, 17
  John 32
  Nathaniel 37
  William 2, 17
Knotts
  Nathaniel 7
Knowles
  Edmund 18
  Richard 13, 18

Lafeld
  Robert 108

Lake
   Henry 73
Lamar
   Susannah 19
Lamb
   George 56
   John 49
   Pearce 87
Lambden
   Robert 2
Lamberson
   Casiah 77
   Elisabeth 77
   Lucy 77
   Saley 77
   Samuel 77, 104, 110
   Sinah 77
   Smith 77
Lambert
   Balser 92
   Eve Catharine 48
Lancaster
   Anthony 65
   Jane 65
   John 65, 110
   Joseph 65
   Mary 65
   Nasey 65
   Raphael 65
Landrum
   Andrew 54
Lane
   James 55, 112
   Samuel 84
   Timothy 1
Langdon
   Joseph 100
Langley
   Jane 10
   John 10, 99
   Mary 99
   William 99
Lanham
   Arsenah 40
   Edward 40, 105
   Eleazar 112
   Henry 40
   Josiah 40
   Mary 40, 89
   Mildred 40
   Rachel 40
   Sarah 40
   Sarah Bias Wilder 40
   Susannah 40, 86
   Zachariah 89, 105, 112
Lanhan
   Bersheba 40
Laramore
   James 13
   Sarah 13
Larsham
   Thomas 109
Latchum
   Dinah 102
   George 102
   Isaiah 102
   John Randall 102
   Joseph 102
   Nehemiah 102
   Peter 102
   Thomas 102, 109
Lattimore
   Benjamin 94
Laurance
   John 29
Laurence
   John 73, 77
   Susannah 73
Laurenson
   Andrew 31

Law
   Acquila 94
Laws
   Panther 13
   Sarah 90
Lawson
   Elisabeth 4
   John 96, 111
Layfield
   George 109, 110
   Isaac 91
   Rebeccah 50
   Robert 50
Layman
   Christopher 35
Laymon
   Rachel 35
Layton
   Charles 59
   James 59, 108, 112
   Nancy 59
League
   James 30
Leatherbury
   Charles 94
Lecompte
   James 9, 83
   John 65
   Mary 20, 25
   Nathaniel 25
   Nehemiah 20
   Philemon 34
Lee
   Alexander 3, 71, 105
   Amos 71
   David 71
   Edward 81
   Elisabeth 71
   Frances 71
   Isaac 21
   Joshua 71
   Kesiah 61
   Rachel 71
   Ruth 71
   Samuel 11
   Sarah Brooke 52
   Solomon 71
   Thomas 52
   Vincent 71
   William 61, 71
Leech
   Elisabeth 48
   Jeremiah 48
Leek
   Joseph 88
   Rebeccah 74
Leeke
   Rhoda 51
Legar
   John 71
   Spencer 39
Legg
   John 47, 102
   Rachel 57
Legor
   Spencer 79
Leigh
   Mary 29
   Peggy 29
Lemar
   Constant 95
Lenard
   Joseph 106
   Michael 110
Lenox
   Richard 107
Leonard
   Elisabeth 64
   John 101
   Joseph 101, 106, 108

   Michael 101, 104
Lester
   Alice 55
Letchworth
   Joseph 59
   THomas 99
Lettick
   Peter 2
Leverton
   Ann 23, 39
   John 23, 39
   John Foster 23, 39
   Thomas 23, 39
Lewin
   Christian 39
   Elisabeth 39
   Frances 39
   Henrietta 39
   Lewis 39
   Margaret 39
   Richard 39
   Samuel 39
   Sarah 39
Lewis
   Ann 63
   Jemima 37
   John 2
   Thomas 63, 76, 85
Lewiston
   John 101
Liddell
   Daniel 72
   David 91
Lighter
   Melcher 97
Limbenstone
   John 101
Lince
   Deborah 1
Linch
   Alexander 109, 110
   Ann 1
   Deborah 1
   Eleanor 1
   Jeremiah 110
   Joshua 1
   Nelly 1
   Sarah 1
   William 1
Lindall
   Peter 110
Lindsay
   Ruth 39
   William 24, 45
Lindsey
   Anthony 72
   William 11
Linegar
   Grace 58
   Jacob 58, 107, 110
Linganfeller
   Abraham 34
Linox
   James 63
   John 63
   Richard 63, 110
Linthicum
   Hezekiah 4
Linthicumb
   Francis 66
   Hezekiah 110
   Richard 41
Little
   Catharine 57
   George 99
   Margaret 57
   Martha 57, 108
   Mary 57, 99
   Robert 57
   Sarah 57

Thomas 57, 99
William 99
Littleton
   Mary 20
Litton
   Caleb 35, 41, 106
   Grace 41
   John 41
   Margaret 35
   Michael 41
Livers
   Arnold 111
Lloyd
   Isaac 48, 61
   James 55
   Mary 61
   Richard 51
Loch
   Meverell 105
Lock
   Meverel 110
   William 86
Lockerman
   Jacob 47, 73
Lockwood
   John 101
   Rebeccah 101
Loflin
   Eleanor 34
   Richard 34
Logar
   Menaper 31
Logg
   John 70
Loit
   Joseph 107
Lomax
   Brazilla 79
   Constant 79
   Margaret 79
   Mark 79
   Rebecca 79
   Seth 79
   Thomas Anderson 79
Loney
   Amos 54
   Arabella 54
   John 54, 108
   Mary 54, 111
   Stephen 54
   William 54
Long
   Aquila 65
   Coulbourn 27
   David 11
   Jefery 27
Lookerman
   Ann 36
   Elisabeth 36
   Jacob 108
   Lilly 36
   Mary 36
Lotan
   John 4
Loughinhouse
   William 34
Love
   Charles 27
   Elisabeth 27, 82
   John 5
   Samuel 82
Loveday
   Thomas 57
Loveless
   Archibald 57
   John Bapt. 109
   John Baptist 57
   Mary Ann 57
   Miliscent 57
   Vachell 57

Lovely
   William 33
Low
   John 107, 111
   Patience 77
   William 48
Lowd
   Charles 47, 108, 112
Lowe
   Isaac 21
   Jacob 21
   Jane 21
   Margaret 21
   Rebecca 21
   Samuel 46
   Sarah 21
Lowell
   Joseph 75
Lowes
   Henry 108
Loy
   Adam 37
   Charles 37
   Frederick 37
   George 37
   Jacob 37, 48, 112
   Mary 48
   Rosinah 37
Loyd
   James 111
Lucas
   James 25
   Jane 25
   John 102
Luckett
   Thomas Hussey 53, 112
   William 9, 27, 63
Lusby
   Betty 27
   Jacob 27
   Joseph 25, 27, 45
   Josiah 25
   Mary 112
   Robert 45
   Thomas 106
Lux
   Darby 94
   William 43, 61
Lyer
   Leonard 75
Lyles
   Zachariah 34
Lynch
   Alice 80
   Anthony 80
   Avarilla 104
   Elisabeth 80
   George 80
   James 5, 80
   Jemima 86
   John 85
   Mary 85
   Nicholas 107, 111
   Patrick 103, 107
   Robuck 103
   William 80
Lynn
   Charles 48
   David 40
   Elisabeth 15
   Josias 15
Lyon
   William 105
Lytle
   Eleanor 15
   Elisabeth 15
   George 15
   Henrietta 15
   James 15
   Margaret 15

   Mary 15
   Thomas 15

Maccatee
   Patrick 107
   Thomas 37
Maccomas
   Sarah 62
Maccubin
   Richard 67
MacDaniel
   Thomas 79
Mace
   Edmund 81
   John 38, 81
Machall
   Benjamin 104
Mackal
   Benjamin 110
Mackall
   Ann 66
   Benjamin 66, 104
   Hanna 66
   Hannah 66
   James 66
   John 66
   Mary 66
   Rebecca 66
   Thomas How 66
Maclanachan
   William 104
Macmans
   Elisabeth 55
Macpherson
   Joseph 90
   Sarah 90
Madcalf
   John Kinnelin 102
Maddock
   James 80
   Sarah 80
Maddocks
   John 80
Maddox
   Ann 72
   Bell 13
   Cornelius 9
   Edward 45
   James 47, 70, 112
   John 33, 45, 67, 109, 111
   Susannah 9, 92
   Theodocia 47
Madkin
   William 58
Magruder
   Enoch 18, 87
   Jeremiah 19
   Mary 19
Mahew
   Ann 37
   Joseph 37
Mahoney
   Samuel 110, 111
Mairman
   Ann 86
   John 86
Makal
   Benjamin 110
Malone
   John 49
Manklin
   Richard 20
Mannery
   John 24
   Mary 24
Manning
   Cornelius 38
   Elisabeth 79

Francis 38
Francis Speak 79
Jane 38
Jeane 38
John 38, 47
Joseph 79
Mary 38
Mary Ann 79
Monica 38
Robert 38
Thomas 21, 57, 107, 112
Mannyngsimmons
   John 17
Mansfield
   John 105
   Richard 71
   Samuel 32
   Sarah 71
Manship
   Charles 21, 59
   Elisabeth 21
Mansill
   Susannah 25
Manycousins
   Michael 113
March
   Charles 104, 111
   John 8
   Sarah 56
Mareer
   James 60
   Judith 60
Marker
   John 100
Markland
   Mary 92
Marloe
   Richard 108
Marquis
   Sarah 9
   William 9
Marriott
   James 39
   John 49
Marshall
   James 86
Martain
   Thomas 108
Marten
   James 106
Martin
   Andrew 16
   Dorothy 11
   Elisabeth 28
   James 76, 109
   John 14, 44, 80
   Mathew 28
   Thomas Green 11, 99
Martiny
   William 24
Mason
   Edward 108
   Martha 20
   Nicholas 16
   William 79
Massey
   Ebenezar 16, 32, 55
   Ebenezer 32
   James 32
   John 72, 108
   Joseph 32, 93
   Nicholas 32
   Samuel 32
   Sarah 32, 33
   Solomon 32
   William 32
Mastin
   Ann 63
   Brittain 63
   Francis 63

   Hamer 63
   James 63
   John 63
   Robert 108, 110
   Samuel 63
   Thomas 63, 107
   William 63
Mathews
   Comfort 20
   Edward 33, 35, 104
   Hugh 62
   James 60
   John 25
   Margaret 20
   Mary 25
   Milcah 25
   Sophia 35
   William 53, 60, 90
Matkins
   Theodore 33
Matthews
   Elijah 101
   John 101
   Rachel 101
Mattingly
   Ignatius 98
   Robert 41
Mauldin
   Benjamin 16
   Elisabeth 16
   Francis 16
   Henry 16
   Mary 16
   Mary Kitridge 16
   Rebecca 16
   William 16
Maxwell
   Alexander 38
   Elisabeth 5
   John 16, 38, 56, 60, 100
   Mary 38
   Peter 38
   Rachel 38, 60
   Robert 21, 56, 60, 104, 107
   Ruth 60
   Sarah 38
   William 60
May
   Mary 108
Mayce
   John 50
Mayhew
   Thomas 66
Mayne
   John 42
Mayo
   Thomas 3, 46, 47, 79
McBride
   Hugh 79
McCallum
   Archibald 107
McCatee
   Eleanor 53
   Elendor 53
   Elisabeth 53
   James 37, 53
   Monicka 53
   Susannah 53
   Thomas 37
   William 37
McCattee
   Agness 37
   Edmond 37
   Elisabeth 37
   John 37
   McCattee 37
   Rosamond 37
   Thomas 37
   William 37

McCawans
   James 104
McClanahan
   William 104
McClean
   John 105
McComas
   Alexander 19
   Daniel 3
McCombs
   Letitia 8
McCool
   Thomas 111
McCosh
   Samuel 38
McCoy
   Henry 21
   James 21
   John 12, 21, 25
   Rebecca 21
McCrady
   Andrew 95
   Edey 95
   Eleanor 95
   Isaac 95
   Mary 95
   Rachel 95
   Sarah 95
   Stephen 95
McCubbin
   Charles 56
   John 38
   Joseph 38
   William 38
McCuddy
   John 90
McCulloch
   David 104
McCullum
   Alexander 55
   Archibald 55
   Fanny 55
   Jane 55
   William 55
McDaniel
   Alexander 24, 45, 111
   Marly 111
   Mary Ann 24, 45
   Patrick 65
   Rebecca 79
   Thomas 106, 108
McDermot
   Charles 113
   Thomas 16
McDonald
   Alexander 18
   Annastatia 18
   Jane 95, 105
   Rachel 95
   Sarah 95
McDonnell
   Sarah 65
McDowell
   Daniel 69
   James 69
   Levina 69
   Thomas 69
McDugging
   Alexander 59
McFarren
   Samuel 75
McGarritty
   Patrick 33
McGarrity
   Patrick 31, 83
McGarvey
   Mary 60
McGay
   Robert 55
McGhuire

Hugh 73
Mary 73
McGill
  John 19
  M. A. 105
McGlachlan
  Dennis 105
McGlachlin
  Jonathon 110
McGraw
  Eleanor 53
McKee
  John 9
McKemmy
  Gideon 80
  Mary 80
  Nathan 80
  Nathaniel 80
  Rachel 80
  Sarah 80
  William 80
McKinley
  George 22
  John 106
McKinnon
  Catharine 40
  Daniel 40
McLane
  Daniel 14
  Elisabeth 23
  Mark 23
McManus
  Philip 3
McPherson
  Alexander 24, 29
  Daniel 64
  Thomas 23, 44, 53
  Walter 79
  William 27
McWherton
  John 60
McWhorter
  John 78
Mead
  Benjamin 16
  Edward 106
Meade
  Edward 39
Meads
  Thomas 23
Meaner
  James 57
  Timothy 57
Medcalf
  Sarah 102
Medford
  George 58
  Jane 49, 107
  Macal 10, 50
  Marmaduke 89
  Robert 108
  Thomas 49
  Unit 50
  Uriel 108
Medley
  Clement 101
Meed
  Elisabeth 40
  John 40
  Patrick 40
  Thomas 40
  William 40
Meeds
  Hester 92
  John 92, 95
  Sarah 95
  Thomas 39
  Walter 95
  William 95
Meek
  Adam 93
  Andrew 93
  Ann 83
  Isaac 14
  James 83, 93
  Jane 83, 93
  Margaret 93
  Mary 93
  Moses 93
  Nancy 93
  Rebecca 93
  Valentine 105
  William 83
Meeke
  Robert 54
Meekin
  Augustine 105
Meekins
  Augustine 105, 110, 113
  Benedict 72, 91
  Catharine 37, 54, 62
  Denwood 91
  Elisabeth 72, 91
  Ezekiel 72, 91
  Hannah 72
  Henry 72, 91
  Henry Holten 91
  Henry Holton 72
  John 37, 54, 62, 108
  John Dennard 72
  Joshua 72, 91
  Mathew 72, 91
  Richard 72, 91, 105, 108, 111
Meeks
  Francis 110
  James 94
  John 89, 94
  Mary 94
  Robert 49
  William 107
Mefford
  John 67
Melson
  Betty 18
  Hannah 18
  John 23
  Joseph 77
  Luke 18
  Nanny 18
  Wharton 18
  William 18, 77
Melton
  Philip 8
Melvill
  David 18, 74
  Rachel 74
  Sarah 59, 74
Mentz
  Casper 97
Mercer
  Robert 106
Meredith
  Ann 1
  James 45
  John 45, 93, 96
  Juliana 1
  Sarah 24, 45
  Thomas 45
  William 45, 79, 96, 112
Meridith
  Benjamin 89
  William 89, 112
Merine
  John 83
Merriken
  John 93
Merrikin
  Hugh 79
Merrill
  Anne 91
  Betty 91
  Elenor 91
  John 92
  Joshua 91, 109, 111
  Leah 91
  Mary 91
  Nancy 91
  Sarah 91
  William 91, 92
Merrit
  William 98
Merritt
  William 86
Methugh
  Aquilla 31
Mezecks
  Fisher 54
Middagh
  John 112
Middlemore
  Francis 15
Middleton
  Elisabeth 23, 44
  George 40
  Ignatius 70
  James 44
  Samuel 23, 44
Miers
  Luke 50
Miffin
  Andrew 95
  Catharine 95
  Eleanor 95
  Mathias 95
  Southy 106
  William 95
Milbourn
  Caleb 69
  John 69, 108, 112
  Thomas 109
Milburn
  Ann 55
  Caleb 95
  John 55, 110
  Sally 55
  Sophia 55
  Susannah 55
Milbury
  Jane 38
Milched
  Ignatius 106
Miles
  Betty 51, 74
  Edward 73
  Elisabeth 46
  Henry 7
  John 22, 30
  John Barton 46, 113
  Joseph 12
  Margaret 97
  Peter 49
  Richard 65
  Thomas 12, 68, 97, 104, 110
  William 7, 30
Mill
  Thomas 39
Millard
  James 105, 107
  Mary 42
  Richard 42, 105
Millars
  Richard 105
Miller
  Ann 66
  Arthur 12, 90
  Charles Sweat 55
  James 66, 92
  Jane 85

John 78
Nancy 84
Rousby 9, 15
Samuel 44
Sarah 44
Simon Stephens 55
Thomas 3, 85
Millington
  Allemby 95
  Mary 95
Mills
  Elisabeth 94
  James 35
  John 18, 90
  Justinian 86
  Robert 6, 24
  Smith 6
  Stephen 66
  Thomas 104
  Wright 39
Millward
  James 58
Milton
  Abraham 12
Minet
  Jacob Andrew 108
Minotree
  Jacob Andrew 106
Minskee
  Ch. 6
Misler
  Ulrick 92
Mitchel
  Ann 65
  Birgin 75
  Edward 8, 80
  Henrietta 65
  Hugh 80
  Ignatius 65
  Rachel 65
  Richard 65
  Richard Bennett 65
  Samuel 65
  Winefred 65
Mitchell
  Ambrose 9
  Edward 84
  Elisabeth 9
  Isaac 100
  John 9, 16
  Joshua 44
  Josiah 5
  Richard B. 51
  Robert 44, 91
  Sarah 5
Mitton
  Abraham 97
Mock
  Adam 113
Mockbee
  Ann 67
  Lessue 67
  Lucia 67
  Lucy 67
  Mary 67
  Ninian 67
  William 67
Molineux
  Richard 110
Monroe
  Thomas 108
Monsh
  John 12
Montgomery
  Francis 106
Moody
  Alexander 81
  David 81
  John 66, 81
  Mary 66

Robert 66, 81
Thomas 81
Mooney
  Charles 69, 111
  Sarah 69
Moor
  Margaret 112
Moore
  Ann 19
  Elisabeth 14
  Henry 58, 68
  Isaac 13
  James 62, 84
  Jane 50
  Jestener 102
  John 20
  Joseph 19
  Joshua 7
  Mathew 50
  Nathaniel 19
  Rudolph 58, 68
  Samuel 19
  Thomas 59, 60
  William 11
Mooth
  Elisabeth 24
  James 24, 82
  Margaret 24, 82
  Mary 24, 82
  Thomas 82, 105, 112
Morgan
  Ann 36
  Avery 109, 111
  Charles 50
  Edward 15
  Elisabeth 36, 44
  James 36
  John 78
  Jonathon 44
  Joseph 94
  Mary 14, 44
  Sarah 36, 50
  Thomas 44, 107
  William 36
Morris
  Beavins 101
  Bevan 101
  Elisabeth 86, 101
  Henry 26
  Isaac 31
  John 94, 110
  Lewisa 101
  Luke 105
  Mary 18, 94
  Thomas 94, 104, 111
Morrison
  John 35
Morriss
  Comfort 77
  Cornelius 77
  Jethro 77
  John 77
  Leah 77
  Lissa 77
  Sarah 77
  Thomas 77
  William 77
Morton
  Elisabeth 83
  Henry 83
  James 74, 83
  John 83
  Jonathon 83
  Mary 83
  Mary Ann 83
  Thomas 83
Mosh
  Samuel 105
Moss
  Elisabeth 58

Richard 58
Samuel 58, 106
Thomas 16
Mossner
  Peter 75
Mouat
  James 104
Mountseir
  Timothy 32
Mudd
  Francis 2
  Henry 2
  Ignatius 2
  James 10
  Joseph 2, 66
  Luke 2
  Richard 2
  Thomas 2
Mullican
  Bazil 55
  Mary 55
Mullikin
  Elisabeth 81
  John 69
  Joseph 81
  Mary 81
  Patrick 81
  Rachel 81
  William 63
Mumford
  James 20, 30
Mundell
  Robert 82
Munroe
  Alexander 14
  Isaac 14
  John 72
  Matthias 14
  Thomas 111
Murphey
  Alley 62
  James 62
  John 62
  Mary 62
Murphy
  Alley 53
  James 53
  John 53, 56
  Margaret 64
  Mary 53
  Philemon 27
  Sarah 36
  William 31
Murray
  Ann 66
  David 107, 108
  William 6, 66, 67
Myers
  John 89
  John Jeremiah 48
  Luke 55
  Rhoda 70
  Stephen 70
  Valentine 50

Nailor
  Joseph Smith 26
Nairn
  John 35
Nairne
  Robert 35
Naitton
  John 98
Nash
  Ann 22
Neale
  Ann 53, 72
  Bennet 65
  Catharine 72

    Edward 106, 109, 110
    Elisabeth 72
    Francis 1
    Henry 110, 112
    John 72
    Joseph 72
    Mary 72
    Mildred 72
    Molly 53
    Raphael 82
    Richard 72
    Sally 72
    William 53, 72, 109
    William Francis 72
Neare
    Daniel 104
Nelson
    Benjamin 78
    Burgess 78, 106
    Henry 78
    John 71
    Joseph 71, 105
    Mary 71
    Rachel 78
    Sarah 78
    William 43, 104, 110
Nesbitt
    Nathaniel 96
Nevitt
    Joseph 99
New
    John 109
Newbold
    John 85
Newman
    Ayres 111
    Elisabeth 103
    Henry 59, 94
    Isaac 59, 94
    Thomas 59
Newton
    Betty 4
    Catharine 42
    Comfort 11
    Edward 4
    Elisabeth 42
    Frances 42
    Job 11
    John 42, 105
    Jonathon 108
    Leonard 42
    Levin 11
    Mary 4
    Nathaniel 100
    Richard 4
    Robert 42
    Willis 4
Nicholas
    Luke 44
Nicholls
    William 94
Nichols
    John 37
Nicholson
    Hannah 66
    Josep 66
    Joseph 13, 51, 99
    Lucy 25
    Mary 13, 38, 90
    Peggy 13
    Roger 112
    Sarah 13
    William 38, 43, 66, 105
Nicolls
    William 93
Nisbit
    Thomas 111
Nixon
    Thomas 20
Noble
    Alice 13
    Ann 107
    George 11, 99
    Isaac 13
    John 13
    Robert 11, 42
    Thomas 18, 87
Noe
    John 92
Norris
    Ann 105
    Catharine 54
    Jos. 45
    Luke 111
    Mark 98
    Martin 9
    Rebecca 19
    Samuel 112
    Thomas 79, 98
Norriss
    Ann 42
    Benjamin 45
    Clement 42
    John 41, 42
    John Baptist 42
    Mathew 42
    Samuel 48
    Stephen 42
    Thomas 42, 45
    William 42
Northcraft
    Ann 92
    Edward 49, 92
    Elisabeth 49, 92
    Frances 92
    Mary Ann 92
    Richard 92
    Susannah 92
Northerly
    Samuel 32
Norton
    Alexander 20
Norwood
    Edward 91
    Mathew 52
Nottingham
    Ann 101
    Athanasius 111
    Athanius 101
    Barbara 101
    Basil 101
    Bennett 101
    Catharine 101
    Eleanor 101
    Elisabeth 101
    Enoch 101
    Mary 101
    Mary Ann 101
    Mathias 111
    Philip 101
Nowell
    Edward 30
    Henry 30
    Lydia 30
Nowland
    Augustine 62
    Benjamin 62
    Daniel 62
    Ephraim 62
    Hannah 62
    Jane 8, 23
    John 62
    Rachel 23
Null
    Valentine 97
Nunam
    Ayres 48
    Frances 48
    John 107
Nuton
    Tamsey 10
Nutter
    Charles 22
    Hewit 112
    James 22
    Nelly 22
    Thomas 22
    William 22

O'Neil
    Thomas 113
Oakly
    John 33
    Sarah 33
Obenhiser
    Elisabeth 101
OBrien
    John 102
Obryan
    Solomon 108
Odell
    Baruch 84
    Eleaner 84
    Martha 48
    Sarah 84
    Thomas 84
Oden
    Eleanor 59
    Elisabeth 59
    Francis 59
    Michael 59
    Sarah 59
Offutt
    Alexander 85
    Hannah 93
    James 84, 93
    Rachel 93
    Rebeccah 93
    Sarah 93
    Thomas 93
    William 84, 93
Ogden
    John 68
Ogle
    Benjamin 98
    Eleanor 98
    James 98
    Joanna 98
    Joseph 98
    Mary 98
    Sarah 98
    Susanna 98
    Thomas 98
    William 98
Oldfield
    Barber 43
    Henry 43
    Lucretia 43
    Margaret 43
    William 61, 111, 112
Oldham
    Ann 92
    Edward 92
    Elisabeth 92
Oldrick
    James 41
Oneal
    Elisabeth 77
    John 77, 104, 111
    Samuel 77
    Thomas 77
Orme
    John 105
Osborn
    Ann 87
    David 87
    James 19, 87
    Mary 87
    Samuel 102

Sarah 102
Violetta 102
William 87
Osborne
　John 102
　Sarah 102
Osbourn
　Ann 37
　Joseph 37, 55
Osbourne
　John 60
　Mary 60
Osburn
　John 106, 113
Osburne
　Samuel 26, 112
Osment
　Jonathon 3
　Priscilla 3
　Richard 3
　Thomas 3
Outten
　Abraham 110
Owen
　Hugh 64
Owens
　Rachel 50
　Robert 50
Owin
　Betty Dashiel 63
　Spicer 104
Owings
　David 50
　Elijah 95
　James 50
　John 50
　Owen 50
　Rachel 50
　Thomas 50
Owins
　David 63
　Elisabeth 63
　James 6
　Mary 63
　Rebecca 63
　Robert 63, 109
　William 63
Owler
　Andrew 100
　Elisabeth 100
　George 100
　Susannah 100
Ozier
　Rebecca 98

Paca
　Elisabeth 15
　Frances 15
　Hannah 15
　John 15, 19, 25
　Martha 15
　Mary 15
Paden
　James 22
　John 22
　Nancy 22
　Sarah 22
Page
　Anthony Deane 86
　Aquila 21
　Araminta 21
　Daniel 86
　George 86, 93
　Hannah 21
　John 21
　Margaret 93
　Mary 21, 100
　Ruth 21
　Temperance 21

Pain
　Ann 20, 25
　Isaac 85
　Joseph 20
　Thomas 104
Palmer
　Isaac 97
　Polly 51
　Rebecca 51
　Thomas 51
Pantain
　Thomas 100, 109
Parish
　Richard 79
Parker
　Abigail 9
　Elisabeth 9
　Samuel 9
　Tabitha 9
Parks
　John 31
Parlton
　James 88
　John 88
Parnham
　Francis 112
Parnon
　John 113
Parran
　Benjamin 24
　Nathaniel 24
　Samuel 9
　Sarah 9
　Young 24
Parratt
　------ 8
　Abner 8
　Elisabeth 8
　Margaret 8
　Mary 8
　William 8
Parrot
　Abner 43
　Francis 43
　George 32
　Mary 43
Parrott
　John 58, 110
　Richard 43
　William 81
Parsley
　Ann 60
　Bartholomew 60, 109
　Benjamin 60
　Eleanor 60
　Elisabeth 60
　Rebeccah 60
　Thomas 60
Parsly
　Bartholomew 106
Parsons
　Benjamin 69
　Hannah 69
　Issabella 6
　Joseph 89, 106, 113
　Joshua 25
　Martha 25
　Michel 79
　Nicholas 6
　Peter 25
　Samuel 79
　Tabitha 27
　Thomas 27
Partridge
　Daubrey Buckley 35
　Isaac 41
　William 35
Patridge
　Jonathon 48, 54
Patterson

Elisabeth 25
Esther 25
John 25
Robert 25
Samuel 25
Patton
　Andrew 36
Paul
　Betty 61, 72
　Desier Griffith 61, 72
　Jane Griffith 61, 72
　John 108, 112
　Lewis Griffith 61, 72
　Mary 61, 72
　Rachel 61, 72
　Slater Griffith 72
　Sliter Griffith 61
Paulson
　Ann 107
　Joseph 48, 104, 111
Payne
　Ann 20, 25
　Daniel 97
　George 105
　Isaac 11
　Jacob 11
　Joseph 20, 25
Peake
　Mary 98
　Peter 98
Pearce
　Andrew 80
　James 56
　John 32, 61
　Joseph 32
　Rebecca 14
　Sarah 104, 108
　Thomas 61
　William 14, 61, 108
Pearman
　Ann 3, 58, 78
　James 3
Pearson
　Richard 107
Pecker
　George 93
Peele
　John 43
　Richard 43
　Robert 43
　Roger 43
　Samuel 43
　William 39, 43
Peirpoint
　Ann 25
Pell
　Charles 109, 112
Pelly
　Ann 87
　Harrison 87
　James 87
　Mary 87
Penn
　Jane 88
　Mary 91
　William 46, 69, 73
Pennington
　Henry 22, 62
　Isaac 14
　John 14
　Mary 14
　Robert 14
　Samuel 11
　Sarah 14
　Thomas 11
Perigoy
　Elisabeth 42
Perkins
　Ann 59, 68
　Betty 76

Comfort 76
Ebenezar 49
Edward 31
John 29, 68, 105, 112
Joseph 52
Mary 29
Philip 59
Phillip 97, 103
Rebecca 31
Samuel 112
Sarah 29, 52, 76
Solomon 31, 103
Tabitha 76
Thomas 49, 76
William 29, 104
Zeporah 76

Perrie
John 62, 65
Thomas 62

Perry
Ann 10
Deborah 10
Francis 62
Hugh 62
John 11, 31, 62
Rachel 62
Rebecca 62
Sarah 10
Thomas 9, 62
William 10, 62

Peter
Lewis 111

Petty
James 109

Phelps
Philemon 40

Philbert
Wharton 9

Philipps
William 107

Philips
John 110
Mary 104

Phillip
John 104

Phillips
Ann 72, 91
Humphrey 45
James 47
John 30, 45, 108
Joseph 65
Mary 65, 111
Nancy 65
Philemon 46
Rebeccah 65
Sarah 59, 65
Thomas 73
William 61, 65, 112

Philpot
Barton 41
Bryan 1
John 107, 111
Mary 109

Philson
John 97
William 97

Phipps
Nathaniel 4
Sarah 4

Pickerine
John 60

Pickering
Francis 86, 93, 102
Margaret 86, 93, 96
Robert 85, 86, 93, 96, 102
Stephen 104

Piddle
John 19

Pierpoint
Francis 35

Pike
Sarah 19
William 19

Piles
Jeremiah 41

Piller
George 58

Piner
Bartus 2, 12
Benjamin 12
Edward 12
Susannah 2, 12

Piper
Christopher 108

Pippen
John 23
Matthias 23

Pisson
William 106

Pitts
John 34

Plowman
James 60

Plumer
Drusilla 104
Zephaniah 109

Plummer
Dorichlar 76
Jeremiah 76
Zephaniah 76

Polk
Charles 85
James 14

Polke
David 20

Pollard
John 3
William 3

Pollitte
William 43

Polson
Joseph 111
Thomas 16
William 16

Pooler
Alexander 108

Pope
Ann 44
John 44
Joyce 44
Mary 44
Naomy 44

Porter
Abraham 49
Alexander 112
Alice 5
Andrew 2
Hugh 13
James 96
John 37
Joseph 35
Richard 5, 110
Robert 23
Ruth 49
William 25, 91

Posey
Ann 41
Belain 80
Benjamin 41
Bennett 41, 106
Blain 15
Blaw 12
Elisabeth 41
John 41
Mary 62

Posten
William 73

Potee
Lewis 104, 106

Poteet
Ann 3
John 3

Pott
John 37

Pottee
Lewis 45

Potter
Sarah 19
Thomas 19

Powel
Thomas 76

Powell
Ann 55, 108
Howell 32, 69
Jane 6
John 11, 76
Levin 108
Thomas 69

Prather
Jeremiah 48
John Smith 48, 112
Rachel 48
Thomas 29

Pratt
Henry 51
Henry Wright 71
James 112
Margaret 89
Philemon 86
Robert 110
Thomas 89, 100

Presbury
George 15
Goldsmith 5
Martha 15
William Robinson 15

Preston
Alexander 71
Ann 45, 62
Benjamin 62
Bernard 62
Clemency 62
Daniel 64
David 71
Elisabeth 69, 71
Eliza 71
James 45, 62, 111
John 62, 69, 71, 105, 113
Martin 62
Mary 62, 69, 71

Previn
Margaret 53
Mary 53

Pribble
Thomas 26

Price
Andrew 8, 35
Ann 11, 92
B. 18
Betty 24
Charles 92
Comfort 24
Daniel 1
Edward 92
Elisabeth 11, 28
Esther 24
Evan 8
Hester 92
Hyland 36
Jacob 8
James 8, 36, 92
Jane 11
John 36, 92
Littleton 24
Lydia 36
Margaret 11
Mary 24, 36, 92, 100
Mordecai 28, 100

Nathan 8
Neal 92
Nicholas 109
Oneal 55, 92
Rebecca 8, 24, 36
Richard 36, 70
Samuel 28
Sarah 36
Sturgis 24
Thomas 11, 70, 109
Webb 24
William 8, 54, 77, 92, 111
Prickett
　George 68
Pries
　Lydia 50
Primrose
　Elisabeth 82
　John 33
Prindell
　Eleanor 55
　John 55
　Philip 55
Pringel
　John 108
Pringle
　Comfort 55
　John 55
Prior
　Andesia 20
　Ann 103
　Betty 20
　Catharine 103
　Comfort 20
　Emory 103
　Esther 20
　James 103
　Joseph 103
　Rebecca 20
　Rosiller 103
　Sturgis 20
　Thomas 103
　Webb 20
　William 103
Pritchard
　Henry 113
　James 87
　Rachel 30, 56
Pritchet
　Edward 7
　James 107
　Levin 107, 112
　Sarah 73
　William 7, 112
Pritchett
　Edward 73
　Elijah 73
　Jabez 73
　Jane 85
　Josebet 73
　Levin 73
　Mary 85
　Sarah 73
　William 73, 85
Proin
　Mary 112
Prouse
　George 8
Provin
　James 47, 106, 108, 112
　Mary 106, 108
Pruce
　William 90
Pryor
　William 82, 112
Puckrell
　Joseph 33
Pullett
　William 14

Pumphrey
　Joseph 106, 112
Purkins
　Tabitha 76
　Thomas 76
　William 76
Purnel
　Samuel 75
Purnell
　Elisha 98, 109
　Hezekiah 91
　Martha 6
　Mathew 6
　Thomas 6, 25
Purney
　Elisabeth 96
Pye
　John 53

Quade
　Ann 44
　John 44
Queen
　Catharine 3
　Edward 3
　Henrietta 3
　Henry 3
　Mary Ann 3
　Monica 26
　Samuel 3
　Walter 3

Raisin
　George 8
　Sarah 8
Rait
　John 110
Raitt
　Ann 44
　Barbara 44
　George 44
　John 44
Raley
　Bennett 101
　Henry 86
　Jane 86
　John 110
Ralph
　Frances 56
　John 56, 63
　Martha 56
　Nancy 56
　William 56
Ralston
　Charles 26
　Mary 26
Ramer
　Michael 92
Ramney
　Ruth 73
Randal
　Theophilus 91
Randall
　Aquilla 92
　John 21, 98
　Richard 70
Ransberg
　Stephen 28, 84
Rape
　Valentine 76
Rapeur
　William 90
Rasin
　Abraham 10
　John 10, 38
　Rosa 10
　Sarah 37
　William 37, 107

Ratcliff
　Peter 33
　Rachel 62
　William 55, 59
Ratcliffe
　William 31, 48
Rathell
　David 21
Ratliff
　Ignatius 70
　Joseph 70
Raven
　Isaac 79
　Lettice 79
　Luke 5, 74, 79
Rawle
　Joseph 112
Rawley
　Betty 112
Rawlings
　Ann 46
　Paul 46, 112
Rawlinson
　John 111
Ray
　Thomas 64
Razin
　Susannah 66
Read
　Benjamin 8
　Eleanor 81
　James 87
　John 81, 84, 96
　Mary 8
　Nathaniel 112
Reardon
　John 64
　Sarah 64
Redden
　Charles 65
　Sarah 65
Redgrave
　Isaac 87, 107
　Joseph 49
　Joshua 57
　Mary 51
　William 51, 87, 113
Reed
　Amos 37
　Ann 37
　Benjamin 37
　Charles 10
　Hezekiah 87
　James 7, 108
　John 37, 40, 113
　Nathaniel 82
　Patrick 35, 107
　Rosannah 35, 40
　Ruth 37
　Sarah 82
　Shadrack 37
　Thomas 7
　Walter 7
　William 7, 37, 60
Reeder
　John 26
　Richard 60
Reesin
　Abraham 32
Reeves
　Edward 98
　Thomas 94
Register
　Arnault 100
　Arnold 100
　David 100
　Elisabeth 100
　John 100, 111
　Mary 100
Reid

Renshaw
  James 35
  John 21
Renshaw
  Joseph 46
  Thomas 46
Resior
  Conrad 8
Reveall
  Bridget 14
Rewell
  John 7
  Mary 7
Reynolds
  ------ 73
  Mary 73
  Richard 112
  William 25, 59
Rhodes
  Jeremiah 29
Rice
  Rachel 8
  Samuel 112
  William 8
Rich
  Cynthia 61
  Peter 61, 106
  Peter Nixon 61
  Susannah 61
  William 61
Richards
  John 50
  Sarah 52
  William 31
Richardson
  Ann 37, 94
  Daniel 95
  Elisabeth 95
  Isabell 69
  James 94
  John 33, 35, 69, 94
  Lucretia 33, 35
  Mary 5
  Milcah 33, 35
  Philip 41, 70
  Phillip 94
  Richard 33, 35
  Robert 94
  Samuel 33, 35
  Susanna 5, 61
  Thomas 5, 33, 35
  William 33, 35, 95
Richarson
  Philip 70
Richey
  Adam 67
  Daniel 67
  Henry 67
  Isaac 67
  Margaret 67
  Mary Ann 49
  William 49, 67
Rickets
  Samuel 39
Ricketts
  Bete 55
  Charlotte 29
  Mary 113
  Nathaniel 29, 52
  Philip 29, 43, 52
  Samuel 106
Ridenour
  Henry 97
Rider
  Peter 64
Ridgaway
  William 86, 95
Ridgely
  Henry 46
Ridgeway
  William 82

Ridgley
  Ann 43
  Elisabeth 84
  John 38, 43, 84, 105, 109
  Nicholas 43
Rigbie
  Henrietta 113
  John 107, 110
  Nathan 46
Rigby
  Arthur 105
Rigdon
  Elisabeth 52
  John 52
  Thomas Baker 52
  William 16
Riggen
  Charles 110
  Jabey 65
Riggin
  Charles 69
Riggs
  Samuel 84
Rikard
  Sidney 101
Riley
  John 32
  Joseph 32
  Sarah 32
Ringer
  Mathias 28
Ringgold
  Charles 17, 65
  James 4, 113
  Josiah 65
  Sarah 66
  Thomas 5, 11, 52, 64, 76, 85
  William 25, 76, 85
Ripley
  John 112
Risen
  Mary 90
  William 90
Risenour
  Tobias 101
Riswick
  John 105, 110
Rix
  Anne 59
  Betty 59
  Nancy 59
Roach
  Betty 111
  Deborah 76
  Elisabeth 74
  James 74, 76
  Levin 74
  Mary 74
  Mary Boazman 74
  Patrick 76
  Samuel 111
  Stephen 74, 76, 104
  Theophilus 66
  William 30, 74, 104
Roads
  Mary 101
Roberson
  Ann 68
Roberts
  Ann 81
  Anthony 75
  Benjamin 105
  Dorothy 1
  Edward 55, 81
  Elisabeth 44, 55
  Harriet 93
  Henrietta 57
  James 55, 57, 64, 81

  John 1, 17, 36, 55, 66, 81, 93
  Mary 14, 24, 55
  Nancy 81
  Rebecca 81
  Rebeccah 81
  Rencher 14
  Richard 44
  Sarah 93
  Susannah 64
  Thomas 55, 81, 97
Robertson
  Alexander 92, 99
  Daniel 92
  Francis 53
  James 90, 96
  John 90
  Mary 53
  Rachel 59
  Richard 53
  Samuel 113
  William 59, 105, 108
Robey
  Annan 71
  Cloe 71
  Eleanor 57, 71
  Elisabeth 71
  John 71
  Linda 71
  Mary 71
  Michael 71
  Mildred 71
  Richard 65
  Thomas 71
  William 53, 71, 112
Robie
  Peter 41
Robinett
  Mary 58, 87
  Richard 58, 87, 107, 108
Robins
  Handley 107
  John 107
  Margaret 41
  William 41, 111
Robinson
  Abraham 15
  Ann 32, 41, 107, 113
  Betty 23
  Charles 33, 41, 105
  Daniel 60
  Elijah 58
  Elisabeth 15
  Francis 47
  George 20, 23
  Isaac 15
  Jacob 15
  John 7, 15, 23, 32, 33, 110
  Joseph 29, 32
  Leek 80
  Mary 20, 23, 56
  Nathaniel 15
  Peter 77
  Rhoda 77
  Richard 15
  Sarah 15
  Sophia 33, 52
  Sophiah 7
  Standley 41
  William 13, 97, 110
Robson
  John 32
  Joseph 22
  Michael 32
Robston
  John 104
Roby
  Jane 41
  Mary 109

Richard 24
Sarah 41
Rochester
  Elisabeth 38
  Francis 38, 45, 47
  Hannah 38
  Henry 38, 47
  James 38
  John 38, 45, 47, 109
Rock
  Jacob 106
  James 59, 60
Rockall
  Thomas 33
Roe
  Abner 12
  Elisabeth 12
  James 95
  Jeanne 74
  John 55, 105
  Mary 14
  Richard 12
  Thomas 12
  William 12
Rogers
  Samuel 10, 106
Rolle
  Feddeman 82
Rolph
  John 90
  William 107
Rorer
  John 106, 108
Ross
  David 40
  George 60
  Robert 42
  Thomas 54
Rottin
  Thomas 108
Rounds
  Catharine 111
Routh
  Christopher Cross 63
Rowles
  David 27
  Jacob 27
  John 27
  William 27
Ruark
  Hannah 91
  Robert 91
  Sarah 72, 91
Ruff
  Hannah 62
Rumbly
  Edward 95
  Jacob 95
Rumsey
  Benjamin 91
  Charles 21
  William 26
Russel
  Andrew 111
Russell
  Andrew 112
Ruth
  Ann 19
  James 3
  John 19, 100
  Walter 96
  William 45, 47
Rutherford
  Joseph 25, 93
Rutland
  Edmund 67
  Elisabeth 67
Rutledge
  Hannah 22
  John 22

Rutter
  Francis 58, 68, 77
  Moses 69
  William 69
Ryan
  Andrew 60
  Ann 91
  Benjamin 91
  Charity 91
  Ignatius 29
  Jacob 91
  John 91
  Joseph 91
  Rachel 91
  Rebeccah 91
  Robert 91
  Susannah 91
  William 91
Rycraft
  Thomas 108
Rye
  Ann 65
Ryland
  Alriches 73
  Frodus 73
  John 73
  Mary 73
  Rebeccah 73
  Stephen 73
  Thomas 73, 106

Saffle
  Elisabeth 35
  Peter 35
Sales
  William 111
Salmon
  William 69
Salsbury
  Enclin 21
  William 54
Saltner
  Catharine 38
  George 38
Sammons
  Grace 41
Sanders
  Ann 28
  Clare 64
  Daniel 104, 111
  Eleanor 37
  John 11, 28, 31
  Mathew 51
  Thomas 28
  William 28, 109
Sands
  Elisabeth 71
  Mary 4, 9
  Thomas 4, 9, 71
Sappington
  Ann 102
  Caleb 43
  James 102
  John 43, 109, 111
  Nathaniel 109
  Rebeccah 43
  Richard 43
  Thomas 43, 98
  William 102
Sarley
  Anthony 104
Satterfield
  William 63
Saunders
  Henry 18
  William 90
Savin
  Richard 96
  William 62

Sawell
  James 15
Scale
  Francis 10
Scandrett
  William 48
Schoolfeild
  Joseph 104
Schoolfield
  Benjamin 20, 23, 101
  Isaac Bozman 101
Scot
  Aquilla 2
  Elisabeth 2
Scott
  Ann 17, 27
  Aquilla 5
  Charles 98
  Daniel 5
  Day George 99
  Elisabeth 2, 5, 94
  George 110
  Jacob 104, 108
  James 2, 5, 17
  John 51, 78
  John Day 99
  Nathaniel 74
  Rebecca 2, 5
  Sarah 2, 5
  Solomon 112
  Zachariah 33
Scrivener
  Hesther 23
  Isaac 93
  John 23
  Joseph 93
  Juliana 95
  Mary 89
  Richard 23, 89
  Robert 93, 95
  William 93
Scrivner
  John 45
Scrogan
  John 45
Scully
  Benjamin 17
Seal
  Priscilla 88
  William 88, 104
Seals
  William 106
Searman
  Ann 105
Sedgwick
  Ann 1
  Catharine 64
  Elisha 64
  Mary 1
  Richard 110, 113
  Thomas 64, 110
  William 64
Sedgwicks
  Elisha 64
  John 64
  Mary 64
  Thomas 64
  William 64
Sedwick
  Benjamin 1, 16
Seeder
  William 92
Seeders
  John 78, 84
Seeney
  John 9, 45, 47
  Nevil 9
  Sollomon 32
  Solomon 9
Seger

Segwick
    John 92
Segwick
    John 64
Seigler
    Elisabeth 2
    John 2
Selbey
    John 112
Selby
    Amelia 63
    Barbary 63
    Cassandra 63
    Daniel 75
    Henrietta 51
    Henry 104, 110
    James 77
    Jemima 89
    John 36, 51, 75, 89, 105
    John Smith 51
    Kenelm Groom 51
    Mary 75
    Mary Ann 63
    Micajah 104
    Parker 36
    Philip 63, 75, 104, 110
    Samuel 63, 110
    Sarah 51
    Thomas 21, 22
    William Harris 63
    William Magruder 63
Selman
    Benjamin 40
    Elisabeth 25, 40, 105
    John 40
    Jonathon 9
    Son 40
    Williams 40
Semans
    Daniel 7
    Fowler 7
    Henry 7
    Jeremiah 7, 23, 35
    Sarah 23, 35
    Solomon 7, 23
    William 7, 23
Semmes
    Alexander 106
    Catharine 82
    Clare 82
    Elisabeth 82
    Ignatius 111
    Jos. Milb. 112
    Joseph 82
    Joseph Melbourn 110
    Joseph Milburn 82
    Marmaduke 82
    Martha 82
    Mary Ann 82
    Rachel 82
    Teresa 82
Semple
    John 49
Seney
    Solomon 109
Sergeant
    John 25
    Mary 25
Serogen
    John 33
Seth
    Charles 96, 112
    Elisabeth 96
    Jacob 96
    John 79
    Rachel 96
    Sarah 96
    Susannah 96
    William 96
Sewall
    Christopher 17
    Henry 28
    James 25
    Joshua 17
    Rachel 25
Sewell
    Charles 70
    Henry 102
    John 50, 107
    Thomas 110
Seymour
    Alexander 52
Seyrims
    Mary 26
    Thomas 26
Shaaf
    Caspar 38
Shaff
    Caspar 48
Shahon
    David 58
Shanahan
    John 81
    Peter 10
Shanks
    Ruth 91
    Thomas 86
Shannahan
    John 66
Sharf
    Casper 27
Sharpe
    Peter 55
    William 21
Shaver
    Peter 37
Shavers
    John 38
Shaw
    Arsenah 79
    Henrietta 36
    John 79
    Joseph 36
    Josiah 33, 36
    Rebecah 36
    Zachariah 36
Shawhan
    James 32
Shawn
    Darby 110
    Dennis 32
Shea
    Thomas 104
Shean
    Ann 4
    Arthur 4
    Bartholomew 4
    Sarah 4
Sheard
    Thomas 17
Shehawn
    Daniel 50
    David 107, 111
Sheil
    Ann 104
Shelton
    Abigal 95
    John 68
    Martha 68
Shemparis
    Thomas 97
Shenton
    Elisabeth 53, 62
    Joseph 61
    Raymond 37, 54, 62
    William 61
Shephard
    James 104
    William 104, 108
Shepherd
    Druzilla 93
    Francis 58
    John 93
    Margaret 93
    Mary 93
    Rebecca 93
    Samuel 60
    Sarah 93
    Thomas 93
    William 67, 68, 93
Sheppard
    Sand. 95
Sherlock
    Abraham 74
Shermond
    John 37
Sherwin
    Stephen 108
Sherwood
    Daniel 111
    John 21, 113
Shever
    Henry 27
Shhea
    Thomas 108
Shield
    John 44
Shiercliff
    Henry 86
    Joseph 86
    Mary 86
    Thomas 86
Shiercliffe
    Henry 112
Shiles
    Elisabeth 105
Shincliffe
    Henry 111
Shingeltaker
    Jacob 104, 109
Shingletaker
    Andrew 75
    Catharine 75
    Elisabeth 75
    George 75
    Jacob 75
    Margaret 75
    Michel 75
Shipley
    George 25
Shirtcliffe
    Henry 110
Shley
    Thomas 48
Shockley
    Isaac 65
Short
    Edward 90
    Elisabeth 90
    Isaac 90
    Jacob 90
    John 90, 104, 111
    Philip 90
    Shadrack 90
    William 90
Shover
    Henry 31, 34
Shroiner
    Valentine 100
Shull
    Christopher 68
Siddle
    Elisabeth 65
Siderman
    Jacob 112
Sile
    Hannah 54
Siler
    Mathias 50
    Maudelina 50
Silo

Robert 54
Sils
　Robert 104
Silson
　John 21
Simcock
　Nathan 107
Simcocks
　Nathan 113
Simm
　Catharine 52
　Joseph 52
　Joseph Walter 52
Simmonds
　Abraham 88
　John 42
　Richard 89
　Sarah 89
Simmons
　Benjamin 31
　George 108
　John 85
　Laurenson 31
　Mary 31
　Richard 32
　Samuel 31
　Sarah 31
　William 39
Simpers
　Anna 96
　Catharine 96
　Francis 96
　George 96
　Jacob 96
　James 96
　John 96
　Mary 96
　Nathaniel 96
　Richard 96
　Thomas 96
　William Howell 96
Simpon
　Aney 82
　Nancy 82
　Sally 82
　Tomsey 82
Simpson
　Alanor 53
　Ann 53
　Basil 82
　Elisabeth 53
　Francis 82
　George 69
　Ignatius 13
　John 50
　Mary 53
　Thomas 53, 108
　William 69
Sims
　Ignatius 29
Simsatt
　Richard 110
Sinners
　Joseph 109
Sirman
　Isaac 111
Sissan
　William 109
Skelton
　Thomas Hyde 33
Skiles
　Elisabeth 101
　Ephraim 101
Skinner
　Ann 11
　Elisha 110
　James 45, 111
　Jeremiah 11
　Sarah 70
　Thomas 30, 41

Skirvin
　William 57
Slacomb
　George 61, 72
Slarrum
　Jacob 68
Slater
　David 102
　Ellis 16, 68
　Jonathon 4
　Richard 28
Slaughter
　Eleanor 19
　James 105
　Thomas 19
Sliawil
　Samuel 78
Sloops
　William 104, 108
Sloss
　Thomas 28, 95
Slowers
　Richard 67
Sluyter
　Peter 16
Slye
　Ginan 109
　John Southern 58
　Mary 58
　Thomas Gerrard 58
Small
　Charles 105
　Sarah 111
Smallwood
　Beane 65
　Beans 24
　Benjamin 24, 65
　Benjamin G. 51
　Frances Ann 51
　Francis Green 24, 65
　James 24, 51, 65, 106
　James Bidon 51
　John 24, 37
　Marbury 51
　Martha 24, 65
　Mary 33
　Mathew 24, 65
　Philip 24, 65
　Priscilla 24, 65
　Samuel 51
　Susannah 51
　Thomas 51
Smalwood
　James 109, 112
Smith
　Addam 35
　Ann 17
　Archibald 6, 34
　Barbara 52
　Charity 58
　Charles 85
　Charlton 98
　Chr. 109
　Christ. 110
　Christian 52, 109
　Clement 52, 66, 110
　Daniel 103, 104
　Deborah 111
　Edward 22
　Eleanor 24
　Eleanor Addison 52
　Elisabeth 99, 110
　Esther 24
　Feryus 36
　Flora 103
　Frances 74
　George 6, 36, 63, 74
　Henrietta 66, 88
　Henry Bacon 105
　James 19, 64, 66, 77,

78, 83, 93, 97
　Jane 26
　John 24, 26, 75, 76, 78, 89, 94, 99
　Jonathon 63, 77
　Joseph 29, 58, 88
　Martin 35, 100
　Mary 66, 74, 78
　Mathew 58
　Nathan 19
　Nicholas 63, 97
　Rachel 18, 59, 74
　Ralph 80
　Rebeccah 75
　Richard 106
　Robert 47, 78
　Roger 53, 88
　Thomas 18, 26, 56, 59, 69, 74, 80, 90, 94, 96, 98
　Turner 6
　William 36, 58, 66, 75, 78, 80, 94, 104, 106, 107, 110
　William Hamilton 46, 113
Smoot
　Charles 70
　Mary 70, 110
Smullen
　Edward 69
Smyley
　James 111
Snavely
　Elisabeth 90
　Henry 90
　Leonard 90
Snelling
　Margaret 34
　William 34
Snow
　William 97
Snowden
　Mary Ann 26
Snulling
　William 30
Soaper
　Thomas 40, 105
Soapers
　Thomas 105
Sollers
　Hugh 35
　James 107
　John 25
　Joseph 25
　Sabret 25
Somerset
　Martha 53
Somervill
　Alexander 9, 100
Somerville
　James 102
Soper
　Basil 76, 93
　Charles 76, 93
　James 76, 93
　John 76, 93
　Mary 93
　Nathan 76, 93
　Rachel 76, 93
　Sarah 76, 93
　Susannah 76, 93
　Thomas 76, 93
Southern
　John 58
　Richard 58
Spalding
　Benedict 110
　Elisabeth 40
　William 40, 105
Spargo

John 50
Sparks
   Absalom 96
   Benjamin 3
   Caleb 96
   Edward 3
   James 3, 74
   John 3, 82
   Joseph 82
   Mary 3
   Nathan 74
   Rebecca 3
   Samuel 3
   William 3
Sparrow
   Dianah 9
   Kensey 9
   Thomas 110
Speake
   Alexander Smith Hawkins 50
   Cordelia 50
   Eleanor Ann 50
   Elisabeth 53
   John 50, 80
   Richard 45, 47, 79
   Thomas 50, 109
Spear
   Andrew 77
   Moses 18
Spearman
   Elisabeth 2
   John 2
   William 32, 65, 69
Spedden
   Hugh 20, 25
   John 20, 25
   Robert 20, 25
Spence
   Adam 75, 76, 98
   Anne 75
   Betty 75
   George 75, 98
   John 75, 98
   Margaret 75
   Mary 75, 98
   Sarah 75
Spencer
   George 84
   Hannah 5
   Isaac 5, 85
   Jervis 5
Spicer
   William 68
Spike
   Lewis 29
Spikernall
   John 32
Spindler
   Jacob 101
Spring
   Sarah 76
Spry
   Abraham 86
   Chr. 105
   Christopher 86, 105, 107, 109
   Franc. 112
   George 86
   Humphry 86
   John 86
   Mary 64, 86
   Rebecca 86
St. Clair
   Mary 85, 104
   William 4, 16, 78, 85
St. Tee
   Christopher 7
   Rachel 7
Stackle
   Valentine 48
Stainer
   Laurance 106
Stainton
   Charles 97, 107, 111
   Jemima 97
   Major 97
   William 97
Staley
   Jacob 37, 84
Stallinges
   Jacob 107
   Mary 107
Standfield
   John 98
   Richard 98
Stanfield
   John 105
Standford
   Elijah 59
Stanley
   Daniel 97
Stanly
   Michael 105
Stansbury
   Bowen 52
   Daniel 86
   Dickson 86
   Edmund 86
   Ellen 52
   Ellin 52
   George 52
   John 86
   Sarah 52
   Thomas 86
   Tobias 52, 103
   William 86
Stant
   James 60
Stanton
   Daniel 19
Stapleford
   John 108
   Raymond 61
Staples
   James 32
   John 47, 112
   Joshua 32
   Margaret 47
Starkey
   Jonathon 16
Start
   Alice 79
   Ann 79
   Benjamin 79
   Elisabeth 79
   John 79
   Martha 79
   Mary 79
   Moses 79
   Rebecca 79
   Sarah 79
Staten
   Sarah 101
Stavely
   James 12, 87
   John 12
   Joseph 12, 87
   Margaret 12
   Mary 12
Stennard
   Nathaniel 49
Stephens
   Ann 5
   Eleanor 30
   John 30
Sterling
   James 51, 111
   John 96
   Mary 66
   Nancy 56, 61
   Rebecca 51
Sterm
   Barbara 31
   John 31
Steuart
   David 3
   Elisabeth 3
   Hannah Morris 31
   James 104
   James Woolford 73
   John 57
   Stephen 27
   Thomas 18, 59
   William 60
Stevens
   Benjamin 90
   Bershaba 57
   Edmondson 61
   Frances 80
   Francis 92
   John 48, 93, 113
   Jonathon 48, 107, 108, 111
   Joseph 100
   Richard 106
   William 28
Stevenson
   Henry 86
   Rachel 17
   William 17
Stevins
   Richard 30
Stewart
   David 3
   Elisabeth 41
   James 108
   James Woolford 47
   John 9, 47, 56
   Mary 3, 65
   Thomas 60
   William 99
Stiger
   Andrew 2
Stiles
   Henry 101
Stilley
   Peter 35
Stilly
   Jacob 35
   Mary 35
Stinchcomb
   John 95
   Lewis 33
Stinson
   Elisabeth 16
Stockett
   Margaret 81
   Thomas 57, 84
Stockley
   John 77
Stockly
   George 48
Stoddert
   John 73, 106, 108
   John T. 30
   Kenelm Trueman 73
   Richard Trueman 73
   Walter Trueman 73
   William Trueman 73
Stoltz
   Nicholas 52
Stone
   Ann 43
   Benedict 37
   D. 108
   Elisabeth 43
   Henry 50
   Ignatius 50
   John 43, 107

Jos. 50
Joseph 50
Littleton 43
Margaret 43
Margret 43
Mary 43
Monica 42
Priscilla 43
Rachel 43
Rebecca 43
Samuel 43
Sarah 50
Susannah 43
Thomas 43
William 43, 50, 70, 110

Stoner
  Frederick 99, 104
  Michael 99
  Peter 99
  Rosanna 99
  Susanna 99

Stoop
  Philip 23

Stoops
  Benjamin Townsend 64
  Cornelia 64
  John 64
  Mary 64
  Rachel 64
  William 64

Stover
  John 97

Strat
  Thomas 84

Street
  Sarah 17
  Thomas 74

Stromatt
  John 45

Strong
  Nathaniel 7
  Rachel 7

Stuart
  James 31

Stull
  Christopher 84
  John 84

Sturgis
  Joshua 76

Sturrum
  Catherine 31
  Jacob 31
  John 27, 31

Sullivane
  Andrew 23
  Ann 112
  Daniel 72
  John 78, 96
  Sarah 24, 78, 96

Sullyvane
  Rachel 34

Summers
  Annastatia 62
  Felix 9

Sunderland
  Benjamin 16
  Elisabeth 16
  John 9
  Sarah 9, 16

Surman
  Isaac 108

Sutherland
  James 11

Sutton
  Ashberry 83
  Christ. 5
  John 44, 63, 87, 106, 109
  Joseph 32, 96
  Rebecca 83

Swabb
  Francis 91

Swain
  John 69

Swale
  Francis 86

Swallow
  Sophiah 4

Swan
  Samuel 26
  Thomas 111

Swann
  Ann 52
  James 52
  John 52, 104, 109
  Thomas 12, 112

Swearingen
  Samuel 33, 35

Swearington
  Samuel 101

Sweeting
  Edward 60

Swift
  Elisabeth 53
  Emanuel 80, 109
  Gideon 53
  Goodwin 49
  James 53
  John 49, 53, 109
  Mable 53
  Martha 80
  Mary 49, 53, 80
  Meade 49
  Rachel 80
  Rebecca 80, 103
  Richard 53
  Sarah 80
  Theophilus 49, 111
  Thomas 49, 53
  Vincent 80

Sworden
  Henry 112

Syffert
  Elisabeth 105
  Stephen 105

Sylvester
  James 54

Tagart
  Cardiff 106
  Samuel 109, 113

Talbert
  Betty 65
  George 65
  John 65
  Joshua 65
  Prisse 65

Talbot
  Edward 42, 104
  William 109

Tall
  Philip 112

Tanahil
  Ninian 67

Taney
  John 113
  Michael 8
  Raphael 26, 30
  Thomas 30

Taneyhill
  Ninian 112

Tanner
  Benjamin 11, 61, 78
  Mary 78
  Philemon 47

Tany
  Sarah 53

Tarboten
  Joseph 92

Tarlton
  John 88

Tasner
  Jacob 111

Tate
  Catharine 38
  George 38

Tatom
  John 101

Tauton
  John 79

Taylor
  Ann 1, 22, 24, 31, 107
  Benjamin 31
  Caleb 4
  Elisabeth 5, 16, 27, 31, 83
  Esther 18
  Gunby 18
  Ignatius 24
  Isaac 4, 16
  James 16, 31, 90
  Jemima 4
  John 27, 31, 45
  Joseph 4, 14, 15, 25, 27
  Mary 4, 16, 31
  Mary Gunby 18
  Mathew 14
  Naomi 18
  Richard 4, 25
  Samuel 4, 21, 22, 31
  Sarah 18, 31
  Solomon 21, 22
  Sophia 4
  Teagle 109
  Thomas 10, 27
  William 31
  William Smallwood 111

Tenley
  Charles 32

Tennant
  Elisabeth 77
  Hannah 77
  James 77
  John 77
  Moses 77, 111
  Sarah 77
  Susannah 77
  William 77

Tennison
  Abraham 86
  Absalom 91
  Ann 91
  Christian 91
  Elisabeth 91
  Jesse 86, 88, 91
  John 86
  Thomas 91

Terrence
  Hugh 14
  Martha 14

Teter
  Devalt 68
  Jacob 68

Tevis
  Nathaniel 72

Thom
  Eliza 5
  John 5

Thomas
  Chloe 19
  Christopher 83
  Daniel 112
  Elisabeth 7
  Henry 4, 5, 10, 32, 106
  James 4, 17
  John 26, 73
  Joseph Cox 89
  Mary 4, 55, 105
  Notley 112

  Philip 17
  Rebecca 17
  Rosanna 8
  Samuel 96
  Sarah 17, 21
  Thomas 17, 55
  Tristram 55, 83
  William 4, 7, 108
Thomlinson
  Grove 67
Thompson
  Absolem 47
  Andrew 16
  Ann 53
  Appelonia 75
  Aquila 97
  Araminta 2
  Dorcas 2
  Edward 14, 70
  Elisabeth 16, 75, 106
  Francis 76, 110
  George 2, 14, 53, 107
  Hannah 16, 67
  Henry 7, 11, 67
  James 11, 75
  Jane 14
  John 14, 27, 53, 106, 109, 110
  John Dockwra 14
  Joseph 11, 80
  Joshua 14, 108
  Leonard 75
  Martha 2, 53
  Mary 2, 14, 27, 75
  Mathew 14
  Richard 11, 35, 111
  Robert 105, 113
  Samuel 53
  Susannah 75
  Thomas 19, 53, 57
  William 48, 53, 75, 87, 110, 112
Thoms
  Jacob 59, 108
  Mary 59
  Sarah 59
  Stephen 59
Thorn
  Benjamin 109
  Daniel 106
  James 105
Thorpe
  Edward 102
  Rachel 102
Thurlow
  John 17
Tilden
  John 106, 113
Tilghman
  Aaron 19
  Catherine 19
  Gideon 101
  Joseph 105
Tillotson
  John 66, 67, 95
Tims
  Joseph 11
Tindal
  Elisabeth 90
Tinnally
  Thomas 34
Tiperary
  Bartholomew 33
  Michael 33
Tippet
  Grace 7
Tippett
  Henry 110, 111
  James 7
Tippins
  Rebeccah 82
Tipton
  John 111
Toadvine
  George 75
Todd
  Benjamin 36, 54
  Betty 54
  David 54
  Henry 93
  John 4
  Levin 36
  Peter 41
  Rachel 92
  Richard 93
  Ruth 92
Tollin
  John 48
Tolson
  Amey 5
  Andrew 5, 49, 89
  Benjamin 5
  John 5, 23
  Thomas 106
Tongue
  Thomas 33
Toward
  John 32
Townsend
  Aaron 12
  Brickhus 31
  James 12
  Jane 12
  Jeremiah 31
  John 31, 65
  Luke 31
  Major 34, 104
  Mary 12, 31
  Sarah 12, 101
  Solomon 12, 44, 74
  Thomas 12
  William 31, 101
  William Barkley 44, 74
Towson
  William 17
Trail
  Charles 28
  Jane 28
  Susannah 28
Train
  Roger 111
Traver
  Henry 2
  Mathew 2
Traverse
  Elisabeth 14
  George 14
  Henry 104
  Levin 35, 41
  Mathew 6
Treadway
  Thomas 24
Tredway
  Thomas 87
Trego
  Betsy 57
  Elisabeth 19, 33
  Henry 19
  James 19, 57, 108
  Levin 57
  Mary 57
  Newton 19
  Priscell 57
  Roger 57
  Rosannah 40
  Sarah 57
  Solomon 40
  Thomas 19, 33
  William 19, 57
Trehearn
  James 94
Trew
  Elisabeth 87
  John 87
  Mary 87
  Sarah 87
  William 4, 87
Trexell
  Frederick 37
Trice
  John 31
Tripe
  Thomas 77
  William 55
Trippe
  Edward 10, 41, 82
  John 10
  Mary 10
  Sarah 82
  William 10, 39
Troth
  Anne 55
  Henry 55
  William 55
Trotter
  Jane 92
True
  William 108
Trueman
  Alexander 78
  Ann 78
  Clara 78
  Cloe 78
  Edward 78
  Henry 78
  James 78
  Jane 78
  Leonard 78
  Sarah 78
  Thomas 78
Truitt
  Martha 110
Trulock
  Henry 95
Trush
  Martin 8
Trussell
  Thomas 89, 106
Tubman
  Richard 106
Tucker
  John 6
  William 41, 106
Tule
  Alice 14
  Ann 14
  Rachel 14
  Rebecca 14
  Susanna 14
Tull
  Andrew 59
  Celia 59
  Edward 104
  Elijah 59
  Jane 59
  Jesse 59, 112
  John 14, 19, 22
  Jonathon 100
  Levin 22, 59
  Mary 22, 59
  Noble 59
  Priscilla 22
  Richard 22
  Sally 59
  Samuel 72
  Thomas 95
  William 22
Tulley
  Charles 104
Tully

Rachel 23
William 7
Tunnell
  William 68, 84
Turbut
  Richard 3
Turner
  Ann 80
  Anna 29
  Anne 80
  Comfort 109
  Deborah 29
  Dorcas 29
  Edward 31, 32
  George 80
  Hannah 31
  Henry 80
  Hezekiah 29
  John 21, 80
  John Beal 29
  Joseph 3, 95
  Martha 29
  Mary 29, 80
  Priscilla 3
  Richard 80
  Samuel 29
  William 80
  Zephaniah 29
Turpin
  Betty 72
  John 72
  Joshua 72
  Nehemiah 27, 72
  Orpha 27
  William 36, 72, 108
Twyford
  John 83
Tyler
  Elisabeth 30
  John 30, 99, 106, 110
  Robert 19
  Sarah 30
  William 30

Ulan
  John 68
Unge
  Elisabeth 102

Van Bebber
  Adam 14
Van Horn
  Barnet 8
  Nicholas 8
Van Horne
  Jacob 8
  Nicholas 8
Vance
  James 106, 113
Vanderford
  James 81
  John 81
Vanhorne
  Barnett 13
  Jacob 13
  Nicholas 13, 23
Vannetson
  Catharine 89
Vanrishwick
  Ann 29
  Milford 29
  Monica 29
Vansant
  Aleatha 86
  Cornelius 28, 78
  Ephraim 49, 57
  George 17, 36, 63
  Peter 86
Vansweringen
  Josep 9
  Joseph 18
Vatts
  George 58
Vaughan
  Abraham 97
  Betty 84
  Charles 42
  Gist 97
Vaul
  Ebenzer 34
Veach
  Daniel 76
  John 112
  Rachel 109
Veazey
  James 11, 106
  John 35, 36
  Robert 62, 113
Veazy
  John 62, 75
Venables
  Charles 109, 110
  George 109
Venebles
  George 106
Vickers
  Ann 21
  Benjamin 21
  John 21
  Mary 21
  Sarah 21
  Solomon 21
  Thomas 21
  William 21
Vincent
  John 73
  Margaret 83
  Sarah 73
  William 73
Vinnent
  Esther 14
Vinson
  Barsheba 18
  Celia 18
  Daniel 18
  Eliab 18, 94
  Elial 80
  James 18
  Sarah 105
Volk
  Worrington 85
Vowles
  Cyrus 86
  Matthew 95
  Richard 95
  Thomas 95

Wade
  Mary 112
  Robert 18, 87
Waggaman
  Elisabeth 62
  George 62
  Henry 62
  John Elliot 62
  Mary 62
  Sarah 62
  William Elliot 62
Waggoner
  Michael 68
Wailes
  Ann 99
  Elisabeth 99
  Helany 99
  Joseph 99
  Sarah 99
Wakeman
  Edward 87
  Elisabeth 87
  Mary 87
  Sarah 87
Walch
  John 17
Wale
  Levin 19
Wales
  Daniel 99
  Elisabeth 99
Waley
  Abraham 3
  Daniel 3
  Esther 3
  Hannah 3
  Joseph 3
  Mary 3
  Rachel 3
  Sarah 3
Walker
  Ann 29
  Catherine 29
  James 105
  Jane 29
  John 29, 71
  Nathan 29
  Sarah 29
  Tamesin 47
  Thomas 13, 20, 47, 83, 105, 109
  William 47, 79
Wall
  Henry 105
  Joshua 61, 108
  Kesiah 61
  Rebecca 10
  Rispy 61
  Robert 10
  Thomas 45
Wallace
  Alexander 42, 107
  Amelia 41
  Bethulia 41, 105
  Charles 41
  David 14
  Hannah 35
  Hugh 35, 75
  Jane 14
  John 9, 50
  Joseph 14, 41
  Leah 14
  Mary 14, 75
  Mathew 14, 41
  Richard 14, 41
  Stapleford 19, 41
  Thomas 36, 41, 62
  William 14, 36
Wallis
  Ann 66
  Elisabeth 66
  Francis 66
  Hannah 28, 66
  Henry 50
  Hugh 28
  James 60
  John 49, 50, 60, 66
  Margaret 66
  Samuel 50, 91, 107, 111
  Sarah 50
Walmsley
  Robert 1, 8
Walston
  Boz 3
  Joy 3
Walter
  Alexander 38
  Ann 24, 78
  Clement 87
  Daniel 87

Frances 24
George 87, 101
John 77, 78, 87
Levi 87
Mary 78
Mitchel 78
Peleg 77
Samuel 87
Sarah 24, 87
Smith 78
Thomas 77, 110
William 87

Walters
  Alexander 35, 57
  Ann 24, 78
  Benjamin 62
  Frances 78
  James 24, 78
  John 8, 62
  Robert 24, 44, 78, 84, 85, 96
  Sarah 78
  Thomas 104

Waltham
  John 89

Walton
  Mary 25
  Meridith 106
  Richard 104
  Stephen 25
  William 25
  Wise 25

Waples
  John 20, 23, 68, 69, 84
  Joshua 23
  Paul 68, 104
  William 20, 23, 68

Ward
  Benjamin 23, 44, 73
  Charity 58
  Edward 42
  James 15
  John 15, 75, 80
  Joseph 41, 104
  Mathias 51, 74
  Nathaniel 80
  Sarah 50
  Stephen 51, 74
  Thomas 15

Warden
  Elisabeth 62
  William 47, 53

Wardrop
  James 110

Ware
  Edward 24
  Francis 9, 24
  James 19
  John 19
  Mary 19

Warfield
  Absalom 112
  Alexander 49, 82
  Brice 82
  Deborah 82
  Elisabeth 82
  Honour 73
  John 35, 49, 82
  Joseph 49
  Luke 49
  Mary 91
  Rachel 49
  Rezin 112
  Richard 49, 109
  Ruth 82
  Seth 49
  Thomas 82, 105, 106
  Vachel 91

Waring
  Robert Marsh. 107

William 43
Warner
  Hannah 9, 49, 66
  Philip 9, 49, 66, 91
  Stephen Garey 57
  Stephen Gary 34

Warren
  Agness 59
  Alefare 59
  Charles 71
  John 19, 59, 111
  Mary Ann 59
  Nicholas 104
  William 59

Warrick
  William 26

Warring
  Basil 31
  Betty 31
  Clark 31
  Henry 31
  James 31
  Marson 31
  Sarah 31
  Thomas 31
  William 31

Warrington
  Nathaniel 9
  Sarah 9

Washington
  Louissa 59

Waters
  Ann 20
  Casandra 20
  Charles 61
  Elisabeth 75
  John 10, 20
  Mathew 20
  Rachel 20
  Richard 20
  Sarah 101
  Thomas 20

Wathen
  Hudson 13
  Sarah 13

Wathin
  Ann 26
  Henry Hudson 26

Watkins
  Benjamin Hudson 42
  Joseph 10

Watson
  Catherine 8
  Edward 8
  Eliza 8
  Hester 8
  Isaac Decon 33
  Jane 8
  John 8, 26, 83
  Jonathon West 77
  Lancelot 35
  Margaret 8
  Mary 83
  Patrick 76
  Pryor 83

Watters
  Sarah 20

Watts
  James 22
  John 22, 60, 106, 111, 112
  Rachel 22
  Sarah 60, 111
  Thomas 22

Waugh
  Elisabeth 68
  William 68, 109, 112

Wayman
  Edmund 40

Weathered
  Dorcas 50
  John 56
  Samuel 56
  William 50, 56, 63, 105, 109

Weatherly
  Charles 20
  Eleanor 20
  James 20
  Jesse 20
  John 20
  Joseph 20
  Mary 20
  Sarah 20

Weaver
  John 106

Weavers
  John 90

Webb
  George 82
  James 65

Webster
  Elisabeth 15
  John 85
  Michael 15

Weems
  Amelia 59
  David 86

Wehaw
  Henry 101

Welch
  Elisabeth 36
  James 89, 98
  John 38
  John McClean 38
  Mary 38
  Milcah 98
  Richard 36
  William 38

Welder
  Samuel Sand. 106
  Samuel Stan. 106

Wells
  George 101, 106
  Richard 88

Welsh
  Edward 75, 110
  Henry Oneal 4
  John 75, 113
  Lewis 63
  Mary 63, 75
  Richard 60
  Robert 81
  Sarah 75

West
  Catha 92
  George 21
  James 52
  John 92
  Thomas 100

Whaley
  Abraham 65
  Daniel 65, 97, 108
  David 111
  Elisabeth 97
  Esther 65
  Hannah 65
  Joseph 3, 16, 65, 104, 106, 111
  Martha 16
  William 3, 16

Whan
  Samuel 12

Wharton
  Charles 69
  Mary 101
  William 69

Wheat
  Mary 97
  William 104

Wheatley
　Daniel 12
　John 60
　Sarah 102
　Silvester 102
Wheatly
　Arthur 61
　Eleanor 13
　James 13
　Sampson 29
　Thomas 21
Wheeler
　Ann 64
　Benjamin 2, 5
　Bennett 42
　Dina 59
　Edward 60, 79
　Eleanor 53
　Elisabeth 20, 51, 80
　George 8
　Henrietta 88
　Ignatius 2, 5, 76, 88
　Jane 8
　John 80
　Leonard 20
　Nathan 42, 108
　Nathaniel 42
　Priscilla 19
　Sarah 60
　Thomas 2, 5, 72
　William 42, 104, 106
　William Benjamin 42
Wheland
　John 32
Whetered
　John 56
Whetred
　William 56
Whinright
　Cannon 21
　Elander 21
　Evans 21
　John 21
　Rebecca 21
　Stephen 21
　William 21
Whinwright
　Evans 59
Whisler
　Esther 108
White
　Abigail 14
　Andrew 1
　Ann 1
　Betty 87
　Catherine 14
　Elias 26
　Elisabeth 5, 70
　Edward 83
　Elias 87
　Francis 14
　Gowen 14
　Hannah 1
　Henrietta 70
　Henry 112
　James 1, 14
　John 14, 80
　Leonard 14
　Martha 14
　Mary 70
　Peter 14
　Prudence 70
　Richard 107
　Ruth 14
　Samuel 27, 70
　Sarah 14
　Stevens 87
　William 70
　William Stevens 87
Whiteford
　Hugh 17
　Mary 17
　Michael 17
Whitehead
　Mary 19
Whiteley
　Abraham 37
　Daniel 37
　Joseph 108
　Solomon 37
　Thomas 73
Whitely
　Edward 45
　Joseph 45
　Thomas 37
　William 45
Whiteman
　Robert 38
Whiting
　Samuel 96
Whitmore
　Robert 19
Whitticoe
　Jane 111
Whittington
　Benjamin 46
　Christian 50, 111
　Elisabeth 46
　James 50, 108
　Jane 46
　John 97
　Joseph 46
　Joshua 112
　Mary 46
　Rachel 65
　Thomas 11
　William 11, 31, 46
Wickes
　Joseph 64
　Lambert 64
　Martha 64
　Mary 56, 64, 106
　Matthias 26
　Richard 64
　Samuel 17, 64, 106
　Sarah 64
Wickham
　Priscilla 19
Wicks
　Mary 66
Wiggens
　Edward 26
Wildman
　Cornelius 26, 46, 84
　John 26
　Mary Anne 26
　Monica 26
　Susanna 26
Wilds
　Jane 50
　John 50
Wiles
　John 109
Wilkes
　Samuel 108
Wilkins
　Thomas 50
Wilkinson
　Joseph 24
　Stephen 27
Willett
　Charles 109
William
　Robert 106
Williams
　Aaron 9
　Alexander 45
　Allan 28
　Ann 71
　Barsheba 85
　Benjamin 4, 7
　Betty 52
　Catharine 54
　Celia 28
　Christopher 5
　Eleanor 70
　Elisabeth 27, 30, 58, 63
　George 63
　Henry 63
　Isaac 52, 108, 111
　James 63, 71, 112
　Jesse 28
　Joanna 70
　Job 28
　John 27, 54, 56, 108
　Joshua 52
　Major 28
　Margaret 63
　Mary 28, 30, 63
　Nathan 63
　Nelly 28
　Polly 28
　Rebecca 28
　Richard 49, 66, 108
　Robert 83
　Ruth 7
　Samuel 52
　Sarah 63
　Spencer 52
　Stephen 52
　Stocket 41
　Susanna 30
　Thomas 28, 70, 72
　William 28, 54
Williamson
　Elisabeth 51
　John 51, 104, 108
Willin
　John 45
　Rachel 45
Willis
　Elijah 96
　Elisabeth 37
　Esther 19
　Grace 96
　Jabus 96
　James 96
　John 37, 96
　Richard 94
　Sarah 96
　Tabitha 96
　William 96, 99
Willson
　Daniel 70
　George 4
　James 4, 23
　John 4, 24
　Mary 4
　Robert 38
　Sarah 4
　Virlinda 39
　William 4, 19
Wilmer
　Edward Price 15
Wilmot
　John 107
Wilmott
　John 102
Wilson
　Abraham 77
　Ann 15, 70, 77
　Aramintha 29
　Catharine 85
　Caty 70
　David 57, 77
　Deborah 81, 85
　Denwood 95
　Elisabeth 19
　Ephraim 57, 62
　George 77

Hannah 77
Hugh 70
Jesse 77
John 29, 57, 85, 109, 112
Jonathon 54, 70
Jos. 77
Larkin 54, 112
Levin 62, 77
Lucia 54
Mary 77, 86, 93, 102
Rachel 7
Rebecca 15
Rebeccah 57
Rhody 77
Robert 85, 111
Rodey 77
Samuel 62, 77
Sarah 54, 77
Sophia 77
Thomas 19, 29, 104
William 7, 57, 70, 77, 81, 111

Wimsatt
  Richard 111
Winchester
  Isaac 5
  John 42
Winder
  Ann 14
Windom
  Thomas 104
Windsor
  Catherford 28
  John 28
  Joseph 50
  Margaret 28
  Reatherford 28
  Rebecca 28
  William 28
Wingate
  John 89
  Philip 84
  Thomas 84, 107, 108, 111
Winright
  Mary 21
Winson
  Barsheba 18
  Bruffit 18
  Celia 18
  James 18
Winter
  George 30
Wirtz
  Jacob 97
  Mary 97
Wise
  Mathew 42
Wiseman
  Elisabeth 29
  John 29
  Richard 29
  Robert 29
Wisler
  John 111
Witchcote
  Paul 28
Withers
  William 21
Withrington
  John 99
Wivell
  Hariott 44
Wolton
  Sarah 91
Wood
  Ann 73
  Anna 37
  Benjamin 73
  Druscilla 73
  Elijah 18
  Elisabeth 73
  Helena 73
  James 99
  James Greenfield 12
  John 37, 53, 73, 90, 112
  Leonard 73
  Peter 110
  Samuel 41
  Thomas 99
Woodall
  John 17, 56
  Mary 56
  William 77
Woodard
  Benjamin 88
  John 89
Woodcraft
  Mary 34
  William 34
Wooderson
  Richard 52, 107
  Sarah 52
Woodland
  Abraham 49
  John 88
  Nancy 88
  Richard 70
Woodward
  Benjamin 9, 52, 65
  Henry 106
  John 90, 110
  Katharine 110
  Katherine 110
  Violetta 90
  William 47
Woodyard
  Henry 47
Woolahand
  Francis 27
Woolen
  Amelia 45
  Anne 45
  Benjamin 45
  Edward 45
  Elisabeth 45
  John 45, 107, 108
  Lettice 45, 61
  Levin 45
  Nancy 61
  William 45
Woolford
  James 21
  Levin 19, 40, 47, 56
Woolhater
  Barbara 33
  George 33
  George Evan 33
Woolhaton
  Barbara 48
Woollen
  Lettice 108, 112
  William 50
Wooters
  John 107
  Jonathon 70
Wootters
  John 112
Wootton
  Elisabeth 81, 112
  Samuel 81
Worell
  Ann 37
Wornall
  Robey 73
Worrel
  James 65
Worrell
  Edward 75
  Joseph 113

Worsley
  Ann 21
  William 21
Worthy
  Samuel 15
Wrench
  Henry 60, 112
  Margaret 71
  Peter 51, 71
  William 71, 93, 105, 109
Wright
  Ann 59
  Anne 60
  Booker 68
  Chloe 60
  Coursey 71
  Daniel 45, 106, 111
  Edward 46, 91
  Elisabeth 4
  Gorey 60
  James 67
  John 68, 95
  Joseph 60, 108, 109
  Leonard 60
  Margarett 60
  Mary 10, 82, 94
  Nathan 43, 82, 108, 109
  Nathan Samuel Turbut 3
  Nathaniel 105
  Prudence 45
  Richard 59
  Robert 82
  Samuel 108
  Sarah 57, 71
  Solomon 71
  Stephen 94
  Thomas 10, 68, 108, 109, 111
  William 4
  Winifred 60
  Zabulon 106
Wrightson
  James 41
Wroth
  James 1
  Kirvin 89
Wroughton
  Thomas 72, 91
Wyatt
  Elisabeth 10
  Thomas 10
Wyley
  William 15
Wynn
  Chloe 24
  John Sharpe 24
  Josiah 24

Yates
  Francis 51, 110
  Jonathon 69
  Robert 51
  Theophilus 51, 59
Yeates
  Robert 113
Yeats
  Jane 90
  Robert 90
Yewell
  Christopher 92
  Isaac 92
  Margaret 92
  Robert 109
  Solomon 92
  Solomon Slaughter 92
Yieldhall
  Benjamin 84
Yoe
  Aaron 44

    Stephen 103
    William 70
Young
    Alexander 30
    Eleanor 50
    Elisabeth 16, 50
    George 16
    Jacob 27
    John 16, 54, 81
    Lovereta 90
    Mary 1, 16
    Parker 66
    Rebecca 16
    Sarah 16
    Sewall 17
    William 16, 108

Zacharias
    Mathias 100
Zoll
    Henry 52
Zuille
    Mathew 106

Other Heritage Books by Vernon L. Skinner, Jr.:

Abstracts of the Administration Accounts of the Prerogative Court of Maryland, 1718–1724, Libers 1–5

Abstracts of the Administration Accounts of the Prerogative Court of Maryland, 1724–1731: Libers 6–10

Abstracts of the Administration Accounts of the Prerogative Court of Maryland, 1731–1737: Libers 11–15

Abstracts of the Administration Accounts of the Prerogative Court of Maryland, 1737–1744: Libers 16–20

Abstracts of the Administration Accounts of the Prerogative Court of Maryland, 1744–1750: Libers 21–28

Abstracts of the Administration Accounts of the Prerogative Court of Maryland, 1750–1754: Libers 29–36

Abstracts of the Administration Accounts of the Prerogative Court of Maryland, 1754–1760: Libers 37–45

Abstracts of the Administration Accounts of the Prerogative Court of Maryland, 1760–1764, Libers 46–51

Abstracts of the Administration Accounts of the Prerogative Court of Maryland, 1764–1768, Libers 52–58

Abstracts of the Administration Accounts of the Prerogative Court of Maryland, 1768–1771, Libers 59–66

Abstracts of the Administration Accounts of the Prerogative Court of Maryland, 1771–1777, Libers 67–74

Abstracts of the Balance Books of the Prerogative Court of Maryland: Libers 2 and 3, 1755–1763

Abstracts of the Balance Books of the Prerogative Court of Maryland: Libers 4 and 5, 1763–1770

Abstracts of the Balance Books of the Prerogative Court of Maryland: Libers 6 and 7, 1770–1777

Abstracts of the Inventories and Accounts of the Prerogative Court of Maryland, 1674–1678, 1699–1703

Abstracts of the Inventories and Accounts of the Prerogative Court of Maryland, 1679–1686

Abstracts of the Inventories and Accounts of the Prerogative Court of Maryland, 1685–1701

Abstracts of the Inventories and Accounts of the Prerogative Court of Maryland, 1688–1698

Abstracts of the Inventories and Accounts of the Prerogative Court of Maryland, 1697–1700: Libers 16, 17, 18, 19, 19½A, 19½B

Abstracts of the Inventories and Accounts of the Prerogative Court of Maryland, 1699–1704: Libers 20–24

Abstracts of the Inventories and Accounts of the Prerogative Court of Maryland, 1708–1711: Libers 29, 30, 31, 32A, 32B

Abstracts of the Inventories and Accounts of the Prerogative Court of Maryland, 1711–1713: Libers 32C, 33A, 33B, 34

Abstracts of the Inventories and Accounts of the Prerogative Court of Maryland, 1712–1716: Libers 35A, 35B, 36A, 36B, 36C

Abstracts of the Inventories and Accounts of the Prerogative Court of Maryland, 1715–1718: Libers 37A, 37B, 37C, 38A, 38B, 39A, 39B, 39C

Abstracts of the Inventories and Accounts of the Prerogative Court of Maryland, 1699–1708: Libers 25–28

Abstracts of the Inventories of the Prerogative Court of Maryland, 1718–1720

Abstracts of the Inventories of the Prerogative Court of Maryland, 1720–1724

Abstracts of the Inventories of the Prerogative Court of Maryland, 1724–1727

Abstracts of the Inventories of the Prerogative Court of Maryland, 1726–1729

Abstracts of the Inventories of the Prerogative Court of Maryland, 1728–1734

Abstracts of the Inventories of the Prerogative Court of Maryland, 1733–1738

Abstracts of the Inventories of the Prerogative Court of Maryland, 1738–1744

Abstracts of the Inventories of the Prerogative Court of Maryland, 1744–1748

Abstracts of the Inventories of the Prerogative Court of Maryland, 1748–1751

Abstracts of the Inventories of the Prerogative Court of Maryland, 1751–1756

Abstracts of the Inventories of the Prerogative Court of Maryland, 1755–1760

Abstracts of the Inventories of the Prerogative Court of Maryland, 1760–1763

Abstracts of the Inventories of the Prerogative Court of Maryland, 1763–1766

Abstracts of the Inventories of the Prerogative Court of Maryland, 1766–1769

Abstracts of the Inventories of the Prerogative Court of Maryland, 1769–1772

Abstracts of the Inventories of the Prerogative Court of Maryland, 1772–1774

Abstracts of the Inventories of the Prerogative Court of Maryland, 1774–1777

Abstracts of the Proceedings of the Orphans' Court of Sussex County, Delaware: Libers 1, 2, 3, 4, A (1708–1709, 1728–1777)

Abstracts of the Proprietary Records of the Provincial Court of Maryland, 1637–1658

Abstracts Worcester County, Maryland Estate Docket, 1742–1820

Other Wills in the Prerogative Court for Somerset and Worcester Counties, 1664–1775

Provincial Families of Maryland, Volume 1

Somerset County Will Books, 1750–1772

Somerset County Will, 1667–1748: Liber EB9

Somerset County Wills, 1770–1777 and 1675–1710: Liber EB5

Supplement Abstracts Inventories and Accounts, Prerogative Court, 1691–1706

Worcester County Inventories and Accounts, 1694–1742: Inventory Book JW15

Worcester County Wills: Will Book MH3, 1666–1742

www.ingramcontent.com/pod-product-compliance
Lightning Source LLC
Chambersburg PA
CBHW080546170426
43195CB00016B/2695